How to Be Like **Walt**

How to Be Like
Walt

Pat Williams
with Jim Denney

Health Communications, Inc.
Deerfield Beach, Florida

www.hcibooks.com

Library of Congress Cataloging-in-Publication Data

Williams, Pat, 1945–
    How to be like Walt : capturing the Disney magic every day of your life / Pat
Williams with Jim Denney.
        p. cm.
    Includes bibliographical references.
    ISBN-13: 978-0-7573-0231-2 (tp)
    ISBN-10: 0-7573-0231-9 (tp)
    1. Disney, Walt, 1901–1966.   2. Animators—United States—Biography.
3. Walt Disney Productions—History.   I. Denney, James.   II. Title.

NC1766.U52D538 2004
791.43'092—dc22
[B]
                                                                    2004047571

Publisher: Health Communications, Inc.
                  3201 S.W. 15th Street
                  Deerfield Beach, FL 33442-8190

R-04-07

Cover photo © Corbis
Cover design by Larissa Hise Henoch
Inside book formatting by Dawn Von Strolley Grove

To Peggy Matthews Rose,
a vital contributor to this book.
Her love for Walt
shines on every page.

Contents

Foreword

Like Walt Disney himself, Art Linkletter is a national treasure. As the host of House Party *(twenty-five years on CBS radio and TV) and* People Are Funny *(nineteen years on NBC radio and TV), Mr. Linkletter has brought laughter and joy into the homes of generations of Americans. He is the author of twenty-three books, including* Kids Say the Darndest Things *and* Old Age Is Not for Sissies. *Art Linkletter is active in many important causes, including fighting drug abuse and improving life for senior citizens.*

WHEN I FIRST MET Walt Disney, he was setting up folding chairs in an empty auditorium. It was 1940, and I was a young broadcaster, working at a local radio station in San Francisco. Walt had come to introduce his new motion picture, *Fantasia.* I arrived early for the press conference, and found the place empty except for one fellow who was busily arranging chairs.

I said, "When is Walt Disney supposed to arrive?"

He grinned and said, "I'm Walt Disney."

I said, "You are? Why are you arranging chairs?"

"Well," he said, "I like to have things just-so."

That was quite an introduction, because it gave me a glimpse of the kind of person Walt was. He wasn't a Hollywood big shot, impressed with his own importance. He was just a friendly, humble guy from the Midwest who happened to be in the movie business. We sat down and talked, and it was as if we had known each other for years.

The next time I encountered Walt was in 1951. My wife Lois and I were on a ship, bound for a European holiday. We were delighted to find Walt and his wife Lillian also aboard. Walt and I had a wonderful time, talking about show business and mutual friends. I had always enjoyed his films, from the Mickey Mouse shorts to *Snow White* and *Fantasia,* and it was fascinating to hear him explain how those films were made.

We became close personal friends, and our families socialized and traveled the world together. We even lived a few blocks from each other in Holmby Hills, near Los Angeles. I enjoyed going to Walt's home and watching him fire up his backyard steam train.

The man was a paradox. He was so down-to-earth and straightforward, yet he continually surprised you with the depth of his thinking. He lived a simple lifestyle, yet he envisioned grand, complex projects like Disneyland and EPCOT, his city of tomorrow. He was so childlike, with his wide-open imagination and his belief that anything is possible. Yet he was amazingly mature in his ability to focus on his goals and make his dreams come true.

Walt delighted in the role of Daddy to his two girls. No matter how busy he was, he made a priority of spending time with his family. He was a Hollywood rarity—a totally involved parent. (My son Jack and Walt's daughter Sharon saw a lot of each other during their teen years. Walt and I used to think that we might one day become in-laws as well as neighbors— but it didn't work out.)

You rarely found Walt at a Hollywood cocktail party. He and Lil enjoyed coming to our house for dinner, because it was always a family affair. There were no photographers, no reporters, no one trying to corner Walt and sell him a movie script. Walt enjoyed relaxing with people he felt comfortable with, and he had no use for the glitz and phoniness of Hollywood.

Unlike Walt, Lil enjoyed social events. She and Lois were very close friends, and she used to say, "Please, Lois, never leave us out of one of your parties. I like to go out and Walt is such a homebody—but he'll always come to a party at your house."

> *"We are all born to be who we are. Walt was a genetically unique individual who was born to be himself. His job, and ours as well, is to finish the job on earth that we were created for."*
>
> RAY BRADBURY
> WRITER

One day in 1954, Walt called me and said, "Art, let me take you for a ride down to Orange County and I'll show you where I'm going to build Disneyland."

Well, I loved to hear Walt talk about his big plans, so we drove down with some researchers from the Stanford Research Institute. We finally got to a place where some bulldozers had cleared out an orange grove. It looked like a big field of dirt clods.

"Well," Walt said, "this is it." He looked around and he could see it all in his imagination: the Disneyland Railroad, Main Street, Sleeping Beauty's Castle, Adventureland, Frontierland, Fantasyland, Tomorrowland. I looked around and saw nothing but a cow pasture. I thought, *My poor, deluded friend! He's going to put a bunch of merry-go-rounds and roller-coasters out here, forty-five minutes from L.A. He'll go broke!*

"Art," he said, "There's a fortune to be made here. If you buy up all the property around Disneyland, in a year or two it'll be worth twenty times what you paid for it."

Well, I was too smart to get caught up in Walt's enthusiasm! I didn't buy any real estate around Disneyland—and by being so "smart," I passed up a chance to make millions!

A year later, in 1955, Walt came to my house and asked if I would emcee the televised grand opening of Disneyland. I was honored, and I chose two friends to assist me. One was actor Robert Cummings, who had just appeared with Grace Kelly in Alfred Hitchcock's *Dial M for Murder*. The other was a charming actor named Ronald Reagan (I understand he later went into government work). So Bob Cummings, Ronnie Reagan and I opened the gates of Walt's Magic Kingdom. Disneyland became a phenomenal success, the Eighth Wonder of the World.

A few years later, I was at a birthday party in Walt's home. He pulled me into a corner and said, "Art, I want your opinion on something. I can get ten-thousand acres in Florida, enough land to do all the things I've ever dreamed of. I can build another Disneyland and have plenty of room for future projects. What do you think?"

"Walt," I said, "when you first told me you were going to build Disneyland, I thought it was a terrible idea. Well, I was wrong then. But now, I think I've got some good advice for you: Don't do it. Don't build another Disneyland in Florida."

He looked at me in dismay. "Why not?"

"Look at what you've got over in Anaheim," I said. "Disneyland is one of a kind. It's like the Pyramids of Egypt or the Grand Canyon—there's nothing else like it in the world. As soon as you build another one, the original isn't unique anymore."

That shows how much I knew!

Of course, Walt had much bigger plans than a second Disneyland. He was going to build an experimental city of the future where people would live and test new ideas and technologies. He wanted to solve tough social problems such as urban congestion, pollution and crime. He had a vision for moving the world beyond the social and political conflicts that divide our nation.

"Walt Disney was an endlessly fascinating man, and mysterious as well. There were men who worked with him for thirty or forty years and they still didn't quite know him. He was a very complex and creative man, and that's what makes him unique."

CHRISTOPHER FINCH
AUTHOR AND DISNEY HISTORIAN

I remember being with him at the 1960 Winter Olympics in Squaw Valley, California. Walt was in charge of the opening and closing ceremonies, and he and I worked together on the nightly entertainment for the athletes in the Olympic Village.

One night, Walt and I looked out over the audience and saw hundreds of Olympic athletes from around the world, people of every race, language and nation. Walt's eyes shone as he said, "Isn't that amazing? Here are all of these people, different in so many ways, yet united by their hopes and goals and dreams. This is how the world should be."

The world knew Walt Disney as a great man who achieved great things. I knew him as a good man, a decent and kind man, and a friend. I miss him to this day. I've often wondered: What if he had been given another twenty years of life? What might he have accomplished?

I'm grateful that Pat Williams has written this book, *How to Be Like Walt*. It's a fitting tribute to Walt's memory and an important contribution to the Disney legacy. There are few people in history whose lives are more deserving of study and emulation than Walt Disney. Now more than ever, we need people with the qualities Walt had: optimism, imagination, creativity, leadership, integrity, courage, boldness, perseverance, commitment to excellence, reverence for the past, hope for tomorrow and faith in God.

How would Walt feel about a book called *How to Be Like Walt?* Well, I suspect he might not like the title. He'd probably arch one eyebrow and say, "I don't want anybody to be like me! I just want everybody to be themselves!"

But that's just the point of this book. Walt was unique—and so are you! The attitudes and traits we learn from Walt's life teach us how to be more uniquely who we are and who we were meant to be. If each of us would dream big dreams, approach life with hope and confidence, and persevere until our dreams come true, then we would not only be more like Walt, but we would become the people God created us to be.

Pat Williams has spent most of his career as an executive in the National Basketball Association, and he is currently senior vice president of the Orlando Magic. He has authored more than thirty books, including *Go for the Magic* and *How to Be Like Jesus.* Pat and his wife Ruth are parents of nineteen children, including fourteen adopted from four nations.

Pat became a serious student of Walt Disney in the late 1980s while working to build the Orlando Magic. He has personally interviewed virtually every living person who knew Walt, including Walt's family and friends, plus Disney artists, actors, composers, studio executives, Imagineers, secretaries and Disneyland "cast members." He and his writing-research team have consulted well over a thousand books, articles and other information sources.

> *"They called Walt a genius, and he was. But in a real sense, Walt was just an average man who could relate to other average people. So what is a genius, really? If we could learn the lessons of Walt's life, maybe we could all be geniuses."*
>
> JOHN KIMBALL
> SON OF ANIMATOR WARD KIMBALL

Pat Williams was assisted by two people who have spent years studying Walt and his accomplishments. Pat's writing partner, Jim Denney, is the author of the *Timebenders* science-fantasy novels for young readers; he cites Walt Disney as a major influence on his writing career. Pat's research partner, Peggy Matthews Rose, has spent most of her adult life with the Disney organization (her first job was as a Disneyland cast member, performing as Peter Pan).

Of all the books written about Walt Disney, this may be the most important. Walt's life was cut short in 1966, and he left many dreams unfulfilled. We are far from his cherished ideal of a world in which people of all races, languages, religions and creeds can come together in a spirit of harmony and brotherhood.

So I encourage you to turn the page, read this book, then go out and carry on Walt's unfinished work. Dream big dreams, and pursue those dreams with courage, optimism and perseverance. Commit yourself to making the world a better place.

I can imagine no finer tribute to Walt than that.

—Art Linkletter

Chapter One

❦

It All Started with a Boy

When Walt Disney was just a boy, his father put him to work in the harsh conditions of a Kansas City blizzard—then kept the money Walt earned. Even so, Walt embraced a nostalgia for his early years while dreaming big dreams of the future.

I came to Orlando, Florida, in 1989 to help build a brand-new NBA basketball team, the Orlando Magic. Soon after I arrived, I discovered that everywhere you look, Orlando bears the imprint of one personality: Walt Disney.

Walt never lived in Orlando. He only visited the town a few times before his death. Yet his vision and values have made Orlando what it is today— a city unlike any other. You sense it in the optimistic spirit of the people you meet. You see it in the clean, broad streets and beautifully designed buildings. Walt's spirit is alive in this town.

We named our team the Magic—not only because the Magic Kingdom is practically next door, but because of the way Walt's magical personality has touched this community. While working to build our organization, I received help and encouragement from Disney executives, and came to know many of them well. Some, such as Bob Matheison, Dick Nunis and Bob Allen, were personally mentored by Walt.

"*Though he wasn't in central
Florida often, no one left bigger
footprints in our sand
than Walt Disney.*"

JOY WALLACE DICKINSON
JOURNALIST, *ORLANDO SENTINEL*

In August 1986, at an event at a Disney hotel, I sat next to Dick Nunis, who was then head of Disney Attractions. Dick began with Disney in 1955 and had known Walt well. So I asked him, "What made Walt Disney so successful?" Then I spread out a napkin and jotted down everything he said. Dick shared story after story of Walt's life—and I wrote each one down. Those stories helped shape my previous Disney-inspired book, *Go for the Magic*.

In the years since I came to Orlando, I've made a second career of studying the life and words of Walt Disney. I've read every book I could find about Walt, and have spent hundreds of hours interviewing people who knew him. Though I never met Walt, I feel I know him well.

Some people have told me it's impossible (even foolhardy) to attempt a book called *How to Be Like Walt*. "The man was one of a kind—nobody can be like Walt!" they told me.

Yes, Walt was unique—but does that mean there is nothing we can learn from him? Don't you believe it, my friend! There isn't a day that goes by that I don't apply one of the lessons of Walt's life to my own career and personal life. Though I never met him, Walt is one of my mentors. My life has been deeply impacted by this man. It would be fair to say that the Orlando Magic would not exist if not for Walt's influence.

The title of this book is *How to Be Like Walt*—but I'm not suggesting that you should open a cartoon studio or build a theme park. Whatever your dreams and goals, the lessons of Walt's life will serve you well. Whether you work in the field of entertainment, the arts, finance, industry, sales, government, philanthropy or religion, you will have greater success and make a greater impact on the world if you apply the principles of Walt's amazing life.

Walt once said, "I only hope that we never lose sight of one thing—that it was all started by a mouse." In reality, it all started with a boy. Here is that boy's story.

The deacon's son

Walter Elias Disney was born in Chicago on December 5, 1901. He was named Walter after Rev. Walter Parr, pastor of Chicago's St. Paul Congregational Church. Young Walter was raised in the strict Congregationalist tradition.

Walt was the youngest of four sons born to Elias and his wife Flora. His three brothers were Herbert (born 1888), Raymond (1890), and Roy Oliver Disney (1893). His sister Ruth was born in 1903. Walt's father traced his lineage back to Hughes d'Isigny, a knight from Isigny-sur-Mer on the coast of Normandy, France. D'Isigny fought in the Norman conquest of England in 1066, then settled in Ireland. Walt's great-grandfather emigrated to Canada in 1834, and his father Elias was born in Ontario in 1859.

Elias married a schoolteacher, Flora Call from Ohio. In the early 1890s, Elias moved his family to Chicago, where he took a job as a carpenter at the 1893 World's Fair (the Columbian Exposition), working seven days a week for a dollar a day.

Elias Disney was an inflexible, un-imaginative, and almost humorless man. Devoutly religious, he maintained a severe approach to child-rearing: "Spare the rod and spoil the child."

Once when Walt was in his early teens, Elias growled at the boy for being slow in handing him a tool. Walt shot back, "I'm working as fast as I can!" Elias ordered Walt to the basement for punishment. Walt's brother Roy told him, "Don't take it from him anymore!" Steeled by Roy's advice, Walt went to the basement with his father. As Elias was about to strike Walt with the handle of his hammer, Walt snatched the hammer from his father's hand.

> "There is a theme to Walt's life and career—a beginning, a middle and a conclusion. There is meaning and continuity to everything he ever did."
>
> RAY WATSON
> FORMER VICE CHAIRMAN,
> WALT DISNEY PRODUCTIONS

"I held both of his hands," Walt recalled in later years. "I was stronger than he was. I just held them. And he cried. He never touched me after that."

There's no excuse for violence against children. Yet it would be a mistake to write off Walt's father as a two-dimensional villain. Elias Disney loved his family, and Walt loved his father despite the man's flaws. Elias possessed a number of good qualities that shaped Walt's life in a positive way.

First, there was Elias Disney's Protestant integrity. He taught his children the importance of honesty and a good reputation—a crucial lesson for young Walter. If Walt Disney had ever sullied his name with scandal, the trusted Walt Disney corporate identity would have become worthless.

Second, there was Elias Disney's Protestant work ethic. Elias worked hard and usually earned a decent living for his family. When misfortune pushed him out of one business, he would start a new business, often in a different part of the country. Young Walter watched his father take risks and battle adversity, and he learned crucial lessons about hard work and persistence.

Walt's father was compassionate toward his fellow man. Elias frequently offered a free meal and a place to sleep to complete strangers. "He'd bring home some of the weirdest characters," Walt later recalled. Walt's sister Ruth remembered Elias as "very sociable. He had such a gracious way with people who came to our house. I always wanted to be like that."

"He was a strict, hard guy with a great sense of honesty and decency," said Walt's brother Roy. "He never drank. I rarely even saw him smoke. . . . He was a good dad."

> *"Walt lived by an intense work ethic that was planted in him at an early age. It came from his mother and father."*
>
> RANDY THORNTON, AWARD-WINNING PRODUCER, WALT DISNEY RECORDS

"I had tremendous respect for him," said Walt. "I worshipped him. Nothing but his family counted." Walt chose to emulate his father's best traits: faith in God, faith in his fellow man, a strong work ethic, honesty and integrity, perseverance, a tolerance for risk, compassion for people, love of music, and love for family.

The farm boy from the big city

Walt's personality was profoundly shaped by his mother. Flora Call Disney was an even-tempered woman who almost never displayed anger, though she was tough and assertive when she had to be. The daughter of a scholar, Flora loved good books. She taught Walt how to read before he started school.

Flora was a skilled seamstress and made most of the children's clothes. She was also good with finances, and often helped in her husband's business enterprises. She drew the plans for the Disney family home at 1249 Tripp Avenue in Chicago. Elias built the house and painted it white with blue trim. Walt was born in an upstairs bedroom of that house.

In 1906, increasingly alarmed about the corrupting influences of the big city, Elias and Flora bought a forty-five-acre farm near Marceline, Missouri, a hundred miles northeast of Kansas City. This move profoundly affected Walt's life. He would later recall nothing of those early Chicago years; his earliest memories were those of a Missouri farm boy.

Though Walt would become a man of the big city, his life was shaped by life in Marceline. Small towns and farms formed the backdrop for most of Walt's cartoons and feature films. Disneyland's Main Street USA is an idealized version of Marceline, Missouri. One of Walt's closest associates on the Disneyland project, Harrison "Buzz" Price, told me, "Walt was rooted to reality in Marceline. He grew up there around real people. He lived close to the earth, close to nature. He maintained that farm boy quality all his life."

Flora had a great sense of humor, enjoying a good joke—even if the joke was on her (young Walter was an incorrigible practical joker). "We had a wonderful mother," Walt's brother Roy recalled. "She could kid the life out of my dad when he was peevish." Flora Disney's love of laughter helped compensate for Elias' austere personality. Her warmth brightened the Disney home and helped shape the optimistic outlook of young Walter Elias Disney.

Increasingly unhappy with life on the farm, Walt's two eldest brothers Herbert and Ray left home one night, taking the train to Chicago. Their departure made life all the harder for Roy, the third Disney brother and only remaining farmhand.

"His parents were plain people who moved from one section of the country to another in futile search of the American dream. Young Walt showed no brilliance as a student; he daydreamed through his classes. Cartooning proved his major interest, but his drawings were uninspired; as soon as he could hire better cartoonists, he gave up drawing entirely. It seems incredible that the unschooled cartoonist from Kansas City . . . could have produced works of unmatched imagination."

BOB THOMAS
DISNEY BIOGRAPHER

Roy Oliver Disney was eight years older than Walt. Despite the gap in their ages, Roy and Walt were close. Roy saw himself as his little brother's protector. Little did Roy know that he would make a career of looking after Walt.

From his earliest years, Walt was a risk-taker. On several occasions, he talked his reluctant sister Ruth into cutting across a nearby pasture. When they did, they were invariably chased by a bull. Sometimes they escaped being trampled by a mere second or two—a memory that was the basis of a scene in Disney's *Song of the South* (1946).

Young Walter saw the animals on the farm as friends and companions. He would go out to the barnyard every morning, greet them all by name, and invent stories about them. One of Walt's closest pals was a fat piglet named Skinny who followed him around like a puppy.

One year, a circus parade came through Marceline. Walter stood on the curb with his mother and sister, watching the parade pass by: clowns, acrobats, elephants, tigers and more. Walt's parents couldn't afford to take him to the circus, so Walt went home, made a tent out of burlap sacks, caged up some farm animals in wooden crates, and charged neighbor kids ten cents to see his homemade "circus." When Flora found out, she made him refund every dime. Walt's love of circuses and parades would last a lifetime.

Marceline was a small but bustling whistlestop on the Santa Fe Railroad. Uncle Mike Martin, a Santa Fe engineer, would bring candy for Roy, Walter and Ruthie, then sit on the front porch swing and talk about life on the rails—everything from his own railroad adventures to the legend of Casey Jones. Walt was fascinated.

Walt's father had once worked as a machinist with the Union Pacific line, and had helped lay track across the Great Plains and the Rocky Mountains. Whenever Uncle Mike was telling railroad stories, Elias would swap a few of his own. One story Walt never tired of hearing was the time Elias met "Buffalo Bill" Cody, the legendary founder of Buffalo Bill's Wild West Show.

In Marceline, Walt saw his first theatrical play—a road performance of *Peter Pan* starring Maude Adams. Walt also saw his first motion picture in a Marceline movie house—a depiction of the crucifixion and resurrection of Jesus Christ. The powerful images made a lasting impression on the boy.

Young Walter spent his happiest days on that farm outside of Marceline. "To tell the truth," Walt once said, "more things of importance happened to me in Marceline than have happened since—or are likely to in the future. . . . I'm glad I'm a small-town boy and I'm glad Marceline was my town."

Young Walter's favorite pastime was drawing pictures. To amuse his sister, who was sick with the measles, nine-year-old Walt created a flip-book animated with walking stick figures. Ruth giggled with delight as she flipped the pages and the stick figures moved.

One of the greatest encouragements Walt received for his budding talent came from Dr. L. I. Sherwood,

> *"As a boy in Missouri, my grandpa loved the railroads because they could take you anywhere—to all kinds of unknown places. He never lost his fascination with trains."*
>
> WALTER DISNEY MILLER
> WALT'S GRANDSON

a retired doctor who lived near the Disney farm. On one occasion, the doctor commissioned Walt to do a drawing of his prize Morgan stallion. "I think the doctor must have held that horse nearly all day, just so I could draw it," Walt later recalled. "Needless to say, the drawing wasn't so hot, but Doc made me think it was tops." The twenty-five cents Walt earned opened his eyes to the possibility of drawing pictures for a living.

Whenever Walt's Uncle Robert and Aunt Margaret came to visit, Aunt Maggie would bring pencils and Crayola paper tablets for Walt to draw on. Aside from Aunt Maggie and Doc Sherwood, though, other grownups were not so encouraging.

Walt's father often rebuked him for "wasting time" drawing pictures at the expense of his farm chores and schoolwork. "He just scoffed at me," Walt recalled, "and said that if I was foolish enough to want to become an artist, I should learn the violin. Then I could always get a job in a band if I was in need of money."

A fourth-grade teacher once scolded Walt for exercising his Disneyesque imagination on a class assignment. The students were shown a bowl of flowers to sketch. Walt drew the flowers with faces—a foretaste of the humanized flowers in the Silly Symphonies and *Alice in Wonderland*. "Flowers," the teacher sternly admonished, "do *not* have faces!"

Electrified in Kansas City

In 1909, Elias became seriously ill. Unable to keep the farm going, Elias sold the property for $5,175—less than he had paid for it. It broke Walt's heart to leave the farm. He cried openly when his favorite animals were auctioned off.

Elias moved his family to Kansas City. From the sale of the farm, he purchased a *Kansas City Star* distributorship. He hired several delivery boys, and made Roy and Walt deliver papers without pay. Every morning at 3:30 A.M. the boys were awakened to deliver newspapers with their father.

Elias insisted on quality work and made the boys place the paper inside the customer's storm door, even if the boys had to walk through four-foot snowdrifts. Some have suggested that Walt's memories of those harsh winters might have been exaggerated. But Disney historian Dan Viets, co-author of *Walt Disney's Missouri*, told me, "Walt told the truth about his boyhood. He talked about one winter in Kansas City with enormous

> *"People who have worked with me say I am 'innocence in action.'*
>
> *They say I have the unself-consciousness of a child. Maybe I have. I still look at the world with uncontaminated wonder, and with all living things I have a terrific sympathy. It was the most natural thing in the world for me to imagine that mice and squirrels might have feelings just like mine."*
>
> WALT DISNEY

chest-high snowdrifts. I checked the weather records for that winter and, sure enough, it was a hard winter with lots of snow."

Between newspaper delivery, school and a job after school, Walt put in the equivalent of an eight-hour workday every day. It's no wonder that, as an adult, Walt rarely took vacations. From boyhood on, working hard was all he ever knew.

Those were traumatic years for Walt. Throughout his life, he experienced recurring nightmares—dreams in which he trudged endlessly through blizzards, or was punished by his father for failing to make a delivery.

At nineteen, Roy decided to leave home. "Dad treats me like a little boy," he told Walt in the summer of 1912. Roy left home in the middle of the night and headed to Kansas, leaving Walt without his longtime friend and protector.

> "I was a little guy and I'd be up to my nose in snow. I still have nightmares about it. What I really liked on those cold mornings was getting to the apartment buildings. I'd drop off the papers and then lie down in the warm apartment corridor and snooze a little and try to get warm. I still wake up with that on my mind."
>
> WALT DISNEY

At the Benton Grammar School, Walt was a mediocre student. His teachers complained that he was more inclined to daydreaming and drawing cartoons than completing assignments. He sometimes fell asleep in class, due to exhaustion from hard work.

Walt's best friend in school, Walter Pfeiffer, recalled an incident from Walt's fifth-grade year. "On Lincoln's birthday," he said, "Walt came to school all dressed up like Lincoln. He had a shawl that I guess he got from his dad. He made this stovepipe hat out of cardboard and shoe polish. He purchased a beard from a place that sold theatrical things. He did this all on his own. Principal Cottingham saw him and said 'Walter, you look like Lincoln. Why are you dressed this way?' Walt said, 'It's Lincoln's birthday and I want to recite his Gettysburg address.' He had memorized it. Walt got up in front of the class and the kids thought this was terrific, so Cottingham took him to each one of the classes in the school. Walt loved that."

Walt considered Mr. Cottingham a friend and sent his family Christmas cards over the years. In 1938, Walt contacted Cottingham, who was still the

Benton School principal (he retired in 1940), and invited the entire student body to see *Snow White and the Seven Dwarfs* for free.

Walt enjoyed his time at Benton School. He entertained friends with convincing impressions of his hero, silent film star Charlie Chaplin. He also displayed his cartooning skills in class. One of his teachers liked to have Walt tell stories to the class and illustrate them on the chalkboard as he spoke.

> *"When I was in school in Kansas City, and later in Chicago, I was both stage-struck and movie-struck."*
>
> WALT DISNEY

Walt and his chum Walter Pfeiffer once performed a skit for a school talent show called "Fun in the Photograph Gallery." The boys pretended to take a classmate's picture with a trick camera. First, the camera squirted water, soaking the unsuspecting classmate. Next, Walt pulled a sheet of paper out of the camera—a caricature of the victimized student (Walt had drawn it in advance, of course). This early show-business experience employed three of Walt's skills: showmanship, comedy and cartooning.

Billing themselves as "The Two Walts," the boys put on skits and comedy routines at amateur night contests around Kansas City. Elias Disney frowned on show business, so Walt would sneak out and meet Walt Pfeiffer at a local theater. "I'd sneak him out of the window, so his dad wouldn't know," Pfeiffer recalled. "When we'd get through [with a show], I'd shove him back in the window and go home."

Walt studied the fine points of acting, including facial expression, gestures, vocal variation, emotion and comedic timing. Throughout his career, Walt used his acting skills to dramatize characters in his cartoons and features. He even invented a comic dance step used as an animation guide for Baloo the Bear in *The Jungle Book*, the last animated feature Walt personally supervised.

Walt was undoubtedly influenced by two amusement parks in Kansas City. One was Fairmount Park on the east side of the city, just two blocks from Walt's first Kansas City home at 2706 East 31st Street (Walt's family later moved to 3028 Bellefontaine Street). It featured giant dipper rides, a nine-hole golf course, a zoo, and swimming and boating on a natural lake.

An elaborate July Fourth fireworks show attracted crowds of over 50,000 people. Walt's sister Ruth once told an interviewer that she and Walt would peer through the fence, longing to enter that "fairyland" (as she called it), but lacking the price of admission.

The other park that influenced Walt's imagination was Electric Park. Located at 46th Street and the Paseo, it was one of the largest amusement parks in America at that time. Like Disneyland, Electric Park featured band concerts, thrill rides (the Spiral Coaster, the Log Flume Plunge, the Ben Hur Racer), and spectacular nighttime fireworks displays. Electric Park also featured a steam-powered train that circled the park, just as a train now circles Disneyland. Perhaps the adult Walt Disney was recalling Electric Park when he said that Disneyland "has that *thing*—the imagination and the feeling of happy excitement—I knew when I was a kid."

Electric Park got its name from the 100,000 electric bulbs that transformed it nightly into a magical fairyland of illumination. Edison's light bulb was still a novelty in those days, and only a third of American homes had electricity. Electric Park hosted crowds of up to 50,000 visitors a day before it burned to the ground in 1925. If you visit Disneyland at night and see the park lit up with thousands of lights, you may be catching a glimpse of the incandescent glory of Electric Park as it shone in Walt's memories.

Walt's teenage years

Walt fell in love with Snow White when he was fourteen years old.

The year was 1916, and Walt was one of scores of Kansas City newsboys invited to a special screening of the silent movie version of *Snow White,* starring Marguerite Clark. It was the first feature-length film Walt had ever seen, and it made a deep impression on him.

When Walt was fifteen, Elias Disney sold the newspaper route to invest in a jelly-canning firm, the O'Zell Company of Chicago. Elias moved his wife and daughter to Chicago and became an O'Zell executive. Walt stayed with brothers Herbert and Roy in the Bellefontaine Street home. Herb was married with a two-year-old daughter, and Roy was an unmarried bank clerk.

Roy helped Walt get a summer job as a "news butcher" for the Van Noyes News Company, selling newpapers, candy and tobacco to passengers on the

Santa Fe Railroad. Walt bought the railroad men cigars and chewing tobacco from his own box, and they let Walt ride with them and blow the steam whistle.

At the end of that summer, Walt joined his parents and sister in Chicago. By day he attended McKinley High School; by night the Chicago Academy of Fine Arts. His art teacher, Carl Wertz, encouraged students to observe and draw live models, both animals and people. Wertz admired the comic touch Walt brought to his drawings.

Leroy Gossett and Carey Orr, two prominent Chicago newspaper cartoonists, mentored Walt, and inspired him to seek a career as a newspaper cartoonist. Walt also worked as a cartoonist on the McKinley High School magazine, *The Voice*. When not in school, Walt worked part-time at the O'Zell Company.

During the summer of 1918, Walt applied for a job with the post office, but was turned down because of his age. Undaunted, the sixteen-year-old Walt put on one of his father's hats and a false mustache, then returned to the post office. The same man who had turned him down an hour earlier promptly hired him.

By the fall of 1918, World War I had been raging for over four years. Roy had joined the Navy and Walt vowed to get into the war as well. He and his friend, Russell Maas, were too young for the Army, so they decided to enlist in the Canadian Army, where the age limit was lower. Russell's mother uncovered their plan and tipped Flora, which ended that scheme.

A few weeks later, Russell told Walt that the American Ambulance Corps had been formed by the Red Cross and was accepting seventeen-year-olds. Walt and Russell showed up at the Red Cross office claiming to be brothers—Walter and Russell St. John. Their plan fell through when the Red Cross asked to see their passports.

Walt told his parents he wanted their permission to join the ambulance corps. Elias refused, but Flora surprised Walt by taking his side. "Three of my sons have left this family in the middle of the night," she said. "Walter's determined to go, Elias, even if he has to sneak out like his brothers. I'd rather sign this paper and know where he is."

After a heated argument, Elias finally said, "Forge my name if you want, but I won't sign!" And he stormed out of the room.

Flora forged his name, and it was done—except that she had entered Walt's real birthdate on the passport application. Walt solved that by changing "1901" to "1900." With the stroke of a pen, Walt became a year older and eligible to volunteer. Walt's Red Cross training was interrupted by the deadly influenza epidemic of 1918.

Though sick herself, Flora took care of Walt and his sister while they suffered fever and delirium. Thanks to Flora's nursing skills (and a lot of quinine water), Walt and Ruthie survived. When Walt recovered, he found that his ambulance unit—and his friend Russell—had shipped out to France. Walt was assigned to a new unit undergoing training in Sound Beach, Connecticut.

There, Walt became acquainted with a fifteen-year-old ambulance corpsman (who also lied about his age) named Ray Kroc. Kroc would later become famous as the founder of the McDonald's fast-food empire. During breaks from training, Kroc and his friends would go into town. Walt stayed by himself in camp. As Kroc later recalled, he and his comrades "regarded Disney as a strange duck, because whenever we had time off and went on the town to chase girls, he stayed in the camp drawing pictures."

"The things I did during those eleven months I was overseas added up to a lifetime of experience. It was such a valuable experience that I feel that if we have to send our boys into the Army we should send them even younger than we do. I know that being on my own at an early age has made me more self-reliant."

WALT DISNEY

On November 11, the Armistice was signed at Compiegne, France, ending the war—and Walt's dreams of glory. The Red Cross still needed ambulance drivers, however, and Walt shipped out on November 18. He sailed to Le Havre, France, aboard the SS *Vaubin,* a converted cattle ship. After passing through mine-infested waters, Walt arrived on December 4, the day before his seventeenth birthday.

Walt took the train from the coast to Paris (he noted that French locomotives were much smaller than the high-powered American engines). After a brief tour of Paris, he reported to Red Cross headquarters at St. Cyr. He slept on a cot in a cell-like room of an unheated chateau, using an old newspaper for a blanket.

Walt chauffeured military officers around Paris—hardly the battlefield duty he volunteered for. Later, he drove relief supplies to war-ravaged areas. He decorated his ambulance with cartoons and picked up extra money by painting discarded German helmets to look like battlefield souvenirs. He sent the money home to Flora via American Express with instructions to buy Ruthie a watch and put the rest in the bank.

While in France, Walt started smoking cigarettes for the first time in his life. Smoking would eventually become a three-pack-a-day habit leading to his premature death (if there is one way you should *not* be like Walt, this is it: *don't smoke*).

In September 1919, Walt's ambulance unit was disbanded. Walt returned to America with the goal of becoming a newspaper cartoonist in Kansas City. On his way back to Kansas City, he stopped by his parents' home in Chicago for a brief visit.

An incorrigible prankster, Walt told his mother that, from the deck of the troop ship, he had seen the words "Prudential Insurance" in neon lights across the Rock of Gibraltar. He also showed her a battlefield souvenir he kept in a little box. When he opened the lid, his mother screamed at the sight of a bloody thumb. It was actually Walt's own thumb, stained with iodine and poking through the bottom of the box.

> *"After World War I, Walt Disney returned home to make a living as a newspaper cartoonist in Kansas City. His father wanted him to come home to Chicago and work in the jelly factory. There was a good-paying job all lined up for him. It would have been the easy thing to do, but Walt said no. He was a young man with a dream."*
>
> BRIAN BURNES
> COAUTHOR, *WALT DISNEY'S MISSOURI*

That evening after dinner, Walt's father called him into the living room for a serious discussion. "Walter," Elias said, "I have a job for you at the jelly factory. It pays twenty-five dollars a week."

"Dad," Walt replied, "I don't want to work at the jelly factory. I want to be an artist."

"You can't make a living drawing pictures," Elias said. "You need a *real* job."

"I'll get a real job," Walt said, "as a newspaper cartoonist." Seventeen-year-old Walt Disney had a dream, and was determined to make his dream come true.

How to Be Like Walt— Lesson 1: Live the Adventure

Walt's boyhood on the farm near Marceline inspired a sense of wonder and imagination that stayed with Walt throughout his life. Yet he also experienced treatment from his father that, by today's standards, can only be considered abusive. Wounds in the flesh will heal; scars in the soul last a lifetime.

The relationship between Elias Disney and his sons was a complex mixture of love and hate, respect and resentment. All four boys loved their father, yet hated the way he forced them to work and donate every cent to the family till. They respected their father's faith, honesty, integrity, charity to strangers and hard work—yet they resented his violent temper and harsh demands. It's significant that all four Disney sons left home between the ages of sixteen and nineteen. They couldn't wait to get out of their father's house and live on their own terms. Clearly, there was an oppressive atmosphere in the Disney home.

Walt's boyhood years are instructive because of the way he chose to deal with his childhood memories. He spoke with heartbreaking candor about having nightmares throughout his life, yet he never let childhood pain darken his optimism. Walt chose to focus on the good in life while letting go of the bad. He shaped his life around warm, nostalgic memories of Marceline, the romance of the railroad, the thrill of his first circus parade, the joy of seeing *Snow White* on the silver screen. He chose to emulate his father's positive traits while disregarding the negative traits.

Walt's positive attitude was a crucial factor in his success and personal happiness. Unfailing optimism was central to the personality of Mickey Mouse, and a consistent theme throughout Walt's cartoons, feature films and television shows. Walt once said, "I always like to look on the optimistic side of life, but I am realistic enough to know that life is a complex matter. With the laughs come the tears, and in developing motion pictures or television shows, you must combine all the facts of life—drama, pathos and humor."

"A strict, hardworking father and a fun-loving mother gave Disney the early traits he needed."

INVESTORS BUSINESS DAILY'S "LEADERS & SUCCESS" COLUMN

Walt's formative years provided the foundation for a lifetime of success. From his mother, Walt learned the value of fun and a good sense of humor. From his father, he learned the value of faith, honesty, integrity, hard work, persistence and a willingness to take risks. Walt sifted his childhood memories, savored the good experiences, and distilled all of those good memories into his films and theme parks.

Stacia Martin is both a Disney character artist and a Disney historian. "My life has been impacted by Walt's unfailing optimism," she told me. "He had a difficult childhood, and received little encouragement to pursue his dreams. But Walt never stopped believing in himself. He kept faith with his dreams, and saw them through to conclusion. You can't undergo as much hardship as Walt did without a great reservoir of optimism down deep in your spirit. Walt's example inspires me every day."

Author Ray Bradbury, a friend and admirer of Walt Disney, told me, "Everything Walt achieved in his life was something he was told he couldn't do. His father told him he could never make a living by drawing cartoons. He spent his entire career proving the doubters wrong. And he had a wonderful time doing it."

Ray once told an interviewer, "Walt Disney was more important than all the politicians we've ever had. They pretended optimism. He *was* optimism. He has done more to change the world for the good than almost any politician who ever lived."

It's true. Walt was so much more than a great showman. He was a great human being who touched and changed our lives. The joy and inspiration he gave the world is far more important, more uplifting to the human race than almost any invention, law or idea in human history. Because Walt walked among us, the world is a kinder, more compassionate, more hopeful place than it would have been without him.

Walt believed in the family and he produced inspiring, illuminating entertainment for the entire family to enjoy together. He enshrined the great legends of American history. In the process, Walt enriched and elevated the way we view ourselves and our place in history.

Today, it's hard to imagine growing up in a world without Disney theme parks, *Snow White* and *Mary Poppins,* Mickey Mouse and Donald Duck. Critics may call the Disney worldview simplistic or unreal. *Pollyanna,* after all, was a Disney movie! Well, let the critics complain. The world would never miss a thousand critics, more or less, but the world would be a much poorer place if there hadn't been just one Walt Disney.

That is why I have written *How to Be Like Walt.* My own life has been transformed by my study of Walt Disney. The more I learn, the more I want to be like Walt.

I'm not claiming Walt was a saint. He was a flawed human being, and in these pages we'll talk honestly about those flaws. But he was also a *great* human being. His life deserves our study and emulation. And the first lessons we learn from Walt's early life are these:

Accept the pain of the past. Learn the lessons of the past. Embrace the nostalgic memories of the past. Then *dream big dreams* of the future and start chasing them!

Above all, live your life as a grand adventure. When Walt was just sixteen, he couldn't wait to break the boundaries of his existence, to rush out into the world, to drive an ambulance through a world war. So be like Walt. Live the adventure. Wade out into the depths of this life and meet it on your own terms.

And the next time you visit a Disney theme park or watch a Disney movie, remember that it all started with a boy—a Missouri farm boy whose father told him to stop dreaming and get a "real job" in a jelly factory. A Missouri farm boy who changed the world.

It doesn't matter where you came from, or who your parents were, or what happened to you when you were a child. All that matters is that you are willing to live the adventure and dream big dreams, then make those dreams come true.

Chapter Two

❧

Anything Is Possible

From the earliest years of his career, Walt demonstrated two qualities that would mark his life and propel his success: his unabashed salesmanship and his unwavering belief that anything is possible.

Walt left his parents' home in Chicago and took the train to Kansas City, back to the house on Bellefontaine Street. On Walt's first night back in Kansas City, he and Roy stayed up late, talking about their adventures and about the future. Walt told Roy about his experiences in France, and Roy recounted the horror of seeing ships in his convoy sunk by German U-boats.

Walt and Roy also talked about the future. Roy was making $90 a month as a teller at the First National Bank of Kansas City; he looked forward to a future in the world of finance. Walt told Roy his plans to become a political cartoonist.

The next day, Walt applied at the Kansas City *Star*, but was turned down because he was too young. Undaunted, Walt decided to start as a copy boy and work his way up. He returned the next day in his Red Cross uniform. The advertising manager took one look at Walt in his uniform and told him he was too old to be a copy boy.

A few days later, Walt landed a job with the Pesmen-Rubin Commercial Art Studio, making $50 a month. There, he met a young artist with the unusual Dutch name of Ubbe Iwwerks. The two eighteen-year-olds became friends and formed their own company, Iwerks-Disney Commercial Artists. Ubbe (who later shortened his name to Ub Iwerks at Walt's suggestion) did illustrating and lettering while Walt handled cartooning and sales.

> *"They were going to call it Disney-Iwerks, but that sounded like an optical company: 'Disney Eye Works.' So they changed it around to Iwerks-Disney."*
>
> DAVE SMITH
> ARCHIVIST, THE WALT DISNEY COMPANY

With the help of his boyhood chum, Walt Pfeiffer, Walt landed the company's first contract: designing the United Leatherworkers' *Journal* (Walt Pfeiffer's dad was an official in the union). Next, Walt showed his drawings to Al Carder, a Kansas City restaurateur who had been a neighbor of the Disney family. Carder also published a trade newspaper, the *Restaurant News*. "You fellas do good work," Carder said, "but the *Restaurant News* is a small publication. I don't have enough work to keep two artists busy."

"Just give us a couple of desks," Walt countered. "We'll do all your artwork for free. You'll have a full-time art department at no charge—and we'll have an office rent-free. Deal?" Even at eighteen, Walt was a great salesman. It was a deal.

In their first month in business, they cleared $135 after expenses. When Walt learned of an opening for a commercial artist at the Kansas City Slide Company, Ub encouraged Walt to apply, promising to keep Iwerks-Disney going. A. Vern Cauger, owner of the company, gave Walt the job, which paid $40 a week. Unfortunately, Ub Iwerks was not the salesman that Walt was, and Iwerks-Disney soon folded.

At Kansas City Slide Company (later called Kansas City Film Ad Company), Walt learned about a new artform called *animation*. After Walt learned the principle of animation with crude cutouts, he wanted to do animated cartoons.

At the Kansas City Public Library, Walt found two books that altered the course of his life. One was Eadweard Muybridge's *The Human Figure in*

Motion, which contains sequential photographs (like frames of movie film) of people engaged in various actions—walking, running, throwing a ball. The other book was *Animated Cartoons: How They Are Made, Their Origins and Development* by Carl Lutz. Walt made photostatic copies of the pictures in those books and kept them as reference guides for his animation experiments.

Of the Lutz book, Walt later said, "Everyone has been remarkably influenced by a book, or books. In my case it was a book on cartoon animation. I discovered it in the Kansas City Library at the time I was preparing to make motion picture animation my life's work. The book told me all I needed to know as a beginner—all about the arts and the mechanics of making drawings that move on the theater screen. . . . Finding that book was one of the most important and useful events in my life."

"When you look at photos of Walt Disney, the young animator, he seems to be enjoying himself so much. The first scene of the first Laugh-O-gram is so telling. Walt is in the picture, smoking his pipe. He seems to be having a blast."

ROBERT W. BUTLER
COAUTHOR, *WALT DISNEY'S MISSOURI*

Walt's career had turned a corner. No longer could he imagine himself drawing static cartoons that would appear in a newspaper one day, then be gone forever. He dreamed of making drawings that lived and moved.

It's interesting to speculate: If A. Vern Cauger had not given Walt a job at his company, it is quite possible that Walt might have never discovered the wonders of animation. I spoke with Ted Cauger, the son of the man who hired Walt. "God sent Walt Disney to the Kansas City Film Ad Company," Ted told me. "It was all destiny—Walt's arrival in Kansas City, my dad owning that company and giving Walt a job, and Walt discovering how animation is done while he was working there. It was all part of God's plan."

Those Kansas City years were lean times for Walt. Though he made decent money, he spent it on equipment for his animation experiments. He set up the equipment in the garage on Bellefontaine Street. Walt's niece Dorothy (his brother Herb's daughter) was five years old at the time, and she recalls, "Walt had me stroll down the walk in front of the house carrying a full milk bottle and wheeling my baby dolly carriage. I pretended to accidentally break the bottle, spilling the milk over everything. Then he reversed the film so that I backed up, and the milk came back up into the bottle."

By this time, Roy was courting Edna Francis, a clerk at the First National Bank. When Walt accompanied Roy to Edna's house, he took it upon himself to serve as chaperone. After dinner, he would sit in a corner, sketching in his notebook, saying, "Don't mind me." He sometimes left notes around the room with cartoons of two love birds in a nest, or with the emphatic command, "No canoodling!" One time, Walt hid a rubber squeak toy under the sofa. When Roy and Edna sat down, the squeak toy squawked, Edna shrieked, and Walt appeared in the doorway, wagging his finger.

I asked Roy and Edna's son, Roy E. Disney (former Vice Chairman of The Walt Disney Company), about his parents' relationship with Walt. "My dad and Walt had a unique relationship throughout their lives," he replied. "I think the key was that Dad was eight years older than Walt, so Walt was always the little brother. In all those years together, Dad felt responsible to take care of his little brother. In addition, Dad married a woman who was three and a half years older than him and twelve years older than Walt. To my mother, Walt was always a little punk kid. She knew just how to stick a pin in his bubble and bring him back to earth. It was a riot to watch Mom do that."

The Laugh-O-gram cartoon factory

Ub Iwerks recalled an incident from his early friendship with Walt that underscores the confidence Walt had in his dreams. It was a slow work day at the Kansas City Film Ad Company, so the artists and cameramen got up a game of penny ante poker. "Hey, Diz," one of them said, "come on, we need your money!"

Walt was at his drawing table, working. "Deal me out," Walt said. "I'm busy."

Ub got up and wandered over to Walt's drawing table. He found Walt practicing his signature. "I knew right then," Iwerks said, "that with his ego, Walt was going to make it."

Walt worked at the ad company during the day and moonlighted producing Newman Laugh-O-grams which sold at a rate of thirty cents per foot of film (which only covered his material costs—he forgot to charge for his time).

By 1920, Roy and Edna were talking seriously about marriage. But Roy suffered two serious attacks of influenza, then underwent a botched tonsillectomy. Soon afterward, Roy was diagnosed with tuberculosis, and the Veterans Administration sent him to a convalescent hospital in New Mexico. It would be years before Roy and Edna would see each other again.

> *"Walt's life proves to us all that you can start with virtually nothing, and if you have passion and love for what you are doing— and above all, if you never give up—you can reach heights that no one ever believed possible."*
>
> LESLIE IWERKS
> GRANDDAUGHTER OF UB IWERKS

Meanwhile, the O'Zell Jelly Company went bankrupt. Elias Disney lost his job and his investment, so he and Flora returned to Kansas City. Walt had no intention of living with his parents, so he moved to an apartment, leaving his camera equipment in his parents' garage. Elias charged him five dollars a month for storage.

In May 1922, Walt quit his job and incorporated a new enterprise, Laugh-O-gram Films, Inc. His plan was to produce New York-style animated shorts, using ink drawings on celluloid transparencies (or "cels"). He moved his camera equipment into a five-room suite in the McConahay Building at 1127 East 31st Street. For operating capital, Walt sold $15,000 worth of stock to several local investors—quite a feat of salesmanship for a twenty-year-old entrepreneur.

Walt coaxed a reluctant Ub Iwerks to join the Laugh-O-gram studio. Iwerks was supporting his mother and worried about being paid in rubber paychecks—a valid concern, as it turned out. Walt attracted five other young artists with a newspaper ad in which he promised animation training (though Walt himself was a novice in the field). Walt also hired a business manager, an inker-painter, a salesman and a secretary.

Walt's youthful exuberance, combined with his lack of business experience, resulted in wasteful spending on a lavish office suite and an over-large staff. Walt had a steep learning curve ahead of him.

"Walt Disney started Laugh-O-gram Films in Kansas City when he was twenty years old. He raised $15,000 to start his company—that's the equivalent of $150,000 today. He had no help from his father. He was completely on his own. Picture this young man in the 1920s, convincing friends and strangers to invest in his vision of something as innovative and unheard-of as a cartoon studio."

BRIAN BURNES
COAUTHOR, *WALT DISNEY'S MISSOURI*

The two twenty-year-olds, Walt and Ub, were the "old men" at Laugh-O-gram. The other employees were still in their teens. (Two of them, Hugh Harmon and Rudolf Ising, would later create the Looney Tunes and Merrie Melodies series for Warner Brothers.) There was no organizational chart—everyone did whatever needed to be done. For example, Walt's friend Walt Pfeiffer manned the animation camera and also inked cels.

Walt's new company quickly landed an $11,000 contract to produce cartoons for Pictorial Clubs, Inc. The distributor paid Walt $100 in earnest money, and his animators went to work. They cranked out cartoons that gave an updated twist to classic fairy tales—*Little Red Riding Hood, Jack and the Beanstalk, Goldilocks and the Three Bears, Puss in Boots* and *Cinderella*.

After six cartoon shorts, Pictorial Clubs went bankrupt. Walt had to lay off employees and cut artists' pay in half. Ub Iwerks returned to Kansas City Film Ad Company (though he continued to moonlight at Laugh-O-gram several nights a week).

By the end of 1922, Laugh-O-gram was approaching bankruptcy. Unable to pay his rent, Walt moved in with Ub and his mother. After two uncomfortable weeks, Walt moved his toothbrush and suitcase to the office and slept on the couch. Once a week, he went to the railroad station, where he could rent a bathtub, towel and soap for a dime.

The studio was temporarily saved when a Kansas City dentist, Dr. Thomas McCrum, paid Walt $500 to produce a film called *Tommy Tucker's Tooth*. In that film, which combined cartoon and live action, Tommy learns the importance of brushing three times a day. The story of how Dr. McCrum commissioned Walt to make that film illustrates how desperate Walt had become.

Walt was alone in his office when Dr. McCrum phoned, ready to conclude the deal. "Could you come to my office tonight?" said Dr. McCrum. "We'll wrap up the details and I'll give you a check for the first payment."

"I can't come," Walt said. "I don't have any shoes."

"No shoes!" said Dr. McCrum.

"I took my only pair to the shoemaker downstairs to have them resoled," Walt explained. "They're ready, but the shoemaker won't let me have them unless I pay him a dollar fifty."

"I'll be right over," the doctor said. He drove to Walt's office, paid the shoemaker for the shoes, then sat down with Walt and concluded the film deal.

Walt hired back some of his animators and made the movie. Twenty years later, after Mickey Mouse made Walt famous, that dental hygiene film continued to be shown around Kansas City.

Alice in Cartoonland

Re-energized by the cash infusion, Walt laid plans for a new cartoon series. He admired Max Fleischer's Out of the Inkwell cartoons, which always opened with Koko the Clown emerging from an ink bottle and jumping into the real world. Walt decided to reverse Fleischer's gimmick by having a real girl jump into a cartoon world. The series was called the Alice Comedies or Alice in Cartoonland.

Walt hired four-year-old Virginia Davis to play Alice. With her charming smile and Mary Pickford curls, little Virginia had screen appeal.

Walt directed Virginia by having her do various actions in front of a neutral background. Animation was added later by Walt, Ub and the other artists. (Forty years later, Walt and Ub would again combine animation and live action in *Mary Poppins*.)

"In order to crack the field, I said, 'I've got to get something a little unique,' you see. Now they had the clown out of the inkwell who played with the live people. So I reversed it. I took the live person and put her into the cartoon. I said, 'That's a new twist.' And it sold. I was surprised myself."

WALT DISNEY
REMEMBERING THE ALICE COMEDIES

When I interviewed Virginia Davis, she told me, "I was four when I first went to work for Walt. He was twenty-one. I just adored him. He was like a favorite uncle to me. I guess I was Walt's first star—the first Disney contract player.

"Walt was a great salesman. He could sell anything to anyone. He was also a very honest man—honest to a fault. When he gave his word, you could count on it. He was a salesman who did what he promised.

"He sold my mother on doing some of the filming for *Alice's Wonderland* in our home in Kansas City. Walt didn't have money to build sets. Instead, he brought all the lights and cameras into our home so that he could shoot the scene where my mother tucks me into bed. Later, after we finished filming *Alice's Wonderland,* Walt sold my mother on letting me go to California to make more Alice Comedies in Hollywood.

"Sometimes we would film in a vacant lot. Walt would have me act out a scene in front of a white tarp that was draped over a billboard to make a pure white background. Drawings would later be added to the white spaces.

"Walt was an excellent storyteller and actor. He would act out the character, so I could see the kind of performance he wanted. He'd say, 'Let's pretend there's a lion chasing you. Here it comes! You're frightened! Now, scream!' Or he'd pretend to be a wolf, and roar, 'Aaarrrggghhh!' Because they were silent films, he could direct me out loud while the camera was rolling.

"Film was expensive, so he had to get those shots in one take. I usually gave him what he wanted in the first take, so Walt was always happy with my performances.

"Walt was very protective of me when I worked for him. He was also protective of his product. He wanted the Alice Comedies to be as good as they could be. I cherish those memories of working with Walt at the very beginning of his career. I fell in love with him and I watched his career over the years. I was heartbroken when he died."

> *"Walt would take stories and act them out at a meeting, and kill you laughing, they were so funny. You'd have the feeling of the whole thing. You'd know exactly what he wanted. We often wondered if Walt could have been a great actor or a comedian."*
>
> DICK HUEMER
> DISNEY ANIMATION
> DIRECTOR AND STORY ARTIST

In May 1923, Walt contacted film distributor Margaret J. Winkler, who distributed Max Fleischer's Out of the Inkwell series. Walt described the Alice series to Miss Winkler, who sent back an encouraging reply (she had seen Walt's Laugh-O-gram cartoons and knew his work).

With live action filming for *Alice's Wonderland* under way, the $500 he'd received from Dr. McCrum quickly ran out. One of Walt's Kansas City investors, Dr. John Vance Cowles, occasionally advanced money to Walt, though he never expected to get his investment back. Dr. Cowles had been the Disney family physician for years, and always liked Walt. (Three decades later, Dr. Cowles' son, John Jr., helped design Disneyland and assisted in building a barn-workshop behind Walt's house.)

During this time, Walt's brother Roy moved from Santa Fe to a veterans facility in Tucson. Hearing of Walt's financial situation, Roy sent Walt a blank check. "Fill in any amount up to $30," Roy's note instructed. Walt made out the check for exactly $30.

Walt ate on credit at a Greek restaurant downstairs from his office. When his tab reached $60, one of the owners cut off Walt's credit. A few days later, the other owner went to Walt's office and found him sitting on a crate, eating cold beans from a can. "Oh, Walter," the man said, "go downstairs and get something to eat! Don't worry about the money."

By mid-June 1923, it was clear that Walt would not have the money to complete *Alice's Wonderland*. In an act of consummate salesmanship, he wrote to Margaret Winkler and said that the film "will be finished very soon" and he would arrive in New York in early July with a print of the film "and an outline of our future program."

Soon afterward, Walt was evicted from the McConahay Building.

> *"Walt once said, 'I think it's important to have a good hard failure when you're young.' His tough experiences gave him the courage of his convictions. He was an enterprising, entrepreneurial risk-taker because he wasn't afraid to fail."*
>
> CRAIG HODGKINS
> DISNEY WRITER AND LECTURER

Deeply discouraged, Walt wrote to Roy, who had moved to the Veterans Hospital in Sawtelle (West Los Angeles). Walt laid out his situation and

Roy wrote back, "Call it quits, kid. You can't do anything more than you've already done."

In early July 1923, Laugh-O-gram Films, Inc., filed for bankruptcy. The court allowed Walt to keep one movie camera and his unfinished Alice film. All his other assets were seized to pay his creditors. Phineas Rosenberg, the attorney appointed to manage the bankruptcy proceedings, recalled, "Most people filing for bankruptcy are disturbed or bitter. Walt wasn't." After the assets were liquidated, Laugh-O-gram's creditors got forty-five cents on the dollar.

In July 1923, Walt went to the Kansas City train station. In his cardboard suitcase were two spare shirts, two sets of underwear, and a can of film—the only print of *Alice's Wonderland.* His wafer-thin wallet contained only $40 in cash—the proceeds from the sale of the movie camera. He wore a checkered jacket, blue trousers and a red bow tie. Walt treated himself to a first class railway ticket to California—a symbol of his optimistic spirit.

Ub Iwerks and Roy's girlfriend, Edna Francis, saw Walt off at the station. "I was just free and happy," he later recalled. "I was twenty-one years old. But I had failed. I think it's important to have a good hard failure when you're young."

Walt's optimism took a beating on the way to California. "I met a guy on the train when I was coming out," he remembered. "He asked me, 'Going to California?' 'Yeah, I'm goin' out there.' 'What business are you in?' I said, 'The motion picture business.' 'What do you do?' I said, 'I make animated cartoons.' 'Oh.' The guy was unimpressed. It was as if I'd said, 'I sweep up the latrines.'"

By the time the train pulled in to Los Angeles, Walt had changed his plans. "I was discouraged with animation," Walt later recalled. "I wanted to be a director." There was just one catch: Walt had barely any experience as a live-action director.

By this time, Walt's Uncle Robert was retired and living in southern California. Walt rented a room at his Uncle Robert's house for five dollars a week.

After he settled into his room, Walt visited Roy in Sawtelle (Roy was confined to a screened-in porch ward so he could breathe the healthfully dry air). Later, Walt toured Hollywood, visiting the abandoned Babylon set from D.W. Griffith's 1916 film *Intolerance* and the modest bungalows of the Charlie Chaplin studio.

Walt had business cards printed that read: "Walt Disney—Selznick News Representative." It was a minor stretch of the truth—he had shot a few newsreels for Selznick News in Kansas City. That business card, plus Walt's confident air, got him past the front gate at Universal Pictures. He wandered around sound stages, the backlot and the post-production facilities, soaking up everything he could learn about filmmaking.

The next day, Walt went to the Universal employment office and asked for a job as a director. He was curtly turned away. By the end of the week, Walt had applied to every studio in town. None would take a chance on a young director, fresh off the train from Kansas City.

> *"Tomorrow was always going to answer all of his problems. Walt was hanging around Hollywood and I kept saying, 'Aren't you going to get a job? Why don't you get a job?' Walt could have gotten a job, but he didn't want a job. He'd get into Universal Studios on the strength of applying for a job, then he'd hang around the studio all day watching what was going on around the sets. MGM was another favorite spot where he could work that stunt."*
>
> ROY O. DISNEY, WALT'S BROTHER

Walt finally landed a temporary job—as a horse-mounted movie extra in a western, *The Light That Failed*. On the day Walt arrived for filming, the shoot was canceled because of rain. "That was the end of my career as an actor," he later mused.

The Disney Brothers Studio

He sent his only copy of the unfinished film, *Alice's Wonderland*, to Margaret Winkler, along with a letter that said, "I am no longer connected with the Laugh-O-gram Films, Inc., of Kansas City. . . . I am establishing a studio in Los Angeles for the purpose of producing the new and novel series of cartoons I have previously written you about." After reviewing the film, Miss Winkler offered him a contract for six Alice Comedies at $1,500 per film. He had no money, no studio—but he was back in the cartoon business.

That night, Roy Disney awoke in his hospital bed to find Walt standing over him, waving a piece of paper. It was nearly midnight.

"What are you doing here?" Roy asked.

"Look at this!" Walt whispered. "We're in! Margaret Winkler wants the Alice Comedies! Can you help me get this thing started?"

"Can you deliver the cartoons on deadline?" Roy asked. "Have you figured your costs and profit margin?"

Walt answered "Yes."

"Okay, kid," Roy said. "I'll help you." Walt left happy.

The next morning, when an X-ray showed that Roy's lungs were clear, he checked out of the hospital and went straight to the bank. He withdrew his savings of $200, then went to persuade Uncle Robert to kick in another $500.

"Walter doesn't pay his debts," Robert protested.

"The distributor has offered him a fat contract," Roy countered. "He'll pay you back."

Robert reluctantly forked over the money.

Margaret Winkler insisted that Walt cast the original Alice, Virginia Davis, in the Alice Comedies. So Walt offered Virginia's mother a one-year contract if she would move to Hollywood. Within days, Virginia and her mom were on a train to California.

Walt signed the contract with M. J. Winkler Productions on October 16, 1923 (that date is considered to be the founding of The Walt Disney Company). For $10 a month, he rented space at the rear of The Holly-Vermont Realty office at 4651 Kingswell Avenue in Hollywood. He taught Roy how to work the $200 second-hand movie camera he bought. Walt handled all the animation chores on the first cartoon and hired two young women to ink the cels. Walt delivered on-time, and Miss Winkler was pleased. *Alice's Day at Sea* debuted on March 1, 1924.

In February 1924, Walt moved next door to a storefront at 4649 Kingswell. Gold-leaf lettering on the window read: "Disney Bros. Studio." He hired one more animator, Rollin "Ham" Hamilton, and the Alice series was under way. With each new entry, Walt's product improved.

In June 1924, Walt convinced Ub Iwerks to move to Hollywood and join the Disney studio—but it took all of Walt's powers of persuasion to win him over. Walt had left Kansas City owing Ub over $1,000 in back salary and could only offer him $40 a week. Finally, Walt offered Ub a twenty-percent interest in the Disney Brothers Studio, and Ub agreed to move.

Ironically, as the Alice Comedies began to find an audience, Walt's distributor cut his income from $1,500 to $900 per film. Margaret Winkler's overbearing, unpleasant new husband, Charles Mintz, thought the Disney brothers were making too much money. He told Walt, in effect, "Take it or leave it," so Walt grudgingly accepted the reduced terms.

By the end of 1924, however, the growing success of the Alice Comedies gave him increased bargaining power. Walt reminded Mintz that other distributors would pay what the Alice Comedies were worth. In December 1924, Walt signed a contract with Mintz for $1,800 per film, plus a percentage of the profits.

Around that time, Walt and Roy moved to a single room in a boarding house. This living arrangement quickly placed a strain on brotherly love. Roy usually did the cooking. One night, Walt shoved his plate away in disgust and headed for the door. Roy swore at him and said, "If you hate my cooking so much, then one of us should move out!"

After the blowup, Roy sent a telegram to Edna Francis and urged her to come to California so they could get married. Edna needed no coaxing. She and her mother arrived by car on April 7, 1925. Roy and Edna were married on April 12 in a small ceremony at Uncle Robert's house. Elias and Flora Disney, who were now living in Portland, Oregon,

> *"Roy and I cooked, ate and slept in that one room, and had to walk about a mile before we reached the bathroom. And yet, when I think back, we had a grand time in those days."*
>
> WALT DISNEY

came down for the wedding. Walt stood beside Roy as best man. Edna's maid of honor was a young inker and painter at the Disney Brothers Studio; her name was Lillian Bounds.

A new suit, a new wife, a new life

Lillian Bounds was born in Spalding, Idaho, in 1899, the tenth and youngest child of Willard and Jeanette Bounds. In 1923, Lilly was living in Los Angeles with her sister Hazel, while attending business college. Kathleen, a friend who worked at the Disney Brothers Studio, urged Lillian to apply for a job as an inker-painter. Kathleen also gave Lillian a word of advice: "Don't flirt with the boss—he's all business."

Lilly had no intention of flirting with the boss. Walt Disney hardly fit her image of a Hollywood studio executive. He was young—two years younger than Lilly, in fact—and his clothes were worn and shabby. He hired Lillian as an inker at a salary of $15 a week.

Although inking the cels was painstaking work, Lillian took to it well. She enjoyed the atmosphere at the studio. Everyone there had a sense that they were doing something good, something important. People were willing to work hard and stay late, and everyone—even Walt—was called by his or her first name.

At the time, Walt and Roy paid themselves less than their animators. Every cent of profit the Disney brothers made was plowed back into the studio. Even so, they often came up short on payday. Whenever the well went dry, Walt and Roy would forgo their own paychecks. Occasionally, Walt would even ask Lilly to hold off cashing her paycheck.

As a boss, Walt was friendly enough, but Lillian detected no romantic spark—nor did she desire any. She enjoyed working at the Disney Brothers Studio and she found her young boss likable enough—but romance? It didn't even cross her mind.

It wasn't love at first sight for Walt, either. Sure, Lilly was pretty and pleasant—but Walt had more important things on his mind than romance. He was totally focused on building the studio and battling deadlines.

Walt owned a beat-up Ford runabout and sometimes gave the girls a lift home from work. First, he would drop Lilly off, then Kathleen. As Lillian later recalled, "When Walt started dropping the other girl off first so he could talk to me, I knew he was interested."

One night, Walt came by the ink department when Lillian was alone and working late. He offered to wait for her and give her a ride home. While he

waited, Lillian became uncomfort-
ably aware that Walt was standing
behind her. She could hardly concentrate on her work. The next thing she
knew, he kissed the back of her neck.
She blushed but pretended not to
notice.

After locking up the studio, Walt
drove her home. The drive was un-
characteristically quiet. Walt walked
her to the door, then blurted, "Lilly,
if I bought myself a decent suit,
would you invite me in to meet your
sister?"

Lillian smiled. "You can come in
now, if you like."

"No," Walt said. "When I get a
suit, you can invite me in." With a
wave, he jumped back in his Ford roadster and sped away.

> *"Walt dreamed of being a Hollywood director, but there he was, stuck in the Midwest. So what did he do? He went to California with little more than the clothes on his back and some pocket change. Then he scraped and struggled and battled to make his dreams happen. The lesson is clear: If you have to get up and move to make your dreams come true, then get up and move!"*
>
> BRUCE GORDON
> DISNEY IMAGINEER AND AUTHOR

The next morning, Walt went to Roy's office. "I need forty bucks for a
new suit," Walt said. "The studio can afford it."

"What do you want a new suit for?" Roy asked.

"Well," Walt said, "maybe I want to get married in it."

Roy gave Walt the money, and he bought a double-breasted gray-green
suit with two pairs of pants. That night, decked out in his new suit, Walt
took Lilly home. He went inside and met Hazel and her seven-year-old
daughter, Marjorie. "How do you like my new suit?" he asked. Hazel and
Marjorie approved of the suit—and of Walt.

Lilly's niece Marjorie recalled, "Walt was at our house an awful lot. . . .
My mother and Aunt Lilly could never really decide whether he was there
because of Aunt Lilly or because of my mother's cooking. But I guess it was
Aunt Lilly."

Walt enjoyed Lilly's family, especially their family singalongs around the
piano. On Sundays, Walt took them all out for a drive, with a stop for ice
cream cones on the way home. He even bought a cone for Lilly's dog.

*"One night he asked, 'If I get
a suit, can I come and see you?'
When he came to meet the family,
he said, 'Well, how do you like
my suit?' My family liked him
immediately. There was never
any embarrassment about Walt.
He met people easily. He was
completely natural."*

LILLIAN BOUNDS DISNEY

One spring night in 1925, soon after Roy and Edna were married, Walt took Lilly to a movie. Afterward, Walt said, "You know, this old Ford is looking kind of shabby. Lilly, you're a practical girl. Which should I buy—a new car or an engagement ring for your finger?"

Lillian knew a proposal when she heard one. "An engagement ring," she said.

"Oh," Walt said, nodding.

Years later, Lillian would laugh and say, "Walt seemed disappointed that I didn't tell him to buy the car." In the end, Walt got the car he wanted as well—a slightly used Moon roadster, dark gray with a rumble seat and a sleek hood ornament.

On July 6, 1925, Walt and Roy made a down payment on a vacant lot at 2719 Hyperion Avenue, in the Silver Lake district of Los Angeles. They also decided to raise their own pay to $40 a week—the same as their top animators. After all, married men had responsibilities.

A few days later, Walt and Lillian took a train to Lewiston, Idaho. On July 13, 1925, they were married in the parlor of the home of Lilly's brother, the Lewiston fire chief.

Walt and Lillian set up housekeeping in a tiny apartment with a view of the alley. They socialized with Roy and Edna, and usually went out to dinner and a movie once or twice a week. Afterward, Walt would often return to the office to finish up a few chores, taking Lilly along. He'd work, she'd fall asleep on the couch, and sometime around two in the morning, he'd gently wake her and take her home.

Walt and Lillian's romance was reminiscent of the comic romances in Walt's later movies, such as *The Absent-Minded Professor*. In fact, screenwriter Bill Walsh claimed he based Professor Brainerd (Fred MacMurray) on Walt. In the movie, Professor Brainerd is so absorbed in his scientific experiments that he misses his own wedding—three times in a row. Walt didn't miss his wedding, but he was prone to absent-mindedness in his private life.

On more than one occasion, Walt became so absorbed in his work that he failed to return home until somewhere between ten and midnight— long after Lillian's carefully prepared dinner had gone cold. After one such episode, Walt brought home a peace offering in a hatbox. Lillian opened the box and found a little chow puppy with a red ribbon around its neck. She fell in love with the dog and named it Sunnee. Lillian later recalled, "I forgave him. You can't stay mad at Walt for very long." Walt would recreate the dog-in-the-hatbox scene in his 1955 animated feature, *Lady and the Tramp*.

A new studio and a new name

The Disney Brothers Studio continued turning out Alice cartoons at a rate of two per month. Unfortunately, distributor Charles Mintz began paying more slowly. Walt wrote Mintz on October 2, 1925, "I intend to continue shipping pictures to you as fast as completed, which is about every sixteen days. I will expect you to take them as delivered and remit immediately. Your failure to do so will constitute a breach of contract."

Walt pushed his animators to deliver both speed and quality. He sometimes insisted that certain sequences be scrapped and redrawn two, three or more times until they met Walt's high standards. During 1925, Walt fired himself as an animator. "I was never happy with anything I ever did as an artist," he once reflected. From then on, Walt would serve as producer, director, coach, cheerleader and head storyteller—but he would never animate another frame of film.

"Walt was not afraid to surround himself with the best artists he could hire. He was not threatened by having better people around him. Eventually all of his old Laugh-O-gram animators from Kansas City came out to California to work for him."

BRIAN BURNES
COAUTHOR, *WALT DISNEY'S MISSOURI*

As the Alice Comedies grew in popularity, Walt urged his animators to find new ways of putting personality and emotion on the screen. Even in those early days of animation, the twenty-four-year-old studio head was pushing his artists toward revolutionary developments in the art of animation.

Animator Friz Freleng recalled working on *Alice's Picnic* in 1927, in which he animated a scene with a mama cat bathing her kittens. Freleng decided to make the bath scene more real by having one little kitten attempting to crawl out of the tub. None of the action he created was in the script—Freleng simply ad libbed.

When Walt saw the pencil tests, he called the animators together. "I want you all to see this scene," he said as the projector rolled. "Look at that one kitten. Friz doesn't have him simply jump out of the water and try to get away. He has this kitten crawl over the side and hang there, like a real kid would do. This is not just a cartoon—this is a character. This kitten has personality. That's what I want to see in our pictures." Walt was quietly but deliberately revolutionizing the way cartoons were made.

> *"Walt's older brother Roy devoted his life to helping Walt finance his dreams. Outside of Walt's own personal drive and creativity, Roy O. Disney was the single most important factor in Walt's ultimate success."*
>
> KEN ANNAKIN
> DISNEY MOVIE DIRECTOR

In January 1926, as the Disney studio was completing its twenty-ninth cartoon in the Alice Comedies series, *Alice's Little Parade,* Walt and Roy moved into their newly constructed studio at 2719 Hyperion Avenue in Los Angeles. It was a one-story white stucco building, completely open inside except for two partitioned spaces for the offices of Walt and Roy. When the Hyperion studio opened for business, it had a new name: The Walt Disney Studio.

There are differing accounts as to how the studio came to be identified by Walt's name alone. Some critics have suggested that the name change was due to Walt's "oversized ego." But shortly before his death, Roy told Disney archivist Dave Smith, "It was my idea. Walt was the creative member of the team. His name deserved to be on the pictures."

The Lucky Rabbit disaster

With the move to the Hyperion Avenue studio, Walt's appearance changed: He added a pencil-thin mustache. The twenty-four-year-old studio head wanted to appear more mature—and perhaps a bit more dashing and self-confident. That mustache would remain Walt's personal trademark for the rest of his life.

At this time, all but one of the animators on Walt's staff were Laugh-O-grams veterans. Walt's animators admired and respected him so much that they eagerly relocated halfway across the country just to work with him again.

Walt's contract with Mintz called for twenty-six Alice Comedies per year—a new cartoon every two weeks. Walt's team delivered like clockwork. In 1926, Mintz told Walt to slow down and deliver a new cartoon every three weeks instead of every two. Walt couldn't afford to do that.

"With my present payroll," Walt wrote Mintz, "on a three weeks schedule I would absolutely be losing money, and to cut down my force is out of the question. You well know, yourself, how hard it is to get men trained in this line of work. My artists are all experienced, capable men, difficult to replace at any salary. How can I afford the loss which a delayed schedule would mean?"

In the summer of 1926, Dr. Thomas McCrum—Walt's Kansas City benefactor—commissioned the Disney studio to produce a companion film to *Tommy Tucker's Tooth* (1922). It starred Walt's niece, Marjorie Sewell, as Clara.

Marjorie Sewell Davis later recalled that her casting was a combination of nepotism and economics: "Walt Disney was my uncle," she said, "and he didn't have to pay me very much!" Her memories of Walt's directing were similar to those of Virginia Davis. "He would act things out himself," Marjorie recalled. "If he told you to do something, he would first go through the facial expressions himself, showing you exactly what he wanted from you."

Near the end of 1926, Carl Laemmle, the head of Universal Pictures, told Charles Mintz he wanted a new cartoon series. The two most popular toons at that time were Felix the Cat and Krazy Kat, so Laemmle wanted something different—how about a rabbit? Mintz told Laemmle he knew just the studio for the job—the Disney studio in Hollywood. Laemmle told Mintz to cut a deal with Disney and start producing rabbit cartoons.

A few days later, Charles Mintz and his wife Margaret toured the new Disney studio. Afterward, Mintz told Walt that The Alice Comedies had run their course and the contract would not be renewed. However, a major studio wanted a series starring a rabbit. Could Disney produce it?

"These Oswald pictures were fairly successful. At the conclusion of our first year, because of the success they had attained, I was of course expecting to be allowed a little more money to build them to a still higher standard. But [Charles Mintz] and I had a difference of opinion on that subject, and he decided he could get along very well without me."

WALT DISNEY

Walt had Ub Iwerks produce character sketches for a new rabbit character. Mintz passed the sketches on to Universal, but refused to tell Walt the name of the studio. Only after Carl Laemmle gave his approval did Mintz tell Walt that the buyer was Universal. A contract was drawn up between Universal, Mintz and the Disney studio for a series Mintz called "Oswald the Lucky Rabbit."

The first Oswald cartoon, *Poor Papa*, was rushed into production in April 1927, while the last few Alices were still being produced. Critics who previewed Poor Papa found Oswald unlikable and gave the cartoon thumbs down. Mintz decided to delay the film's release (it eventually premiered on August 6, 1928).

The second Oswald cartoon, *Trolley Troubles,* appeared on September 5, 1927. The critics loved it. "Oswald is a riot," exulted *Film Daily.* "Funny how the cartoon artists never hit on a rabbit before. Oswald with his long ears has a chance for a lot of new comedy gags, and makes the most of them."

The Lucky Rabbit became a huge star. Dick Huemer, who later became a story director for Disney, was working at the Max Fleischer studio when *Trolley Troubles* was released. "Walt Disney's Oswalds had something more in them than what we in New York were doing at the time," Huemer recalled. "I remember seeing them at the Colony Theatre on Broadway and being considerably impressed—and admittedly jealous. I used to go seek them out and study them."

Oswald was a good vehicle for expressing Walt's belief that anything is possible, that there are no limits to imagination. Walt ruthlessly exploited the elastic possibilities of his cartoon characters in gag after gag.

As the fortunes of the Walt Disney Studio improved, so did the lifestyle of Walt and Lillian Disney. In the fall of 1927, Walt and Roy bought identical prefabricated Tudor-style houses on adjoining lots for $7,000 each. The houses were located on Lyric Avenue in the Silver Lake district, close to the Hyperion studio.

Still, there were signs that all was not well in toonland. Given Oswald's popularity, the studio should have been making more money. Walt's contract with Charles Mintz promised him a flat fee per cartoon *plus* a share of the profits—but Mintz insisted there weren't any profits to share. Walt and Roy found that hard to believe.

At contract-renewal time in February 1928, Walt went to New York with Lillian, intent on cutting a more lucrative deal. As he walked into Mintz's office on 42nd Street, Walt figured Oswald's success gave him the winning hand in a contract showdown.

Walt asked Mintz for a raise, from $2,250 per cartoon to $2,500. Mintz shocked Walt by offering him a pay *cut* instead. "I'll give you eighteen hundred," Mintz countered. That wouldn't even cover Walt's production costs—and Mintz knew it. "Take it," Mintz said, "or I'll ruin you. I already have your key artists signed up."

It was an unbelievable boast. Walt's animators wouldn't desert him for Mintz—would they? Walt had personally taught them the animation trade. He had brought them out from Kansas City. He had paid them well—more, in fact, than he paid himself. They wouldn't sign with Mintz—it was unthinkable.

Walt telephoned Roy from the Hotel Astor and told him of the boast Mintz had made. Roy conducted his own investigation—and found it was true. Charles Mintz had sent his brother-in-law, George Winkler, to the Disney studio, supposedly to collect completed Oswald reels and lobby poster art. Winkler had quietly lured away nearly all of Walt's artists—all except Ub Iwerks and two assistant animators, Johnny Cannon and Les

Clark (Clark would have a long career with Disney and become known as one of Walt's "Nine Old Men" of animation). Mintz and Universal were trying to take over the Disney studio, lock, stock and inkwell.

> "It's hard to know which caused Walt greater pain—the loss of [Oswald], upon which his studio's success rested, or the loss of his staff, whom he regarded as friends."
>
> KATHERINE AND RICHARD GREENE
> DISNEY HISTORIANS

While Walt was in New York, Roy had an attorney look at the contract he and Walt had signed with Mintz and Universal. The fine print assigned legal ownership of the Lucky Rabbit to Universal Pictures. Walt didn't own Oswald. After Walt heard the bad news from Roy, he turned to Lillian and said, "Well, I've learned a lesson. Never again will I work for someone else."

Lillian recalled Walt's amazing calm in reaction to this bitter disappointment. Walt's tone was upbeat as he telephoned Roy. "Keep your chin up, Roy," Walt said. "We'll have the last laugh, and that's the best laugh of all."

Walt was confronted by a stark choice: turn his studio into a subsidiary of the Mintz organization, or walk away and start over. The second option was filled with risks and unknowns—but that's the option Walt chose.

In late March, without telling Roy of his plans, Walt paid a final visit to Charles Mintz. "Charlie," he said, "you want Oswald this badly? Well, you can have him. He's all yours."

Mintz was dismayed. He didn't just want Oswald—he wanted the Disney studio. He started to tell Walt how they could work together on Oswald, but Walt cut him off. "Don't you hear what I'm saying, Charlie? I'm through with Oswald. Just looking at him makes me sick. He's all yours—and good luck with him."

Walt turned to leave—then he paused and added, "But you'd better look out for yourself, Charlie. The people who did this to me will do it to you." Then he walked out.

Walt's final advice to Charles Mintz proved prophetic. With brother-in-law George Winkler in charge, Mintz' Snappy Comedies company created new Oswalds for Universal. It didn't take long, however, for Carl Laemmle to yank the character away from Mintz and put Walter Lantz (the eventual creator of Woody Woodpecker) in charge of the Lucky Rabbit. Mintz learned that what goes around, comes around.

Sometime later, Walt happened to run into Charles Mintz at Universal Studios. Mintz sat in the waiting room, hat in hand, looking nervous and lonely. Setting the past aside, Walt exchanged pleasantries with Mintz. Later, he wrote to Roy and said, "Poor old Charlie. It was sad to see him that way."

"Don't worry, everything okay . . ."

Walt had trusted Mintz, and the man had robbed him blind. As a result, Walt had lost his only cartoon character and nearly his entire animation staff—men he had trusted as friends.

On his way back to the hotel, Walt asked himself, "What now?" He wasn't defeated. He wasn't feeling sorry for himself. He still had Ub Iwerks and a head full of ideas. A door had slammed in his face. It was time to open a window.

"I was all alone and had nothing. Mrs. Disney and I were coming back from New York on the train and I had to have something. I can't tell them I've lost Oswald. So I had this mouse in the back of my head . . ."

WALT DISNEY

The Disney brothers were going to need every ounce of optimism they could muster in order to bounce back. So instead of calling Roy with the news that they had lost Oswald, Walt sent Roy this cheery-sounding telegram, dated March 13, 1928:

LEAVING TONITE STOPPING OVER KC
ARRIVE HOME SUNDAY MORNING SEVEN THIRTY
DON'T WORRY EVERYTHING OK
WILL GIVE DETAILS WHEN ARRIVE
WALT

As Walt and Lilly boarded the 20th Century Limited in Grand Central Station, Walt pondered new plans for the future. During the train ride from New York to Los Angeles, an entertainment legend was born: a spunky little rodent named Mickey.

How to Be Like Walt—
Lesson 2: Be a Salesman

When I spoke with Virginia Davis (Walt's original Alice), I was impressed with this observation she made: "Walt was a great salesman." The more I examined Walt's life, the more I saw what a profound insight this was. From the very beginning of his career, Walt was a salesman—one of the greatest salesmen the world has ever known.

He got his first office rent-free by selling restaurant owner Al Carder on trading artwork for desk space. Later, Walt sold Kansas City businessmen on investing in his animation studio. Without any track record, he sold his Laugh-O-gram cartoons to Pictorial Clubs for an $11,000 contract. After Laugh-O-grams went bankrupt, he sold his Alice Comedies to M.J. Winkler Productions on the basis of an unfinished film—and at a time when he had no staff, no money, no studio and not even a place to live.

On two different occasions, Walt sold Ub Iwerks on the idea of working at his animation studio for lower pay than he was making at the Film Ad Company—and the second time, Walt even talked Ub into moving halfway across the country. Ultimately, Walt persuaded his entire Kansas City animation team to relocate to California. This fact speaks volumes about Walt's ability to inspire others to buy into his dreams.

> "Walt was the best salesman in the world because he felt he wasn't selling."
>
> WOLFGANG REITHERMAN
> DISNEY ANIMATOR

Later in this book, we will see Walt use his formidable powers of persuasion and salesmanship to inspire his artists to create *Snow White and the Seven Dwarfs*—an achievement many said was impossible. We'll watch him finance and build Disneyland with sheer salesmanship. We'll see him go on television and sell Disneyland and the Disney movie magic to millions. Walt succeeded because he was a salesman.

Many people look down on selling as somehow beneath them. I hope you don't make that mistake. All the wealth in America can be traced to the fact that somebody somewhere sold something to somebody else. Selling is one of the most honorable professions around—and one of the most rewarding. It is also one of the toughest.

What does it take to be a great salesman? (I'm using the term "salesman" in a gender-neutral way.) I would suggest five qualities that every great salesman must have. Build these qualities into your life and you can sell like Walt. Those five qualities are honesty, enthusiasm, confidence, courage and persistence. Let's take a closer look:

1. Honesty. All great salesmen are honest. Does that surprise you? That's probably because you have been raised on the stereotype of the fast-talking used-car salesman in the plaid jacket. Sure, shysters abound, and they give a bad name to the honest salesmen who make their living by trading value for value. But the best salesmen are people of integrity.

A great salesman lives on repeat business. The key to repeat business is trust, and the key to trust is integrity. Anybody can sell to one customer one time. A great salesman builds relationships of trust on a foundation of truth.

If a customer catches you in a lie, the trust is broken, the relationship is over. So always tell the truth about your product. Never promise more than you can deliver. It's better to under-promise and over-deliver than the other way around. If you are known as an honest person, you will be known as a successful salesman.

> *"Walt was the consummate salesman. He had the ability to rally the right people around him."*
>
> CRAIG HODGKINS
> DISNEY WRITER AND LECTURER

"Walt was a great salesman," Imagineer Harriet Burns told me, "and his best sales technique was his absolute honesty. I remember many situations where we needed to sell a corporation or a financial backer on some project. When it was a crucial situation, the staff would say, 'Walt, you'll have to go.' In other words, Walt would have to go in person and sell it. And he'd do it every time. He didn't use glib talk or flashy sales methods. He simply sold his ideas with his honesty and sincerity. People could tell that he said what he meant and meant what he said. They trusted him, and that trust relationship made him a great salesman."

2. Enthusiasm. All great salesmen are fired up about their product. Enthusiasm is contagious; it affects everyone around you. How did a twenty-year-old cartoonist convince a group of Kansas City businessmen to part with $15,000 so he could open his studio? Enthusiasm! Voice actor Corey Burton told me, "Walt was excited about his projects, his movies, his theme park. When he was excited about something, his excitement fired up everyone around him. That's how he sold his dreams."

Disney film editor Norman "Stormy" Palmer recalls Walt's power to motivate. "Walt's enthusiasm made over-achievers out of all of us," he told me. "You got caught up with his energy, you believed in his ideas, and you wanted to please him. He transmitted his excitement to all of us. If it hadn't been for Walt, there would have been a lot of times we would have settled for less than our best. But Walt made us believe we could do better."

Disney matte artist Peter Ellenshaw agrees. "Walt Disney had an over-powering aura of enthusiasm about him, and it was contagious. We all felt it. Walt's enthusiasm powered everything we did."

Retired Disneyland executive Jack Lindquist shared a story with me that demonstrates the amazing selling power of Walt's enthusiasm. "In 1955, before Disneyland opened," he said, "Walt attended a board meeting of the Atlantic Richfield Company (now known as Arco). He wanted the company to sponsor the Autopia attraction in Tomorrowland. Walt made his pitch to the board. He had artwork showing these small cars on the Autopia freeway driving past Atlantic Richfield billboards. He said, 'We'll put the Richfield name on all the billboards in the attraction.' He had them in the palm of his hand—the man could really sell.

"Walt finished his presentation, and someone asked, 'How much will it cost us to sponsor this attraction?' Walt said, 'Two-hundred-fifty thousand dollars—that's twenty-five thousand per year for ten years.' You could see the board members picking up his enthusiasm. It was very infectious.

"Walt was the world's best salesman because he believed in his product. It wasn't just a con job with him."

WARD KIMBALL
DISNEY ANIMATOR

"Finally, they asked Walt to step outside while they deliberated. A little later, they brought Walt back and said, 'We think this is a good deal for our company, and we've decided to sponsor it.' Walt said, 'Would it be possible to take the first check with me today?' And darned if they didn't go downstairs and write Walt a check for twenty-five thousand dollars on the spot. After Walt left, Leonard Firestone, one of the board members, said to the rest of the board, 'I have a question. What did we just buy?'"

Disney Imagineer Sam McKim saw scenes like that played out again and again during his years at Walt's side. "Walt was a salesman," Sam told me, "and he could really sell the corporate sponsors on his ideas and projects for the theme park. Executives from those big companies were fascinated by him and loved to be around him. They absorbed his enthusiasm, and their sponsorship made Disneyland possible."

3. Confidence. Great salesmen always brim with confidence, even in tough times. Walt was dead broke, nearly shoeless, and eating cold beans out of a can—yet he confidently told Margaret Winkler that his first Alice film would "be finished very soon" and he would come to New York and present "an outline of our future program." What's more, Walt wasn't just blowing smoke. He believed every word of it. He had a salesman's confident optimism.

Lillian Disney once said, "Walt never thought he was beaten at anything—ever." No matter how bad things seemed, Walt believed in himself, his product and his future.

When Walt tried to get a job directing motion pictures, his experience level was practically nil—but his confidence level was limitless. "When Walt went to Hollywood," media critic Neil Gabler told me, "he didn't know if he would make it or not. He had already experienced a big failure—the bankruptcy of Laugh-O-gram Films. He was starting over in a new place, without any money, but he was carried along by his own confidence. Walt didn't doubt himself. He believed he could make it in Hollywood, and he did."

"Walt had the ability to inspire us by selling us on ourselves," said Disney sculptor Blaine Gibson. "Walt had more confidence in us as artists than we had in ourselves. I'm a sculptor now, but I used to be an animator, and I loved it. I didn't want to leave animation and go work in the theme parks. But Walt saw me as a sculptor, and he sold me on it. He made me believe I could do it. He gave us the confidence to do things we never imagined were possible."

Selling is all about attitude. You must believe you can sell your product even in a down economy, even in an off season, even if you've been in a slump. Confidence is not a feeling, it's an attitude choice. Even if you don't *feel* confident, you can still adopt an *attitude* of confidence.

You may not be comfortable selling yourself or your product, but so what? Nobody is comfortable selling. Nobody ever became successful by staying within their comfort zone. If you want to succeed, you have to do what Walt did: take a big, confident step outside your comfort zone, and start selling your dreams.

"Walt Disney worked hard and sold his ideas from the earliest days of his career. He had no MBA, not even a college degree. But Walt had the right idea and the right spirit, and he was willing to go out and sell his ideas. He was a world-class salesman."

PETER CLARK
RETIRED DISNEY EXECUTIVE

4. Courage. The biggest obstacle every salesman faces is the fear of rejection. So in order to sell like Walt, you must have courage. The fear of rejection is expressed in such questions as, "What will other people think of me?" or "What if people say no?" Psychological studies show that high-achieving, successful people are not overly concerned about what others think. This was true of Walt Disney. He never catered to his critics. He never worried about rejection. He kept selling his dreams.

"Walt was completely focused on his product and his goals, not on himself," said Craig Hodgkins, a Disney historian. "He wasn't concerned about what people thought of him. He had more important things to think about, and that's why he was so effective at selling his dreams."

One thing is certain: If you sell, you will be rejected. It's not a question of if you'll be rejected, but *how many times a day* you will be rejected. So get used to it, accept the reality of rejection, and don't take it personally. Rejection comes with the territory.

5. Persistence. The most important part of selling is persistence. Jean-Pierre Isbouts, director of the documentary *Walt: The Man Behind the Myth,* recalls being profoundly impacted by the lessons of Walt Disney's life and personality.

"The life lesson that I learned from Walt while researching and directing the film," said Isbouts, "is that it takes perseverance and faith in your own abilities. Nothing that is worthwhile comes easy. Walt wanted to start a business creating cartoons, and before long was faced with bankruptcy. A lot of us would have given up and taken a job somewhere. Walt didn't; he simply changed venue, left for California and picked up where he left off. And this time, it worked.

"That is not to say that everything was smooth sailing from there. The loss of the Oswald character must have been devastating to Walt, as was the defection of most of his animator crew. . . . Walt absorbed the blows and soldiered on, fueled by a total and utter belief that his vision was right."

Disney biographer Bob Thomas told me, "Walt succeeded because he was persistent and determined. He didn't let rejection and criticism stop him. He didn't listen to the naysayers who told him he couldn't do this or that. Walt was a finisher." And Wendell Warner, a longtime Disney engineer and draftsman, said, "Walt was successful because of one rock-solid Midwestern value. It's called perseverance."

A great salesman can't be stopped. So be a great salesman—be honest, enthusiastic, confident, courageous and persistent. Sell your dreams, and make them come true.

How to Be Like Walt— Lesson 3: Dare to Do the Impossible

When Walt returned from France after World War I, he believed that anything was possible. He was just audacious enough to believe that an eighteen-year-old with one year of art school could go to the Kansas City *Star* and get a job as a political cartoonist. He was just brash enough to believe that, after learning how to animate crude paper cutouts and reading two books from the library, he could teach animation to other artists. He was reckless enough that, after going bankrupt in Kansas City, he went to Hollywood to start over in animated cartoons when all the animation studios were in New York City.

Walt didn't care about doing what was safe, sensible, respectable. He didn't care about past failures or being flat broke. For Walt, anything was possible.

Walt arrived in Hollywood with his dreams, a can of half-finished movie film, and little else. Yet when he wrote to Margaret Winkler, his letter brimmed with confidence, optimism and bold plans for the future. Why? Because, to Walt, anything is possible.

Later, when Walt lost Oswald and most of his animators, he was discouraged, but not defeated. Before returning home, Walt wired Roy these words: "Don't worry, everything okay." And he meant it. Walt believed everything would be okay. Why? Because anything is possible.

> "Actually, it's kind of fun
> to do the impossible."
>
> WALT DISNEY

Walt's anything-is-possible attitude profoundly affected the cartoons his studio produced. He believed that cartoons could be better than they were, and he constantly prodded his artists to attempt the impossible.

Longtime Disney animation director David Hand observed that Walt's limitations as an artist actually helped remove all limitations from his imagination. "Walt couldn't really draw," said Hand. "I've seen him try. It was pathetic. Well, he didn't have to draw, did he? Better he didn't because he would ask us animators to do things that were impossible to do—but he didn't know it! [That was] Walt's strength."

Glen Keane is considered the dean of the new generation of Disney animators. Though he never met Walt Disney (he began his career at The Walt Disney Studios in 1974, eight years after Walt's death), Glen says he has been profoundly influenced by Walt's life, both personally and professionally. Walt's belief that anything is possible has even affected the way Glen Keane approaches the creation of a character.

"Walt was in the business of believing the impossible," Glen told me. "To him, the impossible was always possible. Now, of course, we are getting into the realm of God and faith, because God is in the business of making the impossible possible in our lives. As Jesus once said, 'All things are possible to him who believes.'

"I had the privilege of animating Ariel in *The Little Mermaid*. She dreamed of doing the impossible. She lived underwater, yet she dreamed of walking on land with human legs—and her dream came true. And I animated the Beast in *Beauty and the Beast.* He was so ugly and deformed, it was impossible that anyone could love such a creature. Yet the impossible became possible, and Belle fell in love with the Beast. Then there was Aladdin, a street urchin who dreamed he could live in a palace with the princess—impossible! Yet the impossible became possible for Aladdin, too. All of these characters had dreams and believed that the impossible could be possible. There was a bit of Walt in all of them."

Wendell Warner told me, "I heard Walt say, many times, 'I'm not interested in what a man can't do. I want to know what he *can* do.' The word 'impossible' wasn't in Walt's vocabulary."

"Walt was never afraid to dream," says Disney historian Jim Korkis, "and he felt no dream is impossible. That song from *Pinocchio*, 'When You Wish Upon a Star,' is the perfect summary of Walt's approach to life: dream big dreams, even hopelessly impossible dreams, because they really can come true. Sure, it takes work, focus and perseverance. But anything is possible. Walt proved it with the impossible things he accomplished.

"Just watch *Snow White.* Just visit Disneyland or Walt Disney World in Florida—he was laying the plans for the Florida park while he was on his death bed. People kept telling him his dreams were impossible. Walt knew better. He had wished upon a star.

"Today, you hear people talk about 'thinking outside the box.' But Walt would say, 'No! Don't think outside the box! Once you say that, you've established that there is a box.' Walt would refuse to accept the existence of the box."

Paul F. Anderson, in his fine Disney-oriented publication *Persistence of Vision,* told a story that illustrates Walt's conviction that anything is possible. In *Pinocchio,* there is a

> *"If you can dream it, you can do it."*
>
> WALT DISNEY

scene in the shop of the old toy-maker, Geppetto, featuring a large number of cuckoo clocks. Each clock is unique, depicting scenes ranging from a brass band to a mother spanking a naughty child. When Walt saw the sequence for the first time, he told his artists, "It's a good thing this is only a cartoon. It would be impossible to build a real clock that works the way they do."

Walt's animators took that as a challenge! They decided to build one of Geppetto's clocks, just to show Walt that it could be done. They designed a clock shaped like a saloon. When the hour was struck, the saloon doors would open, a drunk would stumble out, his head would pop up, his nose would light up, and he would hiccup—all in one smooth, continuous motion.

First, they bought a pair of Swiss cuckoo clocks and broke them open to see what made them tick. Then they talked to experts, from clock-makers to electrical engineers, and all the experts agreed that the task was impossible.

"At that point," animator Frank Thomas recalled, "we had to go on. We couldn't admit we were wrong. Finally, after all the pieces had been carefully carved and all the gears and levers were assembled the way we thought they should work, it actually worked!"

They showed the clock to Walt, expecting him to be bowled over by their "impossible" accomplishment. "I knew you could do it all along," Walt said. "I just wanted to see how long it would take you."

If you want to be like Walt, then dare to do the impossible. Dream big dreams—and don't be surprised when your impossible dreams come true.

Chapter Three

❧

Imagination Unlimited

When his "Lucky Rabbit" was stolen from him, Walt simply focused his creative energies on the situation and came up with a Mouse. The story of Walt and his alter ego, Mickey Mouse, is a story of creative problem-solving.

On the train ride from New York to California, Walt faced an uncertain future. He had lost nearly everything and was starting over once more. In Walt's mind, however, the loss of Oswald was just one more problem to be solved with imagination and creativity.

This part of Walt's story is somewhat obscured by legend, so it is difficult to know how much is fact and how much is invention. According to the official account, Walt was pondering a replacement for Oswald during the train ride home from New York and recalled a mouse he had tamed at the Laugh-O-gram studio in Kansas City. That memory inspired the creation of a mouse he named Mortimer.

Lilly liked the mouse but thought the name Mortimer sounded pretentious. She suggested a name with more panache: Mickey Mouse. As soon as Walt heard it, he loved it.

Though some Disney biographers doubt the authenticity of this account, it is probably based in fact. Just three years after Mickey's debut,

Walt authored an article in *The Windsor Magazine*, published in England. He didn't mention Lillian's contribution, but he did refer to the train ride:

> *Why did I choose a mouse . . . ? Principally because I needed a small animal. I couldn't use a rabbit, because there already was a rabbit on the screen [a reference to Oswald]. So I decided upon a mouse, as I have always thought they were very interesting little creatures. At first I decided to call him Mortimer Mouse, but changed his name to Mickey as the name has a more friendly sound. . . . While returning from a visit to New York, I plotted out the first story.*

Also in 1931, Walt gave an interview to *American Magazine*. Asked who or what inspired the creation of Mickey Mouse, Walt credited his longtime hero, Charlie Chaplin:

> *I can't say just how the idea came. We wanted another animal. We had already had a cat [a reference to Julius the cat in The Alice Comedies]. A mouse naturally came to mind. We felt that the public—especially children—liked animals that are cute and little. I think we were rather indebted to Charlie Chaplin for the idea. We wanted something appealing, and we thought of a tiny bit of a mouse that would have something of the wistfulness of Chaplin—a little fellow trying to do the best he could.*

In 1934, Walt authored a second article for *The Windsor Magazine*, expanding his account of the train trip. In this account, he boarded the train with no idea what the future held—and no ideas for a new character:

> *But was I downhearted? Not a bit! I was happy at heart. For out of the trouble and confusion stood a mocking, merry little figure. Vague and indefinite at first. But it grew and grew and grew. And finally arrived— a mouse. A romping, rollicking little mouse. . . . By the time my train had reached the Middle West I had dressed my dream mouse in a pair of red velvet pants with two huge pearl buttons, had composed the first scenario and was all set.*

Some animation historians doubt that Walt actually conceived Mickey during that train trip. But the fact that Walt was giving that account as early as 1931 suggests it is more than a myth. Walt's mind was always awhirl with ideas. It's not likely that he simply sat on the train and stared at the passing scenery. He must have been engaged in solving the problem.

Before Ub Iwerks died in 1971, he told a somewhat different version: When the train arrived at the Pasadena station on Sunday, March 18, 1928, Ub and Roy were there, along with two loyal assistants, Les Clark and Johnny Cannon. Stepping off the train, Walt told them, "We lost Oswald, but that's okay—we're going to start a new series with a new character."

Walt also had a word of warning about the defecting animators: "Keep an eye on those guys," he said, "and keep them busy. Don't even give them a moment to wipe their noses. They're working for Charlie Mintz, not us." There were three Oswald car-

> *"I only hope that we never lose sight of one thing—that it was all started by a mouse."*
>
> WALT DISNEY

toons left on the old contract, and Walt wanted the disloyal animators to finish those three cartoons—then clear out.

That evening, Walt called a secret meeting at his Lyric Avenue home. In the Iwerks version, Ub first suggested a mouse character at that meeting. Walt liked the idea and assigned Ub to develop the drawing, while Walt worked on the story.

Walt decided to parody the trans-Atlantic flight of Charles Lindbergh, which had taken place a year earlier. Walt devised a story in which the plucky mouse builds an airplane so he can be like his hero, Lindbergh. Walt told the story to Iwerks, and Iwerks drew up continuity sheets (which looked like a newspaper comic strip). The cartoon would be called *Plane Crazy.*

Though Ub recalled that he, not Walt, came up with the idea of a mouse, Ub gave Walt all the credit for Mickey's success. Ub supplied the look of the character, but Walt created Mickey's personality and guided the career of the Mouse for the next four decades.

Ub agreed that the original plan was to call him Mortimer, and that Lilly named him Mickey. Though Walt saw Mickey as Chaplinesque, Ub recalled patterning Mickey's exploits after swashbuckling actor Douglas

Fairbanks. Ub's sons, Donald and David, have stated that their father never resented Mickey's success nor claimed to be Mickey's creator. They often heard their dad say, "It's what Walt did with Mickey that was important—not who drew him."

Roy Edward Disney, the son of Walt's brother Roy, laments the fact that we can never really know the precise story of Mickey's creation. "It's been told so many times," he said, "that you don't know what's true." But Roy is certain of one fact: Mickey's original name was indeed Mortimer. "The name part I'm sure of," he says. "I often heard my father and Walt say, 'Thank God we didn't name him Mortimer!'"

Mickey's silent debut

There is another account of the naming of Mickey Mouse involving actor Mickey Rooney—and this version was told to me by Mickey Rooney himself. Some people ascribe this version to an overactive imagination, but I'm convinced Rooney believes it. As a child actor, he starred in a series of silent films based on Fontaine Fox's comic strip *Toonerville Folks*. In fact, Rooney's mother had his name legally changed from Joe Yule Jr. to Mickey Rooney so that he would have the same first name as his character, "Mickey 'Himself' McGuire."

Mickey Rooney told me he was seven years old when he met Walt Disney. It was lunch time and Mickey was on his way to the studio commissary. Walking past an open door, Mickey saw a man sitting in an office. Rooney walked in and said, "Hi, I'm Mickey! Who are you?" The man replied, "My name is Walt Disney. Come here, Mickey. Let me show you something." So Rooney walked closer. Walt had some paper and a pencil, and with a few quick strokes, he sketched a cartoon of a mouse.

"Wow!" the boy said, "you draw a good-looking mouse, Mr. Disney!"

Walt said, "How would you like me to name this mouse after you?"

"I'd like that," the boy replied, "but I've got to go now and get a tuna sandwich!" And he took off like a shot.

This story doesn't necessarily contradict Walt's version or Ub's version. True, we know that Walt didn't name his mouse after Mickey Rooney. But he easily could have had such a conversation with young Mickey Rooney after the mouse had already been named by Lillian.

Mickey Rooney's story is reminiscent of a story told to me by film editor Norman "Stormy" Palmer. One day in 1953, Stormy passed Walt in the hall. "Hi, Stormy," Walt said. "By the way, did you hear about our next feature? We're naming the picture after you—*Stormy the Thoroughbred.*" Did Walt and his writers really name the movie after Stormy Palmer? Or did Walt just want to put a smile on Stormy Palmer's face? And could it be that, back in 1928, he also wanted to put a smile on the face of a young Mickey Rooney?

> *"Walt was a hundred percent in sync with what his audiences wanted. If it felt right to Walt, he knew it would feel right to the audience."*
>
> TED THOMAS
> SON OF ANIMATOR FRANK THOMAS

Once Mickey Mouse had been created, Walt took no chances. He gave Ub Iwerks a room to himself, away from the rest of the staff. There, Ub single-handedly animated the entire cartoon behind a locked door. It took Ub six weeks to draw *Plane Crazy,* turning out as many as 700 drawings per day. Ub's drawings were hand-inked on cels in Walt's garage by Walt, Lilly, and Roy's wife, Edna, then taken to the studio and photographed late at night.

Finally, on May 15, 1928, the first Mickey Mouse cartoon, *Plane Crazy,* was test-screened in Hollywood. It was shown as a silent film, accompanied by the theater's organist. Walt sat in the back of the theater to observe the audience and see which gags worked and which didn't. That night, *everything* worked. The audience loved Mickey.

That first Mickey was very different from today's version. In fact, the early Mickey bore an uncanny resemblance to Oswald the Lucky Rabbit. Both Mickey and Oswald had noses like black olives, shoebutton eyes, short pants and rascally personalities. The only real difference was that Oswald had long ears and a short tail, while Mickey had round ears and a long tail.

Walt explained: "[Mickey] had to be simple. We had to push out seven-hundred feet of film every two weeks, so we couldn't have a character who was tough to draw. His head was a circle with an oblong circle for a snout. The ears were also circles so they could be drawn the same, no matter how he turned his head. His body was like a pear and he had a long tail. His legs were pipestems and we stuck them in big shoes to give him the look of a kid wearing his father's shoes. We didn't want him to have mouse hands, because he was supposed to be more human. So we gave him gloves. Five fingers looked like too much on such a little figure, so we took one away. That was just one less finger to animate. To provide a little detail, we gave him the two-button pants."

Animation scholars say that the key to Mickey's popularity is his pleasing shape. There are no hard edges anywhere on Mickey's body. His head, body, nose and eyes are all soft, flexible circles, giving him a soft, friendly feel.

Immediately after completing *Plane Crazy,* Ub started work on a second silent Mickey Mouse cartoon, *The Gallopin' Gaucho.* It was test-screened in Hollywood on August 2, 1928—and the audience loved it. So Walt boarded a train for New York with copies of the first two Mickey Mouse cartoons, determined to find a distributor and make Mickey a star.

Selling the Moon

In New York, Walt encountered only rejection. The distributors all said that Mickey was just Oswald with round ears. Walt decided that Mickey needed something extra to set him apart from Oswald, Felix the Cat and the other toons. So he decided to teach Mickey to *talk.* He was inspired by the success of Warner Brothers' 1927 release, *The Jazz Singer* (though mostly silent, about a quarter of the film featured music and dialogue). Walt knew that a talking mouse would be a sensation.

Back in Hollywood, Ub was already animating the third Mickey Mouse cartoon, *Steamboat Willie* (a parody of a Buster Keaton comedy, *Steamboat Bill Jr.*). Walt phoned from New York and told Ub to halt work on *Steamboat Willie.* He had an idea that would revolutionize the industry. Returning to Hollywood, Walt

"Now is our chance to get a hold on the industry. So let's take advantage of the situation!"

WALT DISNEY, LETTER TO ROY DISNEY
ABOUT SOUND IN CARTOONS, FEBRUARY 1929

gathered his staff and told them that they were going to make cartoons that *talked.*

Walt envisioned a cartoon in which music, sound effects and dialogue worked in sync with moving images to produce a powerful effect on the audience. As Walt discussed the possibilities, artist Wilfred Jackson offered an idea. Since film moves through a projector at twenty-four frames a second, music could be matched to the animation using multiples of eight, providing a rhythm that would match the beat of the music.

Animation director David Hand talked with interviewer Michael Barrier about Wilfred Jackson's contribution to the sound of Mickey Mouse. "Willie [Jackson] knew the mechanics of music," Hand recalled, "as I did, too, but I didn't have his mechanical know-how. He knew—as anybody should have known—that twenty-four frames make a second, and you make twenty-four drawings, and jump them up and down in a second and it's in beat, in rhythm, and so on. . . . Walt got the jump on all the other studios because he had synchronization."

When David Hand saw Disney's first sound cartoon, he immediately quit his job with Fleischer and applied at Disney. "When [Walt] synchronized the cartoon with the sound," Hand recalled, "it was like a whole new world opening up. . . . So I had to go out to Walt Disney."

Before recording the soundtrack for *Steamboat Willie,* Walt set up a test screening to see how hard it would be to synchronize music, dialogue and sound effects to the moving picture. Walt did the voices of Mickey, Minnie, and a squawking parrot. Ub played the cymbals, Wilfred Jackson played the harmonica, and Johnny Cannon made cow moos and the clank of a brass spittoon. Walt ran the cartoon several times. With practice he and his noisy assistants got the sound perfectly synchronized. No recording was made, but the experiment proved that sound magnified the fun and believability of the cartoon.

Unfortunately, all the sound studios were in New York at that time. So Walt took a train to New York with a stop-over in Kansas City. There, he talked his old friend Carl Stalling into composing a score for *Steamboat Willie.* Stalling, who was then a theater organist, wrote a complete score for *Steamboat Willie* in a couple of days.

On September 3, 1928, Walt arrived in New York City with his film and

Stalling's hand-written score. Now came the hard part: finding the right sound-recording company. There were several sound systems to choose from. The Vitaphone system, used in *The Jazz Singer,* recorded the sound-track in grooves on a 16-inch shellac phonograph disk. Other formats, such as the RCA-General Electric Photophone process and Western Electric's Variable Density system, recorded the sound right onto the film.

> *"Nobody had ever seen a drawing make noise, and there was no way to be sure that the people would believe it. It might just look like some kind of a fake thing, and Walt wanted it to seem real."*
>
> WILFRED JACKSON
> DISNEY ANIMATOR

Walt decided against sound-on-disk. Though a phonograph record provided superior sound quality, it was hard for a projectionist to synchronize a record with the film. In animation, *Steamboat Willie* had been carefully timed to produce certain comedic effects, as when Mickey plays the xylophone on the teeth of a cow. An unsynchronized soundtrack would destroy the illusion. Though sound-on-film processes had their drawbacks (such as background hiss), they provided perfect synchronization.

After Walt learned that RCA's Photophone system was far beyond his price range, Walt met a man named Patrick A. Powers, whose studio employed a sound-on-film process called Cinephone. Powers, a former business partner of Universal founder Carl Laemmle, offered to record Walt's soundtrack for a fraction of RCA's quote.

Walt hired Carl Edouarde, pit orchestra conductor for the Strand Theater, to conduct Carl Stalling's musical score. Though Edouarde assured Walt he could match the music to the film by watching the screen as he conducted, the task proved trickier than Edouarde supposed. The session was an expensive disaster.

Broke and discouraged, Walt phoned Roy and said, "We need more money to finish the soundtrack." Roy asked where the money would come from. Walt replied, "Sell the Moon." The Moon in question was Walt's most prized possession, his sporty Moon roadster. So Roy sold the Moon, and the money he got for it was just enough for one more recording session.

But how would they solve the synchronization problem? Wilfred Jackson suggested superimposing a bouncing ball over one corner, giving the conductor beat cues for the music. Walt again assembled the orchestra at the Powers studio. This time, the music and picture synchronized perfectly.

Walt had his soundtrack—but he would soon wish he'd never heard of Patrick A. Powers.

A star is born

Walt screened *Steamboat Willie* for the New York distributors—and once again met with rejection. So he turned to Harry Reichenbach, a flamboyant film promoter (he had once released apes and lions in posh New York hotels to publicize the *Tarzan* movies). "Walter," Reichenbach said, "those guys don't know what's good until the public tells them. You need to run that cartoon in a big New York theater. When the public starts talking about it, you won't have any trouble finding a distributor."

Reichenbach set up a meeting between Walt and S. I. "Roxy" Rothefel, manager of the Universal-owned Colony Theatre in New York. Rothefel booked *Steamboat Willie* at the Colony for a two-week run, paying Disney the unheard-of sum of $500 a week. The film premiered on November 18, 1928, opening for a crime drama, *Gang War*. After the first showing, the audience gave Mickey a standing ovation. The Walt Disney Company observes November 18, 1928, as the official birthday of Mickey Mouse.

The Disney studio added sound to the previously silent cartoons, *The Gallopin' Gaucho* (officially released December 30, 1929) and *Plane Crazy* (March 17, 1929). Mickey Mouse cartoons began out-drawing the main features. People would often ask at the box office, "Are you running a Mickey Mouse?" If the answer was no, the movie-goer would find another theater.

Soon, more money was pouring into the Disney Studio than Walt had ever seen before. Just eight months after Charles Mintz had snatched Oswald away, Walt was at the top of the cartoon industry. Like the indestructible Mouse himself, Walt had been decked by the villain only to bounce right back.

In 1929, the first Mickey Mouse Club was formed at the Fox Dome Theater in Ocean Park, California. By 1931, Mickey Mouse fan club membership topped one million. Kids attended Saturday meetings,

> *"Mickey Mouse to me is the symbol of independence. Born of necessity, the little fellow literally freed us of immediate worry."*
>
> WALT DISNEY

watched Mickey Mouse cartoons, and sang the official Mickey Mouse Club song, "Minnie's Yoo Hoo."

Though the family of Disney characters grew with the introduction of Goofy, Donald Duck, Pluto, and more, Mickey remained the distinctive Disney symbol. He appeared in every conceivable guise, from a cowboy to a fireman, from a ghost-buster to a giant-killer. He was Walt's alter ego. His battles against Pegleg Pete symbolized Walt's battles over adversity. Mickey always found creative ways to triumph—and so did Walt.

President Franklin D. Roosevelt admired the spirit and resourcefulness of Mickey Mouse, and ordered that the cartoons be shown at the White House. England's King George V demanded that Mickey Mouse cartoons accompany every film shown at Buckingham Palace. Mickey brought cheer and hope to a world falling under the shadow of the Great Depression. His relentless optimism, so much like Walt's, was good medicine for an ailing society.

Mickey's last black-and-white cartoon (*Mickey's Kangaroo*) and his first color cartoon (*The Band Concert*) premiered in 1935. That year, the Macy's Thanksgiving Day Parade featured a fifty-foot-tall Mickey Mouse—and Walt received a special medal from the League of Nations, recognizing Mickey as "a symbol of universal good will." To top it off, 1935 was the year Adolf Hitler banned Mickey Mouse cartoons from German theaters.

Later, during World War II, Mickey Mouse encouraged Americans to support the war effort by purchasing War Bonds. During the London blitz, English children were issued gas masks with pictures of Mickey on them. The terror of the bombing raids was made more bearable because the Mouse was there. When Allied forces prepared to storm the beaches of Normandy on D-Day, June 6, 1944, soldiers were given a password by which all friendly forces would be recognized: "Mickey Mouse."

Walt himself provided the voice of Mickey from 1928 until 1946—a fact that demonstrates Walt's versatility and his underestimated acting abilities. Bob Thomas, in *Walt Disney: An American Original,* described Walt's vocal characterization: "His nervous, flustery falsetto—a line of dialogue was often preceded with a shy 'heh-heh-heh'—was just right for Mickey. . . . No one else could capture the gulping, ingenuous, half-brave quality."

Disney sound effects man Jim Macdonald became the voice of Mickey from 1946 to 1974, and he was succeeded in the early 1980s by the versatile Wayne Allwine. Both are excellent Mickeys, but neither has

"Always an inventive problem solver, Mickey would become a symbol of the unconquerably chipper American spirit in the depths of the Depression."

RICHARD SCHICKEL
FILM CRITIC, *TIME* MAGAZINE

that unique quality that Walt imparted to the Mouse. There's a special sense in which Walt truly *was* Mickey—and Mickey *was* Walt.

In animating Mickey, many Disney artists found they could best capture the personality of the Mouse by imagining Mickey as Walt. Mickey not only had Walt's voice, but his sense of adventure, his unsophisticated farm-boy outlook, and his absolute loyalty to his sweetheart. It's interesting to note that both Walt and Mickey started out poor and shoeless.

For the 1939 Mickey Mouse short *The Pointer*, animator Fred Moore coaxed Walt into being filmed as a reference model for the Mouse. There is a scene in the cartoon where Mickey, as a gun-toting hunter, encounters a wild bear in the forest. Mickey gulps and stammers, "I'm Mickey Mouse. . . . You've heard of me . . . I hope?" When voicing the scene, Walt put out his hand at about waist-height—an indication of his own sense of Mickey's stature. When you watch that scene, you actually see Walt's own gestures and expressions as captured by Fred Moore's pencil.

"Mickey really is Walt in a lot of ways," observes Roy E. Disney, Walt's nephew. "Mickey has all those nice impulses Walt had, the kind of gut-level nice guy he was."

To Walt, Mickey Mouse was a symbol of joy and laughter. "All we ever intended for him, or expected of him," he said, "was that he should continue to make people everywhere chuckle with him and at him. We didn't burden him with any social symbolism, we made him no mouthpiece for frustrations or harsh satire. Mickey was simply a little personality assigned to the purposes of laughter."

To me, Mickey is a symbol of the power of imagination to transform our lives and our world. The story of Walt and his Mouse is the story of *imagi-nation unlimited.*

How to Be Like Walt—
Lesson 4: Unleash Your Imagination

After losing Oswald the Lucky Rabbit, Walt had a decision to make: Would he respond destructively or creatively? Most people would have said, "I'll sue! I'll get even! I'll show Charlie Mintz he can't do this to me!"

But Walt chose to respond creatively. He responded with imagination instead of retaliation. He said, in effect, "I'll solve this problem by creating something new, something the world has never seen before." So Walt created Mickey Mouse.

> *"Mickey was the first cartoon character to stress personality. I thought of him from the first as a distinct individual, not just a cartoon type or symbol going through a comedy routine."*
>
> WALT DISNEY

Poor Charlie Mintz. He thought he could take Walt's rabbit and his artists, and Walt would have no choice but to surrender. Mintz didn't understand the power of Walt's creativity. He didn't understand that Walt's limitless imagination made him invincible.

Creativity is the ability to unleash the imagination so that we can envision what has never existed before. It is the ability to solve problems by drawing upon the boundless resources of the imagination. As Walt wrote in an article for *The Journal of the Society of Motion Picture Editors* (January 1941), "How very fortunate we are as artists to have a medium whose potential limits are still far off in the future; a medium of entertainment where, theoretically at least, the only limit is the imagination of the artist."

Some people believe that creativity is a talent you are either born with or not. I'm convinced that creativity is a skill that can be learned and nurtured. All people are essentially creative because we are all made in the image of a creative God. Creativity is our birthright; imagination is the essence of our being. Only when we are dreaming big dreams are we truly fulfilling our God-given purpose in life.

Creativity is not so much an ability as a state of awareness. I had the privilege of interviewing Disney story artist Joe Grant, whose Disney career began with *Snow White and the Seven Dwarfs* (1937). In fact, Joe is the only artist to have worked on both the original *Fantasia* (1940) and on *Fantasia 2000*.

"Walt Disney was an extraordinary individual," Joe told me. "He had an astounding creative awareness. He not only stored up ideas and material in his mind, but he was alert to ideas and story material in the world around him. He was thinking and creating on many different levels, at all times, twenty-four hours a day. It was exciting and stimulating to be around him, because ideas were constantly whirling around him. If you stood next to him, you caught some of his creative awareness. You began to see the world the way he saw it. You began to inhabit his world of ideas."

Actress Ilene Woods, the voice of Cinderella, recalls an incident that illustrates the great creative awareness of Walt Disney. She was in the sound booth, recording the song "Oh Sing Sweet Nightingale," which accompanies a touching scene where Cinderella scrubs the floor and longs to be carried away from her life of drudgery. As Ilene sang, Walt listened with his eyes closed, head resting in his hands, visualizing the images that would accompany the song.

As Ilene finished, Walt looked at her and said, "Ilene, can you sing harmony with yourself?" Walt was referring to multi-track recording, a technology invented by Disney sound engineers for *Fantasia*. It enabled a singer to record her own voice, then sing in harmony with that recording. Ilene had never tried it before.

"As I was listening to you sing," Walt continued, "I got a picture in my mind. Cinderella is scrubbing the floor. As she sings, a soap bubble rises, and her image is reflected in that soap bubble. Her image in the bubble sings in two-part harmony with Cinderella. Then another soap bubble rises, and we have three-part harmony. And another bubble, and Cinderella becomes a quartet, and eventually a choir. I see all of these images in the floating bubbles, and I hear your sweet voice repeated again and again, and it all blends so beautifully."

Ilene was eager to try Walt's idea. So Walt had the song re-scored for multiple voices, Ilene recorded it, and the Disney animators created images for that scene that are among the most memorable in animation history.

Months later, when Walt saw the finished sequence, he turned to Ilene and said, "How about that? I used to pay three salaries for the Andrews Sisters when I could have paid for just one of you!"

We can all become more creative. We can set our imaginations free, just as Walt did, so that we can achieve our goals, solve our problems, and create a better world for ourselves and the people around us. Here are some creative insights drawn from Walt's life:

1. Draw on all of your life experiences. Everything that has ever happened to you is grist for the mill of your imagination. Don't waste your experiences. Remember them, reflect on them, and let them inspire you.

Walt's imagination was drenched with nostalgia and memories of his own past. His boyhood in Marceline, Missouri, was the foundation of many of his cartoons, feature films, and theme park attractions. Throughout his career, Walt continually gathered up the events of his life and creatively rearranged them into imaginative new experiences for the world to enjoy.

Animator Ben Sharpstein recalled that the 1931 Mickey cartoon, *Traffic Troubles,* was inspired by Walt's actual experience of being stopped by a traffic cop. "Walt returned to the studio and he was fuming! But as he told it, we could all see the comedic side of this encounter—and pretty soon, Walt could see on our faces that it really was kind of funny.

"[Walt] kept retelling the story to people who hadn't heard it. Each time he told it, he changed some dialogue or added some details, and it just got funnier and funnier with each retelling. Before we knew it, Walt had this whole scenario worked out—and instead of all of these things happening to Walt, they were happening to Mickey."

2. Remove the limits from your imagination. Most of our limitations

> *"Ideas percolated in Walt's memory for years, from his childhood to the trips he made to South America and Europe. On one European vacation, he bought an armload of mechanical toys—birds, poodles, and so forth—and those toys inspired him to build a system of robotics called Audio-Animatronics. That invention changed entertainment history."*
>
> STACIA MARTIN
> DISNEY ARTIST AND HISTORIAN

are actually self-imposed. We limit ourselves by worrying about the "right" or "proper" way to do things. The moment we place limits on imagination, creativity shuts down.

"I must explore and experiment," Walt once said. "I am never satisfied with my work. I resent the limitations of my own imagination." And so should we. A creative mind is an open mind—a mind that questions assumptions and seeks new ideas and new approaches. Sometimes creative thinking demands that we set aside the rules of logic and make an intuitive leap to a completely new range of ideas.

Again, the cartoon *Traffic Troubles* illustrates how to unleash your imagination. After animation director David Hand finished animating one sequence, Walt sat down with him and watched the pencil test (cartoons were always shot in pencil first, so that corrections could be made before the cels were inked and painted). After viewing the sequence, Walt said, "Nope, it needs to be more wacky, more exaggerated. Try it again."

Hand re-drew the sequence, tossing in more chaotic action, more peril, more exaggeration. Then he showed it to Walt. Again, Walt sent him back to the drawing board. And again, and again, and again. After he had re-drawn the same sequence five times, Hand asked himself, "What does this crazy man want? I'll show him! I'll make this scene so outlandish, he'll say, 'Whoa! I didn't mean to exaggerate it *that* much!"

At the next screening, Walt watched the scene in stony silence while David Hand sweated. When it was over, Walt turned and smiled. "Dave, you did it!" he said. "Why didn't you do it that way the first time?"

> *"Walt's mind was always churning up new ideas for new ways to entertain people. His mind was always in motion. When he wasn't sleeping, his brain was firing on all cylinders. In fact, I'm not sure it wasn't working at full speed when he was sleeping!"*
>
> KEN ANNAKIN
> DISNEY FILM DIRECTOR

The moral to the story: Free your imagination. Don't be afraid to go to the extreme limits of your creativity. "That lesson," David Hand later said, "stuck with me throughout my career."

In 1955, when Walt was building Disneyland, he assigned two top designers, Claude Coats and Herb Ryman, to the Fantasyland "dark rides" such as the "Peter Pan Flight." Walt always wanted to achieve the impossible with his Fantasyland attractions. Coats and Ryman would show him their drawings, and he'd say, "Couldn't we fly the pirate ship over the backyard? And could we have the dog, Nana, float up in the air like she does in the movie?"

If they ever said, "We can't do that," Walt would frown and the air would crackle with tension. Ryman and Coats learned that the only acceptable answer was, "We'll find a way."

3. Consider all possible solutions to every problem. Creative people look at problems and challenges from every angle. They don't want one solution. They want hundreds.

Alice Davis, wife of the late Disney artist Marc Davis and a Disney designer in her own right, told me, "Walt wanted you to figure out three or four or ten or twenty ways of doing something. Marc once told me about a young artist who did a single rendering for a project, and he took it to Walt and asked him what he thought. Walt smiled at him and said, 'Well, it's kind of hard to choose between one.'"

Marvin Davis, one of the original Disneyland designers, once mapped out 129 different plans for the Disneyland entrance. "The first scheme you had, Walt would completely tear apart," Davis observed. "Eventually, you would come up with something better. He wanted to see every idea that you could possibly have before he settled on something."

4. Silence your inner critic. We all have a little voice inside us that criticizes our ideas and inhibits our creativity. Our inner critic nags at us and warns us not to take chances or color outside the lines. Creative people learn to shut off that critical voice so they can explore the outer limits of their imagination.

Children are naturally creative because they haven't yet learned to inhibit their own creativity. They still see the world with childlike wonder. They look up at the clouds and see castles, pirate ships, and dinosaurs; adults look up and see only clouds. "Every child is born blessed with a vivid imagination," said Walt. "But just as a muscle grows flabby with disuse, so the bright imagination of a child pales in later years if he ceases to exercise it."

Animator Ollie Johnston remembers one incident that illustrates Walt's childlike approach to the world of ideas. It was 1941 and story artist Ralph Wright was assigned to develop storyboards for a cartoon short, *Pluto, Junior.* "Ralph had never been in a meeting with Walt before," Ollie recalled, "and he was apprehensive about it. He had these drawings of Pluto waking up in the morning and he was concerned whether Walt would like them or not."

Wright sat down with Walt and began making his pitch—then became unnerved as Walt's expression gradually changed to a look of sheer idiocy. Walt's eyes sagged, his mouth drooped at the corners, and his jaw worked up and down. Wright thought Walt was going to start drooling on the spot!

Then Walt said, "You know how it is when you wake up in the morning and you've got this bad taste in your mouth?" And he smacked his lips distastefully a couple of times while wrinkling his nose. "Couldn't we have Pluto do a little more of that type of thing?"

> *"Everybody in the world was once a child. So in planning a new picture, we don't think of grownups and we don't think of children, but just of that fine, clean, unspoiled spot down deep in every one of us, that maybe the world has made us forget, and that maybe our pictures can help us recall."*
>
> WALT DISNEY

Walt had been acting out Pluto's part! He had imaginatively put himself inside Pluto's skin. Wright realized then that Walt had actually done a brilliant impression of Pluto, and had completely captured Pluto's look of comic stupidity.

That was one of Walt's many gifts—that childlike ability to *become* a cartoon character! No inner critic told Walt to grow up and act like an adult. He lived a life of unfettered imagination, and that was one of the keys to his creativity.

5. To be creative, be courageous. Robert Butler, coauthor of *Walt Disney's Missouri,* told me, "Walt lived the life of his own imagination. Most people are afraid to do that, but Walt was fearless in that way."

"People called Walt a dreamer, and he was," said Bob Thomas. "But he was so much more, because he dared to risk everything to make his dreams come true. He imagined things most people had never thought of. He was an innovator—the first to create a cartoon character with a real personality, the first to use synchronized sound, the first to use color, the first to produce a feature-length cartoon, the first to build a pleasure park—and he mortgaged himself to the hilt to build it. Every creative, innovative thing he did was ridiculed by the so-called 'experts.' They called Disneyland 'Disney's Folly.' But it turned out that the real folly lay in ridiculing Walt's wonderful ideas."

J. B. Kaufman is a film historian and coauthor (with Russell Merritt) of *Walt in Wonderland.* "You can't think of Walt Disney without thinking of creativity," Kaufman told me. "That's his leading quality. His mind was always seeking new and creative ways to do things. He wouldn't let anything or anyone limit the scope of his vision, and he never lost his capacity to dream in a big way. He dared to dream big—but he learned to be daring a little at a time.

"He started with small goals—first, a little studio in Kansas City, then a bigger one in Hollywood, then a massive studio in Burbank, then a theme park in Anaheim, then an entire city in Florida. Each goal was a big one at the time, but once he accomplished it, he would get restless and he would want to go beyond it, to something bigger and more daring. He was not just a man of ideas. He was a man of daring and courage."

Tom Nabbe started his Disney career at age twelve, selling *The Disneyland News* on Main Street. He impressed Walt with his spunk and enthusiasm. When Tom Sawyer Island opened in 1956, Walt cast him as Disneyland's first official Tom Sawyer. Nabbe spent his entire career with Disney.

"One day I was walking to Tom Sawyer Island with Walt," Nabbe told me. "He said, 'Tom, there are paths on that island, but those paths are really for the moms and dads. I want young people to make their own paths and explore the island in their own way.'

"I've often thought about what Walt was really telling me. He wasn't just talking about that island. He was talking about life. Walt was saying that we all need to approach life creatively and courageously. We shouldn't just stick to the paths that are laid out for us. We need to explore. It takes courage to step off the path and blaze a new trail, but that's what creativity is all about. Walt really believed that. What's more, he lived it."

If you want to be creative, then dream bold dreams—then dare to make them come true. As Walt said, "All our dreams can come true, if we have the courage to pursue them."

"Walt was a dreamer, but one who pursued his goals with clarity and an almost ferocious intensity."

JACK KINNEY
DISNEY ANIMATOR

6. Work hard. Authentic creativity doesn't just dream; it builds. It turns fairy tale dreams into castles. "If you can *dream* it," Walt said, "you can *do* it."

"Some people are dreamers; others are builders," said Tom Connellan, author of *Inside the Magic Kingdom*. "Walt was both—a unique combination. He didn't just dream. He executed his dreams. That's why the lessons of his life are so important to us today. We need people today who have the vision to dream as he did, plus the skills and the energy to pull it off and make the dreams come true."

I had the pleasure of speaking with a truly legendary singer and voice actor, Thurl Ravenscroft. Among many other accomplishments, Thurl was the voice of Fritz the Parrot in "The Enchanted Tiki Room," and Buff the Buffalo in the "Country Bear Jamboree" (he is probably best known as Tony the Tiger in the Kellogg's commercials).

"Walt was the greatest dreamer ever," Thurl told me, "but what made him so creative was that he saw his dreams through to fruition. Anyone can imagine a talking mouse or a castle in a park, but it takes hard work to make those dreams real. Walt made his dreams come true, and he was never satisfied until they were built the right way, exactly as he envisioned.

"Walt dreamed up the idea for the 'Pirates of the Caribbean' attraction. He told his artists what he wanted it to look like, and they drew up the plans and constructed a scale model. One day, Walt walked me through the model and showed me where everything would be—the waterfall, the pirate ship, the burning town. He had dreamed it in exacting detail, and he was excited to watch it take shape.

"There is so much that we can learn from Walt's life, but one of the most important lessons his life teaches us is this: Dream big—then go after your dreams, see them through, make them real. Don't be satisfied until your dreams are completed. Walt is remembered to this day, not because he dreamed, but because he created and constructed what he had dreamed. When you walk into Disneyland, you enter his world of dreams. Walt's imaginary world is there for us to enjoy because he made it real."

7. Ask yourself, "What if—?" Creative people don't say, "I always do it this way." They question assumptions. They ask, "What if we could find a better way?"

Walt was a master of "What if?" thinking. Imagineer Bob Gurr, who designed many of the most popular attractions at Disneyland, told me, "Walt had a unique way of drawing out your creativity and poking holes in your assumptions. He wouldn't push you—he would pull you, he would lead you through new ideas. He would get you to ask, 'What if?'

"Many times, I'd be drawing up designs for an attraction, and Walt would come in to check on my progress. He'd see a drawing I had hanging on the wall, and he'd tap his finger on it and say, 'Hey, Bobby, this is starting to look good! But what if—?' And he would give me an insight into a totally new approach. I'd think, 'That's a great insight! Why didn't I think of that?' Then Walt would say, 'Let's look at this again next Tuesday.'

"So I'd work on the concept some more, and I couldn't wait to show it to him on Tuesday. Finally, he'd come back and look at what I'd done and say, 'Hey, Bobby, this is great. But what if—?' And the cycle would begin all over again. Walt kept pulling me to be more creative, and soon I would be operating at two-hundred percent of my natural ability. Why? Because Walt was getting me to think more creatively. Instead of saying, 'That's good enough,' he was always saying, 'What if—?' That's a great question for expanding your creativity."

In the late 1930s, when Walt was intensively working on his concert masterpiece, *Fantasia,* story artist Tom Codrick showed Walt his drawings for the "Sorceror's Apprentice" segment. Mickey stood on a high, rocky promontory as ocean waves crashed around him. His arms were outstretched as if he were an orchestra conductor.

"Yes, very lovely pictures," said Walt. "You have Mickey conducting the ocean." He paused, frowning. "But why just have him conduct an ocean? That's really kind of dull, isn't it? Mickey has all these magical powers—what if we have him conduct the whole universe?"

Codrick gulped. "The whole universe?"

"Yes," Walt said. "What if we have him up there conducting while the stars and comets are whooshing all around him?"

And that's exactly what they did. Walt would always ask, "What if—?" and he would expand a good idea into a *spectacular* idea.

The next time you face a creative challenge, remember these principles from the life of Mickey's creator. And the next time you are cheated or mistreated, as Walt was by Charles Mintz, remember Walt's response. Instead of getting mad or getting even, get creative. Invent your own "Mickey Mouse."

You know, Charlie Mintz actually did Walt a favor by taking Oswald away. If Walt hadn't lost Oswald, we never would have heard of Mickey Mouse—and Walt Disney might never have become a household name. Mickey was not merely the right idea at the right time; he was the creative solution to a crisis in Walt's life.

> *"Walt would approach you and say, 'What if we did this?' He would plant a seed in your mind, and it would grow into a big idea. That was how Walt could get you to think creatively."*
>
> CHRIS CRUMP
> FORMER DISNEY EXECUTIVE AND
> SON OF IMAGINEER ROLLY CRUMP

"Walt Disney couldn't forget his dream," Norman Vincent Peale once observed, "for it grabbed him and wouldn't let go. He just kept on believing in himself and working and dreaming. . . . When you get discouraged and feel like throwing in the sponge, just remember Walt Disney and Mickey Mouse."

Chapter Four

꧁꧂

Animated Leadership

Another early crisis in Walt Disney's career tested his leadership ability and revealed what authentic leadership is all about. There is much we can learn about leadership by emulating Walt's strengths—and avoiding his mistakes.

After the triumphant debut of *Steamboat Willie,* Walt had film distributors lined up outside his door, eager to do business. Unfortunately, they all wanted to make Walt an employee, paying him by the week to produce Mickey Mouse cartoons. After the Oswald debacle, Walt was determined to maintain his independence.

In late 1928, Patrick A. Powers, who had provided the Cinephone sound system for *Steamboat Willie,* offered Walt a distribution deal that preserved Walt's independence. The contract locked Disney into the Cinephone sound system for ten years at $26,000 per year.

Walt trusted Powers. In a letter to Roy, he wrote, "Powers is a very big and influential guy. . . . He is personally taking care of me." Boy, was Powers taking care of Walt! In *Walt Disney: An American Original,* Bob Thomas wrote:

Later Walt was to learn that Pat Powers was known to the film trade as one of the great New York City slickers, his shenanigans in the early days of movies having become legend. An Irish blacksmith from Buffalo, Powers shouldered his way into the infant business by bootlegging cameras from the Patents Company, which owned the rights to film equipment. In 1912 Powers battled with Carl Laemmle for control of Universal. . . . By 1928 he had returned to his beginnings—using pirated equipment. His Cinephone system was based on other people's patents.

Walt had again fallen into the clutches of an unscrupulous distributor. Roy read the contract Walt proudly showed him—and exploded! "Oh, Walt!" Roy groaned. "How could you sign this thing? Didn't you read it?"

"We needed that sound equipment," Walt said defensively. "Besides, Powers isn't a crook like Charlie Mintz. Everything's going to work out fine."

"Badgered and bulldozed"

Meanwhile, Walt brought Kansas City musician Carl Stalling to California and made him the first musical director in the history of animation. Soon after his arrival, Stalling suggested a cartoon series constructed around musical themes. Walt loved the idea, because the new series would allow the Disney animators to explore new techniques and approaches to storytelling. Walt called the series Silly Symphonies.

> *"Walt knew that his animated films would come to life with the use of music."*
>
> RICHARD SHERMAN
> DISNEY SONGWRITER

First in the series was *The Skeleton Dance*, animated by Ub Iwerks (assisted by Les Clark). Carl Stalling's musical score was inspired by Edvard Grieg's "March of the Trolls." Consisting of little more than skeletons rising out of graves and dancing in the moonlight, the cartoon had no plot or dialogue, but was rich in music and visual gags.

Walt sent a print of *The Skeleton Dance* to Pat Powers, who responded curtly, "The public doesn't want this. *More mice!*" Walt didn't like being told what to produce, so he booked *The Skeleton Dance* at the Carthay Circle Theatre in Los Angeles. It received a standing ovation. Walt sent the reviews to Powers, who reluctantly agreed to distribute the Silly Symphonies.

Soon, however, Walt had even bigger problems with Pat Powers—problems that involved Mickey Mouse. Mickey's popularity was soaring, yet the meager checks from Powers scarcely covered Disney's expenses. Like Charles Mintz, Pat Powers would never give Walt and Roy a financial accounting. Reluctantly, Walt concluded that Powers was cheating them.

In late 1929, the Disney brothers hired attorney Gunther Lessing to protect their rights. Lessing, who had once brokered a movie deal between the Mutual Film Corporation and Mexican bandit Pancho Villa, was noted in Hollywood for his hard-headed negotiating skills.

In early January 1930, Walt, Lillian and Lessing boarded a train for New York. Walt intended to confront Pat Powers about an estimated $150,000 in missing royalties. Walt went alone to Powers' office and demanded to see the ledgers. Powers said he would only open his books after Walt signed a new five-year distribution deal. Walt refused—as Powers expected.

Then Pat Powers dropped his bombshell. He told Walt that he had hired Ub Iwerks to create a new cartoon series for Powers' company. Powers would pay Iwerks $300 a week—double his salary at Disney.

Walt couldn't believe it. He and Ub had been friends since they founded Iwerks-Disney Commercial Artists in 1919. Walt had brought Ub out to Hollywood from Kansas City, and Ub was the only animator to remain loyal during the Mintz debacle. Walt and Roy had even made Ub a twenty-percent owner of the Disney studio! How could Ub turn against them?

Then Walt recalled how Ub had complained when Walt altered Ub's drawings or exposure sheets. He remembered how Ub had balked when Walt tried to get him to use inbetweeners—apprentice animators—to increase his productivity (Ub stubbornly insisted on drawing every frame himself). And there was the time Walt found Ub in front of the studio, tinkering under the hood of his car. Walt had snapped, "Hire a mechanic and get back to the drawing board!" Ub ignored Walt and continued working on his car the rest of the day.

"Throughout the 1930s, Ub Iwerks forged a career and identity separate from Walt Disney. Beginning in 1930, he ran his own cartoon studio named Celebrity Productions, and the cartoons that he produced were widely distributed by one of the world's largest studios—Metro-Goldwyn-Mayer. However, mention the names of Iwerks' two main cartoon characters, Flip the Frog and Willie Whopper, and you'll most likely get blank stares."

GARY JOHNSON
MEDIA CRITIC, PUBLISHER OF *IMAGES* JOURNAL

Walt didn't see these clashes as major rifts in their friendship—but Ub apparently did.

"Look," Powers said. "You don't have to lose Ub Iwerks. Sign a new contract, and you and Ub will still be under one roof."

"Forget it," Walt said. "If Ub feels this way, I can't work with him."

Powers was stunned. It never occurred to him that Walt would let Ub go. The big Irishman had overplayed his hand.

Desperate to keep Walt under his control, Powers raised his offer to $2,500 a week. A lot of money—but Walt didn't consider it for an instant. He walked out of Powers' office without a backward glance.

Meanwhile, back at the Hyperion studio, Ub Iwerks was in Roy's office, submitting his resignation. Ub's reason for leaving: artistic differences. Roy wrote a check to Ub for $2,920—Ub's twenty percent share of the Disney company (had Ub stayed, his twenty percent share would have been worth millions during his lifetime).

When Carl Stalling heard that Ub had resigned, he mistakenly assumed that Walt couldn't survive without Iwerks, so he also quit. (Stalling later helped launch the Looney Tunes and Merrie Melodies cartoons at Warner Brothers.) Like Pat Powers, Stalling underestimated Walt's contribution to Mickey's success. No matter who wielded the pencil, Walt was the driving force behind every cartoon, contributing most of the story ideas, sight gags and insight into the character.

Walt immediately sought a new distributor for Mickey Mouse and the Silly Symponies. He approached Metro-Goldwyn-Mayer, but when Powers heard about it, he threatened to sue MGM. The threat worked. MGM backed away from Disney.

Columbia film director Frank Capra heard that Powers was trying to ruin Walt Disney, so he asked Columbia Pictures studio head Harry Cohn to become Disney's distributor. Cohn was one of the toughest characters in Hollywood, and Powers' legal threats didn't worry Cohn in the least. Cohn paid the Disney studio a huge advance. With the money from Harry Cohn, Walt and Roy paid Powers $100,000 to buy back the rights to the first twenty-one Mickey Mouse cartoons and cancel Disney's ten-year obligation to use the Cinephone sound system.

Harry Cohn's toughness got Walt out of his contract with Powers, but gave the twenty-eight-year-old cartoon maker a new set of headaches. Cohn's abrasive management style was summed up in his personal motto: "I don't get ulcers, I give them!" Cohn relied on his tough-guy image to give him the upper hand. His office featured a towering portrait of his hero, Italian dictator Benito Mussolini.

> *"We started the business here in 1923, and if it hadn't been for my big brother, Roy, I swear I'd have been in jail several times for bouncing checks. I never knew what was in the bank. Roy kept me on the straight and narrow."*
>
> WALT DISNEY

Walt became one of the people to whom Harry Cohn gave ulcers. Though Cohn's checks always arrived on time, Walt found Cohn impossible to deal with. As Frank Capra later recalled, Walt was continually "badgered and bulldozed" by Harry Cohn.

A breakdown—and a "gypsy jaunt"

It was a stressful period at the Disney studio. Walt's relentless quest for excellence cut deeply into the profit margin on every cartoon. He continually clashed with artists who failed to satisfy his perfectionist demands.

Lillian worried that Walt was working himself to death. He was plagued by insomnia and often spent nights working at the studio instead of sleeping. His mind went blank in story meetings, and he chain-smoked, using the smoldering stub of one cigarette to light the next. Sometimes, when speaking on the phone, his voice would choke and he'd cry for no reason.

In 1931, he suffered a major breakdown. "I went all to pieces," he later recalled. He checked into Good Samaritan Hospital, where he underwent an operation on his throat. The doctors believed that his voice work on the Mickey Mouse cartoons had overtaxed Walt's larynx—but it's possible the sheer stress of running the studio while dealing with Harry Cohn had caused Walt's throat to constrict.

Walt's doctor prescribed exercise and a vacation. So Walt and Lilly set off on what they called their "gypsy jaunt." They took a train to St. Louis, where they hoped to board a paddlewheeler on the Mississippi. Sadly, the Great Depression had shut down the riverboat business. (If Walt wanted to ride on a Mississippi riverboat, he'd have to build one himself—which he did when he built Disneyland.)

On a whim, Walt and Lillian continued by train to Washington, D.C., to tour the monuments. Then they went to Key West and boarded a boat to Havana. After a relaxing stay in Cuba, they cruised through the Panama Canal and back to Los Angeles. "We had the time of our lives," Walt later said. "I came back a new man."

Returning to the studio, Walt plunged into his exercise program with renewed vigor. He tried wrestling and boxing, then bought a set of golf clubs. After shanking the ball into the woods a few times and throwing a tantrum or two, Walt decided that golf wasn't his game.

The transplanted Missouri farm boy still loved horses, so he and Roy joined the swank Riviera Club and often played polo there, or at Will Rogers' ranch in the Santa Monica hills. Walt would take up his cane mallet, climb into the saddle, and whack the ball around with such luminaries as Spencer Tracy, Douglas Fairbanks and Darryl Zanuck.

Walt loved polo, and plunged his whole studio into the sport. He even hired a polo expert to coach the Disney team. But after injuring his neck in a fall from a polo pony in 1938, Walt had to give up polo. That injury would cause him significant pain for the rest of his life.

Three pigs and a duck

When Harry Cohn refused Walt's request to increase the advance to $15,000 per cartoon, United Artists eagerly stepped up, agreeing to pay Disney a $20,000 advance against 60 percent of the gross for each cartoon. With the dictatorial Harry Cohn out of his life, Walt's spirits soared. Lilly and Roy were happy to see the return of Walt's cheery, optimistic self.

In early 1932, work began on a Silly Symphonies cartoon called *Flowers and Trees.* Midway to completion, Walt halted production and ordered all existing work scrapped. Everything had to be redone—in full color.

Walt had just witnessed a new Technicolor process that combined three color negatives—red, blue and green—to produce brilliant, near-lifelike color. Walt knew that color would be as revolutionary as sound. Over Roy's objections, Walt signed an exclusive contract with Technicolor. For the next two years, Walt would be the world's only producer of Technicolor motion pictures.

> *"When I saw those three rich, true colors on one film, I wanted to shout."*
>
> WALT DISNEY

On July 30, 1932, audiences were stunned as the rich colors of *Flowers and Trees* splashed across the screen. The film won an Academy Award—the first Oscar ever given to an animated cartoon.

In 1933, the Disney studio took animation to the next level with a Silly Symphonies cartoon, *Three Little Pigs.* Walt finally achieved what he had been reaching for since the Alice Comedies: cartoon characters with believable personalities. Each of the three pigs was a distinct and well-defined individual. Audiences cheered the pigs, booed the Big Bad Wolf, and sang along with composer Frank Churchill's bouncy songs. The cartoon became so popular that some theaters listed it on the marquee above the feature film.

Three Little Pigs won an Academy Award and gave Americans an anthem of hope during the worst years of the Great Depression: "Who's Afraid of the Big Bad Wolf?" That song symbolized an optimistic belief that the Big Bad Depression would soon be defeated, and that better days were just around the corner.

> *"There was a moral foundation to Walt's movies that people tapped into—a basic moral foundation. In Disney films, you see strong values and role models. You see the importance of being kind to others, of serving others, of finding joy even in adversity. All of this reflects the Judeo-Christian worldview that Walt was raised in."*
>
> LES PERKINS
> VIDEO PRODUCER AND DISNEY HISTORIAN

Theater owners clamored for sequels, but Walt didn't like to repeat himself. Roy finally persuaded Walt that it was just a matter of giving the public what it wanted. So Walt produced three sequels: *The Big Bad Wolf*, *Three Little Wolves*, and *The Practical Pig*. They were never as successful as the original, proving that (as Walt put it), "You can't top pigs with pigs."

Walt set a high moral standard for his cartoons. Many other cartoon series of the 1930s, such as Max Fleischer's Betty Boop and Ub Iwerks' Flip the Frog, were loaded with sexual innuendo, risque images and adult-oriented humor. Walt wanted to produce cartoons that were safe for young minds. "There's enough ugliness and cynicism in the world without me adding to it," he once said.

As journalist and Disney scholar Tim O'Day observed, "Walt's value system was the foundation of everything he did in the field of entertainment. He never hit you over the head with it, but the Disney product stood for something. It reflected his moral outlook."

Merchandising the Mouse

Roy worried about the cost of Walt's obsessive quest for excellence. In 1930, the cost of one cartoon was $5,400. By 1931, it more than doubled to $13,500. In 1932, Technicolor raised the price to around $23,500-$3,500 more than the advance from United Artists. Disney's costs were so high that it took two years for a cartoon to show a profit.

Only one thing kept Disney afloat during the Great Depression: merchandising. In 1933, a nearly bankrupt timepiece manufacturer, the Ingersoll Waterbury Company, signed a deal to produce Mickey Mouse watches. Macy's department store sold 11,000 Mickey Mouse watches in a single day. By the end of 1933, 900,000 Mickey Mouse watches had sold nationwide; by 1935, more than 3 million.

Mickey worked the same magic for the Lionel Corporation, also nearing bankruptcy in mid-1934. By the end of the year, the electric train company had sold more than 350,000 Mickey and Minnie handcars at a dollar apiece. In just four months, Lionel went from $300,000 in the red to nearly $2 million in the black.

In 1934—one of the worst Depression years—Disney cartoons earned over $600,000, while Disney merchandise added an additional $300,000. Herman "Kay" Kamen was the marketing wizard behind it all. Hired by Walt and Roy in 1932, Kamen established Disney Enterprises, the licensing division. He also created K. K. Publishing to handle Disney-licensed comics and books. Later renamed Western Publishing Company, Kamen's corporation became a major investor in Disneyland in the 1950s.

By 1940, Kamen had generated more than $30 million in revenue for Disney. He single-handedly produced a category of collectibles known today as "Disneyana."

Walt becomes a leader

While the Great Depression meant lean times for America, The Walt Disney Studio was making money hand over fist. Walt plowed most of the studio's profits into improving technology (such as Technicolor), expanding his staff and increasing the number of projects in production. So while Disney cartoons made millions, the company still struggled financially.

Reflecting on the financial stresses of that period, Walt wrote in *The Journal of the Society of Motion Picture Editors* (January 1941), "The suspense has been continuous and sometimes awful. In fact, life might seem rather dull without our annual crisis. But after all, it is stress and challenge and necessity that make an artist grow and outdo himself."

During those years, Walt not only grew as an artist—he also matured as a leader. At the beginning of his career, Walt was overly trusting and easily taken advantage of—but his painful experiences with Charles Mintz and Pat Powers wised him up in a hurry.

> *"I thought we could make Snow White for around two-hundred-fifty thousand. At least that's what I told Roy. . . . Roy was very brave until the costs passed a million. . . . When costs passed the one and one-half million mark, Roy didn't even bat an eye. He couldn't; he was paralyzed."*
>
> WALT DISNEY

He learned, for example, that he wasn't as good a judge of people as he thought he was. Raised in the Midwest where a man's word is his bond, Walt was used to doing business with a handshake. Mintz and Powers took advantage of Walt's trusting nature—and Walt learned that his brother was a better judge of human nature than he was. From then on, Walt never signed a contract without Roy at his side.

Walt also learned that while he was a great entrepreneur, he was a poor manager. He lacked what Roy supplied: pragmatic business sense and strong management skills. Neither Walt nor Roy could have succeeded alone. But together, the Disney brothers became one of the greatest partnerships in the history of American business.

How to Be Like Walt— Lesson 5: Become an Animated Leader

I have made a lifelong study of leadership. In my book *The Paradox of Power* (Warner Books, 2002), I distilled the art of leadership down to seven essential components. Walt Disney perfectly exemplifies every one of them: Vision, Communication Skills, People Skills, Good Character, Competence, Boldness, and a Servant's Heart. Let's take a closer look at each one:

1. Vision

Great leaders are people of vision. Without a vision, how will you know what success looks like? And how will you know how to get there? Your vision is your definition of success. Not all visionaries are leaders, but all leaders are visionaries. You can't lead people without a vision of where you are taking them.

When asked how he was able to achieve so much in one lifetime, Walt replied: "I dream, I test my dreams against my beliefs, I dare to take risks, and I execute my vision to make those dreams come true." Let's break that down:

A. "I dream." Walt began with a vision, a dream of the future.
B. "I test my dreams against my beliefs." Walt made sure his vision was consistent with his beliefs, his core values, his integrity.
C. "I dare to take risks." He acted boldly, betting on himself to win.
D. "I execute my vision to make those dreams come true." He focused all his energies, and those of his organization, on turning his dreams into a reality.

History teacher Lee Suggs uses Walt Disney's life and films as curriculum material. "Walt was an ordinary person with extraordinary vision," Lee told me. "He turned his dreams into reality because he was so determined—because, in his words, 'I execute my vision to make those dreams come true.' Walt teaches us that when we have a dream, we should pursue it with all our might."

In his early years, Walt dreamed big dreams of taking animated cartoons far beyond the primitive level of flickering black-and-white images. He dreamed in sound and color, and soon his cartoons talked and exploded in rainbow hues. He dreamed of cartoon characters with real personalities, and soon audiences cared about the fate of three little pigs.

Amusement Week editor Tim O'Brien, told me, "Walt envisioned animated cartoon characters who were more real than any actor, and he succeeded. Then Walt envisioned a theme park—something that had never existed before. It was hard for other people to see what Walt was building until he actually had it finished. Fifty years later, Disneyland is still alive and flourishing and full of wonder because of the power of Walt's initial vision."

Imagineer Bob Gurr agrees. "When we'd be locked into a major project," he said, "we were immersed in our own private world. All we could see was the Autopia or the Monorail—whatever project we were working on. After completion, we would compare notes with each other, and we discovered that Walt had seen the entire picture the whole time. He was the Grand Master of the Vision."

"Think beyond your lifetime, if you want to do something truly great. Make a fifty-year master plan. A fifty-year master plan will change how you look at the opportunities in the present."

WALT DISNEY

People who knew Walt were continually amazed at the vast range of his vision. "Walt was always thinking far out into the future," said Bob Matheison, former vice president of Theme Park Operations, Walt Disney World Resort. "He was way ahead of the rest of us. After dealing with Disneyland and its limited space issues, we all had a hard time grasping Walt's vision of Walt Disney World. In Florida, we had thousands of acres to work with. It was such a challenging project to get our arms around.

"One day we were meeting with Walt in the 'war room' in California. Walt was irritated because our thinking about the Florida Project was so limited. He roared, 'The trouble is that you aren't thinking far enough ahead! We're just beginning! You have to think beyond Disney World! We haven't even begun to think big!' That's the kind of vision he had."

Though Walt envisioned Walt Disney World in Florida, he died before it was built. On opening day in 1971, almost five years after his death, someone commented to Mike Vance, creative director of Walt Disney Studios, "Isn't it too bad Walt Disney didn't live to see this?"

"He did see it," Vance replied simply. "That's why it's here."

2. Communication Skills

A great leader is also a great communicator. If you have a great vision, but can't communicate it to others, how will your vision ever become reality? Walt was a great leader because he was a great communicator.

Walt was not an orator. He had a simple, direct way of speaking, but when he spoke, people listened. Roy's wife Edna once said, "Walt had a way of telling you about what he wanted to do and explaining it to you in a way that you fell right in line with him. You would go right along with him— you couldn't help it. Walt had very expressive brown eyes, and he used his eyes a lot. He'd use his eyes and his hands and tell you all about everything and explain it all to you. That was his way of making you believe it all— and he was usually right."

Those who worked with Walt told me again and again how approachable he was. Disney sound engineer Gary Carlson said, "One day in late 1965, I was working in my office and Walt knocked on the door. He was carrying two cups of coffee and he gave one to me and sat down. We spent the next two and a half hours just talking. He told me about his life and asked me about mine. We talked about all kinds of things. I wish I'd had a tape recorder. Walt was just a warm, friendly, regular guy. Of course, you always knew he was the boss, but he was not some towering, intimidating boss. He was very approachable."

Irving Ludwig, who headed the Buena Vista distribution division, told me, "I had an office in New York and occasionally Walt would come by when he was in town. One day, he walked into my office and sat on the corner of my desk. We started talking about the current crop of movies, and soon he was explaining his plans for

> "Walt would say to me, 'Peter, I can't paint. All I know is what I want.' He inspired me to do better things with my painting. He could draw out the talent in you."
>
> PETER ELLENSHAW
> DISNEY MATTE ARTIST

future pictures. We talked for a long time, and I was mesmerized by the flow of ideas from his mind. When he talked, you could see his plans and dreams the way he saw them. He connected with your heart as well as your mind."

In 1956, Walt chose renowned orchestra leader Tutti Camarata to establish Disneyland Records (now called Walt Disney Records). "Walt challenged and inspired you by talking to you," Camarata told me. "He wouldn't give you detailed instructions about what he wanted you to do. Instead, he would simply point you in the direction he wanted you to go, then leave the rest up to you. He would get you started on the creative process and inspire you with confidence. As a result, you would go far beyond what you thought you were capable of doing."

John Kimball, son of animator Ward Kimball and a longtime Disney employee, told me, "Walt could talk to his artists and get their juices flowing so that they could produce beyond their capabilities. He would have some wildly impossible idea, and he'd tell an artist, 'I know you can do this. Take this project and get it done.' And the artist would think, 'I never dreamed I could do something like that, but if Walt says I can do it, then maybe I can.' And usually, Walt turned out to be right. He inspired people to do the impossible, and he did it by just talking to people."

"Walt had everyone under a spell," said Tony Baxter, senior vice president of Creative Development at Walt Disney Imagineering. "He was on a mission, and he inspired everyone to join his mission. People bought into Walt's vision one-thousand percent. That's why the things Walt accomplished are bigger than life. He could take these creative geniuses, all brilliant in their own way, and get them to soar in formation. With his ability to communicate and inspire, Walt orchestrated hundreds of creative talents to achieve something beautiful and lasting. And no one ever felt used by Walt—they felt honored to have a part in realizing his vision."

Disney executive Orlando Ferrante has helped develop Disney theme parks around the world. He explained Walt's communicating skills using sports terms: "I would list Walt Disney among the greatest coaches who ever lived. He drew up the plays, gave us our assignments, inspired us and motivated us. That's what great coaches do.

"I would also compare Walt to a great quarterback. He inspired us by his presence. If you're on your own one-yard line, you know you've got to go ninety-nine yards to score. But if you believe in your quarterback, you can do anything. We felt that way about Walt. No matter how impossible the challenge, we could do it because Walt was our quarterback."

"The key to Walt's success was his ability to attract people to his cause, inspire them, and motivate them to work with him on his dreams. He sold people, and they bought in and became loyal followers. They're still following him, and they miss him to this day."

KEN ANNAKIN
DISNEY MOVIE DIRECTOR

Irving Ludwig recalls, "Walt inspired you just by talking to you. He extracted your hidden talents by lighting the fire within you. One time, the music director for *The Living Desert* was in Walt's office, discussing the score for the film. Later, he told me, 'I left Walt's office and went to my piano and just played and played.' That result didn't surprise Walt. He expected it! He'd hire talented people, then fill them with that fire to get the results he wanted."

"Walt had a way of communicating

that was just magical," composer Richard Sherman told me. "Simple, but magical. He would give you a challenge and say, 'I know you can do this.' He made you believe anything was possible. He made you proud to be on his team. And it really was a team effort—Walt would roll up his sleeves and go to work alongside the rest of us.

"He saw potential in people who had never really done anything great. My brother Robert and I really had no track record in the music industry, but Walt heard a few of our songs and he gave us an opportunity and inspired us to keep topping ourselves. Without Walt to inspire us, I don't know where we'd be today.

"Walt always wanted you to find something wonderful in yourself, to believe in it and consider it God's gift to you. God gives you the gift, and the rest is up to you. Walt taught me that what you do with that gift is your gift back to God.

"Walt would never condemn you. If you failed, he'd just steer you in a new direction. At Disney, I attended the most inspiring graduate school in the world. I learned something from Walt every day."

What made Walt such an inspiring communicator? He understood that communication is more than words—we communicate with our eyes, our smile, our hands, our posture and our bearing. Walt had studied Charlie Chaplin—an actor who communicated primarily through his face and body, because his movies were silent. That's why Walt had such an expressive face and such sweeping hand gestures.

"Walt was a visual communicator," said sculptor Blaine Gibson. "He would do whatever it took to illustrate a point and get it across to you in a visual way. One time, he

> *"Walt Disney was a storyteller—a walk-around storyteller."*
>
> BOB GURR
> DISNEY IMAGINEER

wanted to illustrate the action of an elephant. So he got up on a chair and made his pants look bunched and wrinkled like the leg of an elephant. Then he put one arm down to look like an elephant's trunk and he made the motions that an elephant would make. Here's this dignified studio head, and he is up on a chair, pretending to be an elephant!

"He would do exaggerated things like this, because animation is about exaggeration. I've seen him get down on the floor to make a point. He didn't care about his dignity; he cared about communicating effectively. He communicated to your eyes as well as your ears."

Storytelling was one of Walt's greatest communication skills. "Walt was a storyteller above all," said X Atencio, a longtime Disney animator-songwriter-Imagineer. "As an artist, he was more of a doodler. But he had a keen ability to tell stories. He deserves to go down in history alongside Hans Christian Andersen and the Brothers Grimm. Walt didn't write the stories, but he envisioned them. He told stories better than anyone else around, and he got the people around him to turn his stories into movies and theme park attractions."

Actress Margaret Kerry remembers Walt as a storyteller, first and foremost. "When I was working as a reference model for Tinker Bell in *Peter Pan*," she told me, "Walt could act out the whole story himself. Then he could show you how your part fits together with every other part of the story. When he was telling you a story, he had your complete attention. Walt's greatest fear was the fear of boring people. That fear drove him every day."

"I was stumped one day when a little boy asked, 'Do you draw Mickey Mouse?' And I had to admit I do not draw anymore. 'Then you think up all the jokes and ideas?' 'No,' I said, 'I don't do that.' Finally, he looked at me and said, 'Mr. Disney, just what do you do?' 'Well,' I said, 'sometimes I think of myself as a little bee. I go from one area of the studio to another, and I gather pollen. I sort of stimulate everybody. I guess that's the job I do.'"

WALT DISNEY

You can't be a good communicator unless you listen well and really hear what people are saying. Disney historian Paula Sigman told me, "Walt was a great communicator in part because he listened so well. He would sit and listen as his creative people discussed a project. He would gather ideas, insights and opinions—then at the end, he would have the perfect solution based on everything he had just heard. He would get it exactly right."

Disney sound engineer Gary Carlson told me, "Walt was always going from place to place, asking questions and listening to people. When he got input from people, he took it seriously. He implemented ideas and suggestions right away. He would wander around the park, and if he bumped into you, he would ask questions. He wanted to know what you see that he might otherwise miss."

"Walt would listen to all of us in the meetings," said film editor Stormy Palmer, "and he would let you know if he thought you were wrong. But he would think about what you said. Later, he might see you in the hall and say, 'Well, maybe you were right. Why don't we go back and take another look at your idea.' He had his own ideas, but he was always willing to listen to new ideas. Walt was a good listener."

This is what Walt teaches us through his communicating style: To be a great leader, become a great communicator, a great storyteller and a great listener.

3. People Skills

Walt once said, "You can dream, create, design and build the most wonderful place in the world, but it requires people to make the dream a reality." Everything Walt achieved, he achieved through people. Not one of Walt's accomplishments was a solo effort.

To be a leader, you must have people skills: the ability to delegate; the ability to manage the results; the ability to inspire loyalty; the ability to create an atmosphere of creative freedom and informality; the ability to turn a collection of talented individuals into a team; and the ability to create an atmosphere of teamwork.

Delegating requires the ability to trust others. As a leader, you can't do it all yourself; you are the visionary, the motivator, the team-builder. You sell your vision to a team of competent people, trust them to do their jobs, and hold them accountable for the results.

Walt delegated the artistic side of his studio to his story artists, animators, background artists, musicians, and other members of his creative staff. He once said, "I am in no sense of the word a great artist, not even a great animator; I have always had men working for me whose skills were greater than my own. I am an idea man." Aware of his limitations, Walt focused on his strengths.

The proof of Walt's creative genius is the fact that no matter how many artists came or went, the quality of the Disney product remained consistently high. Why? Because Walt was a leader. His artists were brilliant people who supplied talent, skill and experience—but the true genius at the Disney studio was Walt himself. Those who say that Walt was not an artist simply do not understand his kind of creativity. Walt was an artist whose medium was *people*. He expressed his artistic vision through *people*. His canvas, brush and pigments were *people*.

Film historian Leonard Maltin explained Walt to me this way: "Many executives feel threatened by the success of their subordinates. Not Walt. He understood that the success of his staff reflected well on him, and enhanced his own reputation and accomplishments. Yes, Walt had a healthy ego and his name was at the forefront of the company, but he knew it was not a one-man operation. Everything he did, he did through people."

Walt delegated the artistic assignments to his animators and delegated the business side to his brother Roy. "Walt's vision could not have succeeded without Roy," said longtime Disney cast member Pam Dahl. "Walt had wonderful, towering dreams, but it was Roy who laid the concrete for those dreams to stand on. Roy has never gotten the credit he deserves for believing in his brother's dreams and getting them built and paid for. Some people say that Walt was the creative side of their partnership and Roy was the non-creative side. No, Roy was creative, too. His creativity lay in finding the money to support Walt's creativity. He had a gift for creative financing, and that's a rare and important form of creativity."

> *"Walt wanted to manage the creative process without intruding on it. So, after work, he would go study the artists' desks, bulletin boards, and even the wastebaskets. Janitors would say he'd sit there and study his artists' work for hours."*
>
> HARRIET BURNS
> DISNEY IMAGINEER

In addition to delegating, leaders must also have *the ability to manage the results*. Leaders must delegate—but they cannot shrug off responsibility for the results. "Delegate" does not mean "abdicate." When you become a leader, you place yourself at risk. Your success depends on the success of your subordinates. If they fail, you fail—and you are responsible.

One of the ways Walt managed the results of his delegating was by his legendary nighttime visits to the animators' offices. He would often return to the studio after dinner and go from table to table, looking at the work his animators had done during the day.

"We'd do gags," animator Roy Williams once said, "and then we wouldn't like them ourselves, so we would wrinkle them up and throw them in the wastebasket. Walt would come in at night, after we all went home. He'd go through those wastebaskets. The janitor had orders not to touch anything in the room until he went through it. The next morning, we'd come into work and there'd be a bunch of wadded drawings, straightened out, pinned up on the storyboard with Walt's note saying, 'Use this! It's a good gag!'"

Some people have criticized these late-night visits as evidence of Walt's "controlling" personality. But I believe this was Walt's way of managing the results. Having delegated the task to a team of artists, he made a nightly habit of checking on those results, making sure the work met his high standards. Rather than going in during the daytime and standing over an artist's shoulder (imagine how nerve-wracking *that* would be!), Walt did his rounds at night.

Walt didn't try to hide his nighttime visits. He left notes announcing his presence. Even so, the artists sometimes treated Walt's visits like a game of cat and mouse. "We'd position our drawings in such a way," said animator Ollie Johnston, "maybe turn them at a slight angle, so that we could tell if he'd been sifting through them."

Walt was on to them. He once told an interviewer, "I sit down at night and look at story sketches and things. The boys know that I do that. And they pull all kinds of tricks to find out whether I've been there, you know. They arrange papers in a certain way on the chairs, and when they arrive in the morning, they say, 'Well, Walt wasn't in this weekend.' But they don't know that I put the papers right back where they were."

On one occasion, in this game of cat and mouse, the cat got caught. Story artist Bill Peet was in his office late one Sunday night, working on a storyboard. Suddenly, Walt walked in—and stopped dead in his tracks. "What are *you* doing here?" Walt asked.

"Working," Peet said. "What are you doing here?"

Walt couldn't think of an answer, so he turned and walked out.

Another important people skill is *the ability to inspire loyalty*. Loyalty is the glue that holds an organization together. "Walt's inspiration and enthusiasm," said Stormy Palmer, "made over-achievers of all of us at the studio. You wanted to please him. Walt was more than a boss. He was like a father to me."

Something about Walt inspired love and loyalty. Randy Thornton, a producer with Walt Disney Records, put it this way: "Walt was not a man who gushed praise. His biggest words of approval were, 'That'll work.' Yet people would work late, sacrifice, and spend every ounce of energy they had to win those two words from Walt. People wanted to please him."

Winston Hibler worked for Disney as a producer, director, writer, cinematographer and narrator. His son Chris has vivid memories of the years his dad spent at Walt's side. "Walt inspired loyalty among those who worked with him," Chris told me. "He could be difficult and demanding, but he was loving and loyal to his employees. He cared deeply about the people who worked with him. Walt's staff could have made more money working for another studio, but they wouldn't leave Walt. They loved him and they believed they were doing something meaningful."

> *"Whenever anyone called him 'Mr. Disney,' he got upset. It was always Walt. And he always knew your name. In the early days, we didn't wear name tags, but Walt still called you by your first name. Once he knew your name, he never forgot it."*
>
> GARY CARLSON
> DISNEY SOUND ENGINEER

Another crucial people skill is *the ability to create an atmosphere of informality.* From the very earliest days of his studio, Walt cultivated a culture of informality. He put everyone on a first-name basis with everyone else. He didn't merely invite people to call him "Walt"—he insisted on it. He corrected anyone who called him "Mr. Disney"—or worse, "sir."

Walt's secretary, Lucille Martin, told me, "When I first started with Walt, I was nervous and always called him 'sir.' He'd call me on the intercom, and I'd say, 'Yes, sir.' And he'd say, 'Call me Walt.' And I'd say, 'Yes, sir, Walt.' He was my boss, and I couldn't bring myself to call him by his first name, even when he ordered me to! So one day he handed me a piece of paper—a cartoon of himself walking with a protest sign. The sign read,

'Down with Sir!' I had to laugh. I taped it to my intercom as a reminder. I still had to work on it, but Walt's cartoon helped."

Fred Joerger, a Disney model maker, told me his favorite Walt Disney story. "Bob Broughton had just been hired as a courier at the studio," Joerger said (Broughton would eventually become a camera effects artist). "Bob had been told by some fellas at the studio, 'Everyone calls Walt by his first name. Don't ever call him 'Mr. Disney,' he hates that. If you see him in the hall, be sure to say, 'Hi, Walt.' Well, soon after he started work there, he got on an elevator, and there was Walt Disney himself! So Bob did what he was told. He said, 'Hi, Walt!' Walt made no response—he was completely lost in thought about some project.

"Well, Bob was horrified. He figured the other guys at the studio had set him up. He'd called the boss by his first name, and now he was probably going to get canned. So Bob decided to never make that mistake again. Later that same day, Bob was walking down the hall, and there's Walt Disney, coming toward him. This time, Bob ignored Walt—walked right past him without a word.

"Walt put a hand on Bob's shoulder, and said, 'What's the matter? Aren't we speaking?'"

Bob Gurr recalls attending a dinner in Pittsburgh in Walt's honor. At the cocktail party before the dinner, Westinghouse CEO Don Burnham approached Walt. He was nervous and stammering, and Gurr could see that the man was awestruck in Walt's presence. Bob Gurr had seen it before. "People would see Walt on TV every week," he said, "and they idolized him so much that when they saw him in person, they didn't know what to say.

"But Walt had a way of putting people at ease. As Burnham was talking to him, Walt casually reached up and loosened his tie and set it a little askew." It worked. Burnham relaxed, and he had a nice chat with Walt.

"That was how Walt made himself approachable," Gurr concluded. "Whenever he was around people, he would deliberately dress down, make himself a little rumpled, loosen his collar, even wear this beat-up porkpie hat that he kept wadded up in his coat pocket. It was Walt's way of signaling, 'Relax, I'm okay, I'm just a regular guy like you.'"

Another important people skill is *the ability to turn a collection of talented individuals into a team*. "Walt had an uncanny knack for discovering talent," said X Atencio. "He'd see talent in people that they didn't even see in them-selves. He'd move people like chess pieces. He'd move them to different departments, even different careers." X Atencio speaks from experience.

Born Francis Xavier Atencio, X began working for Disney in 1938 as an apprentice animator, making twelve dollars a week. He spent nearly thirty years in feature anima-tion, working on such Disney classics as *Pinocchio* and *Dumbo*. "I was an animator all those years," he told me, "and one day Walt said, 'X, it's time for you to move.' And he sent me over to the WED Enterprises, where they were building attractions for Disneyland. I didn't know anything about building attractions. I was an animator.

"When I got over there, I said, 'Walt sent me. What do you want me to do?' And nobody had a clue what I was supposed to do there. Walt hadn't told anyone. And I was there for a few days without any work to do. Finally, Walt called and said, 'X, I want you to write the script for the "Pirates of the Caribbean" attraction. There will be scenes with pirates and townspeo-ple and so forth, and I want you to write all the dialogue.' I wondered if Walt was talking to the right guy. I had never scripted anything before, but Walt said, 'I know you can do this.' And that's how I became a writer."

X began with a scene where an auctioneer is selling off brides to a bunch of drunken pirates. "That's fine," Walt said. "Keep going, this is good." X kept working until he had scripted the entire attraction.

"I think we should have a song that plays throughout the attraction," X said to Walt. "I have a melody and some lyrics." He sang a few bars for Walt, figuring that Walt would bring in his top songwriters, Richard and Robert Sherman. Instead, Walt said, "Oh, this is good. If you need some help with the music, get George Bruns to score it."

That song became one of the most famous Disney songs of all time—"Yo Ho, Yo Ho, A Pirate's Life For Me." X later wrote the script and songs for Disneyland's "Haunted Mansion."

"Walt Disney was a collector of people," Bob Gurr observed. "He had a good sense of what had to be done and who could do it. He never hesitated to transfer people into a line of work they'd never done before. Sometimes people would resist at first, because most people don't like change. But Walt's sense about people was unerring."

Former Disney executive Jim Cora told me his story. "In 1957," he said, "I was nineteen and just out of the Army. I had started college at Long Beach State and worked during that summer in Fantasyland. I ended up as the foreman on the 'Snow White' ride.

"Early one morning, I was walking to work. I had my schoolbooks and a bunch of papers under my arm. I saw Walt approaching and he said, 'Hi, Jim, can you spare a minute?' Well, yes, for Walt Disney, I had a minute to spare.

"He said, 'What are all those books and papers you have there?' I told him I was writing a manual to train future ride operators. Nobody had asked me to do this, but in the Army, I had trained people and written manuals, so this was a natural thing for me to do.

"Walt was interested in my manual idea. He said, 'Jim, I'd like you to go see Van France about this. I want you to put a training book together.' Van Arsdale France was in charge of training all the personnel at the park, and he helped found the training program now known as Disney University.

"So I went to see Van and he said, 'Who sent you?' I said, 'Walt Disney.' He said, 'No, who sent you?' I guess he couldn't believe that Walt would send a nineteen-year-old raw recruit to him. But that's how I got involved with the Disneyland training program. Walt launched my career because he saw a bunch of papers and books under my arm."

From his earliest days as a studio head, Walt focused on talent, teamwork, and balancing personalities to produce a team chemistry. He was constantly looking for insights into the psychological makeup of his staff.

"My grandfather could recognize talent. He hand-picked different people for different projects. He would spot traits and qualities, and he would ask people to join him."

WALTER DISNEY MILLER
WALT'S GRANDSON

Once, during the early days at the Hyperion studio, Walt sat in the lunchroom, watching his animators eat watermelon. One man worked his way from one end to the other, cutting each bite with a knife and fork. Another started in the middle, scooping with a spoon. One man carefully seeded his melon before eating. Another spit his seeds into a cup. After several minutes, Walt said, "I'm sure the way you eat your watermelon reveals something important about your character—but I can't figure out what it is!"

Australian-born layout artist Frank Armitage told me he was continually impressed by the way Walt mixed and matched people in search of a winning team chemistry. "The way Walt could combine people was amazing," he said. "He mixed people the way we mix paint. He knew how to put the right group of people together to produce the best results. In the early days, Walt would have writers, artists, and story artists all together. These were blue sky sessions and you would see a pattern start snowballing, all because of the way Walt combined people's different talents. They built on each other's ideas and produced amazing results."

When Walt assembled a creative team, he would always seek a balance of contrasting personalities: a few frenetic, high-energy types; one or two quiet, reflective types; some natural leaders; some followers; some risk-takers, some play-it-safers. On many projects, he would pair two animators of highly contrasting styles and personalities on the theory that something unexpected would emerge from a combination of polar opposites. He was rarely disappointed.

Again and again, Walt demonstrated that when you transform a bunch of talented individuals into a well-balanced blend of personalities, you have a *team*. As Walt himself said, "Of all the things I have done, the most vital is coordinating the talents of those who work for us and pointing them toward a certain goal."

Longtime Disney artist-Imagineer John Hench summed up Walt's approach to teamwork this way: "Walt would give you the rope and let you run with it in any direction you wanted—north, south, east or west. But the rope was only so long. Walt wanted your imagination to roam freely during the brainstorming phase, but once the team had a sense of direction, he expected you to get behind one idea and become part of the team."

Walt specialized in *the ability to create an atmosphere of teamwork.* He once said, "I have an organization of people who are really specialists. You can't match them anywhere in the world for what they can do. But they all need to be pulled together, and that's my job."

The organizational structure at the Disney studio in Walt's day was unlike that of any other corporate entity before or since. Yes, there was a hierarchy, and yes, Walt was the top man. But the studio functioned more like a community of relationships than a hierarchy. Walt was in the middle of this community, and he personally interacted with every other part.

Walt conducted meetings with an economical balance of firmness, efficiency and informality. Meetings invariably began on time. There was only one small concession to formality that Walt ever allowed: when he entered the meeting room, everyone rose to their feet. Walt never asked for this show of respect, and no one knows where the custom originated.

"Walt was able to put these talented, creative people in the same harness and get them to pull together—but he always held the reins. That's not easy to do. Creative people like to carve out their own individual roles and work independently. That can destroy an organization. It's a tribute to Walt's leadership that he held his organization together and achieved what he did."

SAM McKIM
DISNEY IMAGINEER

Walt welcomed an open exchange of ideas, including dissent. There were only two things that annoyed him in a meeting: (1) being interrupted, and (2) having someone argue with him once he had decided a matter.

Exchanges at these meetings could be frank, verging on brutal. Dick Nunis, former chairman, Walt Disney Parks and Resorts, recalled one tough meeting early in his Disney career. "I was giving this pitch to Walt," Nunis said, "and he was just killing me. He said, 'Nunis, you don't know what you're talking about,' and walked out of the room. Everybody followed him and I sat there in this big room all by myself. I thought I had been fired and was thinking of where I could go to get a new job when I heard the door open behind me. It was Walt. He put his hand on my shoulder and said, 'Look, young fella, you keep expressing your opinions; I like it.'

"I think he tested people. Later, I would sit in meetings and watch him take a position and see who would go with him. Then he would take the opposite position and see who would go with him. I think the people who stuck to their guns, whether they were right or wrong, were the people he respected the most."

Animation director David Hand recalled that the Disney studio in Walt's day was remarkably free of office politics. Walt simply had no time or patience for employees who engaged in gossip, backstabbing, snitching or one-upsmanship. "Walt didn't encourage political maneuvering," Hand told interviewer Michael Barrier, "and he did not like apple polishing. I'm not a politician; but some people are naturally bent that way, and I think that Walt would sense it, squint and frown, and turn and walk away."

Leaders achieve results through people. Good leaders develop good people skills: the ability to delegate, manage results, inspire loyalty, create an atmosphere of informality, turn a collection of talented individuals into a team, and create an atmosphere of teamwork.

4. Good Character

A leader must have good character in order to inspire other people with his vision for the future. As leadership guru John Maxwell observed, "People buy into the leader before they buy into the leader's vision." The scores of people I've talked to have painted a consistent portrait of Walt as a man of great character.

Former Disney CEO E. Cardon "Card" Walker remembered Walt as "a creative guy who had great ability and great character. He produced upbeat, positive material that is as popular today as it was decades ago. Why? Because it is timeless and true, reflecting Walt's own strong character values and personal integrity."

Mouseketeer Tommy Cole remembers Walt as a man continually aware of his influence on the people around him. "Walt Disney was a man of character," Tommy told me. "He used his influence wisely. Thinking about Walt's influence on my life, I would say that I have applied many of Walt's virtues and beliefs to the way I try to live: Work hard in order to reap the just rewards of your labor. Be loyal to friends and family, and that loyalty will probably be returned."

"I grew up watching Walt Disney on TV," says Pam Dahl. "He was like a member of my family, someone I looked up to. I knew as a child that I wanted to work for The Walt Disney Company, because Walt had such an impact on my life. As a result, I worked for the company for twenty-five years. One thing I learned was that the image I saw on television was, in fact, the real Walt. He stood for integrity. He was worthy, honest and true."

"He created Mickey Mouse and produced the first full-length animated movie. He invented the theme park and originated the modern multimedia corporation. . . . But the most significant thing Walt Disney made was a good name for himself."

RICHARD SCHICKEL
FILM CRITIC, *TIME* MAGAZINE

A flaw in his character

Walt elevated the abilities of his talented creative staff far beyond what they themselves imagined possible. But occasionally, he could be a harsh taskmaster, gruff and insensitive to the emotions of his subordinates.

Directing animator Jack Cutting admired Walt, but occasionally felt the sting of Walt's changeable moods. "I always felt," he said, "that his personality was a little bit like a drop of mercury rolling around on a slab of marble because he changed moods so quickly. . . . Although Walt could exude great charm, he could also be dour and indifferent toward people—but this was usually because he was preoccupied by problems. Sometimes you would pass him in the hall, say hello, and he would not even notice you. The next time he might greet you warmly and start talking about a new project he was excited about."

Some of Walt's animators—including some who loved and admired him—lived in fear of being publicly reprimanded by Walt. "If there was one thing about Walt that I was critical of," Ward Kimball once said, "it's that he jumped on people in front of others. In story meetings, he was very harsh on people who brought up an idea that he felt didn't fit into a discussion. As a result, people would hold back because they didn't want to be bawled out or yelled at."

Carl Barks worked as a Disney animator in the 1930s, and later worked on the Donald Duck comic books. He also created the Disney character Uncle Scrooge McDuck. "All of us respected and feared him," Barks once said. "[In story conferences] he would always let us argue a story point. He'd even let us have the last word in these arguments. We said, 'Yes, Walt.'"

Apologizing didn't come easily for Walt, yet it is clear that he deeply regretted some of his excesses. "I've been a slave driver," he once said. "Sometimes I feel like a dirty heel the way I pound, pound, pound." Walt's short fuse was an unfortunate inheritance from his quick-tempered father. When Walt gave a blistering reprimand to one of his animators, he was demanding the same kind of perfection that his father had so often demanded of him.

Story artist Bill Peet worked for Walt from 1937 to 1964. In his autobiography, Peet wrote, "I believe I knew Walt about as well as any employee could know him, even though he was never the same two days in a row." Peet related an incident that gives us a glimpse into how Walt's painful childhood must have troubled him long into his adult years. One day, Walt came into Peet's office and settled into a chair, sighing deeply.

> "Walt had weaknesses like all of us, but he was a brilliant man."
>
> FRANK THOMAS
> DISNEY ANIMATOR

"What's on your mind, Walt?" Peet asked.

"It gets lonely around here," Walt said. "I just want to talk to somebody."

Then, Walt poured out the story of his boyhood to Peet, including those tough years in Kansas City, delivering newspapers for (as Peet put it) "his tyrant of a father, who was a distributor and kept every cent." As Walt spoke, he reminded Bill Peet of "a hurt little boy."

Peet was about to share some of his own childhood misery to "let him know we had something in common." But Walt sprang out of his chair, muttered, "Gotta get going," and was out the door—embarrassed, perhaps, at having revealed so much.

Pressure at the studio often triggered Walt's ill-tempered outbursts. For much of his career, his studio teetered on the brink of financial ruin. Some paydays, Walt and Roy would summon the staff to the softball diamond, set up a card table, and divide the company's cash-on-hand among the employees. They would also hand out stock certificates—largely worthless paper in those days. "I know you can't buy groceries with these," Walt would tell his employees, "but someday they'll be worth something." It was humiliating for Walt to go before his employees and turn his pockets inside-out.

After one stormy staff meeting in the 1940s, he growled, "You fellas don't know what it's like, running this studio! You don't have the worries I have! I'm the one who has to stay up nights thinking of things for you fellas to do!" Not much of an apology—but quite an insight into Walt's mindset and the immense pressure he was under.

By the mid-1950s, as the studio's financial pressures subsided, his outbursts became less frequent and severe—but they still flared up from time to time. Bob Gurr joined Disney in 1955. "If Walt got upset with you," he told me, "you'd get that forefinger of his rammed into your solar plexus. He'd get angry—but a minute later, he would calm down."

Given that Walt could be difficult to work for, it is all the more significant that so many people loved him and spent decades working at his side. One longtime Disney employee, Bob Kredel, told me, "The criticism most frequently aimed at Walt Disney was that he was a tyrant. Well, he was! Ward Kimball once told me, 'Walt made us work. He drove us and pushed us and forced us to reach levels of perfection.' And you know what? Ward admired Walt for that!"

During Ollie Johnston's forty-four-year career as a Disney animator, he experienced the difficult side of Walt, but he places those experiences within a context of Walt's artistic temperament and pursuit of excellence. "He was a fair man," Ollie once said, "but he had little patience for anything bad or weak. . . . He rarely complimented any of us. Even if he did approve of what you had done, he'd add, 'Of course you'll fix that little wiggle,' or something like that. It was a put-down, but that was good for us. We would work a little harder. Some guys would get cocky when they were complimented, and they wouldn't work for two weeks."

Ken Anderson also spent forty-four years with Disney as an animator, writer, architect and Imagineer. "Walt did things that hurt me terribly," Anderson once said. "But by the same token, if a guy can hurt you that

> *"No matter what the provocation, I never fire a man who is honestly trying to deliver a job. Few workers who become established at the Disney studio ever leave voluntarily or otherwise, and many have been on the payroll all their working lives."*
>
> WALT DISNEY

much, he can also make you love him that much."

"People stayed with him because they loved him," said animator Paul Carlson. "And they loved him because they knew he was pulling for them. Walt wasn't easy to work for, but we all knew that he was in our corner. He wanted us to succeed. He cared about us as people. That's why his people still feel so strongly about him, four decades after his death."

Actor-director Kevin Corcoran agrees that Walt's toughness was sometimes necessary. "Walt had a unique knack of knowing what a person needed," he told me. "Some people needed a pat in the back, some needed a kick in the tail. Walt knew what you needed in order to be the best you could be. I was self-critical, so Walt knew I needed a pat on the back. But with others, he might say, 'Come on, you can do better!' People who listened to him were better for it."

Walt definitely mellowed with age. If he could live his life over again, I suspect Walt might criticize less and praise more. He might follow a principle that has guided me over the years: *Affirm in public; confront in private.* Never humiliate people in front of their peers.

Walt Disney was a great man—and a good man. But Walt had his flaws. I think the best summation of Walt's personality was offered by his grandson, Walter Disney Miller. "My grandpa wasn't always easy to work for," he told me. "He had a temper, and high praise wasn't his style. Yet people were drawn to him and wanted to please him. Many people on his staff stayed with him for twenty, thirty, forty years or more. He inspired loyalty."

5. Competence

Walt once said, "Leadership means that a group, large or small, is willing to entrust authority to a person who has shown judgment, wisdom, personal appeal, and proven competence." The word *competence* means "the state or quality of being well qualified, skilled, knowledgeable, and able to perform a given role." People will only follow your leadership if they believe you are competent to lead.

Notice that the first seven letters of the word "competence" are C-O-M-P-E-T-E. Your people need to know that you are a *competent* and *competitive* leader. If they know you will fight hard to win, they will follow you anywhere.

A competent leader sets high but realistic standards for himself and his team, and maintains those standards by holding himself and his players accountable. A competent leader constantly strives to improve his product—whether that product is (as in Walt's case) an animated cartoon, a theme park, or (as in my case) an NBA basketball team. Walt demonstrated his competence and competitiveness through:

> *"It was all about teamwork with Walt Disney. He was always working to get other people involved in the process. Look at Mickey Mouse. Sure, Walt invented him and created his personality, but Lillian named him and Ub Iwerks drew him."*
>
> ROBERT W. BUTLER
> COAUTHOR, *WALT DISNEY'S MISSOURI*

1. *A strong track record.* People knew Walt was competent because of the string of successes he produced. When people saw his achievements, they wanted to join him. They were willing to follow Walt because he was a proven winner.

2. *A commitment to hard work.* Walt learned the lessons of hard work early in life. No one on his staff ever worked harder than Walt himself. "Walt had a great dedication to his work," said Dick Morrow. "He had a bed in his office. He was usually the last one to leave."

Disney Imagineer Sam McKim told me, "Walt never went on vacations. Even when he went to Europe, he was working and gathering ideas. He drove himself hard every day." When asked by a reporter if he had any hobbies, Walt instantly replied, "Work is my hobby."

3. *A commitment to continual personal growth.* Walt was an avid reader, listener and researcher—a sponge for new information and ideas. His lifelong quest was to improve himself and increase his knowledge and skills. As Ollie Johnston observed, "Walt never went farther in school than the ninth

grade, yet I would consider him very well-educated. That's because he was focused on self-improvement."

4. *A commitment to winning.* Walt loved to win. Competitiveness was in his nature. Though he was not a great athlete by all accounts, he was a tough competitor on the polo field and the softball diamond. Walt's nephew, Roy E. Disney, remembered Sunday afternoon croquet games in which all four Disney brothers—Walt, Roy, Herbert and Ray—would compete with cut-throat intensity and even the occasional fist fight. Walt was a fierce competitor.

Bill Peet noted that Walt's competitiveness as a polo player and his competitiveness as a filmmaker were intertwined. He wanted to win at the box office, just as he wanted to win on the polo field—and his opponents were the same people in both arenas.

In an interview with John Province of the online magazine *Hogan's Alley,* Peet said, "There were rumors all over Hollywood that [*Snow White*] wasn't going to go over and that Walt Disney had gotten too big for his britches. . . . The big producers, of course, were hoping to see Walt Disney fall flat on his face. They thought it was arrogant for the 'Mickey Mouse Man' to rise up and compete. I think it angered them that he wouldn't stay in his place. He played polo with them, you see, and they used to kid him about being a 'Mickey Mouse third-rater.' 'The Little King' they called him, because Walt's ego was quite large."

So Walt had something to prove when he released *Snow White and the Seven Dwarfs* in 1937. The success of *Snow White* was a monument to Walt's competitive spirit.

5. *A commitment to excellence.* Walt set high standards for himself and his staff. "Good enough" was never good enough for Walt. "Walt wouldn't put up with mediocrity," said Larry Pontius, former V.P. of Marketing for Disneyland and Walt Disney World, and author of *Waking Walt.* "Because his standards were so high, he wasn't always as nice to everyone as we might like. But it all went back to Walt's desire for excellence. Walt's relentless drive for excellence drove Roy crazy, because Walt spent so much money to make things right. But everything Walt created has endured because he never settled for less than the best."

Actor Alan Young (Wilbur Post of TV's Mr. Ed) was the voice of Disney's Uncle Scrooge. "Walt insisted on the best," Alan told me. "Everything was about quality with Walt. When he would finish a movie, he'd invite the whole staff to view it. They'd offer

> *"I have been up against tough competition all my life. I wouldn't know how to get along without it."*
> WALT DISNEY

their opinions and if the report was not good, Walt would go back and redo it. That's why those movies are classics today. The shorts and features he made back in the 1930s, '40s, and '50s are still entertaining today because they were made so well. That's a great lesson for all of us."

6. Boldness

Boldness is courage, confidence, an adventurous spirit, and a willingness to take risks. Bold leaders master their fears, act decisively, and accept the consequences of their decisions. Walt was one of the boldest leaders in the history of American business. On more than one occasion, he bet his entire studio on a single project.

Walt once said, "Courage is the main quality of leadership—courage to initiate something and keep it going, a pioneering spirit, an adventurous spirit, the courage to blaze new ways in our land of opportunity." If you are not bold, you are not a leader.

"Walt had a strong belief in his own opinions and instincts," said film historian Leonard Maltin. "He didn't have to turn to a focus group or board of directors because he trusted himself. If he liked something, he believed others would too. Walt was his own test audience. We don't see that much anymore in any field. Today's leaders are so afraid of making crucial decisions, but Walt put himself on the line many times. He would sink or swim on the consequences of his decisions."

Former Disney engineer Wendell Warner told me, "Walt expected his people to take a chance and fly high. If you failed, you'd better not shift the blame to others. Walt was never easygoing about failure. But if you took a chance and failed, he wouldn't fire you or berate you. He wanted you to learn and grow from the experience.

"There were times when I made a mistake on some project, and I'd go to Walt and say, 'I blew it. I tried to pull something off, and I failed.' Walt would say, 'Well, did you learn anything?' And I'd say, 'Yes, absolutely.' And Walt would say, 'Okay, then it's not a total loss, is it? Keep trying—and keep an eye on what other people are doing around the shop. See what you can learn from them.' Failure never feels good, but Walt always made you feel that failure could be redeemed, and he expected you to continue working and risking until you achieved success."

Walt's friend, writer Ray Bradbury, explained the lesson of Walt's life this way: "Walt teaches us that if you really want to accomplish something big in life, don't hesitate. Go to the edge of the cliff and jump off. Then build your wings on the way down. That's what Walt did. If he waited for every condition to be perfect, he wouldn't have done anything. The world would have been deprived of so much joy and we would never have heard of Walt Disney."

7. A Servant's Heart

I believe the ultimate test of leadership is this: Does this person have the heart of a servant? If you don't have a servant's heart, you're not a leader, just a boss.

To me, the greatest leader of all time was Jesus Christ. He laid down the fundamental principle of leadership when he said, "You've observed how godless rulers throw their weight around . . . and when people get a little power how quickly it goes to their heads. It's not going to be that way with you. Whoever wants to be great must become a servant. Whoever wants to be first among you must be your slave" (Mark 10:42–44, *The Message*).

Walt Disney was a leader because he was, above all, a servant. Ruthie Tompson was a Disney camera supervisor. She told me, "I had a friend named Bud Du Brock, a polo trainer who was injured and became a paraplegic. Walt always asked me, 'How's Bud doing? You've got to get him to the park.' I kept telling Bud that Walt was asking about him and wanted him to come to Disneyland, but he never wanted to do that. Being paralyzed, I think he assumed there'd be nothing for him to do. Finally, Bud agreed to come as Walt's guest. Walt rolled out the red carpet and personally took Bud on all the attractions, and got him front-row seats for the shows. Walt really cared about people."

Former Disney publicist C. Thomas Wilck told me that he met his wife

Tommie while they were both working at Disney (her unmarried name was Tommie Blount). "Tommie was Walt's secretary for eight or nine years," Wilck said. "During the years she worked for Walt, he became like a father to her. We got married in 1962, and Walt not only gave the bride away, but he paid for the wedding reception. Tommie was devastated when Walt died, but she stayed on for a couple of years to help with unfinished projects, such as CalArts. Walt had been so kind to Tommie, and she wanted to help complete Walt's last unfinished dreams."

Songwriter Robert Sherman shared this example with me: "Walt had a house for guests in Palm Springs—a really terrific place. General Electric had installed all sorts of household inventions in the house that weren't out on the market yet. Walt would let you sign up in advance if you wanted to use the house. I vacationed there several times.

"On one occasion, I went to the Palm Springs house and Walt sent a golf cart over for me to use. I was wounded in World War II and have been walking with a cane since I was nineteen. Walt was so considerate of me.

"There was another time when we had a meeting at the studio and my back went out on me. Walt carried in a Kennedy rocker for me to sit in so I would feel more comfortable.

> *"We share, to a large extent, one another's fate. We help create those circumstances which favor or challenge us in meeting our objectives and realizing our dreams. There is great comfort and inspiration in this feeling of close human relationships and its bearing on our mutual fortunes—a powerful force to overcome the 'tough breaks' which are certain to come to most of us from time to time."*
>
> WALT DISNEY

He was always doing kind things like that for me and other people in his office. It makes me cry to remember what a good man he was, and all the things he did."

Camera effects artist Bob Broughton told another story. "In the 1950s," he said, "Walt started a scholarship fund for the children of employees. When my son, Danny, was accepted at Princeton, I told Walt what his generosity meant to our family. He said, 'Well, Danny is the kind of kid who deserves this.' So Danny got through Princeton, went on to Georgetown Medical School, and is now at the Mayo Clinic—thanks to Walt."

Actor Dean Jones recounted another incident: A gardener at the Disney studio left some tools in an empty parking space. When a producer drove up and saw the tools in his space, he honked at the gardener and gave the poor man a chewing-out. Walt walked up and interrupted the producer's tirade. "Hold it!" he said. "Don't you ever treat one of my employees like that! This man has been with me longer than you have, so you'd better be good to him!"

That was Walt. To his employees, he was not only a leader. He was their defender and their servant. That's what separates leaders from bosses.

The next challenge

The 1930s were trying but instructive years in the life of Walt Disney. He escaped the clutches of Patrick A. Powers, broke free of Harry Cohn's tyranny, and solidly established his studio with cartoons that lifted the spirits of the nation and won Oscar after Oscar. Disney merchandise provided fully one-third of the studio's annual income.

During the early part of that decade, Walt's abilities as a leader and innovator had been tried, tested and refined. Now Walt would take on his biggest, riskiest challenge ever: *Snow White and the Seven Dwarfs.*

Chapter Five

❧

Betting the Studio

Walt had a comfortable house, a string of polo ponies, and a shelf full of Oscars—but he wasn't satisfied. Some called his latest dream "Disney's Folly." Even his wife and brother thought it was a crazy idea. Walt was about to risk everything—including his studio—on a fairy tale.

Walt and Lillian Disney had a good life—but it was not complete. They wanted children. Lilly's first two pregnancies had ended in miscarriage.

Soon after they moved into their new home in the Los Feliz section, near the Hyperion studio, Lilly became pregnant again. Walt wrote his mother, who was living in Portland, Oregon, "Lilly is partial to a baby girl. I, personally, don't care—just as long as we do not get disappointed again."

A few months later, he wrote her again: "The spare bedroom where you and Dad stayed is all fixed up like a nursery. We have a bassinet and baby things all over the place. . . . I suppose I'll be as bad a parent as anybody else. I've made a lot of vows that my kid won't be spoiled, but I doubt it—it may turn out to be the most spoiled brat in the country."

Appropriately enough, Walt was at a *Parents* magazine ceremony honoring him for his Mickey Mouse cartoons when he received word that Lilly was in labor. He hurried to the hospital, arriving just minutes before she was taken into the delivery room. In those days, delivering mothers were often given general anesthesia. Lilly later said that the last thing she heard as she was going under was Walt's cough.

On December 18, 1933, Walt became a father. He and Lilly named their new daughter Diane Marie Disney.

A big gamble

Walt thought of making a feature-length film as early as 1931, when he asked his friend, Mary Pickford, to play the title role in an adaptation of Lewis Carroll's *Alice in Wonderland*. Walt planned for her to be the only live-action character in an all-cartoon Wonderland. The project never got off the ground.

"If we were going to get anywhere, we had to get beyond the short subject. I knew that if I could crack the feature field, I could really do things. Snow White *was the answer to that."*

WALT DISNEY

Whenever Walt talked about making a feature-length animated picture, people responded, "A cartoon is fun for seven minutes, but nobody will sit through a ninety-minute cartoon." Walt figured that a combination of live action and animation would be more acceptable to audiences.

Still, Walt couldn't help wondering: Why shouldn't audiences enjoy an all-animated feature, as long as it is filled with drama, action and laughter? Walt recalled the books that had enthralled him in his youth, such as the science-fiction adventures of Jules Verne, and the enchanting tales of *Cinderella* and *Sleeping Beauty*. He remembered being captivated by the 1916 film version of *Snow White*.

In the spring of 1934, thirty-two-year-old Walt Disney decided to bet his studio on an idea everyone around him said was crazy. He was going to produce a full-length animated film called *Snow White and the Seven Dwarfs*.

"I have a story to tell you"

At first, Walt told no one about his plans. He spent several weeks in secret, reading, researching, making notes, and blocking out a storyline for the film. Finally, he was ready to tell his two closest confidants, Lillian and Roy—and he knew exactly how they would react.

Lilly was aghast. "Walt," she said, "the short subjects are doing well! The studio is successful! Why risk everything on a movie that could ruin us?"

Roy was equally alarmed. "Walt," he said, "do you have any idea how much a feature-length film would cost?"

Walt knew the cost of producing a single seven-minute Technicolor cartoon was around $23,500. A feature-length film would be about twelve

> *"Walt believed in what he was doing and risked everything to turn his dreams into a reality."*
>
> JACK LINDQUIST
> RETIRED DISNEY EXECUTIVE

times as long. By simple multiplication and rounding off, plus a bit of wishful thinking, Walt arrived at a budget of $250,000 for *Snow White*. Roy knew Walt's tendency to be over-optimistic in money matters, so he doubled Walt's estimate to $500,000.

Lilly and Roy tried to talk Walt out of his dream—but when they saw that he was totally committed to it, they gave up. Once Walt made a decision, no one could change his mind.

Within days, Walt gathered forty of his top animators. Opening his wallet, he handed each man some cash, then said, "I want you fellas to go have dinner and relax a little. Then come back to the studio. I have a story to tell you."

The animators walked out of the studio, buzzing among themselves. After dinner, they gathered in a recording stage where Walt had set up folding chairs in a semicircle. The room was dark, like a movie theater, except at the very front. There stood Walt, under a single light bulb, bouncing on his heels, a secretive smile on his face. Once everyone was present, Walt began to tell the story of *Snow White and the Seven Dwarfs*.

Walt didn't merely *tell* the story. He *performed it,* acting out every part. He *became* every character. His eyebrows arched, and his features twisted into those of the evil Queen. He tilted his face toward the bare light bulb, and its soft glow transformed his face into that of Snow White. Each character had a distinct voice and personality.

Reaching the end of the tale, Walt paused—then said, "That is going to be our first feature-length animated film." If Walt had said those words at the beginning of his presentation, his artists would have thought he was crazy. Everybody knew there was no audience for an all-animated feature.

But after watching Walt act out the story before their eyes, they believed it was not only possible, but practically an accomplished fact! Walt had the whole picture in his head—all they had to do was animate it.

"Walt's greatest talent was his ability to get people fired up," said Disney historian Robert W. Butler. "The greatest show Walt ever put on was when he acted out the story of *Snow White* for his animators. They were so energized and inspired by his performance that it kept them going for the next four years."

Back to school

Though the Disney artists were all accomplished animators of squishy, stretchy, exaggerated cartoon characters—they had almost no experience animating realistic human figures. In the summer of 1934, Walt assigned director Wilfred Jackson and animators Les Clark and Hamilton Luske the task of creating *The Goddess of Spring*, a Silly Symphonies cartoon featuring believably animated human figures.

> *"Look at* The Goddess of Spring, *and then look at* Snow White, *which came out in late 1937. We're looking at three years—but it looks like twenty years of development. It's hard to believe that only three years separated these pictures."*
>
> RUDY BEHLMER
> FILM HISTORIAN

As a test of his studio's readiness for the challenge of *Snow White*, Walt found *The Goddess of Spring*, released November 3, 1934, to be a dismal failure. The goddess Persephone's features seemed to float around on her face. As she danced, her rubbery limbs swayed crazily, like seaweed in an ocean current. The Disney studio was clearly not ready for *Snow White*.

Walt began an intensive art training program for his core group of animators. He brought Don Graham and other instructors from the Chouinard Art Institute into the studio to conduct night classes, focusing on the realistic motion of the human body: How do people actually walk, run, turn, dance, show joy or fear or surprise? How do the folds of their clothing move? How do lightning flashes, dappled sunlight, and shadows appear on real human features?

Walt wanted to inspire and challenge his animators to lift their sights above mere cartooning. He wanted them to think like *artists*. So he brought in some of the nation's leading artists and critics to lecture on a wide range of topics, from the physics of light to the psychology of humor. Included were such notables as architect Frank Lloyd Wright, muralist Jean Charlot, writer Alexander Woolcott, and Italian expressionist Frederico Lebrun.

After one lecture, one of the animators said to Walt, "We're lucky to be able to hear people like him." Walt responded, "Listen, he's lucky, too. He can learn as much from you guys as you can learn from him."

Producers at rival studios scoffed at Walt's art instruction program. But when they saw the artistic growth of Disney's cartoons, they stopped laughing. No longer was the Disney studio regarded as a mere "Mouse Factory." Even the casual observer could see that Disney animation had reached a higher plane than the rest of the industry. No wonder Walt considered his art school well worth the $100,000 annual cost.

By late 1934, artists Hamilton Luske and Myron "Grim" Natwick began creating character sketches of Snow White. Walt brought in a young dancer as a reference model for Snow White. Her motions were broken down frame by frame and

> *"The first thing I did when I got a little money to experiment, I put all my artists back in school. The art school that existed then didn't quite have enough for what we needed so we set up our own art school."*
>
> WALT DISNEY

studied by Disney animators so that Snow White's movements would be realistic and believable.

Six months into the project, Walt examined all of the animation that had been produced for the film—and ordered most of it scrapped. His artists were improving so rapidly that their early efforts seemed crude and amateurish.

Unlike their nameless counterparts in the original Brothers Grimm fairy tale, Walt wanted each dwarf to be distinct and eccentric, with names that defined their characters. Some fifty-odd names were considered; these seven were chosen: Happy, Sneezy, Bashful, Sleepy, Grumpy, Dopey and Doc. Rejected names included Scrappy, Hoppy, Weepy, Gloomy, Snoopy, Silly, Gabby, Blabby, Flabby, Dizzy, Biggy-Wiggy and Awful.

Another important task involved finding voices for all of the characters. Casting director Roy Scott auditioned hundreds of young singers for the title role, but none had the right combination of a strong singing voice plus the innocence and vulnerability Walt wanted.

Finally, Scott called voice coach Guido Caselotti, complaining that he could not find the right singer for the part. Meanwhile, Caselotti's nineteen-year-old daughter, Adriana, picked up an extension phone and heard Scott talking about the search for Snow White. She quickly began singing and chattering in a young girl's voice. Her father ordered her off the phone—but Roy Scott had heard enough. He invited Adriana to audition for Walt.

Equal care was given to the other voices. Pinto Colvig, the voice of Goofy, performed two dwarf voices, Sleepy and Grumpy. Comedian Billy Gilbert, a longtime foil for Laurel and Hardy, got the part of Sneezy. Moroni Olsen, a deep-voiced actor whose career spanned over a hundred films, voiced the Magic Mirror. Harry Stockwell, father of actor Dean Stockwell, was the Prince. And veteran actress Lucille La Verne, whose film career went back to 1915, was the voice of the Wicked Queen and the Old Witch (her last and best-remembered role).

Walt gathered his songwriting team, Frank Churchill, Leigh Harline, Larry Morey and Paul J. Smith. "We should set a new way to use music," he told them. "Weave it into the movie so somebody doesn't just burst into song." Walt's innovative approach influenced Rogers and Hammerstein's Broadway production of *Oklahoma!* (1944), as well as the producers of MGM's *The Wizard of Oz* (1939).

In November 1934, Walt sent a memo to his staff, offering a bonus of five dollars for each gag that ended up in the final film. Animator Ward Kimball, for example, earned five dollars for the scene where Snow White first meets the Seven Dwarfs. As she lies sleeping across their beds, the dwarfs creep up on her. One by one, their heads rise up, and their bulbous noses appear—pop, pop, pop!—over the footboards of the beds. Decades later, Kimball observed that a five-dollar bonus in those days would be like fifty dollars today.

At one story conference, the animators, story artists, and other staffers filled out comment cards, detailing their ideas and suggestions about the story. The majority of comments were positive and enthusiastic—but one card read: "Walt, stick to shorts!"

> *"Walt ran the studio like a university. We were learning all the time and a few of us were going to art school at night. Walt would drive us there and pick us up later."*
>
> LES CLARK
> DISNEY ANIMATOR

Walt was stunned. Someone in his studio was opposed to *Snow White!* Fuming, Walt invited the anonymous critic to meet him in his office, but no one stepped forward. The identity of the unknown critic became a matter of legend. Whenever Walt got irritated with one of his artists, he'd point an accusing finger and say, *"You're* the one who told me to stick to shorts!"

Though Walt never learned who wrote that card, a handful of artists knew the identity of Walt's tormentor—and they delighted in keeping the secret.

It was Walt's own brother, Roy.

An expensive quest for excellence

In 1935, Walt received an invitation to Paris from the League of Nations—the pre-WWII version of the United Nations. The League wished to honor Walt for promoting global goodwill through his best-loved creation, Mickey Mouse. With his studio only a year into production on *Snow White,* Walt was reluctant to be away for long.

But Roy reminded Walt that 1935 marked the tenth anniversary for Walt and Lilly—and for Roy and Edna. The Disney brothers could take their wives on a second honeymoon—and Walt could visit castles and soak up inspiration for *Snow White.* That sold Walt. He would go anywhere to improve his motion picture!

It was a memorable tour—England, France, Holland, Switzerland and Italy. In England, Walt met the royal family and author H. G. Wells. In Italy, he was introduced to the Pope and Italian dictator Benito Mussolini. While escorting their wives around Paris, Walt and Roy were surprised to stumble upon a theater running *eight* Disney cartoons back-to-back—and no feature film! Walt smiled. In Paris, audiences were paying to watch Disney cartoons nonstop! This affirmed that Walt was on the right track with *Snow White*.

> *"Walt was the best story man in the studio. No one else ever approached him."*
>
> WARD KIMBALL
> DISNEY ANIMATOR

Walt returned to Hollywood and *Snow White* with renewed vigor. As work proceeded, Walt spent more and more time inside the cramped projection room under the stairwell. That room was called "the sweatbox" because (as Walt put it) "there was no air conditioning and it was hot in there—plus all the animators had to go in there and sweat this thing out with me."

Whenever an animator completed a scene, he and Walt went into the sweatbox and watched the pencil test together. They would run it at normal speed, in slow motion, forward, reverse, frame by frame. "Fifty percent of my time was spent in the sweatbox," Walt recalled, "going over every scene with every animator, getting the action right. The other half of my time was spent on the story."

During this time, Walt used his animated short subjects, especially the Silly Symphonies, as an experimental laboratory for new approaches and technologies, including the revolutionary multiplane camera which created the illusion of depth from flat drawings on glass. The multiplane camera was first used in the Silly Symphonies cartoon *The Old Mill*—a short with no dialogue and very little plot, but extraordinary visual power. The film earned Walt his sixth Academy Award.

Much of the animation for *Snow White* had already been drawn, inked, and painted by the time the multiplane camera was invented, but Walt saw that this technology could greatly improve many of the already-completed scenes. So once again, he ordered entire sections of the movie scrapped and recreated from scratch—much to the dismay of his brother Roy.

Walt became concerned whenever a scene ran too long or interrupted the flow of the story. Ward Kimball spent eight months creating a four-and-a-half minute sequence called "Music in Your Soup." Kimball completed the sequence in pencil animation, and his drawings were filmed, matched to the soundtrack, and projected in the sweatbox for Walt's approval.

After viewing the footage, Walt told Kimball, "That's beautiful work, Ward. I can't tell you how much it hurts to have to cut it from the picture. It interrupts the flow of the story."

That night, Kimball lay awake, grieving for his lost sequence. Then it hit him: Walt was right. That scene *did* interrupt the story. Kimball had to admire Walt's willingness to sacrifice any amount of labor and expense if the scene detracted from the film.

As word got out about Walt's feature-length cartoon with its half-million-dollar budget, Hollywood pundits labeled *Snow White* "Disney's Folly." Several columnists predicted financial ruin for Disney. Though Roy had faith in his brother's vision, there were times he suspected the pundits might be right. Clearly, *Snow White* was the boldest gamble of Walt's career. He had "bet the farm," wagering the survival of his studio on a single project. If *Snow White* failed, the Disney studio was finished.

> *"There was a continual battle between my brother Roy and myself. My brother worried about getting the money back. I was worried about quality. Between us, we were trying to keep the whole thing going."*
>
> WALT DISNEY

Walt and Charlie

In November 1935, H.G. Wells, author of *The Time Machine* and *The Invisible Man,* arrived in Hollywood as a guest of Charles Chaplin. Wells and Chaplin had a lot in common, including a shared utopian dream of a world beyond racism and war—and a shared admiration for Walt Disney. Wells had met Walt a few months earlier during Walt's European tour. Soon after arriving in Chaplin's home, he asked, "How well do you know Walt Disney?"

"I've never met the man," Chaplin said.

Wells was stunned. For years, Chaplin and Disney had lived and worked within walking distance of each other—yet they had never met. So Wells called the telephone number Walt had given him and he arranged for the three of them to meet at the Hyperion Avenue studio.

That meeting was a dream come true for Walt, who had idolized Chaplin since his boyhood. Walt was thrilled to learn that Chaplin was a confirmed Disney fan. He gave Wells and Chaplin a guided tour of his cartoon factory, and even showed them some of the top-secret work in progress on *Snow White*. That meeting was the beginning of a long, close friendship between Walt and Charlie Chaplin.

On January 12, 1936, an interview with H.G. Wells appeared in the *New York Times,* in which Wells said, "Many do not realize that all Hollywood studios are so busy that they keep very much to themselves. Consequently, Chaplin never visited the Disney studios. Imagine, Charlie and Walt Disney, those two geniuses, never met! I took Charlie there. Disney has the most marvelous machinery and does the most interesting experiments. Like Chaplin, he is a good psychologist and both do the only thing in film today that remains international."

In 1936, Disney's distribution agreement with United Artists came up for renewal. This time around, the UA attorneys inserted a strange clause in the contract, asking Walt to sign over all rights to exhibit his films on an experimental new technology called "television." Walt refused to sign. "I don't even know what television is," he said, "so I'm not going to sign away my rights to something I know nothing about."

After negotiations with UA broke down, Walt cut a deal with RKO Radio Pictures, giving Disney seventy percent of the gross while permitting Disney to retain all television rights. Though no one could have imagined the future importance of television, Walt's decision to retain TV rights for his films would prove to be a stroke of brilliance.

The first Disney film covered by the new RKO distribution contract was *Snow White and the Seven Dwarfs*. RKO would continue as Disney's distributor for almost two decades, until the Disney company created its own distribution arm, Buena Vista Pictures, in 1953.

Cash crisis

In 1936, Lillian suffered another miscarriage, so the Disneys decided to adopt. In January 1937, they brought home a two-week-old baby girl, Sharon Mae Disney. Though Walt and Lilly were open with family and friends about the adoption, they kept this information out of the press. They didn't want Sharon growing up being referred to as "the *adopted* daughter of Walt Disney."

By the summer of 1937, the release date for *Snow White* was just months away. Artists donated evenings and weekends to the project without being asked. They believed they were working on something special, and a "Whistle While You Work" attitude prevailed.

Meanwhile, Walt and Roy were out of money. Any personal possessions Walt could convert to cash were already mortgaged or sold. *Snow White* had gobbled up a million dollars, making it more expensive than any live-action picture produced by that time. Even worse, Walt needed a half million more and had no idea where to get it.

> *"Honestly, my fun has never been in having money. That's the last thing I think about. I just know you have to make dough in order to do things. I've been the most broke guy in Hollywood."*
>
> WALT DISNEY

Then Roy had an idea. "Splice together whatever you've got and show it to Joe Rosenberg," he said. Rosenberg was in charge of studio loans at the Bank of America.

Walt hated the idea. "Show him what we have now?" he said. "It's just bits and pieces! We've got some finished footage, but most of what we have is raw pencil tests!"

"You've got to show Joe *something*," Roy insisted. "He can't lend us a half million bucks without seeing what he's paying for."

Walt reluctantly agreed. He was pacing the sidewalk when Rosenberg arrived at the Hyperion Avenue studio. Roy was supposed to be there for moral support, but failed to show up. So Walt led Rosenberg to the projection room. The two men sat down, Walt signaled the projectionist, and the film began to roll.

The movie opened with a beautiful full-color prologue, "Once upon a time, there lived a lovely little Princess named Snow White . . ." The first few minutes flowed past in beautiful full color—then there appeared patches of crude pencil animation. Walt started to apologize for the poor quality of the film. Rosenberg shushed him. Sometimes the soundtrack went silent for a minute or more. Color came and went. A couple of sequences were spliced in the wrong order. Walt sank into his chair, groaning.

Finally, the film came to an abrupt halt. There was no ending—it hadn't been drawn yet. So Walt talked Rosenberg through the ending, reciting the action and dialogue much as he had done on the night he first announced the project to his artists.

"Well, Walt," Rosenberg said, rising, "thank you for showing this to me."

Walt searched Rosenberg's face for any sign of enthusiasm. The banker was expressionless. Walt's heart sank into his shoes. If Rosenberg refused the loan, *Snow White* was finished—and so was the Disney studio.

The two men walked out to the parking lot. Rosenberg opened the car door and slid in behind the wheel, then looked up at Walt. "You know, Walt," he said, "that movie is going to make a hatful of money. You'll get your loan."

Those words from banker Joe Rosenberg saved the Disney studio.

"Aren't you proud of it, Mr. Disney?"

Walt spent the final weeks of production ruthlessly cutting to keep the film as tight and fast-paced as possible. By the time it was completed, *Snow White and the Seven Dwarfs* had employed more than 750 animation crafts-men. Of an estimated two million drawings created, only 250,000 actually appeared on-screen.

A couple of months before the scheduled premiere, Walt took a rough cut to a theater in Pomona, east of Los Angeles. The marquee announced, "SNEAK PREVIEW!"—but made no mention of the film's title. Curious movie-goers took their seats without any idea what they were about to see. Walt positioned staff members around the theater to take note of the audience reaction. He would use that information to fine-tune the movie before its gala premiere.

At first, everything went fine. People laughed at the gags and leaned forward in their seats as the action became tense. Then, more than halfway through the movie, something went horribly wrong. A few theater patrons got up and headed for the exit, then a few more. Soon, about a third of the audience was walking out. Walt was panic-stricken. Everything was riding on this picture—and the audience hated it!

> *"We had a big premiere at the Carthay Circle Theatre—a big, grand premiere. All of the Hollywood brass turned out for a cartoon!"*
>
> WALT DISNEY

He jumped out of his seat and followed the retreating patrons into the foyer. He cornered one young man and said, "What's wrong? Why didn't you like the picture?"

"Oh, I liked it fine," the young man said. "But I live in the dorm, and I've got to get back before curfew." It turned out that all of the walk-outs were college students observing curfew. The mystery was solved—to Walt's profound relief.

On December 21, 1937, *Snow White and the Seven Dwarfs* premiered at the 1,500-seat Carthay Circle Theatre in Los Angeles. Overhead, searchlights lit up the sky. In the courtyard, a full orchestra played music from the movie soundtrack. The theater grounds were decorated with lifesize mock-ups of the Dwarfs' cottage and a forest scene with trees, mushrooms, and a mill with a running waterfall. The Seven Dwarfs were on hand in full costume to greet the guests.

Dozens of limousines pulled up and Hollywood's biggest stars stepped out: Douglas Fairbanks, Charlie Chaplin, Marlene Dietrich, Mary Pickford, Judy Garland, Mickey Rooney, Shirley Temple, Ginger Rogers, Charles Laughton, George Burns and Gracie Allen, and more. Walt showed up in tie and tails, looking dapper but nervous, with Lillian on his arm.

Inside the theater, the screen came alight, and for the next eighty-three minutes, the audience was transported into another world. Again and again, viewers broke out in spontaneous applause. Disney art director Ken O'Connor sat near John Barrymore, carefully observing the actor's response. "When the shot of the queen's castle above the mist came on,"

"Everybody in the theater was crying. I couldn't believe it. It was supposed to be just a cartoon and everybody was crying."

WARD KIMBALL
DISNEY ANIMATOR

O'Connor recalled, "he was bouncing up and down in his seat, he was so excited. Barrymore was an artist as well as an actor, and he knew the kind of work that went into something like that."

As Snow White fell under the spell of the sleeping death potion, Walt was stunned to hear sobs of grief. The movie worked—even more powerfully than he had hoped. At the end, the audience rose and gave Walt a standing ovation.

Six months after the film's release, the formerly debt-ridden Disney studio had paid off its loans and had millions more in the bank. "Disney's Folly" went on to earn over $8.5 million in its initial release, allowing construction of a new $3.8 million studio in Burbank which remains the hub of Disney animation today.

On February 23, 1939, Walt was honored at the Academy Awards banquet with a special award recognizing *Snow White and the Seven Dwarfs* as a significant screen innovation. The award consisted of one standard-size Oscar, trailed by seven smaller statuettes. Child star Shirley Temple made the presentation, saying, "Aren't you proud of it, Mr. Disney?"

Walt replied, "I'm so proud, I think I'll bust."

How to Be Like Walt— Lesson 6: Take a Risk!

Walt's greatest genius was his boldness. He bet everything he had on one movie—and it paid off handsomely. The payoff, of course, was not just the $8.5 million the picture earned. To Walt, money was a fine thing to have because it enabled him to make more movies—but he didn't care about the money per se. The real payoff for Walt was that *Snow White* was loved by the public. He did something everyone told him was impossible, and he succeeded.

Walt demonstrated that true success lies in going where no one else has gone, in doing what everyone said could not be done. Video producer and

Disney historian Les Perkins told me, "Walt exemplified what it means to live the adventure and his movies reflect his approach to life. In his film *In Search of the Castaways,* there is a song by Richard and Robert Sherman that captures the spirit of Walt Disney. The song says that we should not be afraid of the high mountain—the mountain of life. Let's climb, let's climb! Even if we fall off the mountain and die a terrible death, we've had the joy of the climb!

"Walt was telling us to go for it, to take risks—and he earned the right to preach that message. He had no fear of failure. He wanted us to know that it's all right to fail by trying. The real tragedy is to fail by *not* trying—to cling to your security blanket because you were too timid to take a chance. There are no great accomplishments without courage."

Disney storybook illustrator Peter Emslie told me, *"Snow White and the Seven Dwarfs* is one of the most courageous artistic achievements ever created. Walt succeeded because he had the courage of his convictions. All of his life, people told him, 'You can't do that. It won't sell.' His father told him he would never make a living as a cartoonist. Industry experts told him *Snow White* would fail because no one would sit still for a ninety-minute cartoon. Walt never took counsel of his fears. He led with his courage and achieved great things."

Bold risk-taking means bold decision-making. I have usually found that delaying a decision is far more dangerous than making a bold decision based on partial information. If you don't have all the facts, settle for

> *"The rest of us live in fear.*
> *Walt had no fear."*
>
> JIM KORKIS
> DISNEY HISTORIAN

75 percent. Settle for 50 percent. If need be, settle for 25 percent. Get your best sense of the situation, listen to your intuition, then act decisively.

Of course, there's a downside to risk-taking: Sometimes you lose. What then? Walt's answer would be, "So what if you lose? Learn the lessons of your failure, then try again." Walt failed early in his career, and the experience taught him that he could survive failure and still be successful. It made him invulnerable to the fear of failure."

Understand, I am not suggesting you should take reckless chances. Take risks—but make sure they are calculated risks, not stupid gambles. Disney biographer Bob Thomas once observed, "Some financial people considered Walt Disney a dreamer who devised grandiose plans, then told his brother, 'Here—find the money.' In fact, Walt never entered any project without meticulous planning."

Walt's creation of *Snow White,* though risky, was far from reckless. The entire creative process was planned out on storyboards, continuously re-examined and refined, and painstakingly edited by Walt himself, frame by frame. Before the premiere, he tested his film with a sneak preview. From an artistic perspective, nothing was left to chance. Before the film was released, Walt did everything possible to make *Snow White* a commercial success.

Before he began building Disneyland, he hired the Stanford Research Institute to analyze every aspect of the project, from the best location to construction costs. Walt was willing to bet millions on a dream—but he planned out his dreams to the last decimal place.

Chris Miller, Walt's oldest grandson, told me, "My grandfather had big dreams and goals. He risked everything he had to make them come true, and he persevered until he achieved them. There was an almost naive bold-ness about Granddad. His life teaches all of us to believe in our dreams, to be daring in the pursuit of our goals, and to never back away from a chal-lenge. Walt Disney was an adventurer at heart, and the way he lived is an example to us all."

So what is the big impossible thing you dream of doing? What is your *Snow White,* your Disneyland? Let go of your fears! Live the adventure! Be bold!

Oh, and one final thought (and forgive me if it seems a bit off-topic): I feel a personal affinity to Walt in many ways, not the least of which is the fact that Walt and Lilly were adoptive parents. I am the father of nineteen children—four birth children, one by remarriage, and fourteen by interna-tional adoption.

The way Walt and Lilly brought an adopted daughter into their home was wise and loving. They shielded baby Sharon from the prying eyes of a curious media, but they were open about Sharon's adoption with family and friends, and with Sharon's big sister, Diane.

Once, when Diane was in school, she let it slip to her classmates that her sister had been adopted. Walt and Lilly informed Diane that Sharon's adoption was a family matter, not to be shared elsewhere. Recalling the incident, Diane said, "I was surprised that it was a secret. There was no difference between the two of us. I was one way and Sharon the other way." That says a lot about how Walt and Lilly loved their two daughters. Both were cherished equally.

So I encourage you to consider being like Walt in this respect: Consider sharing your love with children who have no hope in their lives. I especially encourage you to consider the possibility of international adoption. I can't tell you what it has meant to have so much love streaming into our home from Asia, South America, and Eastern Europe.

> "When you're curious, you find lots of interesting things to do. And one thing it takes to accomplish something is courage."
>
> WALT DISNEY

I won't kid you—it hasn't always been easy to ride herd on this big melting pot of a family. Every child we adopted presented a unique set of issues and problems. But would I do it again? Absolutely! Only I would start sooner in life, and I would adopt *more* kids!

Perhaps adoption seems like a risky thing to do. I can only say: Come on, be like Walt! Take a risk and share your home with a child who needs your love.

Chapter Six

❦

Triumph to Tragedy

Snow White and the Seven Dwarfs was an astounding success. For a brief golden moment, it seemed that Walt's own life had become a fairy tale, with a "happily-ever-after" ending. But Walt's life was about to be invaded by tragedy and loss.

While Walt was working on *Snow White,* his parents, Elias and Flora Disney, operated a boarding house in Portland, Oregon. When Flora experienced a series of minor strokes, Walt and Roy became concerned about her health.

By now, all four Disney brothers—Herbert, Raymond, Roy and Walt—lived in the Los Angeles area. They urged their parents to retire and join them. In 1937, as *Snow White* neared completion, Elias and Flora moved to California. Ruth and her husband, Theodore Beecher, remained in Portland.

Walt and Roy bought a house in L.A. for their parents and hired a housekeeper. The Disney clan enjoyed Sunday barbecues and croquet games in Roy's backyard. Walt and Roy invited their older brothers to join them at the Disney studio, but Herbert was happy with his job as a postman and Raymond chose to continue selling insurance.

Walt admitted that he sometimes envied the easygoing contentment he saw in his brother Herbert. Herb was happy to carry the mail during the week and go fishing on weekends. He had no lofty goals or ambitions as Walt had—yet he also never suffered the migraine-inducing stress that Walt endured throughout his career.

By New Year's Day 1938, *Snow White* was in its second week of release and a runaway success. Walt's photo was on the cover of *Time*. Elias Disney was baffled by all the fuss over his youngest son. He was proud of Walt, of course, but he didn't really understand what Walt did for a living. When Walt said he didn't draw anymore, Elias wondered exactly what Walt did do at that studio of his.

Flora didn't understand Walt's business either, but she was justly proud of all that Walt and Roy had accomplished. People's eyes lit up when she introduced herself as Mrs. Disney, and she enjoyed answering the inevitable question: "Are you related to Walt Disney?"

The beginning of 1938 was a golden moment in Walt's life. *Snow White* was a resounding success, and Walt was reaping enormous critical and popular acclaim. He commanded a team of nearly a thousand artists, directors, songwriters and technicians. He enjoyed his home life with Lillian and his two daughters, four-year-old Diane and one-year-old Sharon. His parents and brothers lived nearby. The future looked bright as Walt plunged his studio into its next, even more ambitious project, *Pinocchio*.

> *"Walt's family didn't recognize his genius when he was growing up. Only his brother Roy really understood how gifted Walt was, and he ended up being the financial engine that powered the vehicle of Walt's creativity. Though Roy insisted on staying in the background, he was a genius in finance."*
>
> DICK MORROW
> FORMER GENERAL COUNSEL
> FOR WALT DISNEY PRODUCTIONS

"Before *Snow White*," observed Disney character artist Don "Ducky" Williams, "Walt was continually in hock. After *Snow White*'s explosive success, Walt paid off all his debt in six months. Then he took every nickel of profit and put it back into his company. He was constantly investing back into his product and preparing to do the next project. The minute *Snow White* succeeded, Walt was working on *Pinocchio*."

Initially, *Pinocchio* faithfully followed the nineteenth century Italian story by Carlo Collodi. Five months into the project, however, Walt realized that the story and characters needed to be reworked, so he scrapped most of what had been done and started over. In Collodi's original story, Pinocchio was a juvenile delinquent and the cricket who tried to teach Pinocchio right from wrong was viciously exterminated with a mallet.

Walt decided to reshape Collodi's pine-headed brat into a naive but well-intentioned lad, continually led astray by corrupting influences. Walt named the cricket "Jiminy," and handed him over to master animator Ward Kimball, who dressed him in a top hat and tails, and transformed him into Pinocchio's conscience. Jiminy Cricket would become one of Disney's most enduring characters.

Walt shaped the storyline of *Pinocchio* by telling the story to various people. Each time he told the story, he watched how his listeners reacted. With each retelling, he would add this element, subtract that one, always refining, always improving.

One of the first people to hear Walt's Pinocchio was Roy's eight-year-old son, Roy Edward. The year was 1938, and Walt's nephew was in bed with the chicken pox. Walt went to young Roy's room, sat at the foot of the bed, and said, "We're working on a new movie down at the studio. Would you like me to tell you about it?" The boy nodded eagerly, and for the next half hour, Walt told and acted out the tale. When Roy later saw the film on the screen, he was disappointed. He felt that the movie didn't live up to the way Uncle Walt told it.

I also spoke with Dick Jones, the voice actor who portrayed Pinocchio. "I got the job when I was eleven years old," he told me. "Walt took my mother and me out to lunch to give us the good news. He was a regular guy—very friendly and informal. I was little back then, so I remember Walt as a giant. I had to look way up to see his face.

"When I was recording the part of Pinocchio, I could always see Walt through the glass of the recording booth. I could tell how I was doing by his reaction. If he shook his head, I knew I had to try it again. When we were finished for the day, Walt would always play darts with me."

By the fall of 1938, the *Pinocchio* project was proceeding well, like every other aspect of Walt's happy life. He couldn't have known that tragedy lurked just around the corner.

If only—

One day in November 1938, Walt's mother called him. "Walter," she said, "could you see what can be done about the gas furnace in our house? I'm afraid that if we don't get it fixed, we're going to wake up one morning and find ourselves dead." She said it laughingly, with that same ironic sense of humor that had delighted Walt as a boy.

"I'll send some repairmen right over, Mother," he replied. The repairmen went to the house, found a leaky gas valve in the furnace, worked on it, then left.

A few days later, on the morning of November 26, Flora's housekeeper was fixing oatmeal in the kitchen when she felt dizzy. She knocked over the pot, spilling oatmeal on the floor. Still woozy, she scooped the mess into a dustpan and carried it out to the trash can. As her head cleared, she remembered the leaky gas valve and feared the worst.

Meanwhile, Elias got out of bed and staggered to the bathroom where he found Flora unconscious on the floor. He tried to carry her out of the house, but the fumes overcame him. The housekeeper found Walt's parents unconscious on the floor and pulled them out of the house with the help of a neighbor. Elias survived, but Flora was dead.

Walt was devastated when he heard the news. For years, he couldn't talk about it, even to those closest to him. Because the fatal accident took place in the house he and Roy had purchased, Walt blamed himself for his mother's death. His guilt was compounded whenever he saw his grieving father. Elias Disney never recovered from the loss.

If there was anything good that came from this painful experience, it is probably this: Walt made a point of setting aside more time for his wife and children from that time on. Perhaps the loss impressed upon Walt the brevity of life and importance of balancing his successful career with a strong family life.

Walt's daughter Diane later recalled, "Dad referred to his mother's death obliquely, but we never talked about it. I remember some years later, I was going through his drawers. He always kept an interesting collection of matchboxes and soap packages from hotels in them. In one of the drawers, I found a newspaper with the headline about his mother's accidental death."

His younger daughter Sharon only asked Walt about the incident once. "I took Daddy to work a couple of times. I remember driving down Sunset and asking him where his mother was buried and he said, 'She's in Forest Lawn and I don't want to talk about it.' Tears came to his eyes. Nothing more was said."

Once, in the late 1950s, one of Walt's secretaries asked him about the death of his mother, not realizing that it was a very tender issue. "I don't want that ever mentioned in this office again," he responded, his voice husky with emotion. Then he turned and walked out of the office.

He felt the pain of that loss for the rest of his life.

"This place would make a perfect hospital"

After three years of work and $2.6 million, *Pinocchio* premiered in New York City on February 7, 1940. Artistically, it is regarded as one of Disney's finest productions. Commercially, however, *Pinocchio* was a flop.

The person responsible for undermining *Pinocchio*'s success was an Austrian-born dictator by the name of Adolf Hitler.

Disney's film budgets were partly based on earnings from European distribution. On September 1, 1939—five months before *Pinocchio* opened—Hitler sent his Nazi storm troopers into Poland, igniting World War II. The outbreak of war closed the lucrative European markets to Disney's films and *Pinocchio* failed to earn back its production costs in its initial release.

While *Pinocchio* was in production,

"People mistakenly think of Walt as a creator of children's entertainment. When Walt was at the top of his artistic form, he made movies for everyone, not just children. Snow White and Pinocchio were suitable for children but tremendously sophisticated. It was filmmaking at its best."

J. B. KAUFMAN
FILM HISTORIAN, COAUTHOR OF
WALT IN WONDERLAND

the Disney studio began work on *Fantasia* and *Bambi.* The financial failure of *Pinocchio,* combined with the costs of simultaneous work on two other features, plus the expense of constructing the studio in Burbank, plunged the Disney company deep into debt once more.

Walt and Roy were forced to take their company public. They raised $3 million by issuing 600,000 shares of common stock, which quickly sold out at five dollars per share.

In mid-1940, Walt took his father on a tour of the nearly completed new facility at 500 S. Buena Vista Street, Burbank. It was an impressive complex of buildings, linked by underground tunnels, with extra-wide corridors and spacious offices, studios and stages. The buildings were surrounded by broad lawns and recreation spaces for volleyball, softball and badminton. Finally, Elias said, "But Walter, what can all this be used for?"

"It's a movie studio, Dad," Walt replied. "It's the studio where I'll make my cartoons and feature films."

Elias shook his head. "No, Walter. I mean—what can it be *used* for?"

Then Walt understood. His father wanted to know if the studio buildings had some "practical" use. Elias Disney had never understood Walt's business, and he never would.

Walt sighed. "Well," he said, "if we decided to close the studio, this place would make a perfect hospital." As Walt guided his father around the studio, he didn't say another word about cartoons or feature films. "I went through the whole darn studio," he later recalled, "and I explained the thing to him as a hospital. And he was happy."

Walt's father died in 1941. Years later, when Walt built Disneyland, he had one of the prominent upper windows of the Main Street Emporium adorned with these words: "Elias Disney, Contractor—Est. 1895."

The Iwerks-Disney reunion

In 1940, Ub Iwerks approached Disney animation director Ben Sharpsteen and asked him to act as a go-between with Walt Disney. Sharpsteen and Iwerks had been good friends before Ub's unhappy departure. Now Ub wanted to know: Would Walt take him back?

Ub's ten years away from Walt had not been good years. His Flip the

Frog cartoon series enjoyed only middling success, lasting from 1930 to 1933. His Willie Whopper series, though wildly inventive, lasted only a year. A series of fairy tale adaptations, the Comicolor Cartoons, ran from 1933 to 1936. By 1940, Ub was losing interest in animation. He wanted to get into the technical side of filmmaking.

For his Comicolor Cartoon, *The Headless Horseman* (October 1934), Ub had built a makeshift multiplane camera from a used camera and salvaged parts from an old Chevrolet sedan. Ub's crude but practical device predated Walt's more sophisticated multiplane camera by three years. To Ub, the real fun was in solving technical problems, not drawing pictures.

Sharpsteen talked to Walt, and Walt agreed to a meeting. When Ub came to Walt's office in Burbank, Walt greeted him reservedly but cordially. They shook hands, saying nothing about the past, and Walt offered Ub the job he wanted, working in the studio machine shop.

Ub wandered around the studio, looking for machines to fix and problems to solve. Though Walt

> *"My dad would quote Walt Disney: 'Do a good job. You don't have to worry about the money; it will take care of itself. Just do your best work—then try to trump it.'"*
>
> DON IWERKS
> SON OF UB IWERKS, LONGTIME DISNEY
> EMPLOYEE AND FOUNDER
> OF IWERKS ENTERTAINMENT

signed Ub's paychecks, Ub liked to say, "I'm my own boss." And he was. He never had to report to Walt or anyone else on his activities. Over the years that followed, Ub's innovative tinkering contributed greatly to the quality of Disney films. For example, Ub's improved matte process, combining animation with live action, won an Oscar in 1959. Though Walt and Ub were never as close as they had once been, Walt was glad to have Ub back.

"It made pictures in my head"

On November 13, 1940, Walt Disney premiered his most ambitious feature-length movie yet: *Fantasia*. It opened at New York's Broadway Theater (formerly The Colony), the same theater where Mickey Mouse first debuted in *Steamboat Willie* twelve years earlier.

The story of *Fantasia* begins sometime in 1937. At that time, Walt had two main product lines—Mickey Mouse and the Silly Symphonies. The Mickey Mouse cartoons were action- and story-driven; the Silly Symphonies were music-driven. Walt wondered what would happen if he merged the two series in a single cartoon. Answer: "The Sorcerer's Apprentice."

Based on a tale by Goethe, "The Sorcerer's Apprentice" was a concert composition by French composer Paul Dukas. It's the story of a student magician who misuses his master's powers—with disastrous results. Rich in action, drama and comedy, the tale was perfectly suited for Mickey's talents.

In late 1937, after work was well under way on the cartoon, Walt was having lunch alone at Hollywood's famed Chasen's Restaurant. Looking up from his bowl of Chasen's famous chili, Walt spotted the white-maned conductor of the Philadelphia Orchestra, Leopold Stokowski, sitting a few tables away. Disney went to Stokowski, who was also alone, and said, "Why don't we sit together?"

They ate and talked, and Disney told Stokowski—who was a big Disney fan—of his plans for a Mickey Mouse cartoon based on "The Sorcerer's Apprentice." The flamboyant Stokowski responded enthusiastically and offered to conduct the piece. That day, Walt Disney and Leopold Stokowski entered into a partnership that would produce one of the most extraordinary and controversial films ever made.

Inside the Pathé Studio in Culver City, the recording session for "The Sorcerer's Apprentice" began at midnight on January 9, 1938. At Stokowski's direction, a bowl-shaped enclosure with sound-absorbing partitions was added to the stage, creating separation between sound channels. Three hours later, they had produced a beautiful nine-minute recording. The cost of the session ran into the tens of thousands of dollars, shocking not only cost-conscious Roy but even Walt himself.

While working on "The Sorcerer's Apprentice," Stokowski urged Walt to do something more ambitious than a single cartoon. Roy and Walt could see that the $125,000 cost of "The Sorcerer's Apprentice" could never be recouped as a stand-alone cartoon. So they decided to record more musical pieces and combine them into a grand feature film.

Walt was not a fan of classical music when he began. At the time of the film's premiere, he admitted to a reporter from the *New York World-Telegram*,

"I never liked this stuff. Honest, I just couldn't listen to it. But I can listen to it now." Once he and Roy decided to make *Fantasia,* Walt began steeping himself in classical music. *Fantasia* was Walt's $2.3 million music appreciation course.

"We owe it mostly to Dick Huemer," Ward Kimball said, "for the fact that Walt Disney was weaned away from John Philip Sousa and introduced to the classics. Walt learned all about Beethoven, Tchaikovsky, and Stravinsky through Dick Huemer's tutelage." When Walt introduced Huemer to people, he'd say, "Meet Dick Huemer. He goes to operas."

"Cartoon figures had hard edges before Fantasia *was made in 1940, and many of them moved to rinky-tink music. Walt Disney did not invent animation, but he nurtured it into an art form that could hold its own against any 'realistic' movie."*

ROGER EBERT
FILM CRITIC

As Walt learned to appreciate the music, he visualized it in abstract images. "When I heard the music it made pictures in my head. Then the boys listened and they had ideas. I had a lot of ideas, but they voted some of them down." Walt was later amused by critics who saw deep philosophical symbolism in many of the visual abstractions of the film. To Walt, there was no symbolism—just pictures in his head.

Walt learned to appreciate classical music in his own way. He had no use for the pretentiousness of so-called "highbrows." He believed that anyone, including a Missouri farm boy, could appreciate great music simply for its power and beauty.

Animator Frank Thomas recalled how Walt described a concert he attended as a student in Kansas City. "Gee," Walt told him, "I can remember going to concerts as a kid—the orchestra coming out onto the stage, tuning up, and then they'd start playing. All the fiddles would come up at the same time." That's right, Walt called the violins "fiddles."

"Walt didn't care so much about the highbrow, the background, the esoteric, what the music is supposed to mean," Thomas concluded. "He was reacting emotionally to the visual experience as part of a total experience. His whole concept of *Fantasia* was that way."

Roy, as usual, had his doubts about the latest Disney production. He worried that average movie-goers wouldn't find classical music entertaining. After listening to a variety of selections with Walt, Stokowski and music consultant Deems Taylor, Roy blurted, "My gosh! Can't you put some music in this picture that an ordinary guy like me can enjoy?"

For several seconds, everyone in the room just froze.

Then Walt roared, "Get out! Go back to your office and mind the books!"

Walt invents stereo

As Walt expanded his own appreciation for the classics, he encouraged his artists to broaden their tastes as well. One such artist was John Hench, who joined the Disney studio in 1939 (and was still employed by Disney when he passed away in his mid-nineties in 2004). When Walt asked him to work on the "Nutcracker Suite," a ballet segment, Hench asked for a different assignment. "I don't know anything about ballet," he explained.

"In that case, wait here," Walt said. "I need to make a phone call." Walt was gone for a few minutes, then returned. "The Ballet Russe of Monte Carlo is in town," he said excitedly, "and I got you season tickets! I set it up so you can go backstage and talk to everybody—the dancers, the set designers, the costumers, the works! John, you're going to love it!"

Hench had his doubts, but he threw himself into the experience—and he discovered that Walt was right. He soon learned to *love* ballet. "I made friends and it changed my life," Hench said. "Walt had this great curiosity. He was very excited about what he was doing. He lived and breathed it, and finally it rubbed off on you."

Walt Disney, Leopold Stokowski, and the Disney engineers broke new ground with *Fantasia's* revolutionary Fantasound multi-track sound system. It was not only the first film with stereophonic sound; it was the film that *invented* stereophonic sound. Though "The Sorcerer's Apprentice" was recorded in California, the rest of the music was recorded by Stokowski's Philadelphia Orchestra in the historic Philadelphia Academy of Music.

The Fantasound system utilized nine microphones and ninety-six speakers to recreate the original concert hall experience with astounding realism. Unfortunately, only twelve U.S. theaters could afford the $85,000 Fantasound system. Soon after *Fantasia*'s release, the expanding war in Europe had so disrupted the world economy that stereo had to be abandoned.

Fantasia's final scene was transferred to film just days before the movie's New York premiere. The sequence shows a choir of candle-bearing worshippers walking two-by-two along a forest path just before dawn. As the procession moves through the forest, the viewer is carried along in a single, continuous tracking shot. To achieve that shot, Walt had 150 feet of dolly track laid along the floor of a recording stage. A horizontal multiplane camera was mounted on a dolly and moved along the track, a fraction of an inch per frame of film.

"When I was five or six, Dad told me the whole story of the 'Night on Bald Mountain' sequence from Fantasia *on the way to school one morning. The way he told it, there were the little villagers and the mountain where Satan comes out. I went into school, my eyes wide open, and got some kids in the corner and told the whole story all over again."*

DIANE DISNEY MILLER
WALT'S DAUGHTER

A crew of nine men worked for six days to complete the shot. The day after it was finished, the processed film was screened for Walt and the crew. As the projector rolled, everyone groaned. The entire sequence had been shot with a wide-angle lens. The six-day effort was wasted—and the premiere was now four days away.

The crew went back to the recording stage and worked even faster than before. Powered by pot after pot of industrial-strength coffee, they worked around the clock for the next three days. At 2:24 A.M. on Sunday, November 10, as the crew was re-positioning the multiplane camera, the building trembled. It was an earthquake. The shock was mild, as earthquakes go, and centered up the coast in Santa Barbara. Still, it had shaken everything—the camera, the track, the metal frames that held the painted-glass artwork and animation cels. If any element of that complex array had moved, the shot would be ruined.

There was nothing to do but continue shooting. If the quake had ruined the shot, there would be no time to re-shoot it. As they worked, the crew wondered if *Fantasia* would be the first film in history to debut without an ending.

Finally, the shot was complete. When the footage was screened the following day, it was perfect—exactly as Walt had envisioned it. The film was rushed to the airport and flown to New York, where it was spliced to the final reel just four hours before the premiere. Walt's big gamble had paid off. The picture opened on schedule.

Fantasia was the biggest risk Walt had attempted up to that time—a $2.3 million impressionistic movie with very little storyline, featuring music that audiences usually avoided as "highbrow." Now the big question was: Would audiences flock to see it?

The answer, unfortunately, was no.

"*Fantasia* was a mistake . . ."

To this day, the reasons for *Fantasia*'s dismal debut are a matter of debate. Most film historians agree that mass audiences were simply not ready for a movie that was wall-to-wall classical music. *Fantasia*'s box office failure was a terrible blow to Walt, coming on the heels of *Pinocchio*'s poor returns.

> "Although he never lost his enthusiasm for the film, the failure of Fantasia *was extremely depressing to Walt.*"
>
> JOE GRANT
> STORY ARTIST

When the Academy Awards were presented at the Biltmore Hotel in Los Angeles, February 26, 1942, Walt received the Irving G. Thalberg Memorial Award, given for a filmmaker's entire body of work. *Fantasia* also received two special awards that year. One went to Leopold Stokowski for his artistic achievement in the film, and the other went to Walt for the invention of stereophonic sound. When Walt rose to receive the Thalberg prize, he said, "Thank you so much for this. Maybe I should have a medal for bravery. We all make mistakes. *Fantasia* was a mistake, but an honest one."

Walt didn't believe *Fantasia* was an artistic mistake, of course, but he did see it as a huge commercial blunder. Walt's instincts had never let him down before. In 1940, however, he had produced two box office failures in a row—and Walt's faith in his forecasting ability was shaken. He could blame the war for *Pinocchio*'s lackluster returns, but *Fantasia* was another matter.

"Walt was very disappointed that *Fantasia* didn't go over," said animator Frank Thomas, "because he felt that it was a whole new area of animation. He lost money and finally realized that the audience wanted another *Snow White*. I think the failure of *Fantasia* hurt Walt because it kept him from experimenting."

Walt came to the conclusion that his studio might not survive the next failed experiment. From now on, his films had to have mass appeal.

The strike at the Mouse factory

By early 1941, the Disney studio was in deep financial trouble. Gathering labor unrest threatened to tip the studio into a full-blown crisis. The Max Fleischer Studio (producer of Betty Boop and Popeye) was struck and unionized in 1937. The animation departments at MGM and Warner Brothers capitulated to the unions a few years later. The prestigious Disney cartoon factory, however, had managed to elude the grasp of Big Labor.

Walt and Roy had allowed their employees to form an in-house union, the Federation of Screen Cartoonists. Approved by the National Labor Relations Board in July 1939, its first president was senior animator Art Babbitt, the guiding hand behind the Wicked Queen of *Snow White,* the stork in *Dumbo,* and the lovable Goofy.

Babbitt came to believe, however, that Walt was using the in-house union to keep out Big Labor. In February 1941, Babbitt attended a meeting of the Screen Cartoonists Guild headed by union organizer Herb Sorrell. Afterward, Babbitt resigned as president of the Federation and joined the Guild—and he urged other Disney employees to do the same.

A short time later, Herb Sorrell went to the studio and told Walt and attorney Gunther Lessing that he represented Disney workers. Walt and Lessing told Sorrell to get out and stay out. The studio was a family, Walt said, and everyone in his family was happy.

Through the spring of 1941, Art Babbitt continued to recruit Disney

"Walt Disney teaches us to do what you love. Fall in love and stay in love with what you're doing. With Walt, cartoons started it. They said Snow White *wouldn't work, but Walt did it because he loved it. The same with* Fantasia—*a commercial failure at the time, but what a magnificent failure!* Fantasia *set the standard. Walt lived his loves. His life shouts to us, 'Don't try to please others! Be yourself!'"*

RAY BRADBURY
WRITER

workers to the Guild. When Walt heard about Babbitt's union activities, he hit the roof. Walt had made Art Babbitt one of the best-paid artists in the industry, and had thought of Babbitt as a friend. He viewed Babbitt's union activities as a personal betrayal.

Babbitt, however, didn't consider himself disloyal. Sure, he was well-paid, earning over $300 a week—but he was troubled that the inkers, painters, and inbetweeners were scraping by on $15 to $25 a week. Babbitt even took money out of his own paycheck to supplement the income of his assistants.

Art Babbitt also complained that the only name to appear on a Walt Disney cartoon was Walt Disney's. Why, Babbit asked, couldn't the writers and artists have a few seconds of recognition at the beginning of each cartoon?

It wasn't that Walt wanted to keep his workers toiling in obscurity. He simply believed that people didn't care who drew the characters or painted the backgrounds. The public only wanted to know if it was a Disney picture, because they trusted the Disney name. To Walt, the name "Walt Disney" was no longer his own private handle, but the company trademark. He failed to appreciate the fact that all artists want the chance to "sign" their "canvas."

In Walt's view, he had sacrificed to make his studio a "worker's paradise." He had constructed the spacious new Burbank facility with the comfort and convenience of his artists in mind. It boasted multiple wings and large windows so that all of the artists would have what every artist covets—a northern exposure (north light is desired for its "cool" color properties which promote accurate color perception). Artists' desks and chairs were custom-built for comfort and ease of use. Walt continued to provide art classes at his own expense.

The studio restaurant served excellent food, and Walt insisted that it be priced *below* Disney's cost. Artists could also have coffee, milkshakes, and other snack items delivered right to their desks from the studio snack bar. The old "sweatbox" was replaced by cool, comfortable screening rooms (though the term "sweatbox" stuck). The studio also offered such amenities as a baseball field, volleyball courts, a gymnasium with showers, and a sun deck.

> *"I've worked my whole life to create the image of what 'Walt Disney' is. It's not me. I smoke, and I drink, and all the things we don't want the public to think about. My whole life has been devoted to building up this organization that is represented by the name 'Walt Disney.'"*
>
> WALT DISNEY

Unlike every other studio in the industry, Walt did not impose production quotas on his artists. His sole demand was quality, not quantity. He believed he and his artists were on the same quest—to advance the art of animation to previously unimagined heights. He believed his staff was treated well. As for the low-paid assistants, Walt considered inking and inbetweening to be entry-level jobs. Talented people with a good work ethic would advance and earn greater rewards. He paid all employees as much or more than the industry standard.

The Burbank studio was part of Walt's larger vision for an artistic community. As Disney story artist Joe Grant observed, Walt's ultimate plan had a utopian, even socialist, tinge. "Before the strike [in 1941]," said Grant, "Walt thought socialism was about everybody pulling together. He was an extreme liberal at one time. He even considered putting apartments on the studio lot for his employees, so we'd all live there as one big, happy family."

Paradoxically, Walt's lavish spending on the comfort of his artists was actually used against him. His artists knew that *Snow White* had earned millions. One look at the luxurious Burbank facility convinced the artists that their boss had money to burn. Many employees seemed unaware that the box office failures of *Pinocchio* and *Fantasia* had pushed the studio to the brink of extinction.

The growing dissatisfaction at the studio reached critical mass after Walt and Roy were forced to lay off a number of workers—a direct result of the *Fantasia* debacle. The layoffs frightened and angered many workers, driving them straight into the arms of the Screen Cartoonists Guild. By this time, Art Babbitt had recruited nearly half of the Disney studio to the Guild—and Walt was out of patience. He blamed Babbitt for the disaffection in the ranks.

In May 1941, Walt made one of the worst blunders of his career: He fired Art Babbitt and had him escorted off the studio property. Walt was apparently unaware that firing a worker for union activism was a violation of federal labor law—the 1935 Wagner Act. The firing only fueled the resentment of Babbitt's many friends at the studio.

On May 28, 1941, a group of Disney artists—all Guild members—met to discuss Babbitt's firing. Babbitt's assistant, Bill Hurtz (who later directed Rocky and Bullwinkle cartoons and Cap'n Crunch commercials), made a motion calling for a strike. The motion was approved by a voice vote.

The next morning, Walt found Buena Vista Street lined with picket-bearing strikers. Roughly half of his artists—about three hundred employees—had walked out. It was Walt's first clue that his labor problems extended so far beyond Art Babbitt alone. Even then, Walt didn't grasp the intensity of the strikers' mood.

"I can remember about the second day of the strike," recalled animator Ollie Johnston, a non-striker. "We had just come through the picket line and Walt was standing there, kind of smiling at the guys on the line. He hollered something to one of them in a friendly way and said, 'Aw, they'll be back in a couple of days.' He didn't really realize the true situation."

Walt was dismayed to see a number of his top animators on the picket line—men he never imagined would raise a picket sign against him. One was Vladimir "Bill" Tytla, one of the best-paid animators in the business. Tytla is remembered for animating Stromboli in *Pinocchio* and the Night Demon in *Fantasia*. He was also the lead animator on *Dumbo,* which was nearing completion at that time

The decision to strike was difficult for Tytla. "I went on strike because my friends were on strike," he later recalled. "I never wanted to do anything against Walt."

Twice before, Walt had experienced workforce defections that had deeply hurt him. Now, for a third time Walt felt that much of his staff had stabbed him in the back. The strike, coupled with the studio's deepening financial crisis, left Walt depressed and, at times, nearly immobilized.

The strike was a traumatic experience for Walt. Twice before, workforce defections had deeply hurt him—once in 1928, when most of his animation staff signed with Charles Mintz; then again, in 1930, when Ub Iwerks signed with Pat Powers.

> "The strike changed him. Walt was a decent man. On his own, he was planning to do most of what the strikers were demanding—just as soon as he could afford to. They didn't give him a chance."
>
> JOE GRANT
> STORY ARTIST

As the strike wore on, Walt's attorney, Gunther Lessing, gave him some terrible advice: Hang tough. Refuse to negotiate. Break the strike. The Guild responded by organizing a boycott of theaters showing Disney films.

Just three weeks into the strike, on June 20, 1941, the studio released a new feature, *The Reluctant Dragon,* at the Pantages Theater on Hollywood Boulevard. The film included a Disney studio tour hosted by author Robert Benchley. The segment presented an idyllic picture of life at the Disney studio—a view that contrasted sharply with the mood on the picket line. Strikers showed up and protested the premiere.

The strike continued into the summer months, and the picketers' ranks swelled to over a thousand, including many from other unions. One picket featured a scowling Mickey Mouse with a sign that read, "Disney Unfair!" The strikers' morale was boosted by speeches from actor John Garfield and writer Dorothy Parker. Union chefs from Toluca Lake restaurants set up grills in the vacant lot across from the studio and catered the strike in cordon bleu style.

Walt's financial backers at the Bank of America nervously urged Walt to settle. The strike, they said, was hurting the studio's reputation, not to mention its bottom line. Walt steadfastly refused to allow the union into his studio. He viewed the strike as the work of leftist agitators and Communist agents. He blamed Art Babbitt for destroying the sense of family that he had worked so hard to build.

The strike of 1941 was an unmitigated tragedy. Neither Walt Disney nor Art Babbitt was a villain. Each believed he was doing the right thing. Each had sacrificed his own welfare to benefit the studio workers. Each misunderstood the other. In the end, both labor and management lost something—a sense of trust, a sense of shared mission, a feeling of community. The era of Mickey Mouse and *Snow White* had been a golden age. The strike changed everything.

The golden age was over, and would never return.

The goodwill tour

Some months before the strike, Nelson A. Rockefeller approached Walt and asked him to visit South America. Along with his family's numerous oil and charitable holdings in South America, Rockefeller headed the U.S. Office of the Coordinator of Inter-American Affairs. Because of growing U.S. alarm over pro-Nazi sentiment in South and Central America during the war, Rockefeller was urging prominent Americans, including Leopold Stokowski and Orson Welles, to make goodwill tours of Latin America.

"Your pictures are popular in Latin America," Rockefeller told Walt. "You can help offset the Nazi influence if you'll go down there and show the people what America is all about." Roy Disney favored the trip. He knew Walt needed a break from the daily aggravation of a picket line outside his office window.

Walt left for Brazil on August 11, 1941. His entourage included director Norm Ferguson, story artists Bill Cottrell, Ted Sears and Webb Smith, watercolor artist Mary Blair, art director Herb Ryman, music director Chuck Wolcott, animators Jack Miller, Frank Thomas and Jack Cutting, and other non-striking artists.

The Disney entourage (or "El Groupo," as the travelers dubbed themselves) spoke to hundreds of Latin Americans, compared styles with Latin artists, attended concerts and nightclubs, visited beaches and zoos, learned to samba and rumba, rode llamas in Bolivia, and crossed Lake Titicaca in balsa-wood boats. Walt also took a thirty-mile steamer ride on a Colombian river—a trip that later inspired Disneyland's "Jungle Cruise."

Walt's South American tour was funded by a $70,000 government grant—money that helped the studio weather its cash-flow problems. Out of this goodwill tour came two Disney feature films: *Saludos Amigos* (1943) and *The Three Caballeros* (1945). Disney repaid the grant out of the proceeds from the films. "People thought that Disney needed the subsidy," Walt later reflected, "but [*Saludos Amigos*] went out and did a heck of a business, and the United States government wasn't out one nickel."

Meanwhile in Burbank, the strike continued to grind on. President Roosevelt (a big fan of Mickey Mouse) dispatched James Dewey of the Department of Labor to meet with Roy Disney and Gunther Lessing. On September 9, Roy agreed to accept binding arbitration, though he knew it meant a union victory. The strike ended on September 14.

> *"They first wanted me to go on a hand-shaking goodwill tour. But I said, 'I'm not a good hand-shaker.' Then they said, 'You go down and make some films about these countries,' and I said, 'Well, that's my business, I can do that, I'm a filmmaker.'"*
>
> WALT DISNEY

Walt and his party sailed through the Panama Canal and arrived in New York in time for the premiere of *Dumbo* on October 23, 1941. It was a bittersweet homecoming, because Walt learned upon his return that he had lost the strike.

But that disappointment paled next to a more personal loss. Walt's father, Elias Disney, died at the age of eighty-one while Walt was in South America. It hurt Walt that his father died without ever truly grasping all that Walt had accomplished in his life. A father's approval is important to every man. It may be that some of Walt's drivenness was a quest for the approval and affirmation he never received from his father, Elias Disney.

How to Be Like Walt—
Lesson 7: Dealing with Loss

There was an eleven-month period of Walt's life that could be called a golden moment. It began on December 21, 1937, the day of the triumphant premiere of *Snow White and the Seven Dwarfs*. It ended on the morning of November 26, 1938, when Walt's mother died in a tragic accident. His personal loss was compounded by a major professional loss in 1940, when his studio suffered two box office disasters in a row, *Pinocchio* and *Fantasia*.

Then came the strike of 1941, when people he had considered friends walked the picket line, calling him a "tyrant" and accusing him of running a "sweatshop." Walt felt slandered and betrayed.

And finally, there was the loss of his father.

During this period of Walt's life, almost everything that happened to him was a loss of one sort or another. What do you do when life throws hurt after hurt in your path? What do you do with feelings of grief—and the guilt that often accompanies grief? What do you do when you are unfairly treated or falsely accused? There are no shortcuts to recovery, but here are a few suggestions for surviving a painful time in your life.

1. *When you suffer a loss, let go of the need to know why.* When people suffer, the first question they usually ask is "Why?" They want to know, "Why did this happen? Why now? Why me?" There is usually no answer to the "why" question. Even if there was an answer, it would not take the pain away.

Death is a mystery. When we lose someone we love, the loss sends us reeling. The world no longer makes sense. Loss is one of the most baffling of all human experiences.

One of the most baffling components of grief is denial. "I don't believe it!" we say. "This can't be happening!" But it is happening, and we must accept it. It takes time to adjust to the bafflement of loss.

> *"Walt didn't have an easy life. He worked hard, and had many disappointments and setbacks. What faith he must have had to go through what he did, and still manage to achieve such great things."*
>
> DOROTHY PUDER, WALT'S NIECE

2. *If you feel guilty, learn to forgive yourself.* Grief is often coupled with guilt. Walt's guilt centered on the house he and Roy bought for their parents. Though his mother's death wasn't his fault, he couldn't help thinking that if only he'd made some different decisions, his mother might have lived.

Guilt feelings are common among people who grieve: "Why didn't I visit her more often?" "I didn't say 'I love you' enough." "If only I had been there, this wouldn't have happened." If your loss is accompanied by guilt, make a decision to forgive yourself.

Ask yourself: "Is it realistic for me to feel so guilty?" Walt's guilt was not appropriate guilt. He did nothing wrong. In fact, he did a very loving thing: He bought a home for his parents. He was not responsible for the leaking gas valve; in fact, he tried to repair it. This loss, though painful, was not Walt's fault.

Forgiving ourselves is as important as forgiving others. Ask yourself: "Could I forgive someone else for the same thing I condemn myself for? If someone did this to me, would I hate him or forgive him?" Then give yourself time to accept your loss. Give yourself time to heal.

3. *Look for the meaning in your pain and loss.* One of the worst aspects of a loss is that it seems so pointless and purposeless. Given time, you can gain a perspective on your loss that will enable you to say, "I can see how God can use even this tragedy to produce something good." What are some of the good things we can discover in a personal tragedy?

First, we know that pain and loss can often increase our empathy for others. Painful experiences equip us to comfort others through times of loss.

Second, we know that pain and loss can lead us to a deeper relationship with God. Suffering can drive us deeper into a prayer-relationship with our Creator. As we learn to rely on God in the tough times of life, we grow stronger in our faith.

Third, we know that loss can often produce character strength. We discover inner resources we never knew we had. We develop greater reserves of patience, perseverance, love, hope and faith. Our souls put down deeper roots. Our losses have a meaning—if we will look for that meaning. When you must go through suffering, don't waste the lessons of your pain.

4. *Be patient with yourself.* Loss is a process; cooperate with it and you will be changed for the better. Many people try to short-circuit the process by numbing the pain with alcohol, drugs, or some other anesthetic—and sometimes they end up destroying themselves. When you suffer a loss, the only healthy response is to simply go through it.

Grief is an intensely personal experience. No two people grieve in exactly

> "*There was a song from Disney's* In Search of the Castaways *that captured the way Walt dealt with the tough times in his life. A line from that song said, 'We are on the trail of life's highway, enjoy the trip, each bump and dip.' The message of that song is the message of Walt's life: When bad things happen, make the most of it. Find the joy and love in any situation and let that carry you through.*"
>
> LES PERKINS
> VIDEO PRODUCER AND DISNEY HISTORIAN

the same way. No one can tell you how you should grieve. As you go through the process, it may be best for you to talk about your feelings. Then again, it may be best for you to be silent. You must go through the process in your own time and in your own way.

Don't expect the pain of your loss to ever completely go away. Walt felt the pain of his mother's death for decades. People who say that "time heals all wounds" don't know what they're talking about. Time lessens the sting of loss, but the pain never completely goes away. That doesn't mean you won't experience joy and happiness again; you will. In time, you will begin enjoying the present instead of dwelling on the past.

5. *Learn to accept what you cannot change.* Loss is painful. Losses are inevitable. It is not a question of *if* we will suffer a loss, but *when*. The only question we should ask ourselves is: "When my loss comes, how will I respond?"

Our unwillingness to accept the inevitability of loss is one reason we often feel that such experiences are unfair. In a sense, losses *are* unfair. It is never fair when you lose someone you love or when you suffer a setback in life.

But loss is a universal and inevitable part of the human condition. When loss comes into our lives, when someone we love is taken from us, we are not experiencing anything but what all people experience at one time or another. We must learn to accept what we cannot change.

This sad passage of Walt's life teaches us that life is no fairy tale, and there is no "happily-ever-after" ending. But life is good, and we can face any loss if we maintain our faith in God, our love for others, and our hope for the future.

Chapter Seven

❧

The Plus Factor

A look at the films Walt made in the 1940s and '50s shows us a man who was committed to excellence and to giving his customers more than they expect. Walt had a word for his single-minded obsession with quality. He called it "plussing."

In October 1941, when *Dumbo* premiered in New York, the attack on Pearl Harbor was still a month and a half away. Hitler's war machine had cut off an important source of income for the Disney studio. Walt pondered a tough question: How could he produce quality films on a reduced budget? The answer: *Dumbo*.

Ward Kimball recalled hearing about *Dumbo* for the first time in early 1940. "Walt and I were in the studio parking lot," he said, "and Walt told me about this new circus picture we were going to make. He went through the whole story in about five minutes. Then he said, 'I want you to do the dance sequence, where the crows teach Dumbo how to fly.' Listening to him tell the story, I could tell that the picture was going to work."

"*Dumbo* is my favorite animated film," said film critic Leonard Maltin, "because it makes me cry. Every single time and in the exact same spot. I just have a special affection for *Dumbo*." The movie tugs at our emotions because we all identify with Dumbo, the little circus elephant who is always tripping over his big ears and making a mess of things.

Dumbo is the shortest of all of Walt's animated features, running only sixty-four minutes long. It was also one of the quickest and cheapest to produce. The film took less than a year to animate at a cost of only $812,000. After suffering staggering losses from *Pinocchio, Fantasia,* and the strike, Walt finally got some good news: *Dumbo* grossed over $2.5 million on its first release. The film went on to win an Academy Award for best original score, and was nominated for best original song (the sentimental lullaby, "Baby Mine").

The centerpiece of the film is a surrealistic sequence, "Pink Elephants On Parade," animated in record time by animators Howard Swift and Hicks Lokey. Swift was so inspired as he worked that he produced a hundred feet of film in a single week (the average output for a Disney animator was about twenty feet per week).

> *"Originally* Dumbo *was going to be only a half-hour, sort of a special. When Walt saw what we were doing with it, he said it might make a good feature. Well,* Dumbo *made money. In fact, it was the only Disney film to make money until* Cinderella.*"*
>
> BILL PEET
> VETERAN DISNEY STORY ARTIST

"I did it straight ahead," Swift later recalled. "I didn't make any key poses. I just put down a piece of paper and made the next move." The "Pink Elephants" sequence is a feat of improvisational brilliance. Walt was so impressed with Swift's work that, upon viewing the filmed pencil tests, he gave Swift a $25 per week raise—a big pay hike for those days.

Dumbo became the surprise hit of the 1941 season.

Disney goes to war

Tensions remained high at the Disney Burbank studio following the end of the strike. The House of the Mouse was composed almost equally of non-strikers and former strikers. The air of distrust was as thick as the smoke from Walt's unfiltered cigarettes. On December 7, 1941, all of that changed. Suddenly, strikers and non-strikers no longer saw each other as the enemy. There was only one enemy now, and it had attacked America from across the ocean.

Within weeks after the attack on Pearl Harbor, many Disney artists either enlisted or were drafted into the Army, and most were assigned to the Army Motion Picture Unit. Some reported to "Fort Western" (the old Fox Western Studio at the corner of Sunset and Western), while others went to "Fort Roach" (the old Hal Roach Studio in Culver City where the Laurel and Hardy comedies had been filmed). There they made Army training films.

Walt's Burbank studio was also commandeered for the war effort. The Army took over a studio machine shed and filled it with millions of rounds of ammunition for anti-aircraft emplacements in the hills around Los Angeles. A sound stage was turned into a repair shop for Army vehicles and guns. Soldiers were billeted in the Animation Building.

Walt committed his studio to producing films for the government at cost—Disney's contribution to the war effort. Government bookkeepers were baffled. Their ledger system required the payment of costs plus a profit—but Walt refused to take a

> *"It was a very sad time for Walt as well as the rest of us because Walt was cut off at the height of his powers."*
>
> OLLIE JOHNSTON
> DISNEY ANIMATOR, ON THE WAR YEARS

profit. The government was still trying to figure out how to enter the Disney arrangement in its books two years after the war was over.

Walt later recalled, "We produced hundreds of films on such exciting subjects as 'How to Hate Hitler,' 'The Vulnerability of the Japanese Zeros,' 'Fighter Tactics,' 'Bomber Tactics,' and the like. We produced a series on simple sanitation, such as 'How to Control the Malaria Mosquito,' 'How to Avoid the Hookworm,' 'How to Control the Body Louse,' 'How to Build a Privy,' and several other subjects I don't care to mention."

In August 1942, eight months after commandeering the Disney studio, the Army pulled out. The Disney company returned to its original function of producing animated cartoons—only now those cartoons were largely devoted to the war effort. Though Walt lost one-third of his animators to the draft, the studio's output increased 1,000 percent, from 30,000 feet of film per year to 300,000 feet.

The studio continued developing new cartoon shorts, including patriotic and anti-Nazi cartoons, because the government considered them vital for morale. Mickey, Donald Duck, Goofy and Pluto were pressed into service to promote various defense-related activities, including war bond drives, scrap metal drives, blood drives, rationing and victory gardens.

Disney also designed combat insignia for military units. At first, Walt asked artist Hank Porter to design the insignia when he wasn't busy on other projects. By January 1942, demand for insignia had grown to the point where Walt assigned Porter to the project fulltime. By April 1942, Porter had assembled a team of artists who did nothing but design combat insignia. Though his studio was deep in debt, Walt donated these services to Uncle Sam without charge.

Bambi: animated realism

Walt pressed ahead with his masterpiece, *Bambi.* Based on Felix Salten's 1926 novel, *Bambi, a Life in the Woods,* the film is noted for the realism of its animation and the haunting beauty of its background paintings. Because Walt brought in live fawns, rabbits, squirrels, birds, and even skunks for his animators to study, the animals in *Bambi* display a natural grace and believability that has never been equaled.

"I wrote a letter to Walt Disney when I was ten years old and told him I wanted to be a Disney animator. Even at ten I could spot the difference between a Disney cartoon and all the others. I didn't know about the technical stuff but I knew what my eyes told me."

DON WILLIAMS
DISNEY ILLUSTRATOR

Chinese-born background artist Tyrus "Ty" Wong brought an ethereal, Asian-influenced feeling to his feather-edged paintings of the forest. He also taught Disney's team of scenic artists how to paint with the same blend of Eastern and Western influences. In *Bambi,* light, shadow, mist and color combined to produce powerful moods.

Some 4 million drawings, $1.75 million, and nine years of Walt's life went into *Bambi.* Walt had originally planned it as his next feature after *Snow White.* But as the project grew in his mind, more time and money went into training his staff for the unique challenge of the film. It would take the better part of a decade for Walt to recoup his investment.

On February 28, 1942, Walt and his staff took a rough cut of *Bambi* to a theater in Pomona for a sneak preview. During the screening, the audience was unusually quiet. Walt wondered: Is the audience absorbed in the story—or bored?

The audience gasped when a shot rang out in the forest. The horrified audience realized that Bambi's mother was dead. After the gunshot, Bambi wandered alone among the trees, calling, "Mother, where are you?"

From the balcony, a teenage girl called out, "Here I am, Bambi!"

Laughter rippled through the theater. The Disney animators were devastated.

After the screening, Walt and his staff grimly returned to the studio to discuss the film. Several animators pressed Walt to change the crucial scene.

"No," Walt said firmly. "We shouldn't change the scene. It works beautifully just as it is—and it stays." Walt's instincts proved correct.

> *"Walt had a burning desire for excellence in everything he did. He was always thinking, 'We can do it better.' That's a common trait of all successful people."*
>
> ROYAL "MICKEY" CLARK
> FORMER TREASURER OF WED ENTERPRISES

But the death of Bambi's mother would break the hearts of millions of movie-goers, including one eight-year-old girl named Diane Disney. She accompanied her dad to a *Bambi* screening a few days before its premiere. That night, as Walt was tucking Diane into bed, tears streamed down her face.

"Honey," he said, "why are you crying?"

"Bambi's mother died!" Diane sobbed.

"Oh, honey," Walt said, "it was just a movie."

"But Daddy," Diane said, "you could have let Bambi's mother live—and you didn't!"

Bambi premiered at New York's Radio City Music Hall on August 13, 1942, garnering mixed reviews. War-weary audiences flocked to Disney's cheery short cartoons, but avoided the animated realism of *Bambi*. Many parents felt the movie was too disturbing for children. In its initial release,

Bambi earned a million dollars *less* than its production costs. Only after the war did people realize what a significant achievement *Bambi* was.

With the exception of *Dumbo,* every feature Disney produced during World War II initially lost money. Yet *Pinocchio, Fantasia* and *Bambi* have stood the test of time, and over the decades they have returned tens of millions of dollars to the Disney coffers.

The reason they are so durable is something called "the plus factor."

The plus factor

Sometime during the 1940s, Walt coined the term "plussing." Normally, the word "plus" is a conjunction, as in "two plus two equals four." But Walt used the word as a verb—an action word. To "plus" something is to improve it. "Plussing" means giving your customers more than they paid for, more than they expect, more than you have to give them.

If you want to be like Walt, then you have to plus everything you do—

And then you plus the plus.

"Good enough" was never good enough for Walt Disney. He was a pioneer in plussing the artform of animated cartoons. He began by plussing Mickey Mouse with sound, then plussing the Silly Symphonies with color. Walt plussed the skills of his artists by sending them to art school at his own expense. Walt's relentless quest for excellence kept him at the leading edge of his industry—and left his competitors, well, nonplussed.

Sometimes in order to plus, you must subtract. Walt wouldn't hesitate to delete an entire sequence if it slowed the action or detracted from the story. Cutting is plussing when it results in a better product. Sometimes less is more.

Walt spent $400,000 just to have *Fantasia*'s music conducted by the most renowned conductor of his day, Leopold Stokowski—and traveled to Philadelphia to record the music under ideal acoustical conditions. He spent over $100,000 inventing a new technology—stereophonic sound—to reproduce the music with absolute fidelity.

In an interview with Michael Barrier, animator David Hand talked about the legendary battles between the Disney brothers over Walt's relentless (and expensive) obsession with plussing his films. "Walt fought the front office," said Hand, "because they wanted him to make the cartoon for a price. I've heard him. I was with him enough to know that he practically threw Roy out of his office two or three times, because Roy wanted him to make the pictures for a price in keeping with the market returns."

Hand recalls being impressed by the fact that Walt was in complete charge of the situation. When Roy would complain about expenses, Walt would abruptly end the conversation. "Roy," he'd say, "we'll make the pictures—you get the money. Now good-bye, I'm busy."

Roy would sometimes try to go around Walt, appealing directly to the artists. "Fellows, what are we going to do?" he'd say. "You've got to work on Walt and get him to spend less money on each picture!"

> *"Walt Disney was adamant about quality. He always found new ways to 'plus the experience.' He wanted to give people more than they anticipated."*
>
> DAN VIETS
> DISNEY HISTORIAN AND
> COAUTHOR, *WALT DISNEY'S MISSOURI*

"Well," Hand concluded, "you couldn't work on Walt. That's the last thing you could do, work on Walt. Roy would say to us, 'I can't do anything with him. What are we going to do about it? I can't get the money.' But we didn't hear him."

Walt spent the last decade of his life plussing the Disneyland experience. He would continually tell his employees (called "cast members"), "The customer is king," "Every cast member is responsible for the impression we make," and "Take five minutes a day to make a magical memory for one of our guests." Walt would walk around Disneyland with a roll of five-dollar bills in his pocket to tip any cast member who worked extra-hard to plus the experience for a guest.

"Disneyland is something that will never be finished," he once said. "It's something I can keep developing, keep plussing and adding to. It will be a living, breathing thing that will always be changing. Not only can I add new things, but even the trees will keep growing. Disneyland will get more beautiful every year."

If you understand the plus factor, then you have the key to Walt's heart.

Song of the South: A flawed classic

At the close of World War II in 1945, Walt Disney Productions posted its first profit since the release of *Pinocchio.* It was razor-thin—only $50,000—but it meant the studio had weathered the storms of war and debt.

In 1946, Disney released *Song of the South,* a combination of live-action and animation based on the Uncle Remus fables of Joel Chandler Harris. *Song of the South* has been widely praised for its unforgettable characters (Brer Rabbit, Brer Fox, Brer Bear), its strong cinematic values, and its memorable music (its signature song, "Zip-A-Dee-Doo-Dah," won an Academy Award). It is a fine example of Walt's commitment to plussing—the extra, unexpected touches that characterize Disney entertainment.

Walt had been combining animation and live action since the beginning of his career, but *Song of the South* was his most ambitious effort to date. He spent weeks refining the story and characters in story conferences, and every camera shot was mapped out on storyboards. *Song of the South* cost $2.2 million to make—a big budget for those days.

> *"Walt wanted to go into live action because he wanted to do something he'd never done before. He may have grown tired of cartoons. He always kept everybody in turmoil."*
>
> LILLIAN DISNEY

Today, *Song of the South* is Disney's most controversial film. Criticism centers around its presentation of an idealized and unrealistic image of the Old South. Is it, as some critics claim, a "racist" film? No. Uncle Remus, the hero of the story, is a wise former slave who helps the other characters resolve problems and restore broken relationships. A racist film would not present an African-American in such a pivotal and positive role.

But *Song of the South* is racially insensitive, like many other films of the pre-civil rights era, such as *Gone with the Wind.* It's a cruel irony that, when *Song of the South* premiered at the Fox Theater in Atlanta on November 12, 1946, the star, James Baskett, could not attend. No Atlanta hotel would give him a room.

Song of the South pointed the way to a new kind of Disney movie—family-oriented live-action pictures. "Even before *Song of the South* was complete," said Disney producer Bill Anderson, "Walt was ready to do live-action stories. He talked to me about it. He said, 'We won't turn into a live-action studio, but we'll get into this live-action business.'"

Disney's first all-live-action film was Robert Louis Stevenson's *Treasure Island,* released in July 1950. The $1.8 million film was an instant hit and is now considered a screen classic. "Walt always wanted to be a live-action producer," said Disney story artist Joe Grant. "That was his secret dream— though it was really no secret around the studio."

Walt and the capitalist bosses

Throughout the postwar 1940s, Walt was preparing his animators for the challenge of *Cinderella.* Story artist Bill Peet recalled that an atmosphere of crisis surrounded the early stages of the project. "We needed another *Snow White,* another big success," Peet said. "Walt and Roy had been argu- ing for weeks. Roy told him that they couldn't afford to gamble everything they had on one film. If they would sell out now, they could live comfort- ably for the rest of their lives. Roy wanted to pick up the marbles and go home. Walt insisted they do just one more, and he chose *Cinderella.*"

That decision determined the fate of the entire Disney enterprise. Bill Peet concluded that, had it not been for Walt's insistence on making *Cinderella,* Disney's first successful feature since *Dumbo,* "there would have been no Disneyland, no Epcot, and no Disney studio today."

In preparation for *Cinderella,* Walt honed his artists' skills with a series of "package features"—full-length movies comprised of short, self- contained musical stories. The first was *Make Mine Music* (1946), a mix of classical, opera, and popular music. Its storylines are stronger than *Fantasia,* and offer a wider range of music, from Prokofiev's "Peter and

> *"If Walt made a million from one picture, he didn't retire to Miami. He'd take that million, borrow another million and make another picture."*
>
> CHARLES SHOWS
> DISNEY WRITER-DIRECTOR

the Wolf" to Benny Goodman's bobbysoxer swing tune, "All the Cats Join In." Other package features followed: *Fun and Fancy Free* (1947), *Melody Time* (1948) and *The Adventures of Ichabod and Mr. Toad* (1949).

Disney's post-war financial strain brought Walt and Roy into increasingly sharp conflict. Roy was aggravated by Walt's insistence on plussing at the expense of profits. Walt thought Roy's cost-conscious approach to film-making was short-sighted.

Another source of tension: Roy kept pestering Walt to attend stockholder meetings. Walt stubbornly refused. He hated stockholder meetings and considered them a waste of time. But Roy kept pressing, and Walt finally agreed.

Upon entering the room, Walt found himself facing a collection of sober-faced businessmen in black suits—the kind of grim-faced, tight-fisted capitalist bosses he later satirized in *Mary Poppins*. Walt looked around the room with a sour-milk expression. Then he stood up and read a letter from a man in Florida who owned a few shares of Disney stock. The man said how much he enjoyed Disney movies, then added, "I don't care if I ever get any dividends. You just keep up the good work and keep making good pictures."

Walt put the letter down, looked around the room and said, "I wish this company had more shareholders like that one. He understands what Disney is all about. Now, it's been very nice to see all of you, but if you don't mind, I've got a studio to run." And he walked out, leaving his stockholders in stunned silence.

Roy never invited Walt to another stockholder meeting.

Milt Albright, a former Disneyland executive and founder of the Magic Kingdom Club, told me, "Walt had gumption. He was a straight-shooter. He didn't fit in with all the Hollywood smooth-talkers or the financial power-brokers. He was too honest and plain-spoken for them—a fish out of water around all of that Hollywood flash and dash. He was just a good old Missouri farmboy who knew what he liked, and he would spend anything to get it.

"Walt always thought there was a better way to do animation and live action and amusement parks, and he hated to have anyone tell him he

"Walt Disney taught me to always go for the highest quality and never settle for less. Nothing but the best quality products ever left his studio, no matter what it cost."

BOB BRUNNER
DISNEY COMPOSER

couldn't afford to do it his way. He was a down-to-earth guy who wore rumpled old clothes and created all this dazzling, phenomenal stuff."

So dear to Walt's heart

In 1946, the Disney studio was working on the "Mickey and the Beanstalk" segment for *Fun and Fancy Free*. For days, animation director Wolfgang Reitherman asked Walt to go record Mickey's dialogue. Walt kept putting it off. He was busy with studio business, plus his smoker's cough was giving him trouble.

Finally, Walt summoned Jim Macdonald to his office. Jim was the studio's veteran sound effects man. He not only created sounds with crackling cellophane and flapping window shades, but could also imitate mooing cows and sputtering car engines with his voice alone.

"Jim," Walt said, "Woolie's screaming for Mickey's dialogue, and I'm too hoarse to do it. Fact is, I really don't have time to do Mickey's voice anymore. Would you like to try it?"

What a responsibility! Since *Steamboat Willie* in 1928, there had been only one voice for Mickey—Walt himself. "Walt," Macdonald said, "I'd be honored."

So they went to the sound booth and made a test recording. Walt said, "Your Mickey sounds good to me, Jim." There was no higher praise than that. Except for a brief time in the 1950s, when Walt provided Mickey's voice for *The Mickey Mouse Club* TV show, he never voiced Mickey in a cartoon again.

By 1947, it was time to reopen the European movie markets that had shut down in 1939. Walt hired Armand Bigle from France to run his European distribution operation.

"I was Walt's man in Europe," Bigle told me. "I traveled to the different countries, promoting Disney films and merchandise. It was a tough job in those early postwar days. Roy wrote up a contract that guaranteed me fifty percent of the profits—which, because of the weak European economy, was fifty percent of nothing.

"When I was in the States, my family and I would visit Walt in his home in Los Angeles, and he would take us out to eat at Trader Vic's. When Walt came to Europe, he and I would travel together. Walt fit in wherever he was. If he was in England, he acted like an Englishman. If he was in France, he acted like a Frenchman. One time, I took Walt to a flea market in France. He put on a beret and looked just like a native-born Frenchman."

That same year, 1947, Walt bought property at Smoke Tree Ranch, a rustic-but-upscale development in the Palm Springs area. A four-hour drive from Los Angeles, Smoke Tree Ranch would become his personal retreat, the place where his family would spend many weekends and holidays. Walt enjoyed horseback riding, lawn bowling, and hiking in the desert. In his cowboy hat and boots, he fit right in. Walt also enjoyed the sense of community at Smoke Tree Ranch, where all the neighbors shared dinner together in the common dining hall.

In 1949, Disney paired child actors Bobby Driscoll and Luana Patten (who had first appeared in *Song of the South*) in a live-action film, *So Dear to My Heart*. Though it is one of Walt's lesser-known films, it was always one of his favorites. The story reminded him of his boyhood on the farm near Marceline, Missouri. The film earned a special Academy Award for Driscoll, and the song "Lavender Blue," performed by Burl Ives, was nominated for an Oscar.

> *"He'd take me out for hours and devote so much time to getting me over my fear of horses. He'd play with us for hours and hours, whirling us around by our heels or playing with us in the pool. He never seemed to tire of it."*
>
> DIANE DISNEY MILLER
> WALT'S DAUGHTER

Cinderella: plussing a classic

The year 1950 was the year of *Cinderella*. Though Walt felt that *Bambi* was his finest achievement, he believed that *Cinderella* could be both a commercial and artistic success. He chose Charles Perrault's seventeenth-century French version of *Cinderella* for his basic storyline (he thought the Brothers Grimm version too violent). Then he and his story artists began plussing the tale. They added a supporting cast of memorable characters, including Jaq and Gus the mice, Bruno the dog, and Lucifer the evil cat. As a finishing touch, Walt turned Perrault's witchy old hag into a sweet, grandmotherly creature—Cinderella's fairy godmother.

Actress Lucille Bliss was the voice of Cinderella's stepsister, Anastasia, an experience that remains one of her fondest memories. "I was just a teenager when I got the part," she told me. "We'd report to the studio at eight, and I would often pass Walt in the hall. He was always positive and upbeat. 'Hello, Lucille! Ready to go to work?' I'd think, 'He's such an important man, yet he takes such an interest in his cast! He knows my name!' That made me feel special.

> *"We make movies that children are not embarrassed to take their parents to."*
>
> WALT DISNEY

"Walt was so supportive that it took the fear out of it. We were a young cast—Ilene Woods, Rhoda Williams, Mike Douglas, and me—and it really made a difference that Walt was so patient toward us. His personal involvement in the project made us all try harder.

"Walt told me I should feel free to ad-lib during the recording sessions. He had the final say about what went into the film, but he wanted to make full use of everyone's creativity.

"On the fiftieth anniversary of the film, the Disney company put out a commemorative book. There I read that Walt had personally selected me for the part of Anastasia. I had never known that before, and it almost made me cry. I wished I had thanked him."

Cinderella premiered on February 15, 1950, and grossed $1.2 million more than its $3 million production costs. In the early 1940s, Walt had taken costly detours into classical music (*Fantasia*) and realistic story-telling (*Bambi*). *Cinderella* marked a profitable return to the fairy tale realms that audiences loved in *Snow White*. Not only did *Cinderella* revive Disney's fortunes in the 1950s, but movies inspired by fairy tales—*The Little Mermaid, Beauty and the Beast,*

> *"Fantasy, if it's really convincing, can't become dated, for the simple reason that it represents a flight into a dimension that lies beyond the reaches of time."*
>
> WALT DISNEY

and *Aladdin*—would re-energize the company again in the late 1980s and early '90s.

Down the rabbit hole with Alice

Walt's next animated feature was *Alice in Wonderland,* which premiered at London's Leicester Square Theatre on July 26, 1951. Alice is the most fast-paced and surreal of all Disney features, combining elements from two Lewis Carroll classics—*Alice's Adventures in Wonderland* and *Through the Looking Glass.* Along the way, Alice falls down a bottomless rabbit hole, meets a talking doorknob, attends a bizarre tea party with the Mad Hatter and the March Hare, and is nearly beheaded by the Queen of Hearts. The movie crackles with eccentric energy, and remains one of Walt's most imaginatively plussed films.

Alice in Wonderland had been on Walt's mind since the beginning of his career (the book inspired Walt's Alice Comedies in the 1920s). Storyboards and sketches for *Alice* were produced as early as 1931, but Walt shelved the project when a live-action version was released by another studio that year. In 1939, Walt commissioned Hollywood artist David Hall to create hundreds of paintings based on the book illustrations by Sir John Tenniel. Walt saw England as an important market for the film, so when the Nazis bombed Britain in 1940, Walt shelved the project again.

As World War II came to an end, *Alice* came off the shelf. Walt still envisioned a combined animation/live-action feature, so he announced plans to cast Ginger Rogers in the title role. Walt signed English novelist Aldous Huxley (*Brave New World*) as screenwriter. Huxley completed the script in December 1945, but the following year, Walt dropped the idea of having a live actress in the film. "No matter how closely we approximate Alice with a living actress," he told his staff, "the result would be a disappointment."

So Walt decided to produce an all-animation *Alice.* He expected howls from the reviewers. "When you deal with such a popular classic," he said, "you lay yourself wide open to the critics." But Walt knew that a "faithful" adaptation would make a terrible movie. Changes had to be made in order to plus the story for movie audiences.

Walt wanted each character to stand out as a unique individual. The cast of *Alice* reads like a Who's Who of great character actors: Vaudevillian Ed Wynn—radio's "Texaco Fire Chief"—was perfectly cast as The Mad Hatter. Jerry Colonna, a wacky comic with bulging eyes, a handlebar mustache, and a voice that would shatter granite—was The March Hare. Richard Haydn gave the Caterpillar just the right touch of pomposity. Bill Thompson, famous for his eccentric characters on radio's *Fibber McGee and Molly,* fit the bill as The White Rabbit. Sterling Holloway lent his fuzzy tenor to the Cheshire Cat.

"No story in English literature has intrigued me more than Lewis Carroll's Alice in Wonderland. *It fascinated me the first time I read it as a schoolboy, and as soon as I possibly could, after I started making animated cartoons, I acquired the film rights to do it."*

WALT DISNEY

Hardest to cast was Alice herself. Walt was looking for a voice that was "English enough to satisfy British audiences . . . but not so English that it would put off American audiences." One night in 1948, Walt and Lillian went to see *On an Island with You,* starring Esther Williams. On the screen he found his Alice. Ten-year-old Kathryn Beaumont sparkled in a minor role. She was exactly as Walt envisioned Alice: wavy blonde hair, lustrous blue eyes, a prim manner, and just the right accent—English, but not *too* English.

"Walt had been looking all over the world for his Alice," Kathryn told me, "and there I was, living in Los Angeles. I went to the studio and read for the part, and Walt liked the way I sounded."

Walt insisted that Kathryn sit in on the story conferences for *Alice in Wonderland.* "Walt would sit at the back and listen," she said, "and sometimes offer a suggestion or two. He was really involved in the creative process." Kathryn was fascinated by the interaction between the story artists as they plussed and plussed the storyline. Artists would sketch ideas and tack their drawings on the big cork storyboard that lined the wall. "I was seeing this marvelous film evolve before my eyes," Kathryn recalled.

Recording the voices was a fascinating process for Kathryn. She and her fellow actors dressed up in full costume to get into character. For the mad tea party, Ed Wynn wore a green Mad Hatter's hat, Jerry Colonna wore a big orange coat with a red bow tie, and Kathryn wore her blue Alice dress with white apron. Cameras recorded every gesture and facial expression as inspiration for the animators.

Songwriters Bob Hilliard and Sammy Fain wrote fourteen original songs for the film—more songs than in any other Disney feature. At Walt's insistence, Kathryn performed Alice's songs, even though her untrained voice sometimes slipped off-key. Kathryn recalled, "Walt wanted the songs to have a childlike feel, not a professional polish."

Kathryn also modeled the Alice character as a reference for the animators. Disney technicians invented various contraptions that enabled her to fly, spin, tumble, and float through the air. Her motions were filmed and studied by the artists for such scenes as her fall down the rabbit hole.

> *"Alice suffered from too many cooks—each trying to top the other guy and make his sequence the biggest and craziest in the show."*
>
> WARD KIMBALL
> DISNEY ANIMATOR

Alice in Wonderland opened to negative reviews, especially in England. As Walt expected, the film was criticized for taking liberties with the Lewis Carroll classic. Walt was surprised, however, that audiences also gave the film a cool reception. In trying to analyze what went wrong, Walt concluded that he had failed to make the *Alice* character sympathetic enough. In short (as he told interviewer Pete Martin), "There was no heart to it." But like other Disney "failures," *Alice* eventually became extremely profitable in re-release.

From Wonderland to Never Land

The first theatrical play Walt ever saw was James M. Barrie's 1904 play *Peter Pan.* The magic of that performance lingered in Walt's memory for years. In 1939, Walt acquired the film rights from the Great Ormond Street Hospital in London for five-thousand British pounds (Barrie had given the hospital all rights to the play in 1929). Walt immediately put his artists on the project, but had to shelve *Peter Pan* during the war years.

By 1950, the project was moving full-speed ahead—and again, Walt was looking for every possible way to plus the experience. First, Walt filmed the entire picture as a live action film, purely as a reference for the animators. Sets were built for the Darling house, Captain Hook's pirate ship, Peter's tree house, and so forth.

Walt cast Kathryn Beaumont as Wendy Darling. Disney technicians again sent Kathryn flying through the air on cables and pulleys. Recalling the experience, Kathryn said, "Most kids would say, 'What fun!' But I was nervous! I was hoisted up in the air in a harness and I was thinking that the floor of the stage looked so far down."

According to tradition, Peter Pan is always played by a woman. Walt broke with tradition and cast Bobby Driscoll in the title role. Walt kept another stage tradition, however, which holds that the same actor play both Captain Hook and Mr. Darling, the children's father. Walt cast Hans Conreid in those roles. (Kathryn Beaumont enjoyed working with Conreid, whom she grinningly described as "just so marvelously evil.")

Peter Pan is another fine example of Walt's commitment to plussing his films. He could have settled for a "faithful" adaptation; instead, he chose to plus the experience. In Barrie's stage play, for example, Tinker Bell is shown as a bright point of light that flits around the stage. Walt refused to be bound by the limitations of the stage, so he had animator Marc Davis turn Tink into a real character—a winged, womanly pixie with a spitfire personality. As an added plus, Tink leaves a golden trail of pixie dust wherever she goes.

Davis' Tinker Bell is widely rumored to be modeled after Marilyn Monroe. Not true. Davis did use a live model for Tinker Bell, but her name was Margaret Kerry. "There were a lot of people who thought Tink was just a little too sexy," Miss Kerry recalls. "But Marc Davis told me he got away with it by keeping the bottom half womanly while drawing the top half as a young girl."

Miss Kerry remembers Walt as a charming and humble man—not at all the kind of person she expected a studio boss to be. "I was in the sound stage," she told me, "and Walt came over to me and said, 'You went to school with my daughters.' I was surprised he knew that. I said, 'That's

> *"Tinker Bell was designed with the knowledge that her acting would all be done in pantomime, with a face that would register her emotions clearly, a simple costume that would not clutter up her movements, and sex appeal to charm the viewer."*
>
> JOHN CANEMAKER
> AUTHOR AND FILM CRITIC

true, I did.' We chatted for a few moments, and then he excused himself and started to walk away. Then he turned and, with a twinkle in his eye, he added, 'By the way, they liked you.' What a great exit line!

"I've never met anyone who was envious of Walt or resented his success. Everyone was in awe of him. People said, 'Now, there's a man who deserves to succeed.'"

After three years in production, *Peter Pan* was released on February 5, 1953, at a cost of $4 million. The film was both a critical and commercial success. In its theatrical release and re-releases alone, *Peter Pan* earned over $88 million. Like Peter Pan himself, the movie never ages—in large part because Walt was willing to spend any amount of time, money and creative energy in the pursuit of excellence.

Animator Frank Thomas related a story about *Peter Pan* that Walt told him. "During a trip to England," Thomas said, "Walt was walking past a theater in London where *Peter Pan* was being shown. He stopped for a minute and overheard two ladies talking about the film. One of them said, 'Have you seen it yet? I hear that it's terribly Americanized.' And the other lady said, 'Yes it is, but you know, when you see it, you don't mind that so much.' Walt said that when he heard that, he couldn't wait to come back to the studio and tell us."

"Your dog needs to meet my dog!"

You could see the evidence of Walt's commitment to excellence over his fireplace. Walt's mantelpiece groaned beneath the weight of his forty-eight Academy Awards and seven Emmys. Lillian enjoyed accompanying Walt to the Academy Awards ceremonies. In 1953, however, Walt encouraged Lillian not to attend. "It'll be boring," he said. "I'm up for a few awards, but I'm sure I won't win any this year." So Walt went to the ceremony and Lilly stayed home.

That night, Walt won four Academy Awards, the most he'd ever won in a single night. News photographers took pictures of Walt beaming and holding all four Oscars in his arms. But when Walt arrived home, Lilly wouldn't let him inside. She was furious because she had missed the biggest Oscar night of his career! Walt spent the night in his apartment at the studio.

Walt's next animated feature, *Lady and the Tramp,* was Disney's first movie in wide-screen CinemaScope. Though the CinemaScope process inflated the budget by a third, Walt believed it was worth it. "CinemaScope," he said, "gave the artists the opportunity—indeed, the necessity—to experiment with action, groupings, and setting. We were able to do more in our backgrounds and settings because we had a larger canvas on which to work."

"Walt said about the Academy Awards that he was embarrassed to receive an award and he was embarrassed if he didn't get one."

LILLIAN DISNEY

Though released in mid-1955, the origins of *Lady and the Tramp* date back to 1937, when veteran Disney story artist Joe Grant pitched a tale to Walt about a cocker spaniel pup. The twist is that the story is told from the dog's point of view. Walt liked the idea, and asked Grant to develop it further, but the project was shelved when war broke out.

Work resumed in 1943, with Walt planning to produce the story as an animated short. Grant storyboarded the cartoon, then Walt and the boys began plussing it. Walt quickly realized that while the character of Lady was charming, something was missing—that elusive "plus factor." Walt recalled, "We discovered during our preliminary conferences that we had only half the story we wanted. Our prim, well-bred, house-sheltered little Lady, when confronted with a crisis, just up and ran away."

While searching for the "plus factor," Walt chanced upon a short story by Ward Greene entitled "Happy Dan, the Whistling Dog." Happy Dan, a street-wise, happy-go-lucky mutt, was the exact opposite of the refined, faithful Lady. Instantly, Walt began matchmaking. He contacted Ward Greene and told him, "Your dog needs to meet my dog!"

Changing Happy Dan's name to Tramp, Walt merged Joe Grant's story with Ward Greene's story—

"We were free to develop the story as we saw it, unlike the classics where we had to adhere rigidly to the sequence conceived by the author. . . . As the characters came to life and the scenes took shape, we were able to alter, embellish, eliminate, and improve the material."

WALT DISNEY ON *LADY AND THE TRAMP*

and the chemistry between the characters was magical. Suddenly, the dignified and pampered Lady had a rough-edged, roguish charmer to play against. Lady found that Tramp could be insufferable one moment and irresistible the next—so, of course, the romantic possibilities were endless.

Lady and the Tramp was an instant hit when it premiered in Chicago on June 16, 1955. The movie went on to gross nearly $88 million in theatrical releases alone.

A whale of a tale

Walt's next feature was a real "whale of a tale"—Jules Verne's *20,000 Leagues Under the Sea*. The 1950s were the heyday of B-movies filled with monsters, mad scientists, and threats from atomic radiation. Walt shrewdly chose Jules Verne's 1870 novel as the basis for his retro sci-fi adventure—a mad-scientist-and-monster flick with an A-movie budget.

When Walt first approached Roy about *20,000 Leagues*, he expected his brother to put up a fight. After all, Walt's plan called for lavish sets, dazzling special effects, expensive location shooting, and a big-name cast. The price tag: a whopping $4 million. Walt was shocked when Roy instantly loved the idea. "I thought something was wrong with my brother!" Walt said.

Walt's choice of director—Richard Fleischer—was ironic. Fleischer's father was Max Fleischer, Walt's chief cartoon rival in the 1920s and '30s. Richard had been directing films at RKO for a decade when Walt tapped him to direct *20,000 Leagues*.

> "When we hear the name Jules Verne, we think of 20,000 Leagues Under the Sea. *The Disney film is the reason we think of it first.*"
>
> SAMUEL R. DELANEY
> SCIENCE FICTION WRITER

"Walt and my father, Max Fleischer, were intense competitors in the early days of animation," Fleischer told me. "Walt hired a lot of animators away from my father's studio. So I was surprised when Walt wanted to hire me as a director. He showed me a picture of a submarine caught in the tentacles of a giant squid. 'That's the movie I want you to direct,' he said, '*20,000 Leagues Under the Sea.*' I thought there had to be a mistake—I told him I directed live action, not animated pictures. He said, 'This *is* a live action film.'

"I asked him if he knew who my father was. He said, 'Yes, I know.' I said, 'I want to talk to my father first. I wouldn't want to do it if he'd feel hurt by it.' So I called my father and told him about Walt's offer. Dad said, 'It's a great opportunity, you should do it. When you call Walt, tell him Max Fleischer said he has great taste in directors.'

"So I directed the film, and it was a good experience. Walt was very nice to me. He trusted me with a very difficult and expensive picture. He knew what he wanted, and he spent whatever it took to get it."

Walt's friend, Art Linkletter, was present during filming of the most crucial scene in the picture. "Walt called me," Linkletter told me, "and he said, 'How would you like to see a fight between a submarine and a monster squid?' So I went over to the studio with Walt and saw the most awesome battle!"

In that scene, the giant squid has the submarine *Nautilus* wrapped in its tentacles. The sub surfaces in the middle of a raging storm, and Captain Nemo (James Mason), Ned Land (Kirk Douglas), and the crew go up onto the deck for a fierce hand-to-tentacle battle.

The scene was shot in a massive water tank on the Disney sound stage. The huge molded latex squid was controlled by sixty technicians operating a complex cable-and-pulley apparatus. Massive wind machines and wave-makers churned the water. The scene cost a quarter of a million dollars to construct and shoot.

"The scene took some time to film," Linkletter recalled. "There were closeups and retakes and finally the director came over and said, 'Walt, I think we got it.' But Walt said, 'The action on those tentacles wasn't right. I could see the wires.' So they had to rebuild the set and shoot the entire sequence again another day at enormous additional expense. Walt wouldn't hesitate to spend the money to get it right. He was a fanatic about quality."

Irving Ludwig, then head of Disney's newly formed Buena Vista Distribution Company, agreed with Art Linkletter's assessment. "Oh, yes," he said. "Walt was a perfectionist. Everything had to be just right. We had *20,000 Leagues Under the Sea* scheduled for a big opening at a theater on Broadway, but there was a problem with the scene with the giant squid.

"Walt Disney, far and above any of the others, saw visions. And it was always in terms of what can we do now and how can we improve. . . . He was intrigued by Jules Verne, because Jules Verne had this imagination which Disney could relate to."

RUDY BEHLMER
FILM HISTORIAN

The entire scene had to be reshot from scratch. It cost Walt a quarter of a million dollars to reshoot it, and it forced us to delay the Broadway premiere. But Walt didn't care about the expense or the delay. The only thing that mattered to him was getting it done right."

Walt's commitment to plussing paid off. The movie premiered on December 23, 1954, and was an instant hit with audiences. It quickly recovered the $4 million in production costs and went on to earn a huge profit. When the film premiered, Walt was at the halfway mark in the construction of Disneyland, and his company needed the revenue.

Lavishly plussed

While Walt was building Disneyland and filming *20,000 Leagues,* his studio was also hard at work on a $6 million wide-screen production of the fairy tale *Sleeping Beauty.* Many devotees of animation say it has never been surpassed. The score was adapted from Tchaikovsky's "Sleeping Beauty" ballet, and the film was Disney's first in stereo since *Fantasia.* Walt was personally involved in every phase of production, and he spared no expense in his quest to top himself once more.

By 1954, as *Sleeping Beauty* was in the early stages of production, Walt divided his time between the studio and Disneyland. Though increasingly absent from the studio, Walt insisted on personally checking and okaying all of the animation for *Sleeping Beauty.* When an animator finished a sequence, he had to wait for Walt to personally approve the sequence for inking and painting. The artist might wait for days—or weeks. To keep busy, some animators used the time to lavish extra attention on their drawings.

Walt had assigned his very best animators to *Sleeping Beauty,* including Marc Davis, Frank Thomas, Ollie Johnston, Milt Kahl and John Sibley. For a few months in 1953, that list also included Chuck Jones, the famed Warner Brothers animation director responsible for so many classic Bugs Bunny and Road Runner cartoons.

In early 1953, Jones' boss, Jack Warner, concluded that 3D movies were the wave of the future. Rather than converting his cartoon studio to the costly new 3D process, Warner shut down the studio, putting Jones out of a job. So Chuck Jones called Walt and asked if he could work for Disney. "Sure," Walt said. "You can work on *Sleeping Beauty.*"

So Jones spent four months at the Disney studio in Burbank, working on some of the early conceptual work for *Sleeping Beauty.* He soon found that *working* for Walt meant *waiting* for Walt. "You'd finish a sequence," Jones recalled, "and then you'd wait, maybe for weeks. Five or six men, just sitting and waiting for Walt to come around."

Finally, Jones went to Walt's office and explained his frustration.

"What would you like to do, Chuck?" asked Walt. "I'm sure we can work something out."

"Well," Jones replied, deadpan. "There is one job I'd like to have."

"Oh?" Walt said. "Which job is that?"

"Yours," Jones said.

"I'm sorry, Chuck," Walt replied. "I'm afraid that job is filled."

"Well, then," Jones said, "I guess I'll be leaving then. Thanks for everything."

Walt Disney and Chuck Jones shook hands and parted company. By that time, the 3D fad had run its course and Jack Warner had reopened his animation department. Chuck Jones resumed his work at Warner Brothers as if he had never left.

Mary Costa was the voice of Sleeping Beauty. A soprano with a range of three and a half octaves, she was in her twenties when Walt selected her for the part. She remembers Walt not merely as a producer, but as a teacher and mentor.

"Walt told me to always keep my voice clear," she told me. "He said, 'Protect yourself so that you don't get a cold. Be sure to have a warm meal at least two hours before your recording sessions. Make sure you always exercise your vocal cords before you come to the recording studio—hum or read lightly. Get at least nine hours of sleep each night, and always do some physical exercise to get yourself ready.' I wondered how he knew so much about caring for the voice, and then it dawned on me: Walt had done the voice of Mickey Mouse for so many years, and he had to do all of those things to keep that voice high and clear."

Walt also gave Mary Costa some advice that touched her deeply. "When I was a little girl," she recalled, "my father, who had died when I was very young, gave me a kaleidoscope. I would look at it for hours at a time. Walt once asked me, 'Do you like kaleidoscopes?'"

The question startled her, for she had never told Walt about her father's gift. "Walt said, 'That's the way I want you to think. I want those colors to change all the time inside of your mind and translate into your speaking voice. You can tell most anything about a person by the way they speak. You can hear all those different kaleidoscopic colors. I want you to think about that.' Little did Walt know that I would think about that for the rest of my life."

> *"Walt had a simple philosophy:*
> *'Get the job done, but never*
> *sacrifice quality.' It was always*
> *about plussing. He often told us,*
> *'You worry about the quality. Let*
> *me worry about the cost.'"*
>
> ORLANDO FERRANTE
> DISNEY THEME PARK DESIGNER

Sleeping Beauty premiered on January 29, 1959. Enormously expensive for that time, the film failed to earn back its production costs in its initial release—but it ultimately became a hugely profitable film for the Disney company. Today, *Sleeping Beauty* ranks as the sixth highest-grossing animated film in Disney's library.

Sleeping Beauty was the last animated movie that Walt personally supervised from conception to completion. Though he was involved in such films as *101 Dalmatians* (1961), *The Sword in the Stone* (1963) and The *Jungle Book* (released in 1967, after Walt's death), he spent the last ten years of his life concentrating primarily on building and plussing his kingdom of dreams, Disneyland.

How to Be Like Walt—
Lesson 8: Plus Every Experience

Disney historian Les Perkins told me about an incident at Disneyland during the early years of the park. Walt had decided to hold a Christmas parade at the park—a $350,000 extravagance. "Walt called accountants 'bean counters,'" Perkins told me. "That year, the 'bean counters' approached Walt and said, 'Why spend money on a Christmas parade? It won't draw people to the park. The people will already be here, so it's just an expense that we can do without. No one will complain if we dispense with the parade, because nobody's expecting it.'

"Walt said, 'That's just the point. We should do the parade precisely *because* no one's expecting it. Our goal at Disneyland is to always give the people *more* than they expect. As long as we keep surprising them, they'll keep coming back. But if they ever stop coming, it'll cost us ten times that much to get them to come back.'"

Walt was obsessed with quality even in the tiniest details. Hank Block was freshly discharged from the Marines when Walt personally hired him as an engineer at Disneyland. "Walt would show up at my area unannounced, just to look things over," he said. "One morning, Walt and I were talking, and he ran his hand along a gate and felt something rough. It was chipped paint. He said, 'Have you tried to get this fixed?' I told him I'd been calling maintenance for two days and nothing happened. Walt frowned and said, 'You tell them you talked to Walt Disney and he wants this fixed at once.' So I did, and boy, did they come a-running after that."

Peter Ellenshaw was the matte artist for the Davy Crockett episodes of the *Disneyland* TV show. A painstaking artist, Peter strove for results that would look photographically real. As the airdate approached, the producer called Peter and told him to rush the paintings. As he was feverishly working, Walt stopped by to look at his paintings. "Peter," Walt said, "your standards are slipping. This is not your best work."

"Walt," Ellenshaw said, "this is the best I can do with the time I have."

"What do you mean?" Walt asked.

"The producer told me I had to deliver these paintings in three days."

Walt frowned. "They'll always try to push you," he said. "Tell them you can't be pushed. We'll move the airdate if we have to. Just make sure you never do less than your best."

Artist and Imagineer Marc Davis recalled a day Walt came to inspect the robotic pirates for the "Pirates of the Caribbean" attraction, then under construction for Disneyland. Davis was particularly proud of a pirate auctioneer figure. It was so lifelike, it was hard to tell from a living human being. "It's really kind of a waste," Davis told Walt. "All that work and complicated engineering, and people will go by so fast they won't even notice."

> "Once Disneyland was under way, it became his passion. He wanted to plus the Disneyland experience. He wanted to keep adding attractions. He was constantly looking for ways to improve the experience for his guests."
>
> WALTER DISNEY MILLER,
> WALT'S GRANDSON

"Oh, no, Marc," Walt said. "It's not a waste. People will visit this attraction again and again. Each time, they'll see things they never noticed before." Walt knew that even the smallest details get noticed.

Early in his Disney career, Dick Nunis was put in charge of Adventureland's centerpiece attraction, the "Jungle Cruise." One morning, Walt arrived for a surprise inspection and boarded one of the "Jungle Cruise" boats along with the paying customers. Nunis stood on the dock, anxiously watching Walt's departure. When Walt returned to the dock, he was not happy.

"How long is that trip supposed to take, Dick?" Walt asked.

"Seven minutes," Nunis replied.

"It lasted just over four minutes by my watch," Walt said. "We shot through there so fast, I couldn't tell the hippos from the elephants! Do something about it."

So Dick went to work, drilling his boat operators until they could run the cruise in their sleep. Soon, Walt showed up for another inspection.

Dick lined up his best cruise operators in the first couple of boats, figuring that Walt would take the cruise once or twice and be satisfied. But Walt rode every boat and timed each cruise operator. Each one gave Walt a full seven-minute ride.

Art Linkletter summed up Walt's commitment to plussing this way: "Walt could just as well have been a very successful plumber somewhere. He'd be the best plumber, of course, and the plunger would probably play 'Auld Lang Syne' in the toilet." Isn't that the truth!

No matter what business you are in, your success depends on your commitment to excellence and attention to detail. If you deliver more than people expect, you will turn clients into fans. If you go out of your way to make people feel special, they will go out of their way to buy your product.

I once spoke at a Disney resort and afterward visited with the man who introduced me. I said, "How are you enjoying Walt Disney World?"

"Oh, it's incredible," he said. "My family is with me and we're having a great time."

"What was the highlight of your vacation?" I asked, expecting him to talk about the thrill rides or the golfing at the resort. His answer surprised me.

"The highlight of our vacation," he said, "was coming back to the hotel at night." I wondered how a hotel room could top all the wonders of Disney World. He explained. "My five-year-old daughter can't wait to see what the maid does next with her dolls. One night, we found the dolls

> *"Walt was never completely satisfied. I think that's the mark of any artist, any dancer, any scientist, any writer. They may be happy with the day's work they've done—but that night, when they lie awake in bed, they'll be thinking of the things they can correct the next day."*
>
> RAY BRADBURY
> WRITER

perched on the edge of the bathtub. Another night, the dolls were hanging from the light fixture. Last night, the maid fashioned a boat out of a big bath towel and the dolls were in the boat on my daughter's bed."

This maid at a Disney hotel had found a way to be like Walt. She was plussing the hotel experience of a five-year-old girl—and in the process, she made raving Disney fans out of the entire family.

Whether you are an NBA executive, a hotel maid, or a shoestring salesman, you can be like Walt. Pursue excellence in everything you do. Plus every experience—then plus the plus.

Chapter Eight

❧

The Man with Stick-to-it-ivity

By the mid-1950s, Walt had undergone many tests of his character, including tests of his ability to persevere in the face of obstacles and opposition. But the toughest test of all was the challenge of building his dream park—Disneyland.

Walt's dream of a magical kingdom probably goes back to his boyhood in Kansas City, when he peered through the fence at Electric Park, imagining the wonders inside. How long did he dream of building his own fantasy park? We can't know for sure, but we do know he had given it a lot of thought by his early thirties, even before his daughters were born.

In a news story published two days before Disneyland opened, the *Long Beach Independent-Press-Telegram* (Friday, July 15, 1955) reported, "Plans for this wonderland first began to go on paper as far back as 1932 when Walt's magnificent dream began to take form. In cleaning files at the Burbank studio recently, original Disneyland sketches, bearing the 1932 date, were found." Those sketches were dated a year before his first daughter, Diane, was born.

Disneyland was on Walt's mind the night *Snow White and the Seven Dwarfs* premiered at the Carthay Circle Theatre in 1937. Animator Wilfred

Jackson recalled watching Walt inspect the scenery in the forecourt of the theater—the dwarf's cottage, the windmill and waterfall, the giant toadstools, and so forth. Walt told Jackson, "Someday, I want to build a park for kids to play in—a place with fantasy cottages like these, all scaled down to a child's size."

The idea gained momentum after Walt became a father. On weekends, he'd take his daughters to Griffith Park. "I'd sit on a bench, eating peanuts," Walt later recalled, "while the girls rode the merry-go-round. As I sat there, I felt that there should be someplace where the parents and the children could have fun together."

As Walt became more intent on his dream, he researched other amusement parks, including nearby Beverly Park at Beverly and La Cienega Boulevards. It was a clean, well-run, unpretentious little park with a small train, a merry-go-round, and a "waterless boat ride" in which the boats moved around on land. Walt would sit on a bench, observe children at play, and asked them which rides they liked best.

> *"Lillian used to say, 'But why do you want to build an amusement park? They're so dirty.' I told her that was just the point— mine wouldn't be.'"*
>
> WALT DISNEY

Then, in the summer of 1948, Walt took a train ride that put his dream on a fast track.

A steam-powered dream

Ward Kimball's phone rang. "Hey, Kimball," a familiar voice said, "this is Walt."

"Walt who?"

"Walt Disney, for crying out loud!"

Kimball pulled the "Walt who?" bit every time his boss called. Walt never figured out that his leg was being yanked.

Walt asked, "How would you like to go with me to the Railroad Fair in Chicago?"

Kimball's eyes lit up. Like Walt, he was an avid train enthusiast. "When do we leave?" he asked.

On Sunday, July 18, 1948, Walt and Ward boarded the Santa Fe Super Chief at the Pasadena station. It was a forty-hour trip to Chicago, so Walt and Ward had plenty of time to get to know each other better. Walt Disney was a very private man, and Kimball realized he'd never really known his boss until that trip. Walt opened up and talked about his boyhood, his Red Cross duty in France, his painful loss of the Oswald character and more. "Much of what he told me," Kimball later recalled, "I'd never heard before."

The Railroad Fair opened on Tuesday the 20th. Walt and Ward stayed several days, soaking up inspiration and railroad lore. They talked to old-time railroad engineers, walked through vintage railroad cars, and climbed into the cabs of ancient locomotives. Every night, they watched fireworks exploding over Lake Michigan. "That was the most fun I ever had in my life," Walt later said.

Walt was moved to tears by the black-draped replica of President Lincoln's funeral train. It rolled mournfully down the tracks as a band played "The Battle Hymn of the Republic." Walt had always felt a deep bond with Abraham Lincoln.

After the Fair, Walt and Ward boarded a Wabash Railway train and headed to Dearborn, Michigan, to visit the Henry Ford Museum and Greenfield Village. Ford had purchased historical buildings from around the country and moved them to the village. Those buildings included the New Jersey laboratory of Thomas Edison, the Ohio bicycle shop where the Wright Brothers built the first airplane, and the Connecticut home of dictionary publisher Noah Webster. A double-decker sternwheeler, the *Suwanee,* circled an island in a man-made lake, and *The Edison,* an 1870s-style train (built in the 1920s by Ford engineers) ran on a circuit of track.

Walt returned to California, his mind bursting with plans and enthusiasm for a project he called "Mickey Mouse Park," which would be located

> *"While I was in Chicago with Walt, he asked me if there were any places I wanted to go. I told him of a jazz place, and he said 'You can do that anytime! Let's go ride the El.' So we rode that elevated train half the night and he was looking out the window, reliving his childhood."*
>
> WARD KIMBALL
> DISNEY ANIMATOR

on a lot across the street from the Burbank studio. When Roy Disney heard about Walt's latest brainstorm, he hit the roof. He called Mickey Mouse Park "that screwball idea," and told Walt it would be the height of irresponsibility to pour money into such a project.

Walt later recalled, "I had a little dream for Disneyland adjoining the studio. I couldn't get anybody to go along with me because we were going through this financial depression. But I kept working on it, and I worked on it with my own money. Not the studio's money, my own money."

On August 31, 1948, Walt wrote an internal memo with the heading "Mickey Mouse Park." It described a remarkably well-formed vision of what would one day become Disneyland. "The Main Village," he wrote, "which includes the Railroad Station, is built around a village green or informal park. In the park will be benches, a bandstand, drinking fountain, trees and shrubs. It will be a place for people to sit and rest; mothers and grandmothers can watch over small children at play. I want it to be very relaxing, cool and inviting."

The memo went on to describe other features of Mickey Mouse Park: A clean, well-run carnival with Disney-themed rides and a merry-go-round. A self-contained village with a town hall, fire and police stations, and a working post office. A Wild West town, complete with cowboys, horses, stagecoach, and a saloon-style theater. The park would also feature a tour of the Disney studio; a scale-model steam train would take guests from Mickey Mouse Park, over Riverside Drive by trestle, and through the Disney soundstages.

> "Once he got this bug about the park, it was an obsession. It's all he thought about."
>
> WARD KIMBALL
> DISNEY ANIMATOR

For months, the park was all Walt talked about. Disney artist John Hench, who lived near the studio at the time, recalled, "I remember seeing Walt across the street in a weed-filled lot, standing and visualizing all by himself." Hench would eventually become one of Walt's Disneyland architects.

Walt soon had so many ideas for attractions that the vacant lot across from the studio couldn't contain them. He realized he was no longer planning a mere park; he had begun to envision a *kingdom*, with a castle towering over realms of past, future, and pure fantasy. And circling Walt's magical kingdom, like a cast-iron ghost from the past, was a steam-powered train.

The Carolwood Pacific Railroad

In 1949, Walt and Lilly built a new house in the Holmby Hills section of West Los Angeles, between Bel Air and Beverly Hills. The new house at 355 North Carolwood Drive was of modest size, but it sat on a five-acre estate, with plenty of room for Walt's new hobby: steam-powered railroading. "When we built the Holmby Hills house," Lillian recalled, "he had that train in mind. Walt took one look at the property and said, 'That's it!'"

With the help of two master craftsmen from his studio-machinist Roger Broggie and carpenter Ray Fox—Walt built a working one-eighth scale steam locomotive. Roger Broggie did most of the heavy iron work, such as casting and welding. Walt did the finishing, riveting and woodworking. He fashioned the headlight and smokestack of the engine, and built the entire caboose with his own hands. He lavished attention on every detail, including a photographically reduced copy of *The Police Gazette* in the magazine rack of the caboose.

Walt enjoyed learning new metalworking and woodworking skills. He told Broggie, "You know, it does me some good to come down here and find out I don't know everything." Broggie was impressed with Walt's aptitude and skill. "You only had to show Walt once," Broggie marveled, "and he got the picture."

Walt patterned his locomotive after the 1872 Central Pacific No. 173, the first locomotive built in California. He named his train the Carolwood Pacific Railroad (after his Carolwood Drive address), so that the designation "C.P. 173" on the side of the engine would match that of the original locomotive. The engine was painted black with red and gold trim.

Before laying the track in his own backyard, he built out a 300-foot test track in a studio soundstage so his employees could ride it and give him feedback for improvements. On one occasion, *New York Times* film critic Bosley Crowther visited the studio and was shocked to find Walt in the soundstage, riding his train. Crowther noted that Walt "seemed totally

uninterested in movies and wholly, almost weirdly concerned with the
building of a miniature railroad engine and a string of cars. . . . All of his
zest for invention, for creative fantasies, seemed to be going into this play-
thing. I came away feeling sad."

After testing his train at the studio, Walt was ready to build his backyard
railroad. Only one thing stood in the way of Walt's plans: Mrs. Disney.
Lillian wanted a backyard flower garden, not a bunch of tracks, trestles and
tunnels. To win her over, Walt named the engine after her: the Lilly Belle.
He also had his attorney draw up a contract giving Walt a right-of-way for
his railroad in exchange for a promise to build a tunnel under Lillian's garden. Walt and Lillian signed the document, and Walt framed it and hung
it on the wall of their home.

> "He taught me how to run the
> train, how to fire it up and get the
> engine going. I thought it was
> great fun."
>
> SHARON DISNEY LUND
> WALT'S DAUGHTER

Walt hired Bill and Jack Evans to
landscape the acreage around the
railroad (the Evans brothers later
landscaped the Disneyland grounds).
The tracks wound along hillsides,
through a fruit orchard, over a ten-
foot-high redwood trestle, and
through a tunnel. The tunnel was
120 feet long and S-shaped so that passengers would be in complete dark-
ness in the middle of the ride.

When Walt's foreman saw the plans for the tunnel, he said, "You know,
it would be cheaper if we built this tunnel straight."

"No," Walt replied, "it would be cheaper not to build it at all!"

The Carolwood Pacific Railroad began service on May 15, 1950. Roger
Broggie's son Michael shared his memories of Walt's railroad with me.
"Walt and my dad figured out the track layout. They laid a half-mile of
track, including tunnels and trestles. In the middle of the layout was a barn,
modeled after the family barn from Walt's childhood in Missouri. In 1999,
we dismantled the barn and rebuilt it in Griffith Park as a museum for
Walt's memorabilia.

"I remember, as a boy, going to Walt's house with my dad to play on
Walt's trains all day. Walt was like a big kid—very down-to-earth in his
rolled-up dungarees, with grease under his fingernails, his face unshaven.

That train was his escape from the pressures of his studio. He enjoyed sharing his hobby with others."

Backyard railroading was a hobby Walt shared with animators Ollie Johnston and Ward Kimball. Ollie had several scale-model trains, both steam and electric, that ran on an extensive layout around his La Cañada Valley home. Kimball owned a full-size Nevada Central coal-burner and a Southern Pacific passenger coach which he had purchased for a total of $250. His Grizzly Flats Railroad ran on a straight 500-foot ribbon of track through an orange grove.

Ward's son, John Kimball, told me, "When I was eleven or twelve, Walt Disney and his brother Roy would come to our house to discuss plans for Disneyland in a secret setting. My dad had a backyard railroad that included a nicely restored passenger coach that was built around 1840. Walt and Roy would sit in the coach with its old seats and all that railroad history, and they would discuss their plans. Walt liked the peace and quiet at our place, and the railroad surroundings sparked his creative thinking."

There was a strong connection between Walt's backyard railroad and his plans for Disneyland. Walt's biographer, Bob Thomas, told me, "Walt loved to tinker, but his backyard railroad was more than a hobby. That little train was the forerunner of the larger trains that would run around Disneyland and the other parks. Disneyland was an extension of Walt's backyard. When he built the Disneyland Railroad, he was still tinkering, but on a bigger scale."

Researching the dream

By 1950, Walt was intensively researching Disneyland by visiting amusement sites, from parks to fairs to zoos to circuses. He spent countless hours at the Pomona Fair, the Long Beach Pike, and the Santa Monica Pier, asking patrons about their likes and dislikes, which attractions were the most entertaining, and which left them feeling cheated.

Walt also talked to amusement park operators. He told them he was going to build a clean, inviting park; he would charge admission at the front gate (to keep out drunks and other sinister types); and he would staff his park with friendly people. The park operators laughed and predicted

Walt would go broke within a year. "You can't keep cleaning the restrooms all day," they said. "That costs money! And you can't charge admission—nobody will come! And you don't hire 'nice people'—you hire people who work cheap."

Walt rejected the cynicism of the experts. "Walt Disney was focused and determined," said Steve Mannheim, author of *Walt Disney and the Quest for Community*. "He listened politely to the so-called 'experts,' but he was not deterred by those who told him, 'It can't be done.'"

In 1951, Walt and Lilly took a cruise to Europe. Walt was scheduled to host the London premiere of *Alice in Wonderland* on July 26, and he also intended to vacation on the continent. During the ocean crossing, Walt learned that Art and Lois Linkletter were on board. Walt and Art had met in 1940, when Art interviewed Walt on the radio. Renewing their acquaintance, they found that they were neighbors—Art, too, lived in Holmby Hills. That cruise marked the beginning of a close friendship. The Disneys and Linkletters ended up traveling Europe together.

The Disneys and Linkletters visited Tivoli Gardens in Copenhagen, Denmark. Built in 1843, Tivoli is known for its lush flower gardens, fine restaurants, nightly fireworks, and wholesome family atmosphere. In the 1950s, it offered a number of tame rides and attractions, though some extreme thrill rides have been added in recent years.

At night, Tivoli comes alight with over a hundred-thousand light bulbs—a sight that must have reminded Walt of the fairyland atmosphere of Electric Park. Walt later described Tivoli as "spotless, brightly colored, and priced within the reach of everyone. The gaiety of the music, the excellence of the food and drink, the warm courtesy of the employees—everything combined for a pleasurable experience."

Art Linkletter noticed how Walt enjoyed Tivoli Gardens. "As we walked through it," Linkletter recalled, "I had my first experience of Walt Disney's

> *"Walt and I lived a few blocks from each other in Holmby Hills. I was at his house and saw his trains. I was astounded to learn that he did most of the work right there. He was a mechanic, an artist and a craftsman. He was more than just a dreamer."*
>
> Art Linkletter
> Television Personality

childlike delight in the enjoyment of seeing families and in the cleanliness and the orderliness of everything. He was making notes all the time—about the lights, the chairs, the seats, and the food. I asked him what he was doing, and he replied, 'I'm just making notes about something that I've always dreamed of—a great, great playground for the children and the families of America.'"

Journalist and educator John Culhane is the author of *Walt Disney's Fantasia*. In 1951, he was a seventeen-year-old Disney fan living in Rockford, Illinois. When he learned that a friend of a friend knew Walt's daughter, Diane, Culhane decided to use that connection to wangle a meeting with Walt.

"Three friends and I chipped in to buy a car," Culhane told me, "and we drove out to California. On arriving, we learned that Walt was in London for the premiere of *Alice in Wonderland*. We hung around southern California, waiting for Walt's return. Louise talked to Diane, and Diane said she would call when her father returned. On Sunday morning, August 26, Diane called and said, 'Daddy's home. Come on over.'

"I thumbed a ride to the Disneys' house and knocked on the kitchen door. I heard a voice say, 'If you're looking for Diane, she's in the back.' Then I saw Walt himself at the door. I froze. 'Come in,' he said, opening the door. He led me through the house to the backyard.

"As we walked, I had to think of a question to keep the conversation going. 'How does the multiplane camera work?' I asked. His eyebrow went up, and he launched into a detailed explanation. My next question was, 'Why did you take Ub Iwerks back?' He said, 'Don't you think we all deserve another chance?'"

Culhane didn't spend much time with Diane. He spent most of the day talking to his hero. "Walt seemed to be in a mood to talk and teach," Culhane recalled. "He asked me, 'What do you want to be?' I said, 'A writer.' 'What do you want to write?' I said, 'Your biography.' 'Are you good?' 'My teachers think I am.' 'Well, John, teachers are paid to read what you write. The big question is: Can you get people to pay you for your writings?'

"We walked around the Disney property and talked for six hours. Sometimes Walt would talk in long monologues. He reminisced about his boyhood in Missouri. He talked a lot about his dad. He also asked me

> *"Walt's life teaches us to do a good day's work and try to make magic for everyone who crosses your path each day. Make their day happy and lighten their burden by taking notice of them. Take an interest in what they are doing; ask questions the way Walt did."*
>
> RON STARK
> DISNEY HISTORIAN AND
> ANIMATION PRESERVATIONIST

about my life in Rockford, Illinois, and for some reason, he was very interested in my recent job as a soda jerk.

"Walt didn't say a word about his plans for Disneyland, but looking back, I see a lot of clues that the dream of Disneyland was churning in his mind. While he was talking to me, he was actually doing research. A lot of the questions he asked me were aimed at finding out what a seventeen-year-old from the Midwest would like to see and do in Disneyland. He also invited me to spend a day at the Burbank studio on Tuesday.

"As the sun was going down, Lillian Disney called to Walt from the house. They were going out to dinner, so Walt excused himself, but told me I should feel free to stay. 'Use the cabana to change,' he said, 'and go take a swim.' He went to the house and I took a church bulletin from my pocket (I'd been to Mass that morning) and I jotted down notes on everything Walt had taught me that day. A short time later, Walt and Lillian came out, and he introduced us. 'Johnny,' he said, 'meet Mrs. Disney. Stay as long as you like, and close the gate when you leave.' They left, and I couldn't believe that I was all alone on the Disney estate.

"Later, I got dressed and walked back to my friends' house. It was dark by then, and every so often, I would stop under a street light and write down another insight I recalled from my conversation with Walt. One memorable statement Walt made to me was, 'Think of the happy things; it's the same as having wings.' Two days later, when I visited the studio, I learned that it was a line from Walt's next film, *Peter Pan*. He was trying the line out on me, gauging my reaction—but he was also telling me what I truly believed about happiness.

"Walt defined happiness as 'spontaneous delight harmonized with circumstances.' He summed up his philosophy of happiness by singing a song from the Broadway musical *No, No, Nanette.* The key line from the song was, 'I want to be happy, but I won't be happy till I make you happy, too.' He also made a rather wistful statement: 'Life should be a World's Fair of delights. I know that life isn't that way, but I think it should be, I believe it could be, and hope it will be.' I've never forgotten that."

Two days later, Culhane went to the Burbank studio. "Walt had everything set up for me," he recalls. "He had arranged for me to spend time with his creative staff. Why did Walt go to all of that trouble for a seventeen-year-old kid from Illinois? I think it was because he knew he had a disciple for life in me. And he was right."

I'm grateful that John Culhane took good notes on that memorable day in 1951. He preserved for us a fascinating insight into Walt's motivation for building Disneyland. Walt believed that life could—and should—be "a World's Fair of delights." Disneyland—which he called "the happiest place on earth"—was Walt's way of making the world a better place. He believed that by filling people's thoughts with "happy things," he could give them *wings*—wings to soar, wings to attain unbelievable heights.

I believe Walt had something bigger in mind for Disneyland than mere fun and amusement. To Walt, Disneyland was an island of utopian hope and happiness in a sea of human despair. Walt envisioned people coming to Disneyland, finding happiness there, then going out and widening the circle of happiness around the world.

Persevering against opposition

Walt knew that building Disneyland would be the hardest thing he had ever attempted. The park would be incredibly expensive to build, and the studio was already drowning in debt. Moreover, all of the experts told him his dream didn't stand a chance.

Walt's brother Roy begged him to forget this strange obsession. "Walt," he said, "we're in the motion picture business, not the roller coaster business." After a while, Roy stopped trying to change Walt's mind. He just changed the subject. "Whenever I'd go down and talk to my brother about the park," Walt later recalled, "he'd suddenly get busy with financial reports. So I stopped bringing it up around Roy."

> *"Walt wasn't afraid to take a chance with anything. He put up everything he had to build Disneyland, every bit. He sold his second home in Palm Springs, he cashed in his life insurance, he borrowed, begged, whatever he had to do. He held nothing back, he had nothing left. He risked everything on a dream."*
>
> KEN ANDERSON,
> IMAGINEER

Walt decided instead to do an end run around his brother. He began assembling funds, starting with his own personal savings account. Then he borrowed $100,000 against his life insurance and sold his vacation home at Smoke Tree Ranch. Lilly was not happy to see Walt gambling everything on this crazy dream, but she couldn't talk him out of it. One of Walt's strongest traits was a thing he called *stick-to-it-ivity*. Once Walt was committed to an idea, there was no stopping him.

After Walt had borrowed every cent the banks would lend him and sold everything he had to sell, he was still millions short. Where would the rest of the money come from? During one sleepless night in 1953, the answer came to him: *Television!*

The three networks had almost unlimited supplies of money—and Walt's studio had the ability to produce something the networks wanted: Disney programming. Walt had already produced two top-rated Christmas specials in 1950 and '51. Why not give one of the networks a weekly TV show and part ownership of the park in exchange for cash? The network would get a successful weekly series. Walt would get his park. It was the perfect win-win solution.

Walt later recalled, "Every time I thought about television, I thought of this park. I knew that if I did anything like the park, then I would have a medium like television to let the people know about it." Walt went to the two biggest networks, NBC and CBS, both of which were eager to air Disney programming. The moment he mentioned his park, however, the network big-shots tried to change the subject. They wanted no part of Disneyland.

Next, Walt turned to the smaller third network, the American Broadcasting Company. He made his pitch to ABC executive Donn Tatum (who later became a senior exec with Disney). "He didn't have any visual material to refer to," Tatum recalled. "Even so, he drew such a dramatic, vivid description that I left with a great deal of enthusiasm. But our people seemed not to understand what he was talking about." ABC turned Walt down.

Walt refused to accept failure as final. He was obsessed with his dream. There had to be *some* way to finance it. The test of Walt's stick-to-it-ivity was just beginning.

The road to Anaheim

One of the great paradoxes of Walt's life is that he never really cared very much about money, yet he was continually forced to think about money. Why? Because his dreams were so expensive. "If you want to know the real secret of Walt Disney's success," said Ward Kimball, "it's that he never tried to make money."

Imagineer Harriet Burns told me, "Walt was a simple, honest, basic person with Midwestern values. An ethical man. Nothing he did was about money. It was always about the project."

> *"I could never convince the financiers that Disneyland was feasible, because dreams offer too little collateral."*
>
> WALT DISNEY

Walt explained his own views about money this way: "I've always been bored with just making money. I've wanted to do things, I wanted to build things. Get something going. People look at me in different ways. Some of them say, 'The guy has no regard for money.' That's not true. I have had regard for money. But I'm not like some people who worship money as something you've got to have piled up somewhere. I've only thought of money in one way, and that is to do something with it, you see?"

That was Walt's mindset in the early 1950s, as he was looking for ways to finance Disneyland. During that time, he averaged four or five hours of sleep per night. His waking hours were focused on either planning the park or brainstorming new financing schemes.

One unlikely financing scheme turned out to be amazingly effective: He asked his employees to lend him money. The first person Walt asked was

Hazel George, the studio nurse. When Walt hesitantly approached Hazel for money, she said that not only would she invest in the park, but she knew that other employees were also eager to chip in. Hazel organized an informal employees' group called the Disneyland Backers and Boosters. When Roy saw that Disney employees believed in Walt's dream, he was forced to reconsider his opposition.

In 1952, Roy allocated $10,000 to research and develop plans for the park. It was a drop in the bucket, but Walt was cheered by Roy's change of heart. In December of that year, Walt founded Walt Disney, Inc.—later renamed WED Enterprises after the initials for Walter Elias Disney (it is today known as Walt Disney Imagineering, Inc.). The new company had one purpose: to design and build Disneyland.

Walt staffed his new company with people he called "Imagineers," a word that combined "imagination" with "engineers." The first Imagineers came from many backgrounds: artist Ken Anderson (designer of the Fantasyland dark rides), artist John Hench (Tomorrowland designer), vehicle designer Bob Gurr (Main Street vehicles, Autopia cars), machinist Roger Broggie (Audio-Animatronics engineer), and sculptor Wathel Rogers (Audio-Animatronics sculptor).

WED Enterprises was Walt's own company, operating out of space rented from the Disney studio in Burbank. Walt owned all the stock and called all the shots. He enjoyed spending time at WED, huddling with his Imagineers. Harriet Burns recalls, "I worked in the art department at WED. Walt would come down to work with us. He'd sit on a stool and relax with us because we were so informal. He was always up, always positive. How many CEOs would come down to work with his employees like that?"

In July 1953, Walt commissioned the Stanford Research Institute (SRI) to locate the best possible site for the park. The location that headed the list was a little farming town called Anaheim, thirty-five miles south of Los Angeles. Interstate 5 was then under construction and offered easy access via Harbor Boulevard.

Retired Disneyland executive Jack Lindquist told me, "Walt's critics thought, 'This nut is going to build a seventeen-million dollar amusement park in the town Jack Benny always made fun of.' But look what happened. Disneyland turned little Anaheim into a world-class tourist destination. It lifted the economy of the entire area. Knott's Berry Farm in nearby Buena Vista Park became a much bigger attraction merely because of its proximity to Disneyland."

Selling the dream

In the fall of 1953, Walt again decided to approach the TV industry for funding. He took his plan to the Disney board of directors, and the board decided to send Roy to New York to make the pitch. Walt chuckled at the irony. His brother—once Disneyland's staunchest foe—was appointed top salesman for the idea.

Roy contacted the brass at NBC, hoping to set up a meeting within a few weeks. NBC responded: Would next week be all right? Roy agreed— then panicked. The network execs would never grasp Walt's vision unless they could *see* it. Roy told Walt he needed a detailed rendering of the Disneyland plan—and he needed it in a matter of days.

> *"All I know about money is that I have to have it to do things. I neither wish nor intend to amass a personal fortune. Money may worry me, but it does not excite me. Ideas excite me."*
>
> WALT DISNEY

It was a tall order, but Walt knew the man for the job: Herb Ryman, a noted designer with a fine arts background. On Saturday morning, September 26, 1953, Walt called Ryman and asked him to come down to the studio. Ryman met Walt at the Buena Vista entrance twenty minutes later. Walt ushered him inside and they sat down in Walt's office. "Herbie," Walt said, "I'm going to build an amusement park, and I want you to help me."

"You mean, you're finally going to build Mickey Mouse Park across the street?"

"No," Walt said, "we're going to build something big. We don't have the site yet, but it's going to be huge. We're calling it Disneyland. Roy's going to New York on Monday morning. He's got a meeting with the boys with the money. We're going to need millions. Roy wants to take a rendering of Disneyland with him to show the investors."

"Good idea," Ryman said. "Can I see the rendering?"

"You're going to draw it, Herbie. That's why you're here."

Ryman's jaw dropped. "What? You said Roy's leaving Monday morning! Today's Saturday. You want me to do an entire rendering in two days?"

"I know you can do this," Walt said. "And I'll be with you the whole time—even if it takes all night."

"It can't be done, Walt," Ryman insisted. "I'll embarrass both of us."

Walt turned away, and his voice choked. "Herbie," Walt said, "this is my biggest dream. I need your help—you're the only one who can do this."

Herb Ryman couldn't say no to Walt. So they worked together through Saturday and Sunday. Walt filled Herb's mind with word-pictures, and Herb created a visual representation. In two days, working around the clock, Ryman created a beautifully detailed aerial rendering. It was all there—the elevated train station, Town Square, Main Street, the central hub, the castle, the riverboat, the rocket ship towering over Tomorrowland—just as Walt had envisioned.

On Monday morning, armed with Ryman's artwork and a six-page printed prospectus, Roy and WED Enterprises chief Dick Irvine boarded a plane for New York. Over the next few days, they met with executives at NBC and CBS—meetings that Roy later described as "exasperating." As before, both networks wanted Disney TV shows, but rejected the park.

Tired and frustrated, Roy returned to his suite at the Waldorf Astoria and, purely on the spur of the moment, placed a call to Leonard Goldenson at ABC. Goldenson agreed to come to Roy's hotel and discuss a TV deal. After studying the Ryman rendering for a few minutes, Goldenson smiled broadly and said, "Tell Walt he can have whatever he wants. We are ready to go forward with him." And the deal was done.

The ABC network put up half a million dollars and co-signed bank loans for an additional $4.5 million. In return, Walt gave ABC a 34.5 percent share of the Disneyland theme park, plus a weekly hour-long anthology show called *Disneyland*. The other partners in the Disneyland ownership group were Walt Disney Productions ($500,000 invested, 34.5 percent ownership), Western Printing and Lithographing, publishers of Little Golden Books ($200,000 invested, 13.8 percent ownership), and Walt himself ($250,000 invested, 17.2 percent ownership).

The ownership group had assembled just under $6 million in capital and loan guarantees—well short of the $17 million that would eventually be needed. But Walt's television deal would enable him to close the funding gap. When the *Disneyland* show premiered on ABC on October 27, 1954, millions of kids tuned in—but so did a lot of powerful financiers. What they saw looked like $uccess with a capital $. They quickly lined up to lend Walt more money.

Bruce DuMont, founder of Chicago's Museum of Broadcast Communications, praised Walt as a television pioneer. "Walt realized he had a brand name at the motion-picture box office which was indelibly etched in the culture," he said. "Then, along came this new thing called television, and he realized that it would be a phenomenal delivery system for his motion picture business. He also realized that the brand name could be expanded into theme parks. With the television broadcast going into millions of homes, it solidified the association with family entertainment and became the vehicle to promote the theme parks, too. I think that may make him the father of commercial synergy."

> *"Predicting Disneyland would be a colossal flop was my second biggest mistake. My first biggest mistake was not buying Disneyland stock."*
>
> CHARLES SHOWS
> WRITER-PRODUCER

Television had swung the financial momentum in Walt's favor, giving him everything he needed to build his Magic Kingdom. Through hard work and stick-to-it-ivity, Walt had finally sold his dream. Now all he had to do was build it.

A groundbreaking year

In early 1954, the Disney company issued a press release announcing that a site had been located for the new Disney amusement park—in the San Fernando Valley. While the public's attention was diverted fifty miles north of the actual site, Disney quietly bought up 160 acres of orange groves in Anaheim. In all, seventeen families sold their farms to Disney.

Ron Dominguez was born and raised on one of those Anaheim citrus ranches. "I grew up in the farm area of Orange County, California," Ron told me. "At that time, in the early 1950s, the area was ninety-five percent citrus groves and five percent walnut orchards. The only houses around were farm houses. Several times, our family watched as this big black Cadillac drove very slowly past our property, surveying the area. No one had a clue who these people were or what they were up to."

Today, the "Pirates of the Caribbean" attraction covers the land where Ron Dominguez was born. After his family moved out, Ron would come back week after week and watch as bulldozers uprooted orange trees and steam shovels scooped out a river channel.

On Disneyland's opening day in 1955, Ron was there, working as a ticket-taker. He spent the rest of his career with Disney, rising to the position of executive vice president before retiring in 1994. If you visit the Market House on Main Street, you'll notice that one of the windows reads, "Orange Grove Property Mgt.—'We'll care for your property as if it were our own.'—Ron Dominguez, Owner." Ron Dominquez did care for Disneyland as if it were his own, because Disneyland was his birthplace.

Ground was broken for the park on July 16, 1954. The first task after groundbreaking was to clear the land of orange trees. Wanting to preserve as many mature trees as possible, WED landscapers spent days walking the site, tying colored ribbons around the trees. They explained the color codes to the bulldozer operator: blue ribbons on trees to be removed, red ribbons on trees to be spared. A few days later, almost every tree had been uprooted. It seems the bulldozer driver was colorblind.

Soon after excavation began, Walt drove Art Linkletter to the site, along with some of Walt's consultants from the Stanford Research Institute. As Linkletter recalled that day, "We drove and drove out to this remote spot in Orange County. I looked around and I couldn't believe it! We were miles from any major population center. I

> "The greatest piece of urban design in the United States today is Disneyland. . . . I find more to learn in the standards that have been set and the goals that have been achieved in the development of Disneyland than in any other single piece of physical development in the country."
>
> JAMES W. ROUSE
> URBAN PLANNER, URBAN DESIGN
> CONFERENCE, HARVARD UNIVERSITY, 1963

wondered if Walt had lost his mind! I thought, 'My gosh, he wants to put a bunch of roller-coasters out in the middle of these orange groves? Ridiculous!'"

Walt gave Linkletter a tour of a Disneyland that existed only in his own mind. He described in glowing detail the various realms of his Magic Kingdom: Main Street, Adventureland, Frontierland, Fantasyland and Tomorrowland. He envisioned crowds streaming into the place from all over the world. "Art," he said, "you've got to get in on this. Just buy up property all around the park, and in a year or two, you can sell it to developers for hotel and restaurant sites. You'll make a fortune!"

Linkletter looked around—but he couldn't see what Walt saw. So he turned Walt down. Art Linkletter once figured up how much money he would have made if he had taken Walt's advice. According to his calculations, every step he took that day was worth about $3 million dollars—and he let it all slip through his fingers.

Walt always regretted not being able to buy up the land around the park. "If we could have bought more land," he said, "we *would* have bought it. Then we would have had more control and it wouldn't look like a second-rate Las Vegas around here. We'd have had a little better chance to control it. But we ran out of money."

The year 1954 was a groundbreaking year in many ways. Not only was

> "Walt loved the story of Davy Crockett, and he lived by Davy's motto: 'Be sure you are right, then go ahead.' That's why Walt put Davy Crockett on TV. He made the kind of entertainment he liked to watch."
>
> STACIA MARTIN
> DISNEY ARTIST AND HISTORIAN

ground broken at Disneyland that year, but there was a groundbreaking event in Walt's family: On May 9, 1954, Walt's daughter Diane married college football star Ron Miller. Ron played tight end for USC, and later played a season with the Los Angeles Rams before going to work for the Disney company.

More ground was broken on October 27, 1954, with the debut of the *Disneyland* weekly TV series. Walt hosted the show, and his face soon became recognized from coast to coast. On December 15, a *Disneyland* episode, "Davy Crockett, Indian Fighter," ignited the nationwide Davy Crockett craze.

I had the privilege of interviewing "Davy Crockett" star Fess Parker. He even agreed to sing "The Ballad of Davy Crockett" with me (fortunately, no tape recorders were running). I asked Fess to share his memories of Walt and the "Davy Crocket" series.

"The Davy Crockett project was clear in Walt's mind," Fess told me. "He was searching for the right actor. Just about every Hollywood action guy was under consideration for the role—George Montgomery, Ronald Reagan, and others. Someone told Walt he should take a look at a movie called *Them!*, about radioactive giant ants attacking Los Angeles. The star was Jim Arness, and one of Walt's associates thought that Arness would make a good Davy Crockett. Jim went on, of course, to become Marshall Dillon on *Gunsmoke.*

"While Walt was screening the picture to scout Jim Arness, he happened to spot me in a small role—so small that if you looked away to put cream in your coffee, you'd miss me altogether. Walt said, 'Who's that fella?' Nobody knew. So Tom Blackburn, one of Walt's producers, got ahold of Warner Brothers and got my name. They called me out to the studio for an interview."

Even in a minor role, Fess Parker had screen presence. At 6' 6", Fess Parker is truly larger than life—yet he also has a folksy charm that adds an extra dimension to his heroic portrayal of "The King of the Wild Frontier."

> "Walt Disney's 'Davy Crockett' represented values like truth, honor, patriotism, virtue, duty, chivalry and sincerity—the values that Walt Disney himself felt were important."
>
> PAUL F. ANDERSON
> DISNEY HISTORIAN AND EDITOR,
> PERSISTENCE OF VISION

"I was twenty-nine when Walt Disney interviewed me for 'Davy Crockett,'" he said. "I brought my little guitar with me, even though I wasn't much of a singer. After Walt and I talked for a while, he said, 'Why don't you play me a little tune?' I had written a song called 'Lonely,' about a guy who had broken up with his girl and was riding on a train. I did the sound of a train whistle in the song. I later found out that Walt's other passion in life was railroads. I suppose that didn't hurt my chances.

"'Davy Crockett' was a lot of fun to make, but I had no idea it would become so successful. Nobody predicted that, not even Walt. For 'Davy Crockett' to take off like it did, it took a perfect alignment of the heavens and every force in the universe.

"Walt spotted me, yanked me out of obscurity, and opened every door in the world to me. He was awfully happy with the success of 'Davy Crockett,' but no happier than I was. I'll always be grateful to Walt. He gave me something in life that no one else could have given me."

Though Disney would only receive $300,000 from ABC for the Crockett series, Walt lavished $700,000 on the production. He had the series shot in color, even though it was broadcast in black and white. The TV segments were later re-edited into a successful theatrical film, *Davy Crockett, King of the Wild Frontier*, which earned $2.5 million at the box office.

Asking for the impossible

Walt hired a retired Navy admiral, Joseph Fowler, as his senior vice president in charge of Disneyland construction. Fowler had been chief of the San Francisco Naval Yard during WWII, and was known for finding creative solutions to difficult problems.

Walt knew Disneyland inside and out. He could recite every detail of every blueprint from memory. But one thing he couldn't grasp was building codes. After 30 years as a movie producer, he couldn't understand why Disneyland couldn't be built with the same materials used on a movie set—plaster and plywood. That's why Walt needed Joe Fowler.

One day, Walt toured the Disneyland site with Admiral Fowler and Dick Irvine, Disneyland's principal designer. First stop on the tour was the Main Street train station, where the foundation was going in. As tons of wet cement slopped over the framework of steel rebar, Walt turned to Admiral Fowler and complained, "Joe, by the time you've buried all my money in the ground, I won't have enough left to put on a show!"

Fowler patiently but firmly explained the facts of construction life to Walt Disney. He told Walt all about earthquake safety and the need to build Disneyland to last. Walt grudgingly agreed that all those tons of concrete were probably necessary—but he continued to mutter about the cost.

Construction efforts were hampered by frequent rains—the wettest season in Anaheim history. Later, when the weather cooperated, the workforce balked—a plumbers strike and an asphalt workers strike nearly kept Disneyland from opening on schedule. When there was no paving material available in the Anaheim area, Admiral Fowler trucked in asphalt from San Diego at unbelievable expense.

Walt soon realized that assembling the financing for Disneyland—which had seemed impossibly hard at the time—was a piece of cake compared with actually *building* the dream. The construction phase was the supreme test of Walt's stick-to-it-ivity.

> *"I'm afraid if I'd been running this place we would have stopped several times en route because of the problems. Walt has the stick-to-it-iveness."*
>
> ROY DISNEY
> WALT'S BROTHER AND PARTNER

One major problem involved the Rivers of America, home to the Mark Twain riverboat. Engineers dug the river channel then filled it with water. By the next day, the water had soaked into the sandy basin. No wonder the land had been an orange grove before—it had excellent drainage! The construction company trucked in clay, covered the bottom of the channel, and filled it again. The water stayed put—problem solved, lesson learned.

And building Fantasyland was no one's fantasy. The flying elephants of the "Dumbo" ride were built by the same movie special-effects team that constructed the giant squid in *20,000 Leagues Under the Sea*. Molded and painted in Burbank, the Dumbos were shipped to Anaheim and attached to the arms of the ride mechanism. The engineers powered up the ride—but the elephants refused to fly. The Dumbos were too heavy for the motors that raised the arms. A new, more powerful motor was ordered; the ride opened a month late.

The "Casey Junior Circus Train" also posed a problem. There is a point in the ride where the train chugs up a steep grade, huffing, "I think I can, I think I can!" But it couldn't. When the Imagineers tested the train, it stalled, then rolled backward. The track had to be pulled up and the hill re-graded.

Tomorrowland was an even bigger nightmare than Fantasyland. In the early stages of construction, attention was primarily focused on Main Street, Adventureland, Frontierland and Fantasyland. Construction problems were so big and the costs so high elsewhere in the park that it was easy to say, "We'll deal with Tomorrowland tomorrow!" In fall 1954, Admiral Fowler told Walt, "Let's just hang an 'Under Construction' sign at the entrance to Tomorrowland." The idea didn't sit well with Walt—but Admiral Fowler made a convincing case. Tomorrowland would open late.

In January 1955, however, Walt reversed himself. Disneyland, he said, wouldn't be complete without Tomorrowland. One way or another, Walt's world of tomorrow had to open on-time—even though construction on Tomorrowland hadn't even begun!

> *"On my first visit [to Disneyland], I accompanied one of the great theatrical and creative minds of our time, Charles Laughton. I've never had such a day full of zest and high good humor. Mr. Laughton is no easy mark; he has a gimlet eye and a searching mind. Yet he saw (and I found) in Disneyland vast reserves of imagination never before tapped in our country. Disney makes mistakes; what artist doesn't? But when he flies, he really flies."*
>
> RAY BRADBURY
> WRITER

Planting trees upside-down

Bob Gurr joined Disney in 1954 after a year as a car design engineer in Detroit. His job: to design everything on wheels. When Bob started his Disney career in November 1954, he arrived at the Burbank studio machine shop where he met head machinist Roger Broggie and a "slightly rumpled-looking guy" who was introduced only as Walt. That's right—Walt Disney.

Gurr recalls, "Walt was collecting a lot of new folks on the studio lot. We were all gonna design Disneyland. . . . Walt said Disneyland would open in just eight months. Oh my gosh!"

In designing cars for the "Tomorrowland Autopia," Bob Gurr used the same process he had learned in Detroit. After drawing the car, the designer creates a full-size clay model, called a "clay buck." The clay buck is used to make the mold for fiberglass car bodies.

"The clay model weighed about four or five hundred pounds," Bob told me. "I had it built in the garage of Joe Thompson, a teacher at Pasadena's Art Center College of Design. Some of Joe's students volunteered to help me build the model, which was a good thing, because Walt was out of money. So the Autopia attraction was partially built with free student labor.

"We got the clay buck built, but the thing was so big and heavy that it was going to be very hard to move. I was afraid the clay might crack if we tried to move it. We needed to get Walt to approve it, and I was thinking, 'How am I going to get this thing to the studio?' I was new there and I figured a big, important studio head would never come out to the garage.

"So I went to Walt's office and asked him, 'When can I bring the clay model over for you to approve?' He said, 'You're going to bring that big heavy thing over here, just so I can look at it? Why?' I said, 'Well, I just thought you'd be too busy to come out to North Hollywood.' He said, 'Nonsense. We can all drive there in a few minutes. Let's go.'

"So we all piled into Bill Cottrell's Cadillac—Bill was Walt's brother-in-law—and we drove over to the garage. I sat next to Walt and he had his arm over the back of the seat. Bill's car had these white fuzzy seat covers, and the white fuzz got all over Walt's jacket.

"At the garage, Walt walked around the clay buck, checking it from every angle, then he sat down in it. The clay was still sticky, so now Walt had fuzz and clay all over his jacket. He was a mess—but he approved the car for production.

"I never saw Walt act like a big-shot. He had high standards of excellence, but he was never demanding, he never wanted people to go out of their way just to serve him. Fact is, he would go out of his way to save time for us, and that made everything go more smoothly."

Some Disney Imagineers worried about the *Mark Twain* stern-wheel riverboat. The boat was built in two pieces in two different locations—a seeming invitation to Murphy's Law. The 105-foot hull was constructed at the Todd Shipyards in Long Beach, while the three upper decks were constructed in the sound stages at the Disney studio in Burbank. The parts were trucked to Anaheim and joined together in Frontierland. Amazingly, all the parts fit perfectly.

Another attraction built with few hitches was the "Jungle Cruise." Walt and attraction designer Harper Goff originally wanted to use live animals on the ride, but experts convinced Walt it would be impractical. The animals would be difficult to keep in captivity, and tended to sleep during the day. So Walt's movie special-effects team produced a whole zoo of lifelike birds, monkeys, crocodiles, hippos, lions and elephants.

Credit for the realistic look and feel of the "Jungle Cruise" goes to Disneyland's landscaper, Morgan "Bill" Evans. "Trees are living, breathing individuals," Bill Evans once said. "They're alive and respond to the elements. A building doesn't yield to the breeze. I can see the life in the trees by the way they move."

Evans devised some inventive approaches to building a jungle. For example, he took some of the felled orange trees, planted them upside-down, and used their knotted roots to represent exotic jungle vines and branches. He camouflaged pipes, speakers, and utility shacks with dense foliage. Evans' crew secured giant palms and other mature trees by going ahead of freeway construction crews and rescuing trees that had been tagged for destruction.

> *"You could go on the moon trip at Disneyland. You could visit the future! Disneyland was wondrous, because nobody had ever seen anything like it. It gave you the experience. It wasn't just about looking at exhibits—it was about taking rides!"*
>
> GREGORY BENFORD
> SCIENCE FICTION WRITER

Years later, Walt kidded his master landscaper. "When this place opened," he said, "we didn't have enough money to finish the landscaping, and I had Bill Evans go out and put Latin tags on all of the weeds. . . . Of course, to Bill Evans, every weed has a Latin name."

Story artist Art Scott flew with Walt on a chartered plane shortly before Disneyland opened. "As we were taking off," Art recalled, "Walt was saying, 'I spoke to the pilot and I hope he remembers—I asked him to fly over the park. There's nothing like seeing Disneyland from the air!' Then Walt looked out the window and said, 'He's doing it! He's doing it!' He pointed out all the stuff—'There's the train station! There's the castle!' He was all excited, like a little boy with his giant toy down there."

My friend, Peggy Matthews Rose, was growing up in Orange County, California, when Walt's Magic Kingdom was rising up above the orange groves. "On Wednesday nights in 1954," she told me, "our family gathered in front of the magic box in the living room and Walt would tell us about the wonderful kingdom he was building. Sometimes, we would get in the car and drive down Harbor Boulevard. My heart would flutter like Tinker Bell's wings as I spotted the turrets of the castle above the trees. Like most five-year-old girls, I knew I was really a princess. I could hardly wait for my castle to be completed."

For reasons that are still unknown, the Anaheim town planner assigned an unusual address to Disneyland: 1313 Harbor Boulevard. Any odd last digit could have been assigned to the kingdom on the 1300 block of Harbor, so why 1313—a doubly unlucky number? Perhaps Walt asked for that number as a way of thumbing his nose at all the "experts" who had predicted his park would fail. Not only did he defy conventional wisdom by building the park his way, but he even tempted fate by giving Disneyland an "unlucky" address.

The dream becomes reality

An interviewer once asked fantasy writer Ray Bradbury to describe the city of the future. "It would look like Disneyland," Bradbury replied. "They've done everything right. It has hundreds of trees and thousands of flowers they don't need, but which they put in anyway. It has fountains and places to sit. I've visited thirty or forty times over the years, and there's very little I would change."

Bradbury is right. Every city in the world should be as clean, beautiful, and inviting to visit. To call Disneyland an "amusement park" is to miss the point. Disneyland is the city of the future—an idealized and utopian future.

During the earliest design stages of Disneyland, Walt told his designers and Imagineers, "This is a magic place. The important thing is the castle. Make it tall enough to be seen from all around the park. It's got to keep people oriented. And I want a hub at the end of Main Street, where all the other lands will radiate from, like the spokes in a wheel. I've been studying the way people go to museums and other entertainment places. Everybody's got tired feet. I don't want that to happen in this place. I want a place for people to sit down and where old folks can say, 'You kids run on. I'll meet you there in a half hour.' Disneyland is going to be a place where you can't get lost or tired unless you want to."

"When Walt Disney dreams he doesn't fool around. Furthermore, he invariably makes his dreams come true—in a dozen different mediums. 'Maybe it's because I don't know enough to realize what's impossible,' Walt commented at lunch the other day. 'I've found that guys who know too much don't do things.'"

BURRIS JENKINS JR.
HEARST NEWSPAPER COLUMNIST, MAY 1959

Main Street is Walt's red carpet, his visual way of saying, "Welcome to my hometown." Every detail is carefully designed to produce an effect on the senses, including the sense of smell. As you pass the Candy Palace, you are greeted by the scent of vanilla (or, at Christmastime, peppermint). Main Street guides you to the central hub. From the hub, you are just a few steps from any realm you wish to visit, from the Old West to a European fairyland, from exotic jungles to the unexplored reaches of future shock.

Towering above the trees at strategically selected sites in the parks are marquee-like attractions designed to catch the eye from a distance. Walt called them "wienies." A "wienie" (wiener, frankfurter, hot dog) is, of course, a long sausage-like meat product which Walt considered a delicacy. One of his favorite treats, after a long day at the studio, was to come home, head for the kitchen, and eat cold wieners straight from the fridge.

During the design phase, Walt told his designers, "What you need is a wienie, which says to people 'come this way.' People won't go down a long corridor unless there's something promising at the end. You have to have something that beckons to them." In Disneyland, "Sleeping Beauty's Castle" is the grandest wienie of them all—the most visible symbol of Disneyland. The castle draws crowds down Main Street, past the central hub, and across the drawbridge into Fantasyland. Other wienies included the Main Street train station, the rocket ship in Tomorrowland and the twin smokestacks of the *Mark Twain* riverboat in Frontierland.

The "Tempus Fugit" party

As opening day drew near, Walt couldn't have been happier. For one thing, he was now a grandpa! His daughter Diane had given birth to a son, and Walt delighted in his new role as baby Christopher's grandfather. To top it off, Disneyland was about to become a reality.

Just four days before the grand opening, Walt and Lillian celebrated their thirtieth wedding anniversary. Eager to show off his new park, Walt invited family and friends to a "Tempus Fugit Party" at Disneyland (*tempus fugit* is Latin for "time flies"). Scheduled for six in the evening on Wednesday, July 13, the invitation specified, "No gifts please, we have everything, including a grandson!"

For a while, it seemed there would be no party. When six o'clock rolled around, not a single guest had arrived. Jack Sayers, then chairman of Disneyland's Park Operating Committee, recalled, "I was out at the main gate, waiting with Walt for the invited guests. By six o'clock, nobody had shown up. Turned out, the buses and cars had been caught in traffic. Walt was not a patient man. We paced and smoked together, and he kept asking me, 'Where are they?' I think he blamed me for the fact that everyone was late! Finally, the guests began to arrive and Walt quit pacing, greeting each guest by name."

Guests were guided through the gate and on to Main Street. There, horse-drawn surreys chauffeured them to Frontierland for a reception at the Golden Horseshoe Saloon. Once everyone had arrived, the party moved to the *Mark Twain* for the riverboat's maiden voyage.

The evening was warm and a light breeze ruffled the waters. The Firehouse Five Plus Two (a Dixieland band founded by Ward Kimball) played in the grand salon on the second deck as the boat slipped her moorings. Waiters passed among the guests, serving mint juleps in tall glasses. Walt and Lillian moved though the crowd, greeting everyone. Walt's smile couldn't get any broader—his ears were in the way.

When the *Mark Twain* returned to the dock, the party moved back to the Golden Horseshoe Saloon where comedian Wally Boag and singer Donald Novis gave the very first performance of a show that would eventually enter the *Guinness Book of World Records* as the longest-running stage show in history (over 50,000 performances). Years later, Walt recalled how he hired Novis and Boag.

"Walt was a perfectionist. One time he thought the sign in front of the Golden Horseshoe was crooked and told us. We said, 'No, we measured, it's level.' But, to humor him, we checked it again. He was right. Walt had an eye for stuff like that. Things had to be done right."

JIM CORA
FORMER DISNEYLAND EXECUTIVE

"I had known Donald Novis for years," Walt said. "I told him, 'There's something you can do for me, Don. Can you get me a comic?' He said, 'Yes, I know just the fellow.' So I said, 'Let's interview him over at the studio.' So a few days later, in came this fellow. He had a little bag with him, and in the bag he had a dummy and some bagpipes."

Wally Boag vividly recalls that day. "I auditioned for Walt at the Burbank studio," he told me. "I was thirty-four at the time. There was a piano player there for the audition, so I did my dance number, my ventriloquist act, I played the bagpipes, and made some balloon animals. After the audition, Walt told me, 'You know, we're putting on a show at the Golden Horseshoe in Frontierland. Now, this is Disneyland, and we're a family place—' And I stopped him right there. I said, 'I can do the job for you. I have these routines I've been doing in nightclubs—but I can clean them up.' Walt laughed. He liked that."

The night of the anniversary party, Walt and Lillian, with daughters Diane and Sharon, watched the show from their box near the stage. At one point, Wally Boag (as the gun-slinging cowboy Pecos Bill) got into a mock gun battle with Walt. Wally fired blanks, and Walt pointed his fingers and shouted, "Bang! Bang!" The audience roared its approval. Then Walt climbed over the railing and jumped down to the stage.

Diane Disney Miller later recalled how she felt as her father—and her child's grandfather—leaped over that railing. "I think everyone got a bit worried," she said. "I know I did. When Dad got to the stage, he stood

"Walt was a sweetheart, a nice guy. He was a genius, but he saw himself as a regular guy. He was very understanding and I never saw him mad. If I messed up something on the set, he would say, 'Oh, that was funny, Betty, leave it in.'"

BETTY TAYLOR
"SLUE FOOT SUE," STAR OF THE
"GOLDEN HORSESHOE REVUE"

there beaming at everyone. He was so happy."

The audience clapped and stomped, and Lillian went to the stage, trying to pull her ham of a husband off—but Walt refused to go. He was having too much fun! Finally, the band started playing, and Lillian urged Walt to dance with her.

Walt's finest dream had come true, and his family and friends were all at his side to enjoy it with him. The party finally ended, but Walt was still in a party mood as he headed for the car along with Lilly, Diane, and son-in-law Ron Miller.

"Dad just climbed in the back seat of the car," Diane recalls. "He had a map of Disneyland, and he rolled it up and tooted in my ear as if with a toy trumpet. He sang for a while—then, before I knew it, everything was silent in the back seat. I looked around and there he was, his arms folded around the map like a boy with a toy trumpet, sound asleep."

Dateline: Disneyland

The Disneyland opening ceremonies were scheduled for live coverage on the ABC television network. Walt chose his friend, Art Linkletter, to host the show. Several months before the opening, Walt strolled over to Art's house for a visit. "Art," he said, "I want you to be the master of ceremonies for the Disneyland grand opening—but I can't negotiate this kind of thing directly with you. Why don't you have an agent like everyone else?"

"You know me, Walt," Linkletter said. "I've always handled my own business and made my own deals. Just tell me what you want me to do and I'll do it."

"You don't understand," Walt said. "I can't afford to pay you much. We've had some huge cost overruns building this park, and I've had to mortgage the studio. I can't afford to pay you what you're worth."

Linkletter shrugged. "Pay me union scale. That's fine with me."

"Scale!" Walt said, astounded. "But that's only a couple hundred bucks!"

"Walt," Linkletter said, "this is a world event! I want to be part of it." Then he added, with a wink, "Of course, once I have you in my debt, you'll be happy to give me the photo concession at Disneyland for the next ten years. I'll pay your standard concession fee if you'll let me handle all the film and cameras sold at the park."

Walt grinned. "It's a deal," he said. "We'll be broadcasting from various locations, so we need two co-hosts, and they have to be good ad-libbers. Who do you recommend?"

Linkletter didn't hesitate. "I know two fellas who would be perfect for the job: Bob Cummings and Ronnie Reagan." So Walt had his broadcast team—genial TV host Art Linkletter, popular actor Robert Cummings, and future president Ronald Reagan.

Shortly before the park opened, Walt addressed the Disneyland employees. "To make the dream of Disneyland come true," he said, "took the combined skills and talents of artisans, carpenters, engineers, scientists and planners. The dream they built now becomes your heritage. It is you who will make Disneyland truly a magic kingdom and a happy place for the millions of guests who will visit us now and in future years. In creating happiness for our guests, I hope that you will find happiness in your work and in being an important part of Disneyland."

There was still an enormous amount of work to do before opening day. Painters applied second coats, plumbers installed restroom fixtures, and asphalt workers spread blacktop and hoped it would harden in time. Construction crews and TV crews tripped over each other scrambling to get their work done before daybreak.

Walt spent much of Saturday night in the cramped spaces of the

"I had been doing the opening of World's Fairs for many years before the opening of Disneyland. I'm an ad-libber, so chaos is made for me. I love the catch-as-catch-can atmosphere. I love interviewing people who don't even know they're on the air. That's my business. So this show was made to order."

ART LINKLETTER

"20,000 Leagues Under the Sea" exhibit, spray-painting the backdrop behind the giant squid. Imagineer Ken Anderson was there too, trying to get the electrical and mechanical parts of the exhibit to work. Sometime in the wee hours of the morning, Walt and Ken decided to call it quits. They had given it their best shot, but the exhibit would have to open late.

They left the building together, walked up Main Street, and sat down on the curb near Town Square to take a much-needed break. They hadn't been there more than a couple of minutes before someone ran to them, shouting, "There's no power on the Toad ride! Somebody cut the wires!"

Walt groaned.

"Don't worry, Walt," Ken said, rising wearily to his feet. "I'll take care of it."

As Ken left for Fantasyland, Walt stood and stretched. He decided to take a final inspection tour, then try to get some sleep.

Arriving at "Mr. Toad's Wild Ride," Ken Anderson was relieved to find that the power cables hadn't been cut, just disconnected. In fact, several other Fantasyland rides were disconnected as well. Anderson sighed and went to work. "I went through all the wires," he later recalled, "and, with some help from the electrician, we got them fixed so that everything worked." (It turned out that the sabotage was related to a dispute between two unions.)

After an hour or so, Anderson got the power back on. But one thing *wasn't* functioning on opening day: Ken Anderson himself. After fixing the problem with the electrical box, he fell asleep in back of the "Mr. Toad" attraction. He snored through Disneyland's first day.

Walt finished his final inspection tour with a stroll up Main Street. Then he climbed the stairs to his apartment over the firehouse, fell into bed, and was instantly asleep. During the next hour, he was continually awakened by people needing a last-minute decision. Finally, Walt took the phone off the hook. He slept for a couple of hours.

Rising soon after dawn, Walt dressed and mentally prepared himself for the big day. He headed to the door of his apartment, pulled the handle— but the door was stuck. Try as he might, he couldn't open it. Walt was trapped in his own apartment. Tacky paint had sealed the door shut. Walt had to phone for a maintenance crew to free him from the room.

Minutes after being freed, Walt dashed to Town Square, where he huddled with ABC executives and directors, discussing camera setups and logistics for the show. The ninety-minute TV special, *Dateline: Disneyland*, would air live at 4:30 P.M.

Walt's brother Roy, meanwhile, was on the semi-completed Interstate 5, stuck in traffic. It was early Sunday morning, when the roads should have been practically deserted, yet traffic on the southbound 5 was bumper-to-bumper, creeping toward Anaheim at fifteen miles an hour. A helpless victim of the gridlock he had helped create, Roy could do nothing but follow the traffic down the freeway, onto Harbor Boulevard, and through the Disneyland main gate.

> *"Walt practically lived at the park while it was being built."*
>
> LILLIAN DISNEY

No admission was charged on opening day. Only invited guests with VIP passes were supposed to show up. The Disney company had issued 11,000 passes to studio employees, celebrities, and the news media. Unfortunately, someone had forged thousands of passes and sold them on the black market. Instead of 11,000 people, *more than 28,000 showed up*. One enterprising scoundrel had even placed a folding ladder over Disneyland's back fence, near the Frontierland stables. He let people climb into the park for five bucks a head.

The front gates opened promptly at 10 A.M., and the crowd surged past the giant flower-bed face of Mickey Mouse, through the underpass, and onto Main Street. Walt watched from his apartment over the firehouse as his dream came true and his park filled with people. At his side were the Mouseketeers, whose ABC television series, *The Mickey Mouse Club*, would premiere on October 3. Mouseketeer Sharon Baird was twelve years old at the time, and she stood next to Walt, watching from the window as the crowd streamed past.

"When I looked up at him," she recalled, "he had his hands behind his back, a grin from ear to ear, and I could see a lump in his throat and a tear streaming down his cheek. He had realized his dream."

But for many opening day participants, Walt's dream quickly became a nightmare.

Black Sunday

To Disneyland employees, opening day was a disaster—a day they would always remember as "Black Sunday." There were not enough trash cans to contain the litter generated by 28,000 people. Some guests had their clothing ruined by wet paint. Lines were long, and attraction operators compensated by overloading the rides. At one point, the *Mark Twain* riverboat was so crowded that water washed over the deck and the skipper feared that the boat would capsize.

The park had been stocked with food and drink for the 11,000 invited guests—but *more than two and a half times that number* had flooded the park. As a result, Disneyland restaurants ran out of food before the end of the lunch hour.

And then there was the heat. By noon, the temperature topped 100 degrees Fahrenheit. The freshly laid asphalt on Main Street resembled hot fudge. Some women walked right out of their shoes, leaving their high heels stuck in the pavement. Before the day was over, almost every ride had broken down at least once because of over-heating or over-crowding. Conditions were so chaotic that the mayor of Anaheim went home in disgust and watched the event on TV.

Visitors complained of too few drinking fountains. Some saw it as a plot to increase sales at the soda fountain. The truth is that a plumbers strike forced Walt to make a choice: drinking fountains or restrooms. Common sense dictated that restrooms had priority.

Walt himself was unaware of the problems. He was focused on the TV show—and at 4:30 P.M., the show went out live to a then-record audience of 90 million viewers. Ronald Reagan hosted the dedication ceremony at Town Square. All of Disneyland became strangely quiet. On the green of Town Square, Walt stood beside California governor Goodwin Knight, along with three military chaplains representing the Protestant, Catholic and Jewish faiths.

Walt stepped forward, grinning broadly, and said, "To all who come to this happy place, welcome. Disneyland is your land. Here age relives fond memories of the past, and here youth may savor the challenge and promise of the future. Disneyland is dedicated to the ideals, the dreams, and the hard facts which have created America, with the hope that it will be a source of joy and inspiration to all the world."

Then Reverend Glenn Puder, a Presbyterian minister and Walt's nephew, stepped forward and said, "I have long been aware of the spiritual motivation in the heart of this man who has dreamed Disneyland into being. Let us join him, then, in dedicating these wonder-filled acres to those things dear to his heart and ours—to understanding and good will among men, laughter for children, memories for the mature, and aspiration for young people every-where. And beyond the creeds that would divide us, let us unite in a silent prayer that this and every worthy endeavor may prosper at God's hand."

The United States Marine Band played "The Star Spangled Banner" and the flag was raised—a fitting dis-play of Walt's patriotism. As jets of the California National Guard flew over the park, a parade began down Main Street. Walt and the governor rode at the front of the parade in a 1903 Pierce, followed by scores of TV stars, Disney characters, floats and stagecoaches.

Walt put on quite a show. Disney stars Fess Parker and Buddy Ebsen performed songs from the "Davy Crockett" television episodes. The Firehouse Five Plus Two provided musical entertainment along the riverfront. ABC cameras spotted celebrities all around the park: Frank Sinatra on the "Tomorrowland Autopia," Alan Young emerging from the "Peter Pan Flight," Jerry Colonna at the controls of the "Casey Junior Circus Train," Danny Thomas in Tomorrowland, and Irene Dunne christening the *Mark Twain* riverboat.

"I went to Fantasyland to do a standup in front of 'Mr. Toad's Wild Ride.' They told me, 'When you get there, the mike will be waiting for you.' Well, the microphone was there, all right, but they had left it under a pile of lumber. I couldn't find it! Ninety million viewers saw me waving my arms, scrambling around, looking under trash barrels for my microphone. I eventually found it, and the show went on."

Art Linkletter

During a commercial break, Walt hurried to get to his next camera loca-tion, only to find his pathway blocked by a security guard. "You can't go through there," the man said.

"Do you know who I am?" Walt asked.

"Yes, Mr. Disney," the guard said, "but I have my orders. Nobody can go through here."

Walt raised one threatening eyebrow and said, "Mister, if you don't get out of my way, I'll walk right over the top of you!" The guard stepped aside, and Walt barreled past. That moment was symbolic of all the obstacles and opposition Walt had hurdled to achieve his dream.

Art Linkletter guided his viewers into Tomorrowland and said, "The time is 1986. The place is a city of the future, where a trip to the moon is an everyday thing." Linkletter's crystal ball proved to be a bit murky, however. As we now know, there were no daily trips to the moon in 1986—and Linkletter completely missed the fact that by 1986, his Disneyland co-host, Ronald Reagan, would be in the middle of his second term as president of the United States.

The ninety-minute broadcast was filled with unscripted moments. Viewers saw Art Linkletter in front of "Mr. Toad's Wild Ride," frantically searching for his microphone. They also saw Walt stop in the middle of the Tomorrowland dedication, look questioningly at his camera crew, and say, "I thought I got a signal!" From the shaky camera work to the flubbed lines, it was classic live television.

Buckets of money

The news media savaged Disneyland's opening day, calling Walt's Magic Kingdom over-priced and mismanaged. One newspaper called Disneyland "the $17-million people trap that Mickey Mouse built." Another accused Walt of forcing his guests to buy soda pop by means of "a cunning lack of drinking fountains." Most bet on an early demise.

The scorn of the critics stung Walt deeply—especially the charge of gouging his guests. Former Disneyland executive Jim Cora told me, "Walt wanted to keep Disneyland affordable. I remember how alarmed he was when the parking fee went from twenty-five cents to fifty cents. That was huge to him. He once said, 'There will always be ten-cent coffee in Disneyland.'"

On Monday, July 18, Disneyland opened to the paying public (the admission price was one dollar). Though Disneyland's second day wasn't quite the madhouse that Black Sunday had been, it did feature one spectacular problem: a gas leak in Fantasyland caused flames to shoot out of the ground. A maintenance crew dug up the asphalt and quickly sealed the leak.

Because the park opened three years before the invention of credit cards, it was an all-cash business. The task of counting and depositing so much cash was a logistical nightmare, but Walt's staff invented a crude but effective solution. Ticket clerks dumped loose bills and change into metal fire buckets by their feet. When the buckets were full, they ran to the office and dumped out the cash on a big table. As the clerks ran back to their booths, the treasurer weighed the money—so many pounds of quarters equals so many dollars, and so forth.

Though money poured into Disneyland by the bucket-load, expenses were so high that paydays were weekly nail-biters for Walt and Roy. The Disney brothers ordered that hourly workers be paid first, then management. On weeks when there was money left over, Walt and Roy might get a paycheck as well.

> *"Walt Disney built his vision in the 1950s and early 1960s when the Cold War was at its height and the likelihood of nuclear disaster seemed high. He wanted Disneyland to be not just a theme park but a portal to a better time and a different world."*
>
> MARVIN OLASKY
> EDITOR OF *WORLD* MAGAZINE

Mild weather swelled the crowds in late July. In late August, however, the mercury topped 100 degrees for eight straight days, and the crowds stayed home. The day before Labor Day, as the thermometer hit 110, Walt sat in front of the Golden Horseshoe, staring bleakly. Frontierland was a ghost town. In September, however, the heat wave receded and the crowds returned.

On September 8, the park welcomed its millionth visitor. Despite a shaky start, Disneyland was on its way to becoming what Walt had envisioned: the Happiest Place on Earth.

The biggest, brightest toy

In the early years, Disneyland was a cozy, friendly place. Jimmie Dodd and the Mouseketeers often appeared and signed autographs. Fantasyland visitors might find Roy Williams, the *Mickey Mouse Club* co-host, sitting in the shade of "Sleeping Beauty's Castle," drawing portraits of Mickey and Donald and handing them out to fortunate fans. Sharp-eyed visitors might even spot Walt on a park bench, eating an ice cream cone.

"In those early days, Disneyland was like a small town," recalls longtime Disneyland cast member Becky Morris. "It was a close-knit community where everybody knew everybody else. We all felt like we were part of Walt's family. He would come and walk around the park. He was easy to talk to. That was a fun time, but a different era."

"My family was among the first to visit Disneyland in July 1955," recalls Peggy Matthews Rose. "We dined at the Red Wagon Inn on Main Street (now called the Plaza Inn). The waitress told us we were sitting at the table where President Eisenhower and Fess Parker had sat the night before. My parents were excited about being that close to a president—but all I knew was, 'Davy Crockett sat here!' I remember thinking how lucky the waitress was—she got to live in Disneyland! I was only five years old, but that day, I found my goal in life: I was going to live in Disneyland, too!" In fact, Peggy spent most of her career with Disney.

Walt was a kid at heart, and Disneyland was the biggest, brightest, shiniest new toy any kid ever had. Nothing made him happier than spending time at Disneyland, sharing it, tinkering with it and plussing it, continually making it better and better.

Ultimately, Walt's relentless perseverance paid off. In 1957, Walt bought a new home at Smoke Tree Ranch, even bigger and better than the first one. It was a fitting reward for Walt's stick-to-it-ivity.

In 1960, just five years after the park opened, Disney repurchased the ABC network's 34.5 percent share of Disneyland. ABC's $7.5 million return on a $500,000 investment amounted to a 1,400 percent return on investment—not bad! The experts had predicted failure, but Walt achieved unbelievable success. On April 25, 1961, Walt and Roy paid off the last of their loans. After more than two decades in debt to the Bank of America, Walt Disney Productions was finally in the black.

How to Be Like Walt—
Lesson 9: Be a Person of Stick-to-it-ivity

Today we can look at Disneyland and say, "Of course! Just what the world needed! How could it miss?" But in 1955, Disneyland was the biggest gamble in the history of American business. The risk paid off—not because Walt was lucky or favored or a genius. It paid off because *Walt wouldn't quit.* The success of Disneyland is, first and foremost, the result of sheer dogged determination and persistence in the face of obstacles and opposition.

That famous song from *Pinocchio* tells us to "wish upon a star" to make our dreams come true, but Walt knew better. In the real world, if you want your dreams to come true, you've got to have stick-to-it-ivity. That is how an ordinary farm boy with a modest talent for cartooning became the ruler of his own Magic Kingdom. That is how any ordinary person (like you, like me) can accomplish extraordinary things. You can't beat a person who has stick-to-it-ivity.

> *"Dad functions best when things are going badly."*
>
> DIANE DISNEY MILLER
> WALT'S DAUGHTER (1956)

Walt's nephew, Roy E. Disney told me, "If Walt had one great gift, it was that he kept his head down and kept trying. Over the years he was told that his ideas were impractical, impossible and would never work: 'Walt, you'll lose your shirt on *Snow White*,' or, 'Walt, give up this crazy obsession with an amusement park!' Walt knew his ideas were good and the naysayers were wrong. Walt proved that the only way to get things done is by sticking to your ideas and your beliefs."

There was an almost mule-headed perverseness to Walt's stick-to-it-ivity. He once said, "If management likes my projects, I seriously question proceeding. If they disdain them totally, I proceed immediately." That may seem like the statement of someone who is just plain ornery—but in reality, it's an expression of Walt's creative genius. Walt believed that if everyone around him approved of his ideas, then he wasn't dreaming big enough dreams. Only when people opposed his ideas was he sure that the challenge was bold enough!

Walt took himself, his family and his company to the brink of financial ruin to build Disneyland. Opening day was a disaster, with too many people, not enough food, and rides that chronically broke down. For weeks thereafter, a heat wave kept people away in droves. Still, Walt stuck to his dream. Disneyland is a living tribute to Walt's stick-to-it-ivity.

"My husband was the most stubborn individual I ever met," Lillian Disney once said. "He just wouldn't give up if he thought he was right." If we want to be successful like Walt, then we need to be stubborn in the pursuit of our goals, just as he was. We need commitment, perseverance and stick-to-it-ivity because so many obstacles stand between us and our dreams.

"When things are going good, I'm afraid something's going to crack under me any minute. A kick in the pants can be the best thing in the world for you."

WALT DISNEY

One of Walt's biographers, Christopher Finch (*The Art of Walt Disney*), told me, "Walt's greatest gift may have been his enormous tenacity. He absolutely refused to fail, no matter what happened to him. It seemed that the more things went wrong, the stronger he got."

What keeps you from your dreams? Walt couldn't be stopped by anything short of death itself—and even after he died, his dreams were so powerful they continued on. So if you want to succeed like Walt, then don't you dare give up, no matter how tough life gets.

Take it from Walt: "Get a good idea and stay with it. Dog it, and work at it until it's done, and done right. . . . All our dreams can come true—if we have the courage to pursue them."

Chapter Nine

❦

A Sponge
for Ideas

Though Disneyland opened in 1955, it was not completed. In fact, Walt promised that his park would never be finished. He vowed to go on expanding and improving Disneyland by continually soaking up new ideas and inspiration.

Not long after Disneyland opened, one of the grounds-keepers led Walt to a little flower-trimmed area facing "Sleeping Beauty's Castle." He said, "Walt, we've got a problem. I've got a sign here that says 'Keep Off the Grass,' but look at how trampled it is. People are walking right over the flowers so they can take a picture of the castle. We need a fence to keep the people off the grass."

"Oh, no," Walt replied, "we don't want a fence here. The people are right. This is a great place to take pictures. Let's put a pathway right here and a sign that says, 'Best Place for Photographing the Castle.'"

Walt believed the way to improve Disneyland was to observe and listen to people. He took countless walks through the park, talking to guests, asking for ideas, opinions, suggestions and complaints. "Walt liked to visit around the park and check things out for himself," said Bob Matheison, former vice president of Walt Disney World. "Long before Tom Peters wrote *In Search of Excellence,* Walt practiced 'managing by walking around.' In fact, Walt invented it."

Walt's fame as a television personality made it hard for him to walk through his kingdom without being mobbed. He often "hid in plain sight" by wearing rumpled clothes and a floppy-brimmed hat. Walt's young fans fully expected to see Walt at Disneyland, so they frequently spotted him. When a child approached him, Walt would put his finger to his lips, as if to say, "Don't tell anyone who I am!" Then he would hand the child an autograph from the pad he kept in his pocket.

> *"Walt wanted everything done right. He'd walk around the park in old clothes, so that people wouldn't recognize him. If he saw a carpenter doing careless work, he'd say, 'You know, that looks a little sloppy. You should take more pride in your work.' The carpenter would wonder, 'Who does that guy think he is? Walt Disney?'"*
>
> JOHN KIMBALL
> SON OF WARD KIMBALL
> AND LONGTIME DISNEY EMPLOYEE

Art Linkletter recalls walking around the park with Walt in those early days. "Walt had come up with a brilliant way of dealing with autograph-seekers," he said. "He took me to his office and we scribbled our autographs on pads of paper that he had printed up just for that purpose. Then, as we walked along and people came up to us, we could pull out these pads, tear off a sheet, and continue on our way. If you have to stop and write your name, you're sunk, because you'll be mobbed in two seconds. But those autograph pads really worked.

"One time, Walt and I stopped by the Magic Shop on Main Street. We bought fake beards and mustaches and put them on as a disguise. We started down Main Street, but the disguises didn't help. In fact they probably just drew attention to us. We hadn't gotten very far when we were completely surrounded. So we gave out autographs and finally got away. Funny thing, though—not one of those people asked us, 'Why are you wearing those beards?'"

Longtime Disneyland employee Ray McHugh told me, "Walt used to spend a lot of time at Disneyland. My co-foreman on the 'Jungle Cruise' and the 'Mine Train' was Frank McNell. Whenever we saw Walt, Frank and

I would bet on whether or not he'd be spotted and mobbed. Some days, he could stand around in the open with a hot dog in his hand, and nobody would pay any attention. Other days, he couldn't move because people would throng around him."

Retired cast member John Catone remembers the early days at Disneyland. "I often saw Walt around the park early in the morning," John told me. "He'd be dressed in blue jeans and a straw hat, with a red hand-kerchief around his neck. He'd tour the park, talk to the ride operators, and check on everything. If you told Walt that something wasn't right or needed improvement, Walt would act immediately. He'd find out who was respon-sible and he'd say, 'Here's what I want done." At that point, things would happen instantly.

"One day, I took Walt on the 'Jungle Cruise.' As we passed one of the hippos in the river, I noticed that I could see some of the hippo's mechan-ical parts in the clear water. I said, 'Walt, look. You can see the mechanism.' He frowned and took note of it. A week later, I noticed the water was dark and murky. I took a boat out and checked the hippo, and it looked just like a real hippo. Walt had taken care of the problem."

Ray VanDeWarker was foreman of the 'Jungle Cruise' in the early days. He told me, "I was taking the boat out on a deadhead ride— no passengers. I saw Walt standing alone on the dock. He said, 'Mind if I go out with you?' Would I mind? What a privilege! Walt came aboard and we set off down the river. I asked him, 'How did you think up this ride?' He spent thirty minutes telling me where all the ideas came from, about his trip to South America, and so forth. It was fascinating to hear him talk about it."

A positive attitude on the job was crucial to Walt. He was selling happi-ness, and he didn't want to see anyone spoiling his product with a rude or grumpy demeanor. Rod Miller, who has played piano at Coca-Cola Corner for years, told me, "Walt once walked up to a cast member who was look-ing especially sour and told this fellow, 'Young man, you are on my time now, so you need to be happy. You might be surprised how that attitude will last after you clock out.'"

On another occasion, Walt saw one of his Disneyland Railroad conduc-tors behaving rudely toward some guests. Walt went to the man's supervi-sor and said, "See if you can't give that fellow a better understanding of the

"One day, I took my lunch break and sat on the bench at Town Square, near the flag pole. I noticed an old man who came to the park on a regular basis. I said, 'I see you here all the time. Why do you like it here so much?' He said, 'This is the only place I can jaywalk and not get hollered at.' He had probably grown up in a little town somewhere, and he came to Disneyland to relive his youth. That would have pleased Walt."

ANN SALISBURY
LONGTIME DISNEY EMPLOYEE

kind of business we're in. Cheer him up if you can. If he feels sour, he shouldn't work here. We are selling happiness."

Longtime Disneyland employee George Mills remembers Walt as "a gracious man who never met a stranger." He told me, "Walt was eating at the Red Wagon Cafeteria, which is where the employees ate. I came through the line with my lunch tray, and I saw him sitting by himself at a table in his business suit. He looked up and saw me looking for a place to sit, and he asked me to join him for lunch. We had a nice talk. He asked a lot of questions."

Walt liked to see Disneyland from every angle, including that of his employees. You could often find him behind the counter at the Carnation restaurant on Main Street, wearing a striped jacket and straw hat, and scooping ice cream. As he handed you your cone, he'd ask, "Are you enjoying your day? What was your favorite ride? Is there anything we should do differently?" Walt's scoops, by the way, were always the biggest.

Tony Baxter began his Disney career in 1965, working as a sweeper, ride operator, and ice cream scooper at Disneyland. He quickly rose to become Senior Vice President of Creative Development at Walt Disney Imagineering. "I started working in the Carnation Ice Cream stand," he told me. "Walt would come in to see how we were doing. This was less than a year before his death, and he was not well. Yet he was so committed to improving every detail of Disneyland that he continued to walk around, talk to people, and see how things were going. That's what set Walt Disney apart from everyone else: He was committed to making his park not merely good, but the best.

"I used to open the Carnation shop at six in the morning, and I'd see a delivery truck out front, bringing the milk and ice cream. And you won't believe this, but it's true: A number of times, Walt himself drove the milk truck! Can you imagine? The man who built the park was also delivering the milk and ice cream! He wanted to enjoy every aspect of this park he had created. He had a gift for keeping in touch with everyday people, because he learned from them, and he used what he learned to improve the park."

Walt would often purchase a hot dog from a park vendor, then start walking as he ate. When he finished and was left with an empty wrapper, he would take note of where he was. The next morning, a trash container would be placed at that location.

He encouraged his staff to walk around the park to observe and learn, too. Artist-Imagineer John Hench recalled, "When Disneyland first opened, Walt told us to get down there at least twice a month. He said, 'Stand in line with people. Don't go off the lot to eat like you guys have been doing. Eat at the park and listen to people."

Walt liked to personally test all the attractions. "He would ride along with people on the attractions," Ken Anderson recalled, "and they didn't even know it was Walt! They'd climb off the ride and he'd watch their reactions, then he'd say, 'Hello, I'm Walt Disney. Did you enjoy the ride?' And they would be in shock! But that's how Walt learned how to improve Disneyland—by getting out in the park and talking to all sorts of people."

"My one visit to Walt Disney World in Florida made me love the original Disneyland all the more. Disneyland is the only theme park that truly has Walt's fingerprints all over it. It's the only park he actually lived and breathed in."

PEGGY MATTHEWS ROSE
LONGTIME DISNEY EMPLOYEE

The waterfall and the island

The "Rainbow Caverns Mine Train" attraction in Frontierland illustrates Walt's belief that you can achieve the impossible if you sift through enough ideas. The attraction (located where "Big Thunder Mountain Railroad" is today) was a train ride through a colorful desert and a deep cavern. Walt wanted a glowing waterfall in the cavern. He suggested adding fluorescent dyes to the water, with each color in a separate trough to prevent the colors from mixing.

Imagineer Claude Coats checked with chemists and engineers, then reported back to Walt. "The experts all say it's impossible," Coats said. "You can't keep the water from splashing and mixing together. You'll have a fluorescent gray mess within a week."

"Well, Claude," Walt replied with a merry lack of concern, "you just haven't found the right idea yet. I'm sure you'll come up with something."

So Coats huddled with fellow Imagineer John Hench, and they brainstormed and experimented. They came up with dozens of ideas, but none of them worked. Finally, they tried placing braided glass fibers in the water channels—and the splashing problem was eliminated. Claude Coats learned a valuable lesson: All it takes to achieve the impossible is imagination, persistence—and a lot of ideas.

Tom Sawyer Island is the only Disneyland attraction singlehandedly designed by Walt himself. Unhappy with the first set of drawings produced by one of his top artists, Walt took the drawings home and reworked them overnight. The next morning, he handed his drawings to the artist and said, "That's how the island should look."

> *"Disneyland was dedicated to what Walt Disney called 'plussing'—continuous improvement through both new ideas and changes to existing attractions. . . . Its open-endedness appealed to his desire for perfection."*
>
> VIRGINIA POSTREL
> AUTHOR, *THE FUTURE AND ITS ENEMIES*

The island Walt designed is a place where kids and their imaginations can safely run riot. It's filled with secret caves, trails, and passages to explore. Island landmarks have names that suggest danger and excitement: Injun Joe's Cave, Fort Wilderness, Teeter-Totter Rock. Even after Tom Sawyer Island was built, Walt kept his ears open for ideas he could use to plus and improve the attraction. His best ideas came from a twelve-year-old newsboy.

Tom Nabbe recently retired as Manager of Distribution Services at Walt Disney World. "I sold the *Disneyland News* in the park," Tom told me. "I heard that Walt was going to build Tom Sawyer Island, and I was excited because a lot of people told me I looked like Tom Sawyer. So I went to Walt's office and introduced myself. I said, 'If you're going to build that island, I want to be Tom Sawyer.'

"Walt listened politely, then he said, 'You know, Tom, I could build a mannequin that wouldn't run off to get a hot dog and a drink.' I promised I would work hard and stick to the job. Walt said, 'I'll think about it.' I've always thought that Walt was willing to consider it because he admired my spunk—and he'd been a newsboy himself once.

"Whenever I saw Walt around the park, I'd remind him that I wanted to be Tom Sawyer. In late May of 1956, I was selling papers at the Penny Arcade when Dick Nunis came to me and said, 'Come with me.' We went to the raft dock and there was Walt. He said, 'Tom, do you still want to be Tom Sawyer?' I said, 'I sure do!' They opened the island in June, and for the next six years, I was Tom Sawyer.

"Walt would come to the island and we'd walk around and talk. He wanted to hear my ideas. One time, we walked out to Lookout Point and I told him we needed a treehouse and a few other things. He took my suggestions. He listened to people, even to kids, and he was always soliciting new ideas."

The mountain and the Monorail

In 1958, Walt was preparing to fly to Switzerland with director Ken Annakin to begin work on a live action film, *Third Man on the Mountain*. Before he left, Walt stopped by the office of Imagineer Vic Greene. "Vic," he said, "I'd like you to start thinking about new attractions for Tomorrowland. Something big, you know? I'll check in with you when I get back from Switzerland."

In Switzerland, Walt and Ken took a train to the village of Zermatt, which looks out upon the majestic peak known as the Matterhorn. The moment Walt saw the Matterhorn, he was transfixed. He couldn't stop staring. There was something about that mountain—

Suddenly, Walt had a flash of inspiration: *That's it!* He turned and rushed into a souvenir shop. He snatched a picture postcard of the Matterhorn from a revolving rack on the counter. He scrawled a brief message on the back, then mailed it to Vic Greene. The message read simply, "Vic, build this! Walt."

The day Vic Greene received that postcard, he began designing Walt's mountain.

Walt went on to Germany and visited the Alweg Company factory in Cologne. There he watched the construction of bullet-shaped single-rail trains. He decided that he had to have a Monorail train at Disneyland. By showcasing this technology, he hoped to point the way to solving the traffic and pollution problems of America's great cities.

In addition to the Matterhorn and the Monorail, Walt had one more attraction on his mind. Inspired by the success of *20,000 Leagues Under the Sea,* Walt decided to build an underwater attraction for Tomorrowland— the "Submarine Voyage." So Walt had three new dreams: the Matterhorn, the Monorail, and the Submarines—and the obstacle in his path was his brother Roy.

> *"Walt's philosophy has been passed down to generations of Disney employees, and the key to that philosophy is this: The people who come to the park are not customers, they are guests. When you see a person as your guest, it changes the way you relate to them. That concept came straight from Walt, and it's the key to everything Disney does to this day."*
>
> PAULA SIGMAN
> DISNEY HISTORIAN

Disneyland had proven enormously profitable, but the Disney company was still in debt. When Walt approached Roy about adding new attractions, Roy refused to consider it. In two or three years? Maybe. But for the time being, Roy insisted that the Disney company focus on getting debt-free.

Soon after that discussion, Roy left for Europe on a mission to woo foreign investors. As soon as Roy was out of the country, Walt called a meeting at WED Enterprises and told his Imagineers, "We're going to build the Matterhorn, the Monorail, and the Submarines."

The Imagineers were stunned. They knew of Roy's opposition to new projects. "What will Roy say?" one of them asked.

"We're just going to build 'em," Walt replied. "Roy can figure out how to pay for 'em when he gets back."

So work began. Harriet Burns was part of the Imagineering team that designed the Matterhorn. "Nothing like the Matterhorn had ever been built before," she said. "Walt would bring in experts and engineers to advise him on the problems we were likely to encounter. He always wanted the best advice he could get. If the experts said, 'This is impossible, this can't be done,' it rolled right off of him. He wouldn't argue with them, he'd just smile. He had accomplished the so-called 'impossible' so many times in his life that the word no longer had any meaning to him.

"The experts told Walt there was no way to build the Matterhorn with two separate toboggan runs, plus planters for the greenery, plus water flow systems for the waterfalls, plus openings for the Skyway. The experts said that after we had installed all of this machinery, the structure would no longer look anything like the original Swiss Matterhorn. They insisted that what Walt wanted to achieve was simply impossible. And Walt had a simple response: 'Just get it done.' So we put our heads together, solved all the problems, and got it done."

> *"They came back to Walt and said, 'Audio-Animatronics can't be done. There's just no way you can do that.' Walt said, 'If you can visualize it, if you can dream it, there's some way to do it. Now keep after it until we get it!'"*
>
> FLOYD GOTTFREDSON
> DISNEY COMIC STRIP ARTIST

The result of their efforts was a 147-foot steel and concrete replica of the original Swiss mountain peak, built to a 1/100th scale. On June 14, 1959, the "Matterhorn Bobsleds" thrill ride opened to the public. Today, Walt's mountain defines the skyline of Disneyland.

The Submarines and Monorail debuted that same day. Called "a voyage through liquid space," the Submarine ride was built at a cost of $2.5 million. The fleet of undersea boats took visitors past underwater volcanoes, a graveyard of lost ships, the ruins of Atlantis, and the polar ice cap. It was definitely an E-ticket ride.

The futuristic Monorail was designed by Bob Gurr and built by Alweg. Gurr recalled that the ribbon-cutting ceremony was covered on live TV.

"Suddenly," he said, "here comes Walt Disney with Vice President Richard Nixon, the Nixon family, and Art Linkletter. Walt has this impish look on his face as he's showing off his new Tomorrowland train to the Vice President of the United States. Walt introduces me to the Vice President and says, 'I like steam locomotives, but Bobby here likes these modern electric trains, so I let Bobby drive them.'"

Walt invited the Vice President and his family into the red Monorail vehicle to look around. Bob Gurr sat down at the controls to make sure the air conditioning system was working. The Monorail was not supposed to go anyplace—it was purely an inspection tour. But Walt was so full of enthusiasm for his new futuristic train that he turned to Bob Gurr and said, "Let's go!"

So Gurr pulled the Monorail out of the station. As the train passed over the waterfall of the Submarine ride, Mr. Nixon swore. His entire Secret Service detail had been left on the Monorail Station platform. At that moment, Bob Gurr realized that he and Walt had just kidnapped the Vice President of the United States! The train went around the circuit and Gurr was relieved when he saw the Tomorrowland station up ahead. But just then, the Nixon daughters, Tricia and Julie, shouted, "Let's go around again!"

Secret Service men ran alongside the Monorail, shouting as it slowed through the station. Watching his security detail trying to keep pace, Nixon laughed—but Bob Gurr didn't see any humor in the situation. He sped on, leaving the federal agents in his wake. Gurr recalls, "My heart sank and I remember little of the second lap."

The Monorail began continuous operation that day. After two weeks of service with few maintenance problems, the Imagineers received a telegram from Professor Wengatz of the Alweg Company in Germany. His telegram warned, STOP CONSTRUCTION OF MONORAIL TRAIN—IMPOSSIBLE TO WORK.

> *"At the opening ceremonies for the Disneyland Monorail, when Richard Nixon attended, Walt and Nixon took a test ride on the Monorail. Round and round they went. Finally, we had to shut the power off to get Walt to stop at the station."*
>
> JOHN CATONE
> LONGTIME DISNEYLAND EMPLOYEE

Bob Gurr sent a reply telegram, offering Wengatz a ride on the Disneyland Monorail. The Alweg engineers had encountered problems with their Monorail design—problems the Disney Imagineers had already solved. German engineering invented the Monorail, but Disney Imagineering perfected it.

How to Be Like Walt—
Lesson 10: Become a Sponge for Ideas

Walt continually fed his mind with information and ideas. He absorbed inspiration wherever he went.

When Disneyland's "Pirates of the Caribbean" attraction was being built, Walt noticed that one of the construction workers was from the Louisiana bayou country, the setting of the first part of the attraction. So Walt walked the man through the attraction and asked him what he thought of it. Was it realistic? Did it remind him of the bayou country he grew up in?

"It's good," the man said, "but something's missing. I just can't put my finger on it."

"Well," Walt said, "let's walk through it until you figure out what's not right."

So they went through the attraction again. This time, as they were passing through the bayou section,

> "I've got a lot of ideas.
> I haven't worked them out
> and I haven't proved them out.
> I carry ideas around in
> my head for a long time."
>
> WALT DISNEY

the man snapped his fingers. "Fireflies!" he said. "There ought to be fireflies in this swamp!" A few days later, the swamp was alive with electric fireflies.

Some of Walt's best ideas came to him when he traveled. "Always, as you travel," he said, "assimilate the sounds and sights of the world." Walt's friend Ray Bradbury compared Walt to a jackdaw, a bird noted for stealing shiny objects and carrying them to its nest. "Walt was a jackdaw in the meadows of the fields of the Lord," Bradbury said, "He'd find a bright object and he'd think, 'Oh my, that's good!' and he'd carry it back to the studio."

Walt would gather ideas from any source, even bad TV shows. Lillian recalled that, when the children weren't home, he preferred to eat dinner in front of the television. "He looked at everything," she said. "It would be a lousy program and I'd say, 'Do you want me to change it?' And he'd say, 'No, no. I just want to study it.' He was the same with movies. He'd want to see a certain picture and I'd say, 'But that one got a bad review.' He'd say, 'I don't care. I want to see what the director did.'"

"Walt collected ideas and information from the people around him," said Bob Thomas. "He called on people who knew more than he did. He sought out their ideas and viewpoints. He asked for their advice. And when called upon, he would also give advice. He believed that ideas and information were to be shared."

"Walt would walk into a room, throw out some ideas, and get a discussion going right away," composer Richard Sherman recalls. "He wanted people to take his ideas and improve them. He'd tell us, 'Anyone can say, 'I don't like it.' I want to hear you say, 'Here's how we can make it better.' He was like a great coach or a great general. He had a magical way of getting our creative juices flowing. When he was around, he turned our office into an idea factory."

One of the tools Walt used for generating ideas was the storyboard, invented largely by accident at the Hyperion Avenue studio in 1931. Story artist Webb Smith would create drawings for a cartoon, then toss them on the floor, where he could rearrange them into any sequence he liked. When Walt told him to stop making a mess all over the floor, Webb started tacking his drawings to the office wall with pushpins. Again, Walt was dismayed. "You're ruining my walls with all of these holes!" he said.

Finally, Webb began pinning his drawings to four-by-six-foot boards. He could reposition sketches and change the continuity of the story without having to completely redo his drawings. Soon, other story artists were pinning their drawings to four-by-six-foot boards—and when Walt walked in and saw half a dozen story artists with their stories laid out on these boards, he realized that something revolutionary had taken place.

From then on, Walt insisted on storyboarding every project—and not just cartoons. Walt used storyboards to plan every shot of his live action films and every thrill of his Disneyland attractions. Whenever Walt was working on a new film, he would display the storyboards along one long wall in his Burbank studio. Any Disney employee—animator, writer, secretary or custodian—could go to that wall and post suggestions and ideas. Walt personally read every idea, and many were incorporated into the finished project. Storyboards became a powerful tool for drawing upon the imagination and creativity of the entire Disney community.

Because Walt fed his mind with ideas from so many sources, he became an expert in fields far beyond the realm of animation and movie-making. In fact, after building Disneyland, he was an authority in such fields as architecture, interior design, and food service. On one occasion in the 1960s, Walt flew to San Antonio, Texas, in the Disney plane. His pilot, Kelvin Bailey, remembered a particular breakfast he shared with Walt at the hotel.

> *"All of us dream, but Walt made his dreams tangible. When Walt had a dream or an idea, you knew that the reality was on the horizon."*
>
> BLAINE GIBSON
> DISNEY ARTIST, IMAGINEER AND SCULPTOR

When the waiter came to take their order, Walt asked for the manager. The manager came to the table and Walt said, "You have a very nice dining room, but may I make a few suggestions?" On a napkin, he sketched some ideas about the design of the room, the construction of the entryway, the wall colors, and the placement of the chandelier, then he handed his sketches to the manager.

A year later, Bailey stopped in at the same hotel restaurant. The manager had implemented all of Walt's ideas—and he told Bailey, "This restaurant has been a gold mine ever since we took Mr. Disney's advice!"

Disney biographer Bob Thomas told me, "Walt was always thinking, reading, listening, working, gathering ideas. He lived and breathed ideas. He kept a notepad by his bed. When he woke up in the middle of the night with an idea, he would write it down and go back to sleep. The man was a sponge for ideas—and that is why he was so amazingly creative."

If you want to be more like Walt—more creative, more imaginative, more successful—then keep your eyes and ears open. Read. Watch. Travel. Talk to people wherever you go. Ask questions. Invite opinions.

To be like Walt, become a sponge for ideas.

Chapter Ten

❧

The Man Who Saw Tomorrow

Walt was a walking paradox. Though probably the greatest nostalgist who ever lived, he was fascinated by the future. Most important of all, Walt didn't just predict the future and tell stories of the future. He made the future happen.

Ray Bradbury first met Walt Disney in the early 1960s. It was Christmastime, and Ray was shopping at a Beverly Hills department store when he spotted Walt coming toward him, carrying a huge load of gift-wrapped presents. *That's him!* he realized. *That's Walt Disney!*

Ray rushed up to Walt and said, "Mr. Disney?"

Walt stopped in his tracks. "Yes?"

"My name is Ray Bradbury."

"Oh, yes," Walt said. "I know your books."

"Oh, thank God!" said the author of *The Martian Chronicles* and *Fahrenheit 451.*

"Why?"

"Because sometime soon I'd love to take you to lunch."

Walt brightened. "How about tomorrow?"

Ray Bradbury thought, *Isn't that beautiful? 'How about tomorrow?'* Not next week. Not next month. Tomorrow!

The next day, Bradbury and Walt shared soup and sandwiches over a card table in Walt's office. "We babbled like a couple of kids," Ray later recalled. "Walt was like a long-lost brother or a father to me."

Ray told Walt how, as a fourteen-year-old boy, he had gone to the L.A. County Museum of Art on Sunday afternoons and admired original animation cels from *Steamboat Willie* and *The Skeleton Dance*. He described his first visit to Disneyland in the company of his friend, actor Charles Laughton. He recalled how he and Laughton had flown together over London and Never Land, and how, on the 'Jungle Cruise,' Laughton had reverted to his old movie role—Captain Bligh of the HMS *Bounty*. Walt was thrilled to hear it.

> "Walt was a futurist. Walt was a visionary. There was no single more forward-thinking person than Walt Disney."
>
> LEONARD MALTIN
> FILM CRITIC

From then on, Walt and Ray were great friends. They met often for lunch—two great storytellers who lived half their lives in the future. And it all began with the question, "How about tomorrow?"

Walt Disney was a visionary and a futurist. And what is a futurist? Not a fortune-teller or a soothsayer, not a reader of tea leaves or crystal balls. A futurist is a planner and a doer. Futurists look at trends and innovations. They look for patterns of change. Then they act. Futurists don't just predict the future. They make the future happen.

Though Walt loved the past, he looked forward to the future. He was always asking, "How about tomorrow?"

Television: the medium of the future

The first "person" ever to appear on television was Mickey Mouse.

The television medium was invented on January 7, 1927, when a nineteen-year-old farmboy, Philo T. Farnsworth, filed a patent on an invention he called "television" (he named it after a fictional device he'd read about in a science fiction magazine, *Amazing Stories*). Two years after filing his patent, Farnsworth transmitted a Mickey Mouse cartoon, *Steamboat Willie*, from his Philadelphia laboratory to a receiver in his home a few miles away.

The only viewers of this forerunner of The Disney Channel were Farnsworth's wife and toddler son. The boy watched spellbound as the cartoon played over and over.

Eight years later, Walt Disney was reading a contract when he stumbled upon an unfamiliar word: *television.* A clause in his renewal contract with United Artists would have granted the distribution company all television exhibition rights to Walt's movies. At that time, no one—Walt included—had an inkling of how powerful and pervasive television would become. Yet, something told Walt that he should not surrender those rights. Walt had his finger on the pulse of the future.

After World War II, television began to demonstrate its enormous potential—and the Hollywood movie moguls trembled. Across the country,

> *"Instead of considering TV a rival, I said, 'I can use that, I want to be a part of it.'"*
>
> WALT DISNEY

people stopped going to the movies, preferring to stay home and watch *The Texaco Star Theater* with Milton Berle in glorious black and white. Some short-sighted producers saw TV as a fad that would blow over; others, equally short-sighted, saw TV as a competitor to be feared.

Only one filmmaker embraced TV as a friend and ally: Walt Disney.

"Walt had the voice of a prophet," story artist Joe Grant once said. "I remember the time when television was on its way in and I said to Walt, 'Why aren't we on TV?' He said, 'Television will come to us,' and it did. He knew ahead of time."

Television did, indeed, come to Walt. In 1950, NBC asked the Disney company for a Christmas special, and Walt responded with a show called *One Hour in Wonderland.* Along with Walt, the show featured ventriloquist Edgar Bergen, Kathryn Beaumont, and Walt's daughters, Diane and Sharon. The special, which aired on Christmas Day 1950, was viewed by 20 million people—at a time when there were only 10 million homes with TV sets!

That show marked a major transition for Walt's studio. Suddenly, Disney was no longer just a motion picture studio. It had taken the first step toward becoming a multimedia empire. Walt's second TV special, *The Walt Disney Christmas Show,* aired on CBS on Christmas Day 1951, and drew an equally large audience. Clearly, the Disney name was television magic.

The *Disneyland* TV series debuted on October 27, 1954. The show transformed the Disney company in three important ways:

First, the *Disneyland* series was a brilliant piece of entertainment synergy: The show sold the Disneyland theme park to the public, and the park generated public interest in the show, making it one of the top-rated programs on television.

Second, the *Disneyland* series was a brilliant piece of marketing synergy: A December 1954 episode introduced Fess Parker as Davy Crockett, igniting a nationwide Crockett craze and producing a $100 million merchandising windfall—everything from Davy Crockett coonskin caps to 45 rpm records of "The Ballad of Davy Crockett."

Third, because Walt personally hosted the show, he immediately became "Uncle Walt" to generations of Americans. His warm and genial personality played well on television, and American families welcomed him into their homes as if he were a member of the family.

ABC president Robert E. Kintner recommended the show to his programming heads with these words: "You will be buying more than a great franchise on a most important show. You will be able to capitalize on the greatest reservoir of good will in America—Walt Disney himself."

> *"They called him 'Uncle Walt' and that was because he was such an 'old shoe,' such a comfortable man to be around."*
>
> DICK VAN DYKE
> ACTOR

Walt's studio followed the *Disneyland* show with two more series for ABC. First was *The Mickey Mouse Club,* an after-school program for kids. The show debuted on October 3, 1955, at 5 P.M. During that time slot, seventy-five percent of all TV viewers were watching *The Mickey Mouse Club.* (We'll take a closer look at that show in the next chapter.)

The second Disney show for ABC was *Zorro,* a weekly adventure series. The half-hour adventure drama, set in Spanish colonial California, first aired in 1957 and was an immediate hit.

It was the era of the TV western, of *Wagon Train, Maverick* and *Gunsmoke.* So ABC executives demanded that Walt put more horse operas on the *Disneyland* show. Walt resisted the network pressure. He liked to set trends, not follow them. At some point, however, he decided to give the network what it clamored for—but on his own terms.

Donn Tatum, then an ABC executive, recalled, "We had a meeting set up and in came Walt wearing a cowboy outfit and two guns. He threw the guns on the table and said, 'Okay, you want Westerns, you're gonna have Westerns.' He proceeded to recount the whole story of Texas John Slaughter, and then the story of Elfego Baca, a self-appointed sheriff in old New Mexico. The network executives' eyes were all bugging out and Walt said, 'We're gonna give you the *true* heroes and the *true* West!'" And that's how Walt appeared on camera when he introduced those western serials on the *Disneyland* show—as Walt the cowboy.

In the fall of 1958, the show's title was changed from *Disneyland* to *Walt Disney Presents,* though the format remained unchanged. Later that season, Disney produced yet another innovation: the first TV broadcast in simulcast stereo. On January 30, 1959, Disney aired "The Peter Tchaikovsky Story." In some cities, the audio portion was broadcast by a pair of radio stations. If you had two radios, you could tune one to receive the right channel and the other to receive the left.

Through television, Walt was able to multiply his influence many times over. Though his initial reason for entering television was to promote Disneyland, he soon found that television could virtually guarantee success for his theatrical films.

Walt never feared the future; he embraced it. Disney historian Dan Viets (*Walt Disney's Missouri*) explains Walt's futuristic spirit this way: "Walt was quick to embrace new innovations and use new technologies. He led the way with synchronized sound cartoons, Technicolor, feature-length animation, and television. Were he alive today, Walt would instantly grasp the Internet and use it very effectively."

"Man in Space"

Walt saw tomorrow with a rare sense of clarity and optimism. One of Walt's grandest, most optimistic visions was in the field of space exploration.

Sometime in late 1953, Ward Kimball showed him a series of six articles on space exploration that had appeared in *Collier's* magazine, beginning with the March 22, 1952, issue. The *Collier's* series was authored by some of Kimball's heroes, including rocket scientist Wernher von Braun, science fiction writer Willy Ley, physicist Heinz Haber, astronomer Fred Whipple, and others. The articles laid out a detailed plan for building a space program, from the first piloted rockets to an orbital space station to manned missions to the moon and Mars.

By this time, Walt and Herb Ryman had already drawn up plans for Disneyland which included The World of Tomorrow (later renamed Tomorrowland)—but Walt didn't know exactly what kinds of attractions to put there. The *Collier's* articles provided the answers. Walt wasted no time in arranging a meeting with Wernher von Braun.

> *"My career as an artist was influenced and motivated by Walt Disney. He fired my imagination as a youngster. In the 1950s, Walt's presence was ubiquitous. His TV shows covered a wide range of topics, including one of my favorites—space exploration."*
>
> VINCENT DiFATE
> SCIENCE FICTION ILLUSTRATOR

During World War II, von Braun had served the Nazi war effort, helping to build V2 rockets. He had no sympathy for Hitler's war in Europe, and had once been arrested by the Gestapo for advocating the peaceful use of rockets for colonizing the moon and planets. After the war, von Braun emigrated to America and became one of the leaders of the U.S. space program.

Both Walt and Wernher von Braun were profoundly influenced by the science fiction writings of Jules Verne. Both believed science and technology could improve life for the human race. And both were eager to ignite public support for an American space program.

Walt asked von Braun to serve as his technical advisor for Disneyland and for a program he was planning for the *Disneyland* TV series. Von Braun eagerly agreed, and also brought colleagues Willy Ley and Heinz Haber into the Disney fold.

Since Ward Kimball was a passionate space enthusiast, Walt chose him to produce and direct the space episode for the *Disneyland* program. He chose newcomer Charles Shows to write the script.

Kimball and Shows spent several weeks researching and developing the project, then they met with Walt and showed him drawings and a script for a show called "Man in Space." The script began a thousand years in the past, with the invention of the first rockets in ancient China; and it looked far ahead, to the construction of orbiting space stations and the exploration of the moon and Mars.

After seeing what Kimball and Shows had produced, Walt was quiet for a long time. Then he said, "You know, boys, you don't have a story here."

Kimball and Shows were dismayed. "We don't have a story?" gulped Shows.

"You have *three* stories here," Walt said, "three different episodes. The first should be called 'Man in Space,' about the development of rockets and manned spaceflight. The second should be on how to put the first men on the moon. We'll call it 'Tomorrow the Moon.' The third will be on Mars and the search for life beyond the Earth. We'll call it 'Mars and Beyond.'"

With that, Walt launched three of the most important episodes ever shown on his anthology series. "Man in Space" aired on March 9, 1955, and was seen by 42 million viewers. The show featured on-screen appearances by Walt, Ward Kimball, Wernher von Braun, and Heinz Haber (the appearance of von Braun and Haber helped popularize the stereotype of rocket scientists as men in white coats with thick German accents). Von Braun made a straightforward pitch for public support of an ambitious national space effort.

> *"He loved the past and used it, but he also loved the future and was always reaching out to unknown areas."*
>
> WALTER DISNEY MILLER
> WALT DISNEY'S GRANDSON

The second episode, "Tomorrow the Moon," aired on December 28, 1955. "Mars and Beyond" was shown on December 4, 1957, less than three months after the Soviet Union shocked the world by launching the first artificial satellite, Sputnik I.

The Disney space series proved to be enormously influential. President Dwight Eisenhower requested copies of the three episodes to show his staff. The series inspired thousands of young people to become space engineers, astronomers, physicists and astronauts. It undoubtedly played a big role in launching America's space program.

Almost fourteen years later, as astronauts Neil Armstrong and Buzz Aldrin approached the moon in Apollo 11, von Braun phoned Kimball and said, "Ward, have you been watching? NASA has been following your script for 'Man and the Moon'!"

Walt was a true futurist. He predicted the future, and he made it happen.

The nostalgic futurist

Walt Disney was a walking paradox. He was probably the greatest nostalgist who ever lived—a man who treasured and revered the past. He spent millions recreating the Main Street of his boyhood, the frontier era of Davy Crockett, and Mississippi riverfront of Mark Twain's time. He also went to considerable trouble and expense in resurrecting Abraham Lincoln.

Yet, for all his love of yesterday, Walt had an obsession with tomorrow. As Imagineer John Hench put it, "Walt had one foot in the past and one foot in the future."

To Walt, Tomorrowland was always as important as Adventureland, Frontierland, and Fantasyland. "Walt was an optimistic futurist," songwriter Richard Sherman told me. "My brother and I wrote a song about Walt's view of the future. It's called 'There's a Great Big Beautiful Tomorrow.' When we wrote lines like 'Tomorrow's just a dream away,' we were really writing about Walt."

Tomorrowland is a visible, steel-and-concrete reflection of the mind of Walt Disney—a mind that was curious about the possibilities of science, the exploration of space, and the expansion of new frontiers. Walt was an avid science fiction reader long before the term "science fiction" was coined by Hugo Gernsback in 1926. Walt grew up on the scientific tales of Jules Verne and H.G. Wells, and the adventures of the boy inventor, Tom Swift.

Of all the realms of Disneyland, Tomorrowland is the most frequently remodeled. Why? Because Today keeps catching up with Tomorrow. The future must be continually revised and updated or it is not the future anymore. As Imagineering executive Dick Irvine noted, "Walt could never get hold of Tomorrowland. He always said, 'The minute we do Tomorrowland, it's today and past.'"

In 1966, Walt said, "Now, when we opened Disneyland, outer space was Buck Rogers. I did put in a trip to the moon, and I got Wernher von Braun to help me plan the thing. . . . And since then has come Sputnik and then has come our great program in outer space. So I had to tear down my Tomorrowland that I built eleven years ago and rebuild it to keep pace."

Walt looked forward to a better world—and he built it. Tomorrowland is Walt's way of transmitting his optimism to future generations. "Walt built Tomorrowland to inspire young people about the future," said Imagineer Bruce Gordon. "He wanted them to stay in school, get a good education and good careers, and help build a brighter tomorrow."

> "A lot of young people think the future is closed to them, that everything has been done. This is not so. There are still plenty of avenues to be explored."
>
> WALT DISNEY

When Walt built Disneyland, he was not just putting on a show. He was thinking of the future of humanity—of the grand dream of moving out into space, colonizing other worlds, and harnessing the energies of the atom. He envisioned the entire human race living together in peace and harmony. Had he lived longer, our world would be a much better place than it is. Shortly before he died, Walt told his son-in-law, Ron Miller, "If I could live for fifteen more years, I would surpass everything I've done over the past forty-five years."

The march of human progress fascinated Walt. During his lifetime, he saw enormous changes in the world. He was born two years before the Wright Brothers flew at Kitty Hawk, and he lived to see America and the Soviet Union racing into space. "One of man's greatest desires," he said, "has been for space travel, to visit other worlds. Until recently, this idea seemed impossible. But great new discoveries have brought us to the threshold of a new frontier."

After Walt's death in 1966, his Imagineers faced the challenge of keeping Tomorrowland fresh and forward-looking. As the world changed, the task grew increasingly more complex. Tomorrowland attractions of the 1950s looked quaintly archaic by the 1970s. In the late 1990s, Disney Imagineers gave Tomorrowland a major facelift, a retro look. Tomorrowland's new slogan sums it up: "The future that never was is finally here."

Today's Tomorrowland is a kaleidoscopic fusion of Jules Verne, Flash Gordon, and The Jetsons, adorned in eye-popping neon, burnished bronze, and shades of deep blue and purple. It's an exciting place—but it's not about the future anymore. Along with Main Street, Frontierland, and other Disney realms, Tomorrowland has become a new kind of Nostalgialand.

Would Walt approve? I'm not sure.

Walt would undoubtedly appreciate the ingenious solution to the biggest problem of Tomorrowland: obsolescence. The Eisenhower-era Tomorrowland could never have survived unchanged into the Eisner era. Change is inevitable, but a retro future never goes out of style. The new Tomorrowland can retain its nostalgic-futuristic charm for decades to come—and that will save the Disney company millions in remodeling costs.

But Walt would probably mourn the loss of a truly futuristic dimension to Disneyland. The new Tomorrowland no longer gives us a window on "new frontiers in science," or on "the challenge of outer space." The new Tomorrowland no longer points us toward "the hope for a peaceful and united world."

In many ways, the future we live in is not the future Walt hoped it would be. In 1958, he said, "We step into the future and find fantastic atomic-powered machines working for us. The world is unified and peaceful, outer space is the new frontier. We walk for a time among the strange mechanical wonders of tomorrow, and then blast off on a rocket to the moon."

Well, we have home computers and the Internet and hundreds of TV channels, but our presence in space is pretty limited—no tour rockets to the moon, no colonies on Mars. And our world is far from unified and peaceful. In short, the future isn't what it used to be.

Was Walt all wrong about the future?

I don't think so. Walt Disney truly was the man who saw tomorrow. He was the great popularizer of our dreams of a future among the stars. But those dreams sputtered to a standstill within a few years after Walt passed away. Maybe there's no connection, but then again. . . . Perhaps we lost our way to the future because we no longer had Walt as our tour guide.

How to Be Like Walt—
Lesson 11: Ask Yourself "How About Tomorrow?"

Walt embraced the future and put the stamp of his own personality on tomorrow. So should we. If we want to help shape a better tomorrow, then we need to continually ask ourselves the same question Walt asked Ray Bradbury: "How about tomorrow?"

The difference between today and tomorrow is something called *change*. It takes courage to embrace the future, because the future is about change, and change brings uncertainty and anxiety. We fear change; we prefer the comfort of the familiar.

But change is inevitable. If we do not become future-focused, we are doomed to obsolescence when tomorrow arrives. To seize the future as Walt did, we must do three things:

1. *Embrace change*. Walt taught Mickey Mouse to talk while other movie producers dismissed "talkies" as a passing fad. Walt jumped into television while other movie-makers shunned it. Walt succeeded where others failed because he was quick to embrace change.

If you and I want to experience a successful and effective life, we need to welcome new technologies, new ideas, new information, and new opportunities. Since change is inevitable, we might as well learn to enjoy it. Don't be afraid to dip your toe into the ocean of tomorrow. Catch the next wave and ride it into the future.

2. *Identify ideas and trends that produce change*. When he was laying plans for EPCOT, his city of tomorrow in Florida, Walt surrounded himself with stacks of books on urban planning, such as Victor Gruen's *Out of a Fair, a City* (which describes how a World's Fair can be transformed into a planned community).

> "Walt Disney had a larger view of the future than most people. Even more important, Walt knew how to make the future happen."
>
> ALAN COATS
> SON OF IMAGINEER CLAUDE COATS

Walt surrounded himself with Imagineers and experts in many fields of knowledge, so he always had the latest information on dealing with change. Walt was continually monitoring trends that affected his industry.

Here are some ways you can identify the ideas and trends that will change your life: Scan newspapers, magazines, journals and the Internet for articles and information. Look for trends in society, the economy, your customer base, your audience, your competitors, your shareholders. Watch for legislation that affects your life and your industry. Take note of innovative technologies. Ask yourself, "How will this change affect me? How can it hurt me or help me? How can I take advantage of it? What new skills or knowledge must I acquire in order to deal effectively with these changes?"

Avoid basing major decisions about the future upon isolated events. Instead, focus on large-scale trends and emerging patterns. As you monitor trends, remember that the further into the future you try to track certain trends, the less accurate your forecast is likely to be.

Also, be aware of cycles—trends that tend to repeat at intervals, over and over again. We see cycles in the changing seasons, in the weather, in the economy, in fashion, in entertainment, in politics. An awareness of how cycles affect change can improve your ability to look into the future.

Scan the horizon for emerging issues. These are so-called "seeds of change" that could produce the trends of tomorrow. "In this volatile business of ours," Walt once said, "we can ill afford to rest on our laurels, even to pause in retrospect. Times and conditions change so rapidly that we must keep our aim constantly focused on the future." Here are some possible seeds of change (both positive and negative) that are just over the horizon:

Cars and planes that run on pollution-free hydrogen. Smart cars and automated freeways that make collisions and mechanical failures a thing of the past. Aquaculture—harvesting foods from the oceans. Robotic insects that control pests without chemicals while pollinating crops with computerized effectiveness.

Increasingly sophisticated terrorists with more accurate and destructive weapons, resulting in the elimination of all privacy rights. Wars in Africa over the water-rich Sahara aquifer. Animals with human rights. Designer babies.

Computers that operate by thought recognition. Airport security systems that read minds. All of your ID information, credit information, medical information, and passport information reduced to a single chip implanted in your hand.

Watch out for so-called "wildcard events," events of sudden and discontinuous change. Some can be good for your future. Some can be disastrous. The assassination of JFK, the loss of the space shuttles *Challenger* and *Columbia,* the collapse of Soviet communism, and the terrorist attack of September 11, 2001, were all wildcard events. Sudden and unexpected change can abruptly terminate trends and throw your forecasts into complete uncertainty.

As you scan the horizon for change, maintain a healthy balance between open-mindedness and skepticism. Sometimes there's a very thin line between a visionary genius and a total looney. The green movement, for example, was considered a "wacko" fringe movement twenty or thirty years ago; today, environmental concerns are very much in the mainstream of our society.

As you learn to identify trends and ideas that produce change, you will be empowered to more effectively, pro-actively respond to the trends and events going on around you. The more you understand about change, the better you will manage your future.

3. *Learn to effectively plan for change.* Consider all possible implications of change in your life and your organization. Picture both best-case and worst-case scenarios, then devise strategies to enable you to survive and thrive in the midst of change.

Develop a vision for change. Walt was more than a futurist. He was a visionary. A vision is an optimistic dream of tomorrow that pulls you toward a desirable future. Envision the future as you want it to be, then spend the next ten, twenty, thirty years of your life turning that dream into a reality. Don't accept any limits on your vision; reach for the sky.

As you envision the future, be boldly optimistic. Preach optimism and inspire people around you with your positive view of tomorrow. As you talk up your optimistic view of the future,

> *"He became preoccupied—then later obsessed—with building a city of the future; a real place where people would sleep, work and play. No slums. No pollution. No crime."*
>
> KATHERINE AND RICHARD GREENE
> DISNEY BIOGRAPHERS

expect opposition from the naysayers. There will always be a few poor souls who thrive on doom and gloom, who insist that the end is near. They are to be pitied—but don't let them distract you from your vision for a brighter tomorrow.

If the pessimists prevail, our world is headed for a dark and gloomy future. But if we keep preaching our message of optimism, then this world will get better and better. Optimism is a powerful force for building a brighter tomorrow.

Influential, successful people like Walt Disney don't see the world as most people see it. They don't see reality as it is, but as it could be—and even as it should be. They envision a shining and hopeful future, and then they create practical strategies for making their beautiful dreams come true. Walt showed us that predicting the future is really not difficult at all. You simply make a prediction—then you go out and make that prediction come true.

Every day, ask yourself the question Walt asked Ray Bradbury: "How about tomorrow?" The answer to the question is largely up to you. The answer cannot be found in a crystal ball or a deck of tarot cards. The answer is in your hands and between your ears.

There are so many possible futures. Which one will you choose?

Chapter Eleven

❦

Living for the
Next Generation

In the late 1950s, Walt became increasingly concerned about the needs of future generations. The result of this concern was an innovative blend of entertainment and education called The Mickey Mouse Club. *And that was just the beginning . . .*

Walt Disney had an uncanny talent for recognizing and developing creative talent. Take Bill Walsh, for example. A graduate of the University of Missouri, Walsh had knocked around the world of print and broadcast media for nearly twenty years before he met Walt Disney. During his first few months at Disney, Walsh had no direct contact with Walt. He didn't think Walt even knew his name.

One day in 1950, Walt stepped into Walsh's office. "Bill," he said, "you're going to be a television producer."

"Me?" Walsh said, stunned. "I don't know anything about television."

Walt shrugged. "Who does?"

Just like that, Bill Walsh was a producer. He produced Disney's first two Christmas specials, and went on to produce the *Disneyland* Sunday night show on ABC.

In late 1954, after the *Disneyland* series was up and running, Walt again approached Walsh. "Bill," he said, "I'm taking you off the weekly TV show."

Walsh breathed a sigh of relief. Producing an hour-long show every week had left him in a state of exhaustion.

"I'm going to put you on a new show," Walt continued. "It's called *The Mickey Mouse Club,* and it's an hour-long show, five days a week."

Walsh groaned. Walt had just quintupled his weekly quota!

Jimmie and the Big Mooseketeer

Bill Walsh wrote up a plan for the new show, based on Walt's ideas. The name of the show, *The Mickey Mouse Club,* was inspired by the Mickey Mouse fan clubs of the 1930s. The cast members would be called "Mouseketeers," after the 1936 Silly Symphonies cartoon, *Three Blind Mouseketeers.*

For the adult leader of the Mouseketeers, Walt wanted a warm and likable Mr. Nice Guy, and he found one in Jimmie Dodd. Born in Ohio in 1910, Dodd was an actor, guitarist, singer, songwriter and devout Christian. He had worked steadily in movies during the 1940s. Though a heart condition kept Jimmie out of World War II, he joined the USO and entertained the troops overseas.

After the war, he returned to California to resume his movie career—but no one would hire him. "When we got back to Hollywood," Jimmie's wife Ruth recalled, "it was like every door was closed. We felt that maybe the Lord didn't want him in show business anymore." So one night, Jimmie and Ruth prayed and asked God to open a door.

The very next day, Jimmie's phone rang—and his prayer was answered. It was one of Jimmie's tennis buddies, Disney animator Bill Justice. "Walt Disney needs a songwriter," Justice said. "I recommended you. I hope that's okay."

"That's great!" Jimmie said. "What kind of a song does he need?"

"We're going to animate a pencil, and we need a pencil song. Can you do it?"

A pencil song? It was a strange assignment—but Jimmie wrote and recorded a pencil song and sent it to the studio. Walt loved the song so much that he hired Jimmie as a songwriter. Not long afterward, Walt chose Jimmie as host for *The Mickey Mouse Club.*

Walt not only admired Jimmie's talent, but he liked Jimmie as a person—

his strong moral character, his humility, his positive attitude. Jimmie's
personality was the perfect reflection
of what *The Mickey Mouse Club* was
all about.

Jimmie Dodd put his heart and
soul into the show and wrote most of
its songs, including the "The Mickey
Mouse Club March." His sunny
charm and strong Christian faith
were evident in several songs he

> *"Very few individuals have
> impacted our lives like Walt has.
> If you grew up in the 1950s
> and '60s, your view of popular
> culture was shaped by Walt
> Disney. You couldn't escape it."*
>
> TED THOMAS
> SON OF DISNEY ANIMATOR FRANK THOMAS

wrote, such as "Good Samaritan" and "Do What the Good Book Says."

Jimmie was more than a songwriter and performer; he became a friend
and mentor to the Mouseketeers. They looked up to him, and he was
always ready to give the young performers a word of spiritual, moral or
motivational encouragement.

Mouseketeer Lonnie Burr observed, "The amazing thing, given the
notoriety of most child stars, is that the original Mouseketeers do not
appear in the tabloids." Of the thirty-nine Mouseketeers, Burr added, only
two ever got into any trouble with the law—and not until forty years after
they were on the show.

Mouseketeer Tommy Cole remembers Jimmie as a guiding presence on
the show. "He would never tell an off-color joke," Cole said. "Jimmie was
sort of a father figure, like Walt Disney. He was a great influence on me."

Jimmie's co-host, Roy Williams, was also hand-picked by Walt. His TV
nickname, "The Big Mooseketeer," came from a nickname he picked up
playing high school football. He was still known as "Moose Williams"
when he joined the Disney studio as an animator and story artist.

Roy Williams first met Walt in 1929 when he applied for a job as an animator. He went to Walt's studio and the secretary told him to wait in the
office. So Roy sat with his portfolio across his knees and waited. After a few
minutes, an office boy came in and started shuffling some papers on the
desk. "Are you waiting to see Walt Disney?" the office boy asked.

"Yeah," Roy said. "I want to be an animator." They chatted for about ten
minutes, then Roy said, "Tell me—what is Walt Disney really like?"

The office boy grinned. "I'm Walt Disney," he said.

Roy was so startled that he dropped his portfolio and his drawings went flying across the floor. While Roy turned red with embarrassment, Walt picked up some of the drawings and held them up in front of his face so that Roy wouldn't see him grinning. That was the beginning of a long friendship between Walt Disney and "Moose" Williams.

Roy Williams became one of Walt's favorite gag artists. He was a wild practical joker who could do no wrong in Walt's eyes. On one occasion in the 1930s, Williams showed up late for work and the studio office manager docked his salary. In retaliation, Williams rigged a bucket of water over a door. When the manager opened the door, he got soaked.

The manager burst into Walt's office and roared, "You've got to fire Moose Williams!"

"That's between you and Moose," Walt said, repressing a chuckle. "Now, go change your clothes. You're dripping all over my carpet."

Disney voice actress Ginny Tyler told me, "In the early 1950s, Roy started goofing off and doing too much late-night partying. It affected his work so, around 1953, Walt had to fire him. Roy tried to act unfazed—he said he could get a job at any studio in town. But he couldn't find animation work, so he ended up at an iron foundry in L.A. It was hot, miserable work.

"One day, Roy looked up and there was Walt, standing with his arms folded. Roy walked over to talk to him, and Walt asked, 'Are you ready to come back?' Roy was ready, and Walt took him back to the studio."

Roy Williams' biggest contribution to *The Mickey Mouse Club* is probably his least known: He designed the Mickey Mouse ears worn by the Mouseketeers. The idea came from a 1929 Mickey Mouse cartoon that Roy had animated. In that short, *The Karnival Kid,* Roy had Mickey tip his hat to Minnie—and Mickey's "hat," of course, was his ears.

Those mouse ears became the visual signature of *The Mickey Mouse Club,* and a hugely popular merchandise item at Disneyland souvenir shops. At the height of the show's popularity, the mouse ears sold at a rate of 20,000 per day.

One day in early 1955, Walt was sitting in Roy's office, talking over ideas for the show, when his face suddenly lit up. "Say, Moose," Walt said, "you're kind of fat and funny-looking. I'm going to put you on the show. We'll call you 'The Big Mooseketeer.'"

Roy thought Walt was kidding. When he saw that Walt was serious, he panicked. "I was scared to death," he later recalled. "I was no actor, but I had faith in Walt's vision." And that's how Roy was added to the cast.

Mouseketeer roll call

In March 1955, casting directors Lee Traver and Jack Lavin began casting the show in the usual Hollywood manner: They put out "cattle calls" for child actors. It was a time-consuming process, and Walt was not happy with the candidates he saw.

"I don't want those kids that tap-dance or blow trumpets," a frustrated Walt finally told Bill Walsh. "And I don't want to deal with their nutty stage mothers. I just want ordinary kids."

"Walt," Walsh said, "where are we going to find these 'ordinary kids'?"

"We'll just go where the kids are," Walt said. "Visit some schools. Watch the kids at recess. You'll always find one kid you can't help watching. That's the one with star quality. Find a few kids like that and let's put on a show."

"Walt sent his producers to schoolyards to look for natural kids to be Mouseketeers. He didn't want that slick, professional look. He wanted real kids."

BOBBY BURGESS
MOUSEKETEER

One of the first Mouseketeers cast was Sharon Baird, who was personally recommended by Jimmie Dodd. "I always thought of Walt Disney as a shy man," Sharon later recalled. "I could tell he was always watching out for us, and I remember him in coveralls with paint all over them, just like any of many workers on the lot. And he knew everyone on a first-name basis, whether it was a producer or director, or a gardener or electrician."

The two youngest Mouseketeers, Karen and Cubby, were usually paired together. At his audition, nine-year-old Carl "Cubby" O'Brien played the drums—a talent that was put to good use on the show.

Karen Pendleton was eight when she auditioned. "I didn't have a clue what was going on," she recalled. "I just did my little dance—and I got the giggles right in the middle of it. Then I looked around the room, and I recognized Jimmie Dodd. He had sung at my church the previous Sunday." Seeing a familiar face put Karen at ease. She finished her dance, and won her mouse ears.

Another original Mouseketeer was Lonnie Burr. "We were kids playing ourselves," he said, "and there was nothing else like that on television at the time."

Mouseketeer Tommy Cole is now one of Hollywood's leading makeup artists. He recalls being nervous when Walt was on the set. "I was doing a scene one day," he said, "and having a hard time with the cue cards when Walt came in. I was so nervous with him there I just couldn't get it right and had to ask him to leave. . . . Once he left, I was fine."

> "He wanted the Mouseketeers to call him 'Uncle Walt.' We respected him so much that we couldn't. We called him 'Mr. Disney.' But if he were here today, I would call him 'Uncle Walt.' Now that I'm older, I understand what it would have meant to him."
>
> SHARON BAIRD
> MOUSEKETEER

Doreen Tracey remembers Walt as more of a kindly uncle than a boss. "He never talked down to me," she said. One time in 1956, Doreen was at Disneyland with Walt and the other Mouseketeers to shoot a musical sequence with the Firehouse Five Plus Two. Between takes, Walt turned to her and said, "Do you realize that being a Mouseketeer is the greatest thing you'll ever do in your whole life?"

"At first, I thought, 'What does he mean by that?'" Doreen recalls. "But I never forgot it and boy, was he right."

Canadian-born Darlene Gillespie sang "The Ballad of Davy Crockett" at her audition. During her first year on the show, she had her own serial, "Corky and White Shadow." After the series ended, she got her degree in nursing and raised two children.

"When the show was syndicated on television," Darlene said, "I never told my children that the pigtailed girl named Darlene was their mom. I thought it would embarrass them or that they would think the show was silly. Finally, one of my neighbors told my children that Mouseketeer

Darlene was their mother. Fortunately, they liked the show and were very proud of me. That made it all worthwhile."

The undisputed sweetheart of *The Mickey Mouse Club* was Annette Funicello, who was discovered by Walt himself. "Walt Disney saw me dancing in a school recital," Annette recalls, "and he invited me to audition for the show. I was told they auditioned over ten thousand kids, and I was the last one chosen. Mr. Disney was so supportive of me. I certainly wasn't the best singer and I wasn't the best dancer on the show, but he always made me feel better about myself."

Annette's mother, Virginia Funicello, was intimidated in Walt's presence. "I actually hid when I saw him coming," she recalled. "But he was really so nice and he knew I was scared. He always tried to make me feel comfortable by talking about Annette and telling me what a wonderful girl she was."

> *"I owe everything to those ears."*
> ANNETTE FUNICELLO
> ACTRESS AND MOUSEKETEER

Annette became better acquainted with Walt during her post-Mouseketeer career. "I would go to him for advice at times," she said. She was concerned about her shyness and asked Walt if she should see a psychologist about it. "Absolutely not!" Walt told her. "People love you just the way you are. If you were to change that, you wouldn't be you."

In 1992, Annette disclosed her battle with multiple sclerosis (MS), a crippling disorder of the central nervous system. "When I was first diagnosed with multiple sclerosis," she said, "my family was foremost in my mind. Although I also thought, 'If Mr. Disney were here, I could ask him what I should do. He would know.'"

Mickey in the classroom

Walt envisioned *The Mickey Mouse Club* as a show that would educate by entertaining. The show was so much fun, with made-for-TV serials, skits and cartoons from the Disney vault, that young viewers didn't realize they were learning as they watched.

For *The Mickey Mouse Club's* science segments, Walt tapped physicist Julius Sumner Miller to appear in the recurring role of "Professor

Wonderful." Though Miller looked like a mad scientist with his intense eyes and unruly white mane, his energetic personality made science come alive for his young audience. Miller, who studied under Albert Einstein, inspired many young viewers to seek careers in science.

Walt also recruited Pinocchio's conscience, Jiminy Cricket, to lecture on safety topics. The theme of these segments was "I'm No Fool" and featured segments on water safety, recreational safety, safety with electricity, and more.

Educators praised *The Mickey Mouse Club* for its seamless blend of educational and entertainment values. Disney and ABC developed a booklet called the *Disney Television Classroom Guide,* which was sent to teachers. Walt described the mission of the show in his foreword to the *Classroom Guide:* "We have the greatest respect for the basic intelligence of our future adults and their desire to learn. We, likewise, are aware of a sometimes prevalent habit of 'talking down' to audiences of this type. To the best of our ability we aim to 'talk up' as much as possible as we program our material, remembering that we will accomplish more if we entertain as we go along."

The Disney company also published *The Mickey Mouse Club Magazine* as a companion to the show. Again, this publication reflected Walt's commitment to stimulating a love of learning among his viewers. Each issue featured stories about the Mouseketeers, serialized fiction based on the *Mickey Mouse Club* serials, Disney comic strips, and articles on history, science, and places around the world. Walt wanted *The Mickey Mouse Club* to encourage a love of reading and learning.

> *"It wasn't just cartoons and Mouseketeers. Kids were taught how Christmas was celebrated in other lands and how life was lived on a farm. They learned something while they were being entertained."*
>
> LONNIE BURR
> MOUSEKETEER

Walt also sent his Mouseketeers out to area hospitals to visit, sign autographs, and perform. In her book *A Dream Is a Wish Your Heart Makes,* Annette Funicello recalled that hospital visits often left her feeling "emotionally exhausted after seeing a badly disfigured, burned or critically ill child." Yet she was glad that she and her fellow Mouseketeers had the experience of giving of themselves to these children.

The Mickey Mouse Club was canceled in 1959 after a contractual dispute between the ABC network and Disney. The demise of *The Mickey Mouse Club* was a devastating blow to the young cast. During the show's four seasons, the Mouseketeers became a close-knit family. The kids couldn't understand why the show was ending while it was so popular.

Annette recalled the final day of shooting: "Sharon Baird and I carried our autograph books from friend to friend and made sure that everyone signed them. All of us Mouseketeers cried, and so did our mothers. Making it even more difficult was that last day's work. We were filming reaction shots in which we all had to laugh and smile as if we were the happiest kids on earth. Now, that took acting."

For Jimmie Dodd, Mouseketeer Jimmie was the role of a lifetime. Though a veteran of over seventy motion pictures, he'd never had a starring role before *The Mickey Mouse Club.* Walt gave him the chance to play himself on TV, write and perform his songs, and become a friend to millions of young people. The show defined Jimmie for the rest of his life, and he was always grateful to Walt for giving him that opportunity.

True-Life Adventures

Walt's commitment to educating by entertaining was never more clearly demonstrated than in his nature documentaries, the True-Life Adventures. The series originated with Walt's own true-life adventure in remote western Alaska.

In August 1947, Walt and his ten-year-old daughter Sharon boarded a privately owned Douglas DC-3 airliner as guests of Walt's old polo buddy, Russell Havenstrite. Lilly had originally planned to go too, but changed her mind a few days before departure. Diane was in summer camp and unable to go.

Walt, Sharon, and Havenstrite had a great trip for the first few days. Walt shot 16 mm footage of Mount McKinley from the air. They flew above the Arctic Circle, where the summer sun remained in the sky twenty-four hours a day.

The pleasant jaunt turned into a frightening adventure, however, as they flew to the mining town of Candle. They found themselves over a dense blanket of clouds and couldn't see to land—and the radio chose that moment to go dead. Havenstrite's pilot circled for ninety minutes, hoping for a break in the clouds.

As they circled, Havenstrite broke the seal on a bottle of 80-proof libation and shared a drink with Walt—just to steady the old nerves. As the plane's fuel tanks grew steadily more dry, Havenstrite reminded Walt that their old polo partner, Will Rogers, had been killed in a 1935 plane crash near Barrow, not 400 miles north of their position. On that cheery note, Walt requested another drink.

With the plane running on fumes, the pilot decided to get beneath the clouds and hope there was no mountainside waiting for them. As they broke through the cloud cover, the pilot and passengers saw an amazing sight: the town of Candle. By sheer chance, they had come through the clouds right over their destination. When Walt came down the gangplank, he fell face-down onto the tarmac. He later said, "I don't know whether I kissed the ground or fell on it."

> *"Walt was a genius, but in a different sense than Isaac Newton or Einstein. I think Walt was one of the fifty brightest people of all time. But I don't think Walt ever considered himself a genius. He was too humble for that. He described himself as a storyteller."*
>
> BOB PENFIELD
> DISNEYLAND FOREMAN

Walt's close call in Alaska fired up his enthusiasm for making documentary films about out-of-the-way places. From footage shot in Alaska by Disney photographers, director James Algar produced a film called *Seal Island,* a half-hour short subject released in 1949. The film explored the cycle of life among seals and birds on a tiny island in the Bering Sea, and became the first of more than a dozen True-Life Adventure films. Other documentaries in the series included *In Beaver Valley* (1950), *The Living Desert* (1953), *Bear Country* (1953), *The Vanishing Prairie* (1954), *The African Lion* (1955) and *White Wilderness* (1958).

The True-Life Adventures were documentaries with a distinctly Disney flair—including a sense of humor. Walt's nephew, Roy E. Disney, began his Disney career as an apprentice film cutter, working on *The Living Desert* and *The Vanishing Prairie*. Roy Edward recalls working with footage of ducks landing on a frozen pond. There was one shot of a duck that didn't realize the pond was frozen. On landing, the bird skidded and tumbled base-over-apex across the ice. It was a funny shot, though the cameraman quit filming before the bird came to a stop.

The duck-landing sequence was used in a rough cut of the film, which was screened for Walt. At the end of the sequence, Walt stood up. "Hold it!" he said. "Where's the footage where that duck skids into the other ducks?"

Film editor Lloyd Richardson was baffled. "We don't have any footage like that, Walt."

"Yes, you do," Walt insisted. "I remember seeing it! The duck rolls across the ice and tumbles right into a bunch of other ducks. You cut out the best part!"

Richardson was sure there was no such footage, but he said, "We'll look for it, Walt." Then he quietly told his young apprentice, Roy E. Disney, to find that footage.

"But it doesn't exist," Roy replied. "Walt thinks he saw it, but he's wrong!"

"If Walt says he saw it," Richardson said, "then it must be there. Find it."

Roy spent countless hours over the next three months, looking through every frame of footage they had, trying to find a duck skidding into a bunch of other ducks. Every so often, Walt would stop by and ask, "Did you find that shot with the duck?"

"Not yet," Roy said, "but if it's in there, we'll find it."

"It's in there," Walt insisted.

But it wasn't in there. It wasn't anywhere. So James Algar sent a cameraman out to a frozen pond in northern Minnesota with a bunch of tame ducks. The cameraman shot dozens of takes as a crewmember repeatedly slid one duck into a group of other ducks. The best footage was spliced in at the end of the duck landing scene and shown to Walt.

"You see?" Walt said triumphantly. "I told you that footage was in there."

Walt created films and TV programs that were not only fun but enriching. He gave young people knowledge to feed their dreams. Perhaps that is why so many of today's environmentalists, naturalists, zoologists, marine biologists, and animal welfare workers credit Walt's True-Life Adventures as a major influence in their lives.

One person profoundly impacted by Disney's nature films is Mignonne Walker Decker, daughter of former Disney CEO Card Walker. "Walt turned me into an environmentalist through his True-Life nature films like *Seal Island*," she told me. "He was so ahead of his time on this topic. I was deeply impacted by *Bambi* and the Silly Symphonies. The cartoon *Little Hiawatha* made me hate hunters, and *Lady and the Tramp* taught me about animal rights."

> *"I have learned from the animal world, and what everyone will learn who studies it is a renewed sense of kinship with the earth and all its inhabitants."*
>
> WALT DISNEY

Walt once said that his goal for the True-Life Adventures was to "open the eyes of young and old to the beauties of the outdoor world" and encourage people to "conserve priceless natural assets." He added, "In all my years of picturemaking, I have never had more satisfaction or felt more useful in the business of entertainment than I have in making the True-Life Adventures."

Walt Disney didn't merely live for balance sheets and return on investment. He lived for the next generation. He lived to inspire young hearts and nourish young minds. He once said, "A child is helpless in choosing what is to be engraved on his mind during the formative years. The awsome responsibility is assumed, for better or worse, by us as adults. Today we are shapers of the world of tomorrow. That is the plain truth. There is no way we can duck the responsibility and there is no reason, except sloth and cowardice, why we should."

It's a responsibility Walt took very seriously. And so should we.

A born teacher

In his later years, Walt's thoughts turned to the task of preparing the next generation to face the challenge of the future. In 1961, Walt and his brother Roy gave a generous endowment to establish the California Institute of the Arts (CalArts), a university-level school for the creative and performing arts. The Disney brothers also guided the process of forming CalArts through the merger of the Los Angeles Conservatory of Music (founded 1883) and the Chouinard Art Institute (founded 1921).

Walt had a great admiration for both institutions. Beginning in 1934, Chouinard instructors had helped prepare Walt's artists for the task of animating *Snow White and the Seven Dwarfs*. He remembered the generosity of the school's founder, Mrs. Nelbert M. Chouinard, who didn't charge for classes when Walt and Roy were having cash-flow problems. In the late 1950s, when the Chouinard school developed ruinous financial problems, Walt paid Buzz Price and his Economic Research Associates to examine the school's finances. Price traced the school's problems to an employee who had embezzled $75,000. Disney attorney Luther Marr helped resolve the school's financial and legal problems.

The Los Angeles Conservatory of Music had trained many of the musicians and songwriters Walt worked with over the years, including Marty Paich, who arranged the music for *Lady and the Tramp*. Coincidentally, the Conservatory was also undergoing financial problems due to an embezzler. Together with Conservatory patron Mrs. Lulu May Von Hagen, Walt helped devise a plan for combining the Conservatory with the art school and creating a university of the arts, modeled after the California Institute of Technology. The merger formally took place in 1963.

Walt envisioned CalArts as a community of the arts where creative talent from every discipline could learn together in a synergistic way. Walt had seen how an interdisciplinary approach had magnified the creativity of his own studio. His artists, for example, were much better prepared if they also knew about music, storytelling, acting, dance, and even engineering.

Animator-Imagineer Marc Davis recalls that Walt wanted to bring great artists to CalArts as guest professors—artists such as Salvador Dali and Pablo Picasso. Walt once told Davis, "Maybe I could teach a class there myself." Davis must have had a surprised look on his face, because Walt frowned and added, "I don't mean to teach drawing—but I'm a good story man! I could teach story!"

Amazingly, CalArts was more important to Walt than his films, his television shows, and even his beloved Disneyland. "It's the principal thing I hope to leave when I move on to greener pastures," he once said. "If I can help provide a place to develop the talent of the future, I think I will have accomplished something."

> *"Walt felt people would come to CalArts from around the world. This was his dream—to attract people with outstanding talent and put them in this environment where they would experience absolutely everything."*
>
> MARC DAVIS
> DISNEY ANIMATOR

"He wanted to build that school!" Buzz Price recalled. "It was the most pervasive objective in a man's mind that I've ever run into. He was very close to the evolution of CalArts. He was passionate all the way." Walt's commitment to CalArts was demonstrated by his donation of thirty-eight wooded acres from the Disney studio's Golden Oak ranch near Newhall, California—a site often used by the studio for location filming. When Walt died, he left forty-five percent of his estate to CalArts.

"Walt was a born teacher," his friend Ray Bradbury once said. "Everything he did pointed to a moral or indicated a route for us to take. It was very important, for a teacher, as he often said, to give the proper information to people."

In the last decade of his life, he helped create one of the most forward-thinking fine arts, film arts, and graphic arts institutions in the world. "This is the thing I'm going to be remembered for," he said. In view of all of Walt's many other accomplishments, that's quite a statement. But Walt was intensely committed to CalArts because he wanted to leave something of lasting value to the next generation.

Walt's friend, Art Linkletter, shared a memory with me that reveals Walt's heart for young people. "Walt gave me a gift on my birthday one year," he said. "It's a four-by-six photo of a small boy looking off in the distance. There is a single word across the bottom of the photo—'Priorities'—and below that word is this statement: 'A hundred years from now it will not matter what is in your bank account, or what kind of car you drive. It will only matter that you made a difference in the life of a child.'

"That's what drove Walt," Art Linkletter concluded. "He wanted to impact children in a positive way. Walt wasn't just living for himself, for his own success or pride. He was living for future generations."

If we want to be like Walt, then that must become your goal and mine. We must be people who live not merely for ourselves, but for generations to come.

How to Be Like Walt—
Lesson 12: Live for the Next Generation

In the 1950s, Walt called Santa Monica High School and asked the drama teacher if there were any promising students in the graduating class. The teacher gave Walt the name of a talented senior—Ken Wales. Walt invited Ken to be his guest at the Burbank studio. For three days, Walt mentored Ken. He took him around the studio and showed him every aspect of filmmaking, from crafting a story to creating vivid sound effects.

"I spent three days with Walt," Ken Wales told me, "and he was my friend for life. He didn't just teach me the fundamentals of filmmaking. He taught me the fundamentals of creativity. From Walt, I learned that we should not merely dream big—we should dream *beautifully.* Walt's films are timeless because they are full of imagination, values, warmth and delight."

Those three days with Walt Disney changed Ken's life forever. On the last day, Walt wrote a $5,000 check from his personal account. Walt gave Ken a fully paid scholarship to study filmmaking at the University of Southern California. "I was at USC for five years," Ken told me, "and that laid the foundation for my life."

Upon graduating, Ken Wales was hired by director Blake Edwards. During his fifteen-year partnership with Edwards, Ken helped create such films as *The Great Race, The Party* and *Revenge of the Pink Panther.* He also produced such films as *The Tamarind Seed* with Julie Andrews, *Islands in the Stream* with George C. Scott, *The Prodigal* for Billy Graham, and the highly acclaimed TV series *Christy.* He also became an executive with the Walt Disney Studio and The Disney Channel.

Today, Ken Wales teaches filmmaking at USC. "It's a way of giving back what I was given," he says. "Walt Disney mentored me, and now I mentor my students as a way of honoring Walt and repaying him for the kindness and generosity he showed to me when I was a high school senior."

The story of how Walt Disney mentored Ken Wales is just one of the many examples of how Walt lived for the next generation. He didn't just create educational films and TV programs. He didn't just endow a school of the arts. He involved himself in the lives of people. He mentored. He taught. He trained. He coached. In the process, he set a fine example for you and me—an example of how to live for the next generation.

Even if you are not a television producer or a filmmaker, even if you do not have the wherewithal to endow a university, you can still live for the next generation as Walt did. Here are some suggestions to get you started:

Become inspirationally involved in the lives of young people. Become a learning partner or reading tutor for children in your neighborhood or at a local elementary school. Volunteer to read with a child on a regular basis. Help children learn to use the library. Volunteer to read to groups of children in a local kindergarten or early elementary class.

Create a neighborhood study site at a school, private home, or community center. Provide resource materials and organize tutors to help kids with their homework. Play math games with kids and help them with spelling exercises.

Volunteer to spend time in classrooms, helping overburdened teachers. Offer your talents in teaching music, crafts, drama and art. Help decorate the classroom, grade papers, or perform other chores. Purchase or collect items needed for educational or crafts activities.

Become a mentor to children or teens. Become a Big Brother or Big Sister. Get involved in Scouting. Contact a teen shelter or crisis pregnancy center and volunteer to help counsel a troubled or pregnant teen. Open your home and become a foster parent.

Become a Sunday school teacher or youth advisor at your place of worship. When you teach, don't just educate—entertain! Make it fun! Use audio-visual aids that rivet the attention of young listeners—a PowerPoint presentation or a video with music and images young people enjoy. Dress up in a costume that reflects your subject matter. Bring an exotic animal to class (make sure it doesn't bite!). Seek new ways to provoke curiosity and fire the imagination of your students. Never let them get bored.

"Think beyond your lifetime if you want to accomplish something truly worthwhile."

WALT DISNEY

Do you want to change the world and make it a better place for the next generation? Then start by becoming what you wish the world to be. If you want the world to be more loving, then live out your love in your actions.

If you want the next generation to know a world of peace, then live at peace with others around you. If you want the world to be a welcoming and nurturing place for children, then open your heart to the children around you.

During the last years of Walt's life, he clearly gave a lot of thought to his legacy. What will you be remembered for? A hundred years from now, will it matter what is in your bank account? Will it matter what kind of car you drive? Will it matter if someone puts up a statue of you in the park or carves your face on Mount Rushmore?

No. The one thing that will matter to future generations is that you made a difference in the life of a child.

Chapter Twelve

❧

A Man of
Singular Focus

*By the early 1960s, Walt was in the home stretch of his life.
He knew he had much to do and only limited time to do it. His
closing years became the ultimate test of his ability to focus on
his dreams.*

In April 1906, Flora Disney stepped off the Santa Fe train, accompanied
by her three youngest children—thirteen-year-old Roy, five-year-old
Walter, and three-year-old Ruth. They had traveled from Chicago to Fort
Madison, Iowa, where Uncle Mike Martin lived. Elias and the two older
boys had left Chicago a few days earlier with a wagonload of family furnish-
ings, headed for the new farm Elias had bought just outside of Marceline,
Missouri.

During their stay at the Martin house, Roy and Walter enjoyed going
out and exploring the town. While they were walking together, Walt spotted something shiny in the street. He picked it up and admired it. "Roy,
look!" he said. "A pocketknife!"

"Gimme that!" Roy said, snatching the knife from Walt's hands.

"Hey!" Walt said. "That's mine! I found it!"

"You're not old enough to have a knife," big brother Roy said. "I'm keeping this for your own good."

Years passed. The Disney brothers grew up, moved to California, and went into business together. They made cartoons and feature films and they built a park called Disneyland. Through those years, they had their share of clashes, yet Walt never said a word about the pocketknife.

One day in the early 1960s, Walt and Roy were in the throes of a sharp disagreement over one of Walt's projects. As usual, Walt wanted to gamble with a few million dollars of the studio's money, and also as usual, Roy said no, the studio couldn't afford it.

"That's what you always do!" Walt shouted, pointing an accusing finger at Roy. "You're always bossing me around, treating me like a little kid! It's just like when we were in Fort Madison and you took that pocketknife from me!"

Roy was stunned. He and Walt hadn't talked about the pocketknife in almost sixty years—but Walt hadn't forgotten! That knife symbolized their entire relationship, both as brothers and business partners. Roy had spent his whole life, man and boy, looking after Walt, protecting him from danger. Sure, Roy had sometimes bullied Walt—but always for Walt's own good.

Over their long and extraordinary partnership, a predictable pattern had emerged: Walt would propose an expensive idea. Roy would say no. Walt would bamboozle Roy every way he could. Ultimately, Roy would give in and find some way to finance Walt's latest obsession.

> "Walt and Roy needed each other. I've often wondered what might have happened if they hadn't been together. Walt might have ended up working for Walter Lantz, because he wasn't a businessman. And Roy could have ended up as a manager of a Bank of America in Glendale."
>
> JACK LINDQUIST
> RETIRED DISNEYLAND EXECUTIVE

One of Walt's longtime friends, Rush Johnson from Marceline, Missouri, worked with Walt on "The Marceline Project," a plan to restore Walt's childhood home and turn it into a park. Rush shared a story with me that provides an insight into the Disney brothers' unique relationship. "In 1956," Rush said, "when Walt and Roy Disney came back to Marceline, Roy took me aside and said, 'You've got to watch Walt. You have to stand firm and tell him no, because he gets all carried away with his projects.' Later, Walt pulled me aside and said, 'Here's how we'll handle Roy. You say this and I'll say that. Then you say this and I'll say that. Then we'll shut up and Roy will go for it.'"

The yin and yang between Walt and Roy was legendary. They clashed repeatedly through the years, yet their conflicts were *creative* conflicts between two contrasting and complementary personalities. Walt supplied the dreams and energy; Roy supplied the prudent judgment and financial savvy. Neither man could have achieved greatness alone; together, they were an unstoppable force.

The polar opposition of their personalities was the source of their success—but also the source of their many clashes. No matter how loudly they fought, Walt and Roy knew they loved each other as brothers and needed each other as partners. Soon after the 1956 breakup of Dean Martin and Jerry Lewis, Walt remarked, "Roy and I must have a guardian angel. We could never split up like Martin and Lewis, because Roy doesn't know if it's my guardian angel who made us successful, and I don't know if it's his."

In the 1950s, as the Disney company diversified into so many different entertainment fields, the company's structure and business relationships became increasingly more complex. Contrary to popular belief, Walt no longer ran Walt Disney Productions. He was far more than a figurehead, certainly, and he still oversaw every major creative project at the studio and the park.

But Walt didn't call the shots. Operational decision-making was concentrated in the hands of Roy and the board of directors, all of whom answered to the stockholders, not to Walt. As a result, the relationship between Walt and Roy became increasingly tense.

A major area of tension involved Walt's creation of WED Enterprises to build attractions for the Disneyland theme park and the holding company Retlaw, ("Walter" spelled backwards). Most of the attractions built by WED Enterprises were sold to Walt Disney Productions on a cost-plus-overhead basis. WED Enterprises retained ownership of the Disneyland Railroad and the Monorail, staffing them with WED employees. Walt Disney Productions leased those attractions from WED for cash and royalties on merchandise sold in the park.

In forming these companies, Walt granted exclusive use of the Walt Disney name to WED and Retlaw, the companies he personally owned.

Then he demanded that publicly owned Walt Disney Productions pay a leasing fee for the right to use his name. Walt felt it was only right that he be compensated for the commercial use of his good name, but Roy considered Walt's demand an affront verging on betrayal.

Angry but pragmatic, Roy reined in his emotions and tried to settle his differences with Walt. Roy arranged for a working vacation—just Roy and Edna with Walt and Lillian at Walt's Smoke Tree Ranch retreat. Roy saw it as a time when the Disney brothers could resolve their differences, once and for all.

It was not to be.

Lilly and Edna huddled together at one end of the house, while at the other, Walt and Roy shouted at each other until they were hoarse. Walt insisted that he only sought what was fair, after his years of sacrifice. Roy argued that the arrangement Walt wanted would provoke a stockholder revolt. Walt's demands might be fair, but they gave an appearance of conflict of interest—a cozy deal for Walt that would rob stockholders of return on investment. The faintest whiff of impropriety could open the door to costly litigation.

The battle dragged on for three days, punctuated by the harshest language and worst accusations ever exchanged between the two brothers. Roy's intended peace conference had erupted into World War III.

It was the beginning of a cold war that lasted well over a year. During that time, Walt and Roy didn't speak to each other. When they needed to communicate, they exchanged memos or sent messages through intermediaries. An outside observer might have thought that Walt and Roy hated each other. In reality, their brotherly love was as strong as ever. Neither Walt nor Roy saw the feud as a matter of hatred.

> "Walt was highly creative, but his brother Roy was the left brain of the family."
>
> HARRIET BURNS
> IMAGINEER

Dick Morrow was general counsel for Walt Disney Productions at the time. "The love between the two brothers never diminished in the slightest," Morrow said, "and I heard that from each of them individually. People who tried to take advantage of [the feud] and tried to play off one against the other faced trouble."

In the end, love proved stronger than anger. At one point, Roy sent a delegation of attorneys to meet with Walt and his agent. The meeting went badly, with shouting on both sides. Walt talked about making movies for a rival studio. The attorneys threatened legal action. Roy heard the entire shouting match from his office down the hall.

As Roy had done for most of his life, he came to Walt's defense. He strode into the conference room and confronted his negotiators. "You forget how important Walt Disney has been to your careers. None of us would be here in this studio if it hadn't been for Walt. Your jobs, your benefits, everything you have are the result of Walt's sacrifices. He deserves a lot better treatment than he's been shown here today."

At that point, the atmosphere of the negotiations changed, and Walt got most of what he wanted. The studio bought WED Enterprises and Walt retained ownership of Retlaw.

The atmosphere changed between Walt and Roy as well. Walt showed up in Roy's office with a gift-wrapped present for Roy's birthday. Roy opened it and found a Native American peace pipe. For the first time in months, they laughed together. Then they filled the pipe with tobacco and smoked it in turn. Afterward, Walt hand-wrote this letter to his brother Roy:

> It was wonderful to smoke the pipe of peace with you again—the clouds that rise are very beautiful. I think, between us over the years, we have accomplished something. There was a time when we couldn't borrow a thousand dollars and now I understand we owe twenty-four million!
>
> But in all sincerity, Happy Birthday and many more—
>
> And I love you.
> Walt

Roy had the pipe framed and hung in his office next to a portrait of Walt by photographer Yousuf Karsh. The feud between Walt and Roy passed into Disney legend.

Walt at the World's Fair

By the early 1960s, Walt was nearing the time in his life when most people start thinking about slowing down and enjoying those "golden years"—but Walt had no intention of slowing down. He was accelerating into the future at full throttle.

In a March 1960 meeting at WED Enterprises in Burbank, Walt told his Imagineers, "There's going to be a big fair in New York in 1964. All of the big corporations in the country are going to spend a lot of money building exhibits there. They don't know why they're doing it, except that the other corporations are doing it and they need to keep up with the Joneses.

"They'll want something that will make them stand out from the others, and that's what we can offer them. We've proved we can do it at Disneyland. This is a great opportunity for us to grow. We can use their financing to develop technologies that will help us in the future—and we'll be getting new attractions for Disneyland, too."

It was a brilliant yes-yes concept—but the first few companies said no. The Coca-Cola Company turned down a chance to underwrite the "Enchanted Tiki Room," which Walt wanted to premiere at the fair, then move to Disneyland. General Motors also turned it down. One GM official laughingly said, "You know who you oughta talk to? Those guys over at Ford. They don't have a clue what they're doing when it comes to the World's Fair."

> *"The World's Fair proved that the Disney magic was just as strong on the East Coast as in California. Walt's success in New York gave him the confidence to build the Florida Project."*
>
> JACK LINDQUIST
> RETIRED DISNEYLAND EXECUTIVE

The GM exec meant it as a joke, but Walt went to Ford, and Ford accepted Disney's offer. Disney Imagineers went to Dearborn, Michigan, toured the Ford plant, and were inspired by what they saw. John Hench noted that Ford cars started out as molten metal from a smelter at one end of a half-mile-long assembly line, and emerged as shiny new cars at the other end. Why not move people through an attraction the same way cars move down an assembly line?

The result was Disney's Omnimover system, now used in many Disney attractions, such as the "Haunted Mansion." For the Ford exhibit, the Omnimover used Ford convertibles as people-moving vehicles, carrying visitors along a track lined with 127 Audio-Animatronics figures. The attraction depicted the stages of evolutionary development, from the dinosaur age to the space age, and was called "The Magic Skyway."

The Ford exhibit was the first of four attractions Disney built for the World's Fair. The second was General Electric's Progressland, a circular theater in which the auditorium revolved around a stage with mechanically animated scenes of human progress. Progressland was renamed the "Carousel of Progress" when it was moved to Disneyland after the close of the fair.

The third attraction was the Illinois state exhibit. "Great Moments with Mr. Lincoln," featured an Audio-Animatronics version of President Abraham Lincoln, the rail-splitter from Illinois. Accepting this assignment was a huge risk for Walt. His Imagineers had never before constructed a truly convincing human-looking robot—yet Walt promised to deliver a robot that could fool Abe's own mother.

As a guide to programming the robot's speech and movements, Walt filmed actor Royal Dano (who bore a remarkable likeness to Lincoln) delivering a speech by the late president. The Imagineers studied Dano's performance in order to program the robot's facial expressions and gestures.

Royal Dano's first performance was a good reading—but Walt interrupted and shouted, "No, no! That's not what I want!" The actor did several more takes, and each time Walt said it was all wrong. When Dano was thoroughly tired and discouraged, Walt stood and directed the entire studio crew in singing "The Battle Hymn of the Republic." The soundstage tingled with emotion. There wasn't a dry eye in the place.

At the end of the song, Walt cued

> *"The Imagineering team had an incredibly difficult time getting Lincoln to move in a believable way. Walt kept saying, 'Keep going, you can do this.' He gave them the money they needed to get it right, and he kept urging them toward perfection."*
>
> FRANK ARMITAGE
> DISNEY ARTIST

Dano, and the actor gave a powerful performance. He was somber and weary, and his voice was on the verge of choking—just as the war-weary Lincoln must have felt as he stood on the blood-drenched battlefield and delivered the Gettysburg Address. It was precisely the performance Walt wanted. That recording became the soundtrack for the exhibit. When people saw "Great Moments with Mr. Lincoln," they marveled at the emotional power and realism of the robot's performance.

World's Fair president Robert Moses later said that his two greatest accomplishments at the World's Fair were bringing Michelangelo's statue "Pieta" to New York and bringing Disney's Lincoln. "Great Moments with Mr. Lincoln" later moved to Disneyland's Main Street Opera House, where it opened on the park's tenth anniversary, July 17, 1965.

The fourth attraction Walt produced for the World's Fair was the Pepsi-Cola exhibit, "It's a Small World." Amazingly, this enduring attraction was actually a rush job that Walt's team assembled at the last minute. Pepsi was working in partnership with UNICEF (the United Nations Children's Fund), but after spending months producing one failed design after another, Pepsi ran to Disney's Imagineers, pleading for help.

Admiral Joe Fowler, head of WED Enterprises, told Pepsi there was not enough time to design a decent attraction. Then Fowler went to Walt and told him he had turned Pepsi down.

Walt was stunned. "You did *what*?" he said. "Call them back, Joe! Tell them we're going to build it!" So work began on "It's a Small World."

> *"Walt came to me and said, 'Rolly, I want to do this big tower out in front of Small World, with nothing but mobiles and propellers.' I got the assignment because he had remembered my interest in kinetic sculpture."*
>
> ROLLY CRUMP
> IMAGINEER

Walt knew that this attraction had to compete for attention while remaining true to its small-scale theme. So Walt determined that it should have a tall marquee structure—a "weenie"—to attract visitors to the Pepsi-Cola pavilion.

Walt commissioned Imagineer Rolly Crump to create that marquee—a fanciful arrangement of spires, arches, propellers, and mobiles called the Tower of the Four Winds. Images of birds, butterflies and dragons were suspended from the 120-foot-tall, hundred-ton structure. Long Island winds kept its propellers and dancing animals in a state of perpetual motion. Rolly's tower became the most recognized landmark at the World's Fair.

Walt carefully selected the design team for the interior of "It's a Small World." He chose Mary Blair because of her gift for bold, vibrant color design. She created individualized color schemes for each nation and culture. Europe was multi-hued, Africa blue and green, the Middle East yellow, and Latin America pink and orange. The rest of the design team consisted of Bob Gurr, Rolly Crump, Marc Davis, and Marc's wife, Alice.

I asked Alice Davis how she was selected to work on the attraction. "One night," she said, "soon after Marc and I got married, I spent the day stripping wallpaper in our new house. I called Marc and told him I couldn't fix dinner—I was too tired. So we went to the Tam O'Shanter for dinner. In the middle of dinner, Marc felt a hand on his shoulder. It was Walt! He said, 'Is this your new wife?' Walt joined us, and I felt very comfortable with him.

"Before he left, Walt said, 'It may be a while, but I am going to call you. I want you to come work with me.' Sure enough, a few months later, Walt had a job for me, and I went to work designing costumes for 'It's a Small World.'"

Walt originally wanted the dolls in the exhibit to sing their own national anthems. The idea was tested—and the result was an ear-splitting cacophony of voices. So Walt had songwriters Richard and Robert Sherman write one song for all the children of the world.

The Shermans brothers looked at the drawings of Mary Blair and Marc Davis for inspiration. Then they went back to the piano and dashed off a little tune that could be sung in a round. When they showed the song to Walt, they apologized for writing something so mindlessly simple, and promised that their next try would be better.

"No, no, no!" Walt said. "This is it! This is perfect!"

And the song "It's a Small World After All" was born.

The attraction was a huge hit at the World's Fair. In 1966, after the fair closed, "It's a Small World" opened at Disneyland. The enduring popularity of this attraction is doubly amazing, since it was the most hastily created attraction in Disney history.

The four attractions Disney designed for the World's Fair were a shrewd move on Walt's part. Walt's Imagineers crammed a decade's worth of research and development into two years. The technological lessons they learned were applied to numerous Disneyland attractions, including "The Enchanted Tiki Room," "Pirates of the Caribbean," and the "Haunted Mansion." Best of all, Walt got three corporations and the state of Illinois to foot the bill.

Walt's cinematic obsession

Four months after the opening of the New York World's Fair, Walt unveiled his crowning achievement as a filmmaker—*Mary Poppins.* Based on the 1934 children's classic by P.L. Travers, *Mary Poppins* is the story of the magical English nanny who disturbs the well-ordered routine of the Banks family on London's Cherry Tree Lane.

Walt first encountered the book in 1939 when he found his daughter Diane reading it with her sister Sharon. In January 1944, Walt learned that P.L. Travers had moved to New York to escape the Nazi bombing raids over London. He sent Roy to meet with her and secure the adaptation rights. Pamela Lyndon Travers (a pseudonym for Australian-born Helen Lyndon Goff) refused to sell. "I cannot conceive of Mary Poppins as a cartoon character," she said. Roy returned to California empty-handed.

Walt wouldn't give up. He thought: *If Ms. Travers can't imagine Mary Poppins as a cartoon character, then let's do a live-action picture.* He made a new offer to Ms. Travers, and she refused again. Over the next seventeen years, Walt and Roy continued to write, phone, and meet with P.L. Travers, and were repeatedly turned down. In 1960, Walt offered Ms. Travers the right to approve both the script and the casting of the title role. She finally agreed.

Walt's first task was to translate the book into a filmable story. He decided *Mary Poppins* would be a musical, so the story had to be structured around the music. So Walt placed the project in the hands of his composers, Richard and Robert Sherman. He gave them a copy of the book and said, "My wife and my daughters think this would make a good movie. Read it and tell me what you think."

The Sherman brothers read the book from cover to cover, then went to the table of contents and circled six of the book's twelve chapters. They believed that those six chapters formed the core of a strong plot. When they showed Walt the chapters they had circled, Walt smiled, opened his own copy of the book, and showed it to them.

Walt had circled the same six chapters.

Now Walt had a storyline. So he put Richard and Robert Sherman together with Don DaGradi, one of the studio's top story artists. Walt wanted to encourage a creative synergy between his composers and his story man—and it worked. The Sherman brothers' music inspired DaGradi as he created the storyboards, and his storyboards inspired the Shermans to write more music. Once the story was blocked out in songs and images, Bill Walsh wrote the screenplay.

> "Mary Poppins *is the culmination of Walt's career. It draws on everything he'd learned how to do—blending animation with live action, integrating songs with story, and of course, his great eye for talent. After all, he's the one who brought Julie Andrews to Hollywood."*
>
> LEONARD MALTIN
> FILM CRITIC

Robert Sherman described the synergistic relationship between music and story. "Don DaGradi came in one day," he said, "with a sketch of a chimney sweep who was whistling and carrying his brooms. I saw it and said, 'This is a song!'" The song sparked by that drawing was "Chim-Chim-Cher-ee," which won an Academy Award.

Ideas might come from anyone. One of the film's key musical sequences was suggested by Peter Ellenshaw, Disney's British-born special effects artist. Bill Walsh was admiring Ellenshaw's paintings of the rooftops of London and happened to mention that the Sherman brothers were having trouble writing a dance song for the rooftop scene.

"I know the kind of song you need," Ellenshaw said. "It's an English pub song called 'Knees Up, Mother Brown.'" Then he demonstrated the dance.

Walsh excitedly called Don DaGradi and the Sherman brothers to Ellenshaw's office. Ellenshaw taught them all how to link elbows, kick up their knees, and dance to the old English knockabout song. The Shermans loved it! The whole group moved down the hall to Walt's office and demonstrated the dance for him. Walt said, "Can I do that?" and he joined right in, linking arms with DaGradi and Ellenshaw. "We only performed it once," Ellenshaw recalls. "Walt was out of breath afterward—but what a wonderful memory."

The Sherman brothers composed a similar song and called it "Step in Time."

I asked Richard Sherman what it was like to work with Walt on *Mary Poppins*. "Walt believed in teamwork," he said. "We all chipped in and felt we were part of something special. We were proud to be on Walt's team, and this made us want to make *Mary Poppins* work. We all had our own little bailiwicks, but we felt free to make suggestions to each other and learn from each other."

Whether in his studio, or in his Imagineering team, or at CalArts, Walt continually tried to break down the walls that separated creative people. He encouraged the creation of open communities where talented people—artists, musicians, writers, actors, dancers and filmmakers—could challenge and inspire each other to greater heights.

The mercurial Ms. Travers

It took Walt four years to take Mary Poppins from conception to completion—and they were four of the toughest years of Walt's career. His greatest challenge was dealing with P. L. Travers. The temperamental author had script approval—and she rejected draft after draft.

The biggest source of conflict was Mary Poppins herself. The original book portrays her as proud, demanding, fussy and vain—in short, a reflection of her creator, P. L. Travers. Walt wanted to soften Mary's character and make her more charming and sympathetic. Ms. Travers opposed any tampering with Mary's character—but she failed to reckon with Walt's determination to get his film made his way.

P. L. Travers also insisted that there be no animation in the film, but her stubbornness was no match for Walt's. "When he was making *Mary Poppins*," said Diane Disney Miller, "the people involved with the picture would go to the daily rushes, and they'd see *Song of the South*. They were confused. They thought, 'Jiminy Christmas, does Walt want to put animation in this picture?' They knew that P. L. Travers had said she didn't want any animation. What Dad was doing was planting the seed. He might want to use animation in *Mary Poppins*. And he did."

Walt revealed his intention to use animation while listening to a new song that the Sherman brothers had just written. Richard Sherman recalled, "I was in the middle of singing a song that Bob and I had just written, 'Jolly Holiday.' We came to a section where a quartet of waiters comes out and sings, 'Order what you will, there'll be no bill, it's complimentary.' Walt said, 'Hold it!' I thought he didn't like the tune or something.

"As the original Mary Poppins *budget of five million dollars continued to grow, I never saw a sad face around the entire studio. And this made me nervous. I knew the picture would have to gross ten million dollars for us to break even. But still there was no negative head-shaking. No prophets of doom. Even Roy was happy. He didn't even ask me to show the finished picture to a banker. The horrible thought struck me: Suppose the staff had finally conceded that I knew what I was doing."*

WALT DISNEY

"Then Walt said, 'Waiters always remind me of penguins. I think the waiters should be penguins.' I said, 'How can you teach penguins to sing?' Walt said, 'We'll animate the penguins. All the principal characters will be live action, and everything else will be animation.'

"Walt came up with that idea in a flash of inspiration, and 'Jolly Holiday' became one of the film's most memorable sequences. It could have been a very ordinary scene, but Walt made it extraordinary."

P. L. Travers spent a month at the Burbank studio during the early stages of production. She attended story meetings and lectured the artists and writers about every detail of each character. She demanded that an entire animated sequence—the fantasy world inside the sidewalk chalk drawing—be eliminated. She hated the Sherman brothers' musical score and insisted that only authentic songs of the period (like "Ta Ra Ra Boom De

Ay") be used. She even demanded that the Disney wardrobe department purchase the cloth for Mary Poppins' skirt from a certain dressmaker on Kensington Road in London.

"When we sat down with Mrs. Travers to present our treatment," Richard Sherman recalled, "she hated everything we had done. Disliked it with a passion! For every chapter we developed, she had a definite feeling we had selected the worst one. She started naming the chapters she felt we should adapt, and they were the ones we thought were absolutely unusable."

Walt worried that, at any moment, the mercurial Ms. Travers might pull the plug in mid-production and demand the rights back. It was during this time that Walt purchased the rights to Mary Norton's *The Magic Bed-Knob*. If need be, he could fall back on Ms. Norton's tale of three English children and an apprentice witch. (The movie *Bedknobs and Broomsticks* was, in fact, produced after Walt's death).

Julie Andrews: Worried about her nose

Walt personally made all of the casting decisions for *Mary Poppins*. His first choice for Mary was surprising—Bette Davis. One of the reigning queens of moviedom, Ms. Davis was in her fifties at the time. In voice and appearance, she couldn't have been more different from the twenty-seven-year-old singer Walt ultimately chose. Yet P. L. Travers had given no hint of Mary's age in the books—most readers at the time assumed her to be a middle-aged woman. So the choice of Bette Davis seemed logical.

But as the Sherman brothers developed the score for the film, there were several songs written for Mary Poppins to sing. Bette Davis was not a singer. Walt contacted Mary Martin, famed as *Peter Pan* on Broadway and TV, but Ms. Martin turned down the role.

> *"I was brought up on the* Mary Poppins *books. . . . When I was a kid my friends even suggested I should play Mary one day, but I never thought I would. Certainly Walt Disney didn't consider me for the role when he first planned the film."*
>
> JULIE ANDREWS
> ACTRESS

Walt was in a quandry until his secretary, Tommie Wilck, suggested a young actress who was a big hit on Broadway as Eliza Doolittle in *My Fair Lady* and Queen Guenevere in *Camelot*. Her name was Julie Andrews.

In late 1961, Walt went to New York and attended a performance of *Camelot*. He was impressed by the acting ability and lovely soprano voice of Julie Andrews. After the show, Walt went backstage and told her he wanted her to play Mary Poppins. Then he launched into a scene-by-scene narration of the story.

Ms. Andrews was impressed—but not convinced it was the right role for her screen debut. She was being considered to play Eliza Doolittle in the Warner Brothers production of *My Fair Lady*, a role she had created on Broadway. Ms. Andrews agreed to appear in *Mary Poppins* only if she didn't get *My Fair Lady*. When Jack Warner chose Audrey Hepburn to play Eliza, Walt had his Mary Poppins.

The biggest concern Walt had about Julie Andrews was her age. What if Ms. Travers rejected her as too young? So Walt called Ms. Travers and asked, "How old is Mary Poppins?" The author replied, "I've always thought of her as about twenty-seven." Walt was amazed, for that was Julie Andrews' exact age.

In late November 1962, Walt arranged a telephone meeting between Julie Andrews and P. L. Travers. At the time, Ms. Andrews was in a London hospital following the birth of her first daughter, Emma Kate. The author and the Broadway star had a long talk by phone. Ms. Travers approved Julie Andrews, based on her voice alone.

Julie Andrews was nervous about her first motion picture role. She was accustomed to acting and singing on a stage, but worried about acting before cameras. In an article in Showtime magazine, January 1965, she recalled her feelings of anxiety. "Would I be self-conscious?" she wrote. "How big would my nose look on the wide screen? . . . My nose worried me particularly. I had been thinking of having it fixed (it tilts up!) but my husband objected. 'Leave it alone,' he said, 'It's a good nose. You can see it against the scenery!'"

An interviewer once asked Ms. Andrews to describe Walt Disney. "He was a charming man with a twinkling personality," she replied, "and he put in an enormous number of hours at his studio each week. Among all of his skills, one of his great talents was an almost phenomenal ability for picking nice people to work with. His studio had a special charm—it still does."

When I met Julie Andrews at a Chicago book convention, I asked her what she remembered most about Walt. "Oh!" she said, "His sparkling eyes!" Walt's presence, it seems, had that effect on everyone who met him.

Dick Van Dyke: A serendipitous thing

Though Bert the chimney sweep was a minor character in P. L. Travers' original book, the Sherman brothers saw a much bigger role for him in the movie. So Walt and his story artists built Bert into a full-fledged leading man. In a casting decision that raised many eyebrows, Walt picked All-American TV star Dick Van Dyke to play the Cockney chimney—sweep/kite-peddler/sidewalk artist/one-man band.

The beanpole comedian had already achieved fame as comedy writer Rob Petrie on *The Dick Van Dyke Show*, yet Walt had never heard of him. After a private screening of an episode of the CBS comedy, Walt chose him on the spot—no audition needed. While working on *Mary Poppins*, Van Dyke and his wife Margie became friends with Walt and Lillian Disney.

"It's my third motion picture, but the best one I've ever been in, and the best one I ever will be in if I live to be a hundred and fifty years old. To me, this is the greatest family classic of all time."

DICK VAN DYKE
ACTOR

Some critics panned the casting of Dick Van Dyke, claiming his Cockney accent is, well, less than authentic. Maybe so. But Walt wasn't as interested in Van Dyke's accent as his on-screen chemistry with Julie Andrews. What's more, the Sherman brothers had created a demanding part for Bert, requiring an actor who could sing, dance, do physical comedy, and create a believable, likable character. The multi-talented Van Dyke was uniquely qualified.

When Dick Van Dyke heard that the role of the old bank chairman, Mr. Dawes, had not yet been cast, he told Walt, "I'd like to play Mr. Dawes—and I won't charge you a nickel."

"The price is right," said Walt, "but you'll have to test for the part."

So Van Dyke went to the studio and did a screen test as doddering old Mr. Dawes, long white beard and all. The actor improvised a slapstick scene of a wobble-kneed oldster descending the steps with a cane. Walt loved it so much he had a step added to the boardroom set so Van Dyke could do the bit in the movie.

Because of union rules, Dick Van Dyke wasn't allowed to do the role for free—but Walt suggested an alternative. The Disney company paid Van Dyke $4,000 to play the part of Mr. Dawes, and the actor donated that amount to Walt's favorite cause, CalArts.

Dick Van Dyke remembers the months he spent filming *Mary Poppins* as "the happiest, most fun few months I ever spent in my life." The best part was working with Walt. "What I liked about him," the actor recalled, "was that he had the enthusiasm of a ten-year-old about the work. To work with him was one of the most serendipitous things that ever happened to me."

Practically perfect in every way

Walt put as much care into casting the secondary roles as he did in casting the leads. He looked for screen chemistry, even in his child stars. Child actors Karen Dotrice and Matthew Garber, who had previously starred in Disney's *The Three Lives Of Thomasina*, were together again as the Banks children, Jane and Michael. "Uncle Walt" paid to bring Karen's family over from England so she wouldn't be homesick.

David Tomlinson was cast as the stuffy father, George Banks, and Glynis Johns was his dizzy suffragette wife, Winifred. Other memorable performers included Reginald Owen as Admiral Boom, Arthur Treacher as Constable Jones, and Elsa Lanchester as Katie Nanna.

> "Walt Disney was magical. He would give you a challenge and say, 'I know you can do this.' It was electric to be around him."
>
> RICHARD SHERMAN,
> DISNEY SONGWRITER

For the role of the old bird woman, Walt chose Jane Darwell, who had won an Oscar as Ma Joad in *The Grapes of Wrath*. Her career went back to the silent era, and at the time Walt cast her, she was living in the Motion Picture Country Home and could no longer walk. Darwell gave a touching performance, the last of her long career.

The casting of Glynis Johns required some agile thinking on Walt's part. He invited her to lunch one Friday in the Coral Room, the executive restaurant just off the main commissary of the studio. Joining them were Bill Walsh, Don DaGradi, and the Sherman brothers. Walt began by saying that he was casting a new movie, *Mary Poppins*. He didn't even finish his sentence before Ms. Johns began thanking him. "Oh," she said, "I've always wanted to play Mary Poppins!"

There was an awkward silence—then Walt explained that Julie Andrews had already been cast in the title role. "You see," Walt added, "I want you to play Winifred Banks."

Ms. Johns was crestfallen. "I really wouldn't be interested—"

"And just wait," Walt continued smoothly, "until you hear the wonderful musical number that Richard and Robert have written especially for you." He glanced at the Sherman brothers and they looked back as if to say, *What musical number?*

"When can I hear it?" Ms. Johns asked.

"Come back next week," Walt said. "Dick and Bob will be happy to play it for you."

Dick and Bob grinned bravely. "Yes, absolutely," they said.

After Ms. Johns left, the Sherman brothers asked Walt what song he was talking about.

"I'm sure you boys will come up with something," Walt replied.

So the Sherman brothers worked through the weekend, racking their brains for a good tune and lyrics. Finally, they adapted a tune they had originally written for the nursery scene, a song called "Practically Perfect in Every Way." They wrote new lyrics, called it "Sister Suffragette," and they played it for Glynis Johns the next Tuesday. She took the part.

Walt cast Elsa Lanchester as Katie Nanna a short time after the death of her husband, actor Charles Laughton. Laughton and Lanchester had enjoyed one of the longest marriages in Hollywood, and she was deeply depressed over her loss. Elsa Lanchester happened to be the godmother of Karen Dotrice, so Karen's mother suggested that Walt cast Ms. Lanchester in the film. Walt agreed. The role helped Elsa Lanchester through her grief, and her role in *Mary Poppins* marked her successful return to acting after a six-year absence.

Filming of *Mary Poppins* began in May 1963 and was completed in September. Post-production and animation took another eleven months to complete. *Mary Poppins* premiered at Grauman's Chinese Theater in Hollywood on August 27, 1964, and was universally acclaimed.

Well, there was one dissenter: P. L. Travers.

At the party following the premiere, Ms. Travers told Walt, "The movie was quite nice, and Miss Andrews is satisfactory as Mary Poppins. But I'm afraid Mr. Van Dyke is all wrong as Bert. And I don't really like mixing the little cartoon figures with the live actors. When do we start cutting the film?"

Walt smiled. "The picture is completed," he said. "We aren't going to change a thing."

Mary Poppins went on to earn $44 million in its initial release. It was nominated for thirteen Academy Awards, and won five. Though it didn't win best picture (that award went to *My Fair Lady*), Julie Andrews captured the Oscar for best actress in her very first screen role (ironically, Audrey Hepburn wasn't even nominated). As Julie Andrews accepted the award, she looked to Walt and said, "I know where to start. Mr. Disney gets the biggest thanks."

Tuppence is all it takes

In a phone conversation, Richard Sherman told me how, during the last year or two of Walt Disney's life, he would stop by the Sherman Brothers' office at the close of every Friday. "We had our own little private ceremony," Richard told me. "He'd ask us what we were working on, and we'd tell him. Then he'd say, 'Play the song, Richard.' And I knew which song he meant. I'd play 'Feed the Birds' from *Mary Poppins*.

"Walt would look out the north window of his office while I played the song. And when it was over, he'd say, 'Yep, that's what it is all about. Have a good weekend, boys.' And with that, he'd send us home.

"Walt understood what Bob and I were saying through that song, and I think that's why it became his favorite song. It was the first song we wrote for the picture—our first inspiration after we read 'The Bird Woman' chapter in the book. It was the song we played for Walt at our first story meeting, and it was the last thing we played for him. When we wrote it, we knew it was the metaphor for the whole picture.

"It's a song about the bird woman who sells bread crumbs in front of St. Paul's Cathedral. The old woman says, 'Feed the birds, tuppence a bag.' That's the theme of the picture: It doesn't take much to do an act of kindness—just tuppence, just a penny or two.

"That's what everyone learns by the end of the film. The children just needed some love and attention from their parents. They didn't care about their mother's causes or their father's money. They just wanted to know that Mum and Dad were interested in them. And that's what Mary Poppins taught them. It's a subtle thing, but Walt loved the meaning of that song. That's what he was all about.

"Even after Walt left us, I continued to play the song every Friday afternoon in his honor. It was a very personal thing for me. I'd feel his presence.

"On Walt's hundredth birthday, they had a big celebration in the middle of Disneyland. I was there, and I spoke about Walt. They had a piano and they asked me to sing 'Feed the Birds.' I sang it, and I choked up, but I got through it. As I was singing, a beautiful gray dove flew right by me and then up again into the sky. Don't tell me there is no God in the heavens!

"My love for Walt Disney is stronger now than when he was alive. It keeps compounding. All the lessons he instilled in me are becoming more clear as the years go on. Hindsight gives me more appreciation for him. Walt was a humble man—a sweet, humble man. Very rarely, a special man comes to Earth and I got to be around that very special man."

As Richard told me this, he was moved to tears—and so was I.

After a few moments, I said, "Richard, could I ask a favor of you? Could we sing that song together?" And over the phone, without accompaniment, and with me remembering only half the words, we sang "Feed the Birds" together.

And I felt a little closer to Walt Disney.

Project X

While Walt was building World's Fair attractions and producing *Mary Poppins,* he was also devoting time and effort to his last and most ambitious dream, "the Florida Project" or "Project X." Walt's inspiration for the Florida Project dates back to the first few years after Disneyland opened. His great regret was that he lacked money to create a buffer zone to keep the park from being surrounded by cheap motels and other unsavory establishments.

Soon after Disneyland opened, the public clamored for an East Coast Disneyland. At first, Walt said he would never build another Disneyland. Sometime in the late 1950s, however, he experienced a change of heart and began laying plans for a vast resort complex east of the Mississippi. But Walt's new venture—his "Project X"—was more than just a theme park. He was determined to build the Community of Tomorrow.

In 1959, Walt contacted Harrison "Buzz" Price, the former Stanford Research Institute consultant who had helped find the Disneyland site in Anaheim. Price had formed his own company, Economics Research Associates, in Los Angeles. Walt commissioned ERA to find the best East Coast location for Project X. After looking at all the factors, ERA identified three Florida sites: Palm Beach on the Atlantic coast, Ocala in the center of the state, and dead-last on the list, the little citrus town of Orlando.

Walt rejected Palm Beach—an ocean-side location meant hurricanes and high humidity—and he zeroed in on Ocala. He set aside a back room at the WED design studios where he held top-secret brain-storming sessions with a few trusted Imagineers. The plan for Project X moved forward in secrecy.

> *"It's like the city of tomorrow ought to be. A city that caters to the people as a service function. It will be a planned, controlled community, a showcase for American industry and research, schools, cultural and educational opportunities."*
>
> WALT DISNEY

In 1963, Walt learned that a freeway was under construction, linking Tampa-St. Petersburg on Florida's gulf coast with Daytona Beach on the

Atlantic coast. That freeway—Interstate 4—would pass right by Orlando. Walt had ERA take another look at Orlando, and the connection to I–4 completely changed the equation. Orlando shot to the top of the list.

In November 1963, Walt and several associates (including Donn Tatum, Card Walker and Buzz Price) boarded the Disney Beechcraft in Burbank and set off on a cross-country journey. They stopped in St. Louis and talked with city officials about building a park on the banks of the Mississipi, but there wasn't enough available land. They visited Niagra Falls and Baltimore, but the bitter winters ruled out both locations.

On November 22, Walt and his team flew down to central Florida. The Beechcraft passed over the sleepy little community of Orlando and approached a large freeway construction project—the interchange between the Florida Turnpike and the brand-new Interstate 4. Walt pointed and exclaimed, "This is it!" Walt had made his decision. Project X would be built near Orlando. Within thirty years, that little community of 60,000 people would become a global tourist destination with over a million and a half residents.

The plane continued on to New Orleans. Arriving at their hotel, Walt and his team learned that President John F. Kennedy had been assassinated during a motorcade ride through Dallas. It was a quiet and somber flight home the next day.

Soon after his arrival, Walt informed Roy that he had selected the site for the Florida Project. Roy was not enthusiastic—but he knew it was pointless to oppose Walt's vision. For one thing, Walt never took "no" for an answer. For another, Walt was usually right.

> *"Solving the problems of the city obsessed him."*
>
> JOHN HENCH,
> DISNEY ARTIST AND IMAGINEER

The scope of Walt's latest, greatest dream was truly breathtaking. He didn't just want to build a theme park. He wanted to build a *city*—a real, working community of the future where American industries could experiment with innovative solutions to human problems. But to build it, Disney would have to acquire a vast amount of property.

Building Disneyland had been a back-breaking challenge. Project X appeared a hundred times more complex. There would be financial, legal, and governmental problems to be solved. Walt wanted to build everything at once—the city of tomorrow, the futuristic transportation system, the second Disneyland, everything. Roy suggested it be built in stages.

"Let's build the new Disneyland first," Roy said. "We'll get the park up and running, and that will give us an income stream that we can use to build everything else." The duplicate Disneyland would become, in effect, the "wienie" that would attract people and money to Disney's Florida operation.

Roy's plan made sense. Walt agreed to make a new Disneyland-style theme park as "Phase One" of a larger Florida Project.

In the summer of 1964, as *Mary Poppins* premiered on the West Coast, a number of anonymous land buyers began purchasing real estate near Orlando, Florida. Much of it was swampland, and the going price was around $200 per acre. The buyers operated under various names and purchased the land in separate parcels. For months, the people of central Florida had no clue that Walt Disney was moving into their neighborhood.

The success of *Mary Poppins* made the Florida land acquisition possible. The movie brought millions into the Disney treasury just when it was needed for the land purchase. In fact, the Disney-created company that planned and built the Florida Project was called Mapo (combining "Mary" and "Poppins"). Mapo later merged with Walt Disney Imagineering.

Walt desperately wanted to go to Florida, but Roy reminded him that his face was too recognizable. Finally, Walt could resist no longer. Against

"We had a lot of fun writing the songs of The Jungle Book *. . . It was the last animated movie supervised by Walt Disney and he was very involved in every aspect of the project. You can find all his humor and sensibility in this movie, which is why it's been so successful."*

RICHARD SHERMAN,
DISNEY SONGWRITER

Roy's wishes, he took some studio executives down to Florida and walked around the Orlando property. Afterward, he and his associates dined in a hotel restaurant. A waitress came over and said, "Sir, did anyone ever tell you that you look just like Walt Disney?"

"Look like Walt Disney?" he said. "I *am* Walt Disney!"

The other men at the table dropped their jaws in shock.

"You're pulling my leg!" the waitress said.

"I'll prove it to you," Walt said. He took out his wallet and showed the waitress his driver's license. The other men groaned silently.

Fortunately, the waitress never told her story to the newspapers.

Fun in the jungle

Though Project X consumed most of Walt's time, he continued hosting the weekly television show while guiding the development of new Disneyland attractions. He also became deeply involved with a new animated feature, *The Jungle Book*.

Walt assigned *The Jungle Book* to veteran story artist Bill Peet, who produced a faithful adaptation of Rudyard Kipling's original book. Songwriter Terry Gilkyson composed a musical score to match Peet's artwork. When Walt saw the storyboards and heard Gilkyson's score, he said, "This isn't the movie I want to make! It's too dark and depressing!"

"But that's what the book is like," Peet said. "That's the way Kipling wrote it."

"I know it is," Walt said, "but that's not the way Disney will make it. I want this to be a funny movie. There's nothing funny in these story-boards—and there's only one good song in the score." The song Walt liked was "The Bare Necessities."

Embittered over the rejection, Peet angrily resigned, ending a relationship with Walt that went back to 1937. Walt assembled a new creative team: Richard and Robert Sherman would write the score, Larry Clemmons (a former comedy writer for Jack Benny) would develop the storyline and gags, and Wolfgang Reitherman would draw the story-boards. Walt began by asking them if they had ever read Kipling's original book. All said no.

"Well," Walt said, "make sure you don't. We're not doing Kipling's *Jungle Book*—we're doing Disney's *Jungle Book*. All you need to know is the storyline, and I'll give it to you right now: It's the story of a boy named Mowgli who is raised by wolves. He's lived his whole life with the jungle animals. Now, for his own good, he must return to the human world. The villain is a tiger named Shere Khan, who wants to kill Mowgli. That's all you need to know about the story. Dick and Bob, I want you to write as many funny songs as you can. Larry and Woolie, I want you to come up with the funniest jungle animals anyone has ever seen."

Under Woolie Reitherman's direction, the film was animated by Disney's top artists, including Milt Kahl, Ollie Johnston, Frank Thomas and John Lounsbery. Walt attended most of the story sessions and contributed extensively to the characters and story of the film.

While *The Jungle Book* was in production, Beatlemania was in full swing. In the summer of 1965, The Beatles' manager, Brian Epstein, met with Walt to discuss the possibility of The Beatles performing songs for *The Jungle Book*. An agreement was worked out between Walt and Epstein, but when The Beatles' manager told the band, John Lennon exploded, "There's no way The Beatles are gonna sing for Mickey blankety-blank Mouse!" So much for that idea.

The Jungle Book was the last film to benefit from Walt's own personal touch. Released on October 18, 1967, after Walt's death, it was one of Disney's biggest hits.

> *"The last scene of* The Jungle Book, *when this pretty girl sings and flirts with Mowgli and he shrugs and goes off with her— that was the Disney touch. Walt put that little bit of heart in there. For the most part, the film was fun, slam-bam and socko stuff. But, like Chaplin, Walt had that secret of always putting in a little tear someplace."*
>
> RICHARD SHERMAN
> DISNEY SONGWRITER

Walt's utopian vision

By October 1965, land acquisition for Project X was nearly complete— fewer than 300 acres remained to be purchased. By this time, rumors about the mysterious land buyer ran wild. Here and there, the name of Walt Disney was mentioned.

Back in California, in the Coral Room at the Disney studio, Walt hosted a luncheon with newspaper reporters who were covering the tenth anniversary of Disneyland. One of those journalists was Emily Bavar, Sunday magazine editor of the *Orlando Sentinel*. During lunch, she surprised Walt by asking, "Is the Disney company buying up land in central Florida?"

"He looked like I had thrown a bucket of water in his face," Ms. Bavar later recalled.

Caught off-guard, Walt hesitated—then said, "Why would we want to locate way out there?" It was not a denial. To Emily Bavar, a non-denial was as good as a "yes." The next morning, the *Orlando Sentinel*'s headline read, "We Say It's Disney." The secret was out.

> *"I heard [Walt] talk over and over again about EPCOT. He wanted to build an ideal city, which would be pleasant living for families, give them education, recreation, amusement."*
>
> BOB THOMAS
> DISNEY BIOGRAPHER

Instantly, real estate prices shot up to over $1,000 per acre. By that time, however, the acquisition was 99 percent complete. In the end, the Disney company spent $5 million to acquire 27,400 acres of Florida real estate—about 43 square miles. Walt now had a patch of land to play with that was roughly twice the area of Manhattan and nearly 150 times the size of Disneyland.

On November 15, 1965, Walt appeared with his brother Roy and Florida governor Haydon Burns at a press conference at Orlando's Cherry Plaza Hotel. There he announced his most ambitious project yet—a vast undertaking called Disney World.

I have studied Walt's last and finest vision, and I am convinced that Walt's plan would have profoundly improved the world we live in, if only he had lived to make it come true. Walt was not merely thinking of building a theme park. He envisioned nothing less than a planned community in which thousands of people would live, work, play and dream. It would be his gift to the human race—a clean, healthy, crime-free community where new technologies could be tested and showcased.

One day, while having lunch with his Imagineers, Walt gave his visionary city a name. "What I'm talking about," he said, "is an Experimental

Prototype Community of Tomorrow. What does that spell? E-P-C-O-T. And that's what we'll call it: EPCOT!"

He later described his utopian vision. "In EPCOT," he said, "there will be no slum areas because we won't let them develop. There will be no landowners and therefore no voting control. People will rent houses instead of buying them, and at modest rentals. There will be no retirees; everyone must be employed. One of the requirements is that people who live in EPCOT must keep it alive." Science-fiction writers had dreamed of such a community. Only Walt Disney dared build it.

Picture a city laid out in concentric circles, with a glass-domed, fifty-acre air-conditioned hub, with People-Movers radiating out from that hub and Monorails circling the city. The gentle whoosh of Disney's mass-transit system would make smoggy, car-clogged streets a thing of the past. EPCOT's hub would be a commercial center with gleaming high-rise office buildings, convention centers, entertainment complexes, and hotels.

Surrounding the city hub would be well-planned, tree-lined districts with recreation facilities, schools, churches, sports complexes, shopping districts, and residential neighborhoods. Homes would back up to lush green parks. Children would have room to play. There would be no traffic jams, no traffic cops, no traffic lights, because there would be no traffic. Cars would be used only for out-of-town trips. Trucks and other commercial traffic would move unseen through underground tunnels.

American companies would bring their newest innovations to EPCOT to demonstrate and test them in a real urban environment. Those companies would underwrite the costs of EPCOT with their sponsorship.

Walt's utopian dream did not come out of thin air. He was a serious student of urban problems. He read every book he could find on urban planning. He met with city planners across the country. Walt became a self-taught expert on everything from infrastructure to transportation to emergency services to sanitation.

To oversee the Florida Project, Walt hired a retired Army general, William E. "Joe" Potter, who had

> "If anyone in this century could have pulled off a successful utopia, it would have been Walt Disney."
>
> HOWARD MEANS
> JOURNALIST, *THE ORLANDO SENTINEL*

directed construction of the New York World's Fair. Potter had served with the Army Corps of Engineers, and had once been governor of the Panama Canal Zone.

By 1966, Walt's brother, Roy O. Disney, was in his early seventies. Several times, Roy had talked about retiring. But Walt knew he couldn't build his far-flung dreams without Roy, so once again, Walt talked Roy out of retiring, just as he had several times before.

In October 1966, Walt made a promotional film about EPCOT. "Here in Florida," he said, "we have something special we never enjoyed at Disneyland: the blessing of size. There is enough land here to hold all the ideas and plans we can possibly imagine." He spoke passionately, without a script or prompter. His eyes were alight with enthusiasm for his latest, greatest project. Only those closest to Walt knew that he was in great pain during the filming. When the camera stopped rolling, his body was wracked by a dry, hacking cough.

Two months after making that film, Walt Disney was dead.

The unfinished dream

After Walt's death, his brother Roy pressed on with Walt's unfinished dream. Roy stepped into Walt's shoes and familiarized himself with the operation of WED Enterprises—a part of Walt's life that Roy had once kept at arm's length. On May 30, 1967, ground preparation began at the future site of Walt Disney World in Orlando.

In July 1967, seven months after Walt's death, the GE "Carousel of Progress" opened at Disneyland. Visitors were dazzled by a huge model of Walt's city of the future. The model was called "Progress City" to coordinate with the "Carousel of Progress" theme, but it was actually a model of EPCOT as Walt had envisioned it. The "Progress City" model would remain on display at Disneyland for the next six years.

Working closely with Joe Potter, Roy guided the construction of Phase One, which called for a Disneyland-style theme park, several resort hotels, an advanced Monorail-based transportation system, and many other entertainment and recreational features. As construction proceeded, Roy announced a small but important change to the name of the new Florida theme park. "It's going to be called 'Walt Disney World,'" he said, "so people will always know that it was Walt's dream."

Throughout construction, Roy made frequent trips to Florida to oversee progress on Walt's dream. During one bouncing Jeep trip over a swampy field, Roy looked skyward and called out, "Walt, what have you gotten me into?"

"Everybody can make their dreams come true. It takes a dream, faith in it, and hard work. Yet, the work isn't all that hard because it so much fun you hardly think of it as work."

WALT DISNEY

When Edna Disney worried that Roy was taxing his health, he said, "This was Walt's last dream. Once it's finished, I'll retire and let the younger fellas take over."

On October 1, 1971, Walt Disney World was opened to the public. The price tag for the project: $400 million. Roy O. Disney and Walt's family were on-hand for the dedication. Also present was Art Linkletter, who had hosted the opening day broadcast at Disneyland, sixteen years earlier.

As Roy went to the platform to give his dedication speech, he stopped and looked around as if something was missing. John Hench, who was nearby, heard Roy quietly tell an aide, "Would you go find Mickey for me? We don't have Walt anymore, and Mickey's the nearest thing to Walt we have left." Moments later, Mickey Mouse joined Roy on the platform.

At one point in his dedication speech, Roy looked around at the Magic Kingdom, then he turned to Walt's widow and said, "Lilly, you knew of Walt's ideas and hopes as well as anybody. What would Walt think of it?"

Lillian Disney nodded and said, "I think Walt would have approved."

After dedicating the Florida park, Roy returned to California. Walt Disney World was up and running, and Roy was ready to cut back his busy work schedule.

At the end of one workday in December 1971, Roy met with his secretary and discussed his future plans. He had decided to work half-time at Disney until the summer of 1973. At that point, he would celebrate his fiftieth year in the motion picture business, then retire completely. As he got up to leave, he rubbed the bridge of his nose and mentioned having problems with his vision. "I've been to the eye doctor," he said. "He thinks I may need new glasses." Then Roy left the office for the last time.

A few days later, Roy's wife and son found him on the floor beside his bed, alive but dazed. They took him to St. Joseph's Hospital, where he died of a cerebral hemorrhage on December 20, 1971.

With the death of Roy O. Disney, Donn Tatum became chairman of the board; E. Cardon "Card" Walker became president and CEO. Walt's son-in-law, Ron Miller, became executive producer of the film division. Card Walker assumed the task of carrying on Phase Two of Walt's last dream. From 1972 through 1974, Walker met frequently with the Imagineering team, headed by WED Enterprises executive Marty Sklar. These planning meetings were intended to move Walt's EPCOT concept from dream to reality.

Sometime during that three-year period, however, Walt's original plan for EPCOT evolved into something that was no longer an "Experimental Prototype Community of Tomorrow." In 1973, the "Carousel of Progress" was closed at Disneyland and moved to Walt Disney World, where it opened without the model of Walt's Progress City. That scale model of Walt's original EPCOT disappeared from public view, and has not been seen since.

> *"After Walt's death, the EPCOT project fell apart because no one had the vision to carry it on. The whole company was lost without him."*
>
> RANDY THORNTON
> AWARD-WINNING PRODUCER
> WALT DISNEY RECORDS

On May 15, 1974, Card Walker told a meeting of the American Marketing Association that the Disney company was reconsidering EPCOT "from the point of view of economics, operations, technology, and market potential," and was no longer looking at it as a place where individuals and families would live. In other words, Walt's city of tomorrow would not happen. In its place would be an Epcot theme park.

The groundbreaking for Epcot took place on October 1, 1979; it opened three years later, on October 1, 1982. The first visitors to Epcot were wowed by what they saw—a futuristic World's Fair environment, dominated by a 180-foot-tall geodesic dome called Spaceship Earth. Few visitors knew that this Epcot was not the one Walt had envisioned. In time, EPCOT became Epcot—no longer an acronym for "Experimental Prototype Community of Tomorrow," but simply the name of a theme park.

I have visited Epcot many times, and it's an outstanding achievement in its own right. But today's Epcot is not Walt's EPCOT. His city of tomorrow exists only as a series of drawings, plans and models somewhere in the Disney Archives. Without Walt, his successors didn't know how to build his city. So they settled for the proven formulas of the past.

The people Walt left behind approached every challenge with the question, "What would Walt do?" It was the right question—but they got the wrong answer. Instead of dreaming big dreams as Walt would have done, they merely repeated what Walt had *already* done in the past.

Walt's grandson, Walter Disney Miller, told me, "EPCOT was my grandfather's biggest dream—the city of the future that would point the way to a better world. His dream remains unbuilt. When he died, the company lost the driving personality that focused the organization's energies on a single goal. Bob Gurr once compared the Disney organization to a big orchestra. Walt Disney was the conductor. Without him, the players in the orchestra didn't know what to play, when to come in, or what the tempo was."

For years after Walt's death, actor Kurt Russell was bothered by a statement he kept hearing around the studio: "Nothing's changed." As in, "Even though Walt's gone, nothing's changed. We will continue doing everything just as we did when Walt was here."

Kurt Russell knew that something was terribly wrong with that kind of thinking. Finally, he said to a studio executive, "You know, that's the problem with you guys. You keep saying, 'Walt's gone, but nothing's changed.' Well, things *would* have changed if Walt were still here. He always wanted to change things. He

> *"I started at Disney in 1957. The thing that impressed me most about Walt was his decision-making ability. He always made the right decisions. We'd bring him three new ideas, and he'd choose the right one every time. After Walt died, the company floundered because no one had Walt's knack for making those decisions."*
>
> PETER CLARK
> FORMER DISNEY EXECUTIVE

hated to see things stay the same. He was always looking to the future. You guys are still stuck in the past."

We shouldn't be too hard on Walt's successors for not building Walt's city of the future. It may have been wise, after Walt died, to downsize his dream. The Disney company, after all, is a public company, and has a responsibility to its shareholders. Trying to build Walt's dreams without Walt himself to energize those dreams might have been a disaster.

We'll never know what might have been. Tragically, Walt was taken from us all too soon.

Bob Gurr recalls a time he flew with Walt to Florida to get an aerial look at the EPCOT site. "I vividly remember sitting next to Walt on a plane," he said, "when he pointed to the center of EPCOT, an oval-shaped area. He said, 'When EPCOT gets up and running, there's going to be this spot with a little bench. That's where Lilly and I are going to sit and watch.' I thought this was pretty interesting. Walt could see the big picture, but he could also have in mind this little detail. And he knew where his part was going to be within that little detail."

That was Walt's grand utopian dream: a city of tomorrow, a place of gleaming buildings and green parks, with technological wonders and innovations all around—and in the middle of it all, a quiet little place where he and Lilly could sit and watch.

If only . . .

How to Be Like Walt—
Lesson 13: Build Complementary Partnerships

Walt and Roy had strikingly different personalities. The contrast between them was visible even in their choice of offices at the Burbank studio. Walt chose a spacious third-floor corner suite in the northeast part of the building, close to the artists and the creative hubbub on which he thrived. Roy chose a small, rather austere single room on the second floor of an east wing of the building, where he was surrounded by attorneys and accountants.

The Disney brothers were not merely *different* from each other. Their personalities and leadership styles *complemented* each other. It was the complementary aspects of their personalities that made them such a successful team.

As my friend Peggy Matthews Rose told me, "Every Walt needs a Roy and every Roy needs a Walt." Every dreamer needs a doer. Every starter needs a finisher. Every entrepreneur needs an administrator. And vice versa. A successful team is made up of people with complementary personalities and abilities, all focused on a unified vision.

The problem with complementary personalities is that they tend to conflict with each other. Those very traits that combine to produce a successful team will also produce friction, frustration and conflict. If you are a creative, visionary, Walt-type person, then you need a "Roy" on your team to apply the brakes now and then to keep the train from roaring off the tracks. That means there's going to be conflict between you and your "Roy."

In order to achieve success through teamwork, you must have a healthy tolerance for creative tension and conflict. Conflict produces pain and frustration in any relationship. When conflict occurs, there is only one solution—the solution symbolized by the peace pipe Walt gave to his brother Roy. That solution is called *forgiveness*.

Complementary personalities inevitably clash. If they can forgive each other and tolerate their differences, they can achieve together what neither could achieve alone. But if they are intolerant and unforgiving, they will end up destroying everything they have built together.

If you want to achieve great things, then find that person who supplies what you lack, and who lacks what you supply. Build a complementary partnership. Walt couldn't do everything by himself, and neither can you. If you're a Walt, find your Roy. If you're a Roy, find your Walt. Then build your launching pad together and shoot for the moon. Odds are, you'll reach it.

How to Be Like Walt—
Lesson 14: Stay Focused!

I interviewed Imagineer John Hench on September 10, 2001. He said, "Roy Disney told me about his last visit to Walt in the hospital, when Walt was talking very excitedly about the Florida Project. It was as if Walt could see this map on the ceiling, and he was describing it to Roy, explaining why we'd have to build an east-west road running through, and so on. Walt could see the whole thing in full detail. He died the next morning—but he died the way he had always lived: focused on his dreams. Walt was obsessed, and that's why he achieved the things he did."

Media critic Neil Gabler described Walt in similar terms. "Walt Disney was an obsessive man," he told me. "That obsessive quality made him passionate and kept him focused on his dreams until his dreams became a reality. Of all the influential and successful people I have ever studied, Walt was the most intensely focused on his goals. His ideas possessed him."

When Walt had a dream, it was all he thought about, all he talked about. He drove his dreams, and his dreams drove him. One of Walt's greatest obsessions was Disneyland—a dream that went at least as far back as the 1930s, and perhaps even to Walt's boyhood. The dream drove him through the difficult struggle to finance and build the park. And even after the park was built, he was still focused on Disneyland—on plussing it with new and bigger attractions.

For a while in the early 1960s, some of Walt's associates thought that Walt's attention had wandered from Disneyland to the New York World's Fair. Only after the Fair closed and the attractions came to Disneyland did they see that Walt was focused on Disneyland all along.

Then there was *Mary Poppins*. Walt was relentless in his pursuit of the rights to that book. For years, he persevered through rejection after rejection. Finally, in 1960, after sixteen years of focused effort, Walt obtained the rights from author P. L. Travers.

Walt soon found, however, that his battle with Ms. Travers was far from over. He had to fight her every step of the way through story development and production to make the film he envisioned. *Mary Poppins* is more than a cinematic masterpiece. It is a tribute to Walt's ability to remain focused on his goals.

Finally, there was EPCOT, Walt's last obsession, his experimental community of tomorrow. Walt began planning EPCOT soon after Disneyland opened, and he spent years in secret with his Imagineers, drawing up plans for his futuristic city. Even as he lay on his deathbed, he was focused on his great utopian dream, and he could see its outlines etched into the ceiling tiles over his head.

Ultimately, Walt's focus was so strong and clear that it drove his brother and his associates even after his death. The force of Walt's personality gave the Florida Project so much momentum that it continued on without him. True, the final result was less than Walt envisioned, but the fact that Walt Disney World was built at all is a testament to Walt's singular focus.

In his book *Answers to Satisfy the Soul*, my writing partner Jim Denney observed, "Everybody dreams of success. Only a few ever reach it. Why? Because success demands that we remain intensely, relentlessly focused on our dreams. Only a rare few have the level of focus it takes to keep faith with their dreams and see them through to completion. A dream becomes reality only if you stick to it."

Director Ken Annakin told me, "There are a lot of lessons people can learn from Walt's life—lessons in creativity or taking courageous risks or persevering through adversity. But if you don't understand the absolute extremes of Walt's obsession with his dreams, you can never be like Walt, you can never have anything like the success and influence he had.

"I doubt whether one person in fifty million is capable of the obsessive focus with which Walt lived each day of his life. And it was not in any way a selfish obsession. He was not focused on making money or acquiring fame, although he did both. His grand obsession was simply to bring happiness to others. That was his total focus. It made Walt Disney who he was."

The obsessive focus of Walt Disney is a powerful lesson for you and me. Our dreams will become reality if we remain faithful to them—and never lose our focus.

Chapter Thirteen

✑

The Show Must Go On

*The final year of Walt's life was a time of great productivity—
and great sadness. We can learn how to live meaningful, influential lives by observing Walt's last year on earth. He died just as he
had lived—working to bring happiness to others.*

When Walt was in his twenties, a sideshow fortuneteller told him he
would die before the age of thirty-five, and that his death would take place
near his birthday. Walt wasn't superstitious, and he laughed off the fortuneteller's prediction. But from time to time over the next few years, that
prediction came back to haunt him, even after he was safely past his thirty-
fifth birthday.

We all think about death periodically, yet Walt seemed unusually conscious of his own mortality. There was so much Walt wanted to accomplish,
and so little time. His greatest fear, it seemed, was not death itself, but
dying before his work was done.

Story artist Bill Peet recalled a conversation in Walt's office one afternoon in the early 1960s. The two men were sitting around Walt's coffee
table, talking about a film project. Suddenly, Walt's mood took a melan-
choly turn. He got up and walked over to the window.

"You know, Bill," he said, "I want this Disney thing to go on long after I'm gone. And I'm counting on guys like you to keep it going."

Peet tried to kid him out of it. "Come on, Walt," he said, "you'll outlive all of us."

"If I were a fatalist, or a mystic, which I decidedly am not, it might be appropriate to say I believe in my lucky star. But I reject 'luck'—I feel every person creates his own 'determinism' by discovering his best aptitudes and following them undeviatingly."

WALT DISNEY

"No, no," Walt said softly. "I'm serious, Bill. I want this thing to keep going."

As it turned out, Peet himself left Disney in 1964; two years later, Walt died. But Walt got his wish. "This Disney thing" has indeed outlived him.

Scores of books have been written about Walt Disney, and many of them have searched for the source of his unique combination of drive, achievement, influence and success. I'm convinced there are many sources: His unfailing optimism. An endlessly creative mind. Strong leadership skills. An intense commitment to excellence. A willingness to take bold risks. His ability to anticipate the future and seize its opportunities. Courage. Perseverance. Focus.

But I believe that one of the most crucial traits Walt possessed was his awareness of the brevity of life. It gave him a sense of mission, purpose and urgency. It forced him to focus on his goals.

Most of us go through life pretending that death doesn't apply to us. We avoid facing the fact that God has granted us a limited number of days, hours, seconds and heartbeats in which to accomplish our life's work. When it's over, it's over, whether our work is done or not.

Jesus once told his disciples, "As long as it is day, we must do the work of him who sent me. Night is coming, when no one can work" (John 9:4 NIV). That was the mindset of Walt Disney. He knew that the night was coming. He lived with a sense of urgency.

Walt Disney was a passionate, driven, focused workaholic. What he accomplished in a single lifetime amazed the entire world. Walt was driven by a continual awareness of the Ultimate Deadline.

Walt's final year

On January 1, 1966, Walt rang in the New Year as Grand Marshal of the Tournament of Roses Parade in Pasadena, California. With Mickey Mouse at his side, Walt rode in a white Chrysler Imperial convertible, waving to nearly a million people along the parade route. He didn't know it then, but he had less than a year to live.

Wayne Allwine recalls meeting Walt during that last year. "I was just a teenager when I was first hired to work at Disney studios in Burbank, basically as a gofer or office boy. I was there late one night, up on the executive floor, when someone was coming toward me down the hall. As he got closer, I realized that it was the boss himself, Walt Disney.

"This was toward the end of his life, and he was already pretty sick. Still, he stopped me and asked who I was, and I told him and said, 'Pleased to meet you, Mr. Disney.' He looked at me and said, 'The name is Walt. The only Mr. Disney here is the one who signs the checks,' meaning his brother, Roy. That was it—my brush with greatness."

In a real sense, that office boy eventually became Walt's successor. In the early 1980s, Wayne Allwine became the third voice actor (after Walt Disney and Jim Macdonald) to perform the voice of Mickey Mouse. He continues to be Mickey's voice today.

Walt was in a great deal of pain during 1966. He rarely complained of it to the people around him, except to Hazel George, the studio nurse. Walt's staff had few clues that he was unwell. TV audiences could see that he was aging; his face was more lined than in years past, but the lines in his face just enhanced his image as "Uncle Walt." Only those closest to him suspected how much pain he was going through.

> "Walt's death came as a shock not only to the public at large, but to the studio as well. For most of us, the old saying, 'But I didn't even know he was sick!' was amazingly close to the truth. We did know he was ill; we didn't suspect he would leave us so quickly."
>
> HARRY TYTLE
> DISNEY WRITER AND TELEVISION PRODUCER

Walt's old polo injury, suffered in a spill from a horse in 1938, had grown more troublesome over the years. Pain throbbed from his neck to his back and down his left leg. Chronic sinus problems required frequent applications of hot compresses to his face—sometimes for as long as forty-five minutes at a time. Every Tuesday, he went to a doctor to have his sinuses drained. Walt was especially susceptible to catching colds. Persistent kidney trouble resulted in several visits to St. John's Hospital in Santa Monica.

Many of these problems were related to his smoking habit. Over the years, his family had urged him to quit. As a Christmas present one year, one of his daughters gave him two cartons of filtered cigarettes. "Dad," she said, "if you won't quit, at least smoke these filtered ones. Maybe you wouldn't cough so much." He accepted them and smoked them—but he broke off the filters before lighting up.

Ward Kimball told about a time in the late 1950s when he was showing Walt the storyboards for the "Mars and Beyond" segment of the Disney television show. Suddenly, Walt was seized by a coughing fit. Walt's coughing jags were common, but this was one of the worst. Soon, Walt's eyes were watering. Kimball was embarrassed for him—and angry.

"For crying out loud, Walt," he snapped, "why don't you give up smoking?"

Walt replied, "A guy's got to have a few vices, doesn't he?"

"He knew he ought to give up smoking," Kimball reflected, "but he never did. I was kind of mad that here's this guy we all look up to and depend on, and he's destroying himself."

In fact, Walt would have given anything to quit. After reaching middle age he repeatedly tried to stop or cut back, but without success. He even tried switching to filtered or low tar cigarettes, but couldn't stand the taste. So he continued to smoke.

Art Linkletter told me, "I was Walt's friend, but I failed him in one area. Many times I said, 'Walt, you've got to quit smoking.' He'd say, 'Art, I'm going to cut it out.' But he never did."

In some individuals, nicotine addiction is every bit as powerful and unbreakable as addiction to heroin or cocaine. Walt had actually grown to hate his addiction. He once told Hazel George, "You're right about one thing: Smoking and drinking are sins. We're God's creatures and if we don't take care of the bodies He gave us, we're committing a sin."

Cigarettes deprived Walt of an untold number of productive years. Equally tragic, cigarettes deprived the world of an extraordinary and beloved man.

Roy E. Disney, Walt's nephew, told me, "Walt was a lot sicker in those last years than any of us realized. He didn't feel good, and the illness took its toll and slowed him down, yet there was so much he had to do and he kept working. It was terribly hard for him, yet he never lost his motivation and drive. He never stopped pursuing his dreams."

His poor health kept Walt from working the long hours he once had. He spent more time resting at Smoke Tree Ranch, near Palm Springs—usually just on weekends, but occasionally for an entire week. During 1966, his thoughts turned increasingly toward concern for his mortality. Hazel George once told an interviewer that, during that final year, Walt "would be introspective and very vocal" about concerns for his health, his family, and the future of the entire Disney enterprise.

He had always been a devoted husband and father, but in the final year of his life, Walt spent even more time with his family. In July 1966, he took a two-week cruise with Lilly, daughters Diane and Sharon, and the

> "The illnesses seemed to reinforce the old premonition that he would die before finishing his work."
>
> BOB THOMAS
> DISNEY BIOGRAPHER

Disney grandchildren. They chartered a 140-foot yacht with a crew of eight and sailed the island waterways of British Columbia. Roy was relieved to see Walt get away for a couple of weeks.

When Walt returned from vacation, however, Roy was shocked to see that his brother looked worse than before he left. Walt was noticeably thinner, his cough was deeper, and his walk was stiff and painful. Worst of all, Walt's mood seemed to have changed. He was irritable and increasingly lost his temper with those around him.

There was clearly more to Walt's irritability than the pain of an old polo injury. His outbursts often focused on the issue of *time*. For example, Walt had a meeting with Joe Potter on the Florida Project. "We could extend the man-made lake out to here," Potter said, pointing to a map, "but that would cost another million."

Without warning, Walt snapped, "I don't care what it costs! Potter, why are you wasting my time with unimportant details?" With that, the meeting ended—and Walt wouldn't speak to Joe Potter for days.

Finally, Potter was called to Walt's office. After some awkward small talk, Walt got to the point. "I haven't been able to sleep after the way I blew up at you," he said. "I keep asking myself, 'Why did I kick Joe Potter around like that?'"

Despite Walt's touchiness around the office, he and Roy actually grew closer during that last year. A lot of the old friction between them now completely disappeared.

Walt plunged back into his workaholic schedule—long work days at the studio or at WED Enterprises, interspersed with trips to Florida in the company airplane. He was rarely as happy as when he was viewing the future site of Walt Disney World from a helicopter or, on one occasion with Art Linkletter and the governor of Florida, in a hot-air balloon.

On July 24, Walt went to UCLA Medical Center for tests. He believed his chronic pain was the result of his old polo injury, and X-rays did show considerable calcification at the site of the injury. The doctors recommended surgery to relieve the pressure. Citing his busy schedule, Walt decided to postpone the procedure.

In September, Walt appeared alongside California Governor Edmund G. "Pat" Brown for a ceremony at the site of Disney's proposed Mineral King winter ski resort in the Sierras. Walt spoke about the Disney company's plans for the resort, and Governor Brown pledged state support for a highway into the resort. The ceremony took place at a 7,800-foot elevation, and reporters couldn't help noticing that Walt struggled for breath throughout the event. (The project was later derailed by a decade-long legal challenge from the Sierra Club.)

During this time, Lucille Martin, one of Walt's secretaries, became increasingly alarmed about Walt's health. "He was unwell much of the time," she told me. "He was sometimes discouraged about his health, and he was concerned about what would happen to the company's stock value if anything happened to him. He worried about the future of his projects—EPCOT and CalArts.

"Walt was also very concerned about the people around him. He was one of the kindest men I have ever known. When I started working for him in 1965, I was alone with two young children. He was always asking about my girls and how we were doing.

"One day, Walt was sitting in his office with Tommie Wilck and me. It was near the end of the day and he was very tired. As he stood up to leave for the day, he said, 'Sometimes I feel like chucking it all.' Then he smiled and added, 'But Lucille and her girls need me.' I've always treasured that. He went into the hospital just a few days later."

By October 1966, everyone around Walt was worried about his declining health. They could see it in the pallor of his skin, the worsening of his cough, and his stiff and pained footsteps. Despite the pain, Walt maintained an intense schedule. He shot a promotional film for EPCOT, put in long hours with his Imagineers, and spent considerable time overseeing feature films such as *Blackbeard's Ghost* and *The Jungle Book*.

At one story meeting for *The Jungle Book*, animator Milt Kahl finally voiced the question that was on everyone's mind. "What's wrong, Walt?" he said. "Are you worried?"

"You're damned right I am," Walt snapped—but he refused to talk about it.

By Wednesday, November 2, the pain in his neck and back had reached the point where he could no longer put off the surgery. Walt checked into St. Joseph's Hospital, located directly across from the Disney Studio. Walt's doctors took X-rays—and were dismayed to find something they weren't even looking for: a dark spot on Walt's left lung.

As Walt waited for the doctors in his hospital room, he had a surprise visitor: Chuck Jones, the Warner Brothers animator. Walt brightened when he saw Jones at his door. "I went to your office at the studio," Jones said, "and your secretary said you were over here for a check-up. So I just wandered over here to see how you're doing."

They chatted for a while, and Jones reminded Walt about an incident from thirty years earlier. "You won't remember this, but I wrote you back in the thirties, when I was just starting out in cartoons. I told you how much I admired *Three Little Pigs*. And you wrote back."

"I do remember," Walt said. "In fact, I believe I wrote back and said I hoped you'd continue working as an animator."

"What a memory!" Jones said, amazed. "I carried your letter around in my hip pocket for years, and showed it to everyone I met. I wore it out years ago."

Walt laughed.

"You must have gotten hundreds of letters," Jones said, "and you couldn't answer them all. Why did you take the time to answer mine?"

"You were the only animator who ever wrote to me," Walt said.

They visited for a while longer. After Jones left, the doctors returned with bad news.

"I'm going to whip it"

Walt shunned funerals. His daughter Diane recalls that, when Walt's brother Herbert died in 1961, Walt kept an out-of-town appointment just to avoid attending the funeral. In Diane's 1957 biography of her father, *The Story of Walt Disney*, she wrote, "He never goes to a funeral if he can help it. If he has to go to one, it plunges him into a reverie which lasts for hours after he's home. At such times he says, 'When I'm dead I don't want a funeral. I want people to remember me alive.'"

Disney art director Herb Ryman remembered one of the few funerals Walt ever attended. After the death of Disney art director Charlie Phillipi, Walt called Ryman and asked, "Could I ride with you to the funeral?" So they went to the chapel and sat through the service. Walt fidgeted and drummed his fingers. Ryman could tell that his boss was upset and desperately wanted out of there.

When the service finally ended, Walt saw some of his staffers, including Milt Kahl and Marc Davis, standing at the back of the chapel. "Okay, okay!" he growled. "Let's get back to work!" Ryman concluded, "That was one of the last funerals Walt ever went to."

Whenever the subject of death came up, Walt was eager to change the subject. But after the doctors told Walt about the spot on his lung, the subject could no longer be avoided. The spot was detected on Wednesday, November 2; the doctors scheduled Walt for surgery the following Monday. Walt spent Wednesday night in the hospital. Then he returned to the studio the next morning and put in a full day of work. He also attended a CalArts board meeting in a studio conference room.

CalArts board member Buzz Price recalled that meeting. "On the last day I ever saw him," Price said, "we had a board meeting at which [Walt] presented CalArts in model form. Then he took me and Lulu Mae Von Hagen into the side room and handed me a box full of all the reports I had written, which had been stored under his desk. He looked at the two of us and said, 'Look after my school.'"

Price was shaken by Walt's words—and filled with a resolve to honor the trust Walt had placed in him. (Four decades later, Price is still on the CalArts board.)

At the end of that day, Walt called film producer Bill Anderson into his office for a drink. Bluntly, without any preamble, Walt said, "They found a spot on my lung."

Anderson gasped as if he had been punched.

"When my grandfather died our family never was the same. He kept us all together and we all still feel his loss."

JENNY GOFF
WALT'S GRANDDAUGHTER

"Don't worry," Walt added quickly. "I'm gonna whip this thing. They're going to go in and take a biopsy on Monday."

Sometime later, Walt told his brother Roy about the spot on the X-ray, and again he downplayed the seriousness of it. "I'm going to whip it," he repeated. Despite Walt's outward optimism, Roy had a foreboding of doom when he heard those words.

On Sunday, November 6, Walt drove himself to St. Joseph's Hospital. The doctors performed surgery the next morning, on November 7. Though Walt had told Lilly and his daughters not to make a fuss about his operation, they came to the hospital and waited for the doctors' findings. After the procedure, the doctor came out and told them: Walt's left lung was cancerous and they had removed it. By the best medical estimate, Walt had six months to two years of life remaining. As it turned out, that estimate was way off the mark.

Harry Tytle, who was production manager on the Disney TV series, visited Walt in the hospital to discuss script issues on the show. "At the time," Tytle recalled, "Rod Peterson and I were preparing a script on 'Boomerang, Dog of Many Talents.' Walt seemed to take a special interest in the story and I visited him often at the hospital, which was just across the street from the studio. It was during one of these meetings that the doctor came in. I was there when he reported to Walt that they had removed all the cancerous lesion, and if Walt took it easy for a while, he would be as good as ever. . . . His family, though, had been given a much more ominous picture by the doctors."

After the surgery, Roy contacted Walt's doctors and asked them how serious Walt's condition was. The doctors wouldn't give him an answer. Finally, Roy went to Walt's primary physician and said, "Walt and I run a large corporation with thousands of employees and stockholders. As chairman of the corporation, I need to know how sick Walt is."

The doctor hesitated—then took a piece of paper and wrote some Latin words down. "That's all I can tell you," he said, handing Roy the paper.

> When Walt died, he left a big hole in all of our lives. He was a close friend in many ways and yet he always distanced himself from everybody else. He was a genius. He lived his own life in his own mind and his own heart, but he couldn't help but affect all the rest of us very deeply."
>
> FRANK THOMAS
> DISNEY ANIMATOR

Roy took it and left. That evening, he went to the home of his son and daughter-in-law, Roy Edward and Patty Disney. He took the piece of paper from his pocket and showed it to them. "A doctor wrote that," he said, pointing to the Latin words. "Do you know what it means?" Roy didn't mention that it referred to Walt.

Patty examined it, then said, "It means 'small-cell cancer of the lung.'"

Roy swore. Patty was shocked. Her father-in-law had never used that kind of language around her before—but in the next instant she realized that those Latin words were a diagnosis—and she understood whose diagnosis it was.

Walt Disney had terminal cancer.

After that, Roy and the Disney family told no one of the severity of Walt's condition. They didn't even discuss it with Walt. But they didn't need to. Walt knew.

Saying good-bye

Throughout his career, Walt was a prolific letter-writer. The Disney Archives contain several hundred boxes of correspondence from his forty-three years in the motion picture business. Walt continued to write and dictate letters until the end of his life.

Buzz Price told me of a letter he received from Walt sometime after his last CalArts meeting with Walt. "Right before he died," Buzz recalled, "Walt sent me a letter and thanked me for inventing the word 'imagineering.' I didn't even know I did that, but I guess in one of our early meetings I tossed out the word and Walt remembered it."

Walt was not one to pass out praise or thank-yous. During Walt's final days, however, a number of his closest associates received either a note of thanks or a word of praise from him. Walt knew he was dying, and he wanted to make sure he left nothing unsaid that ought to be said. It was his way of saying good-bye.

Walt's son-in-law, Ron Miller, who also was a Disney movie producer, recalled one visit with Walt when he was still in the hospital. "I came in with Diane and Lilly," Miller said, "and he said to the nurse, 'I want you to meet my son.' She said, 'You mean son-in-law.' 'No,' he said, 'my *son*.' It's the greatest thing that's ever been said to me."

Walt also tried to reach out to one old friend who had become estranged from him—Bill Peet, the longtime story artist who had resigned in a dispute over *The Jungle Book*. Peet had written and illustrated a number of highly acclaimed children's books, and Walt sent Peet a letter offering to buy the film rights to his books. It was a lucrative offer—and, in Walt's indirect way, it was a compliment.

Bill Peet didn't see it that way. Still sore after their split, Peet called Walt's direct line, intending to give his old boss a blistering earful. When Tommie Wilck answered Walt's phone, she told Peet that Walt was out of the office. She didn't mention that he was in the hospital.

As Walt recovered from surgery and loss of his left lung, he told visitors he felt "like a new man—good as new." Across the street from the hospital, the Disney studio sent out a press release announcing that Walt had undergone surgery to correct an old polo injury; there was no mention of cancer.

Laid up in bed with nothing to do, Walt grew restless. He asked secretary Tommie Wilck to bring his mail to the hospital room every day, where he read it and dictated replies. He also called director Norman Tokar and producer Bill Anderson to his hospital room for a bedside meeting about *The Happiest Millionaire,* a Fred MacMurray film which was wrapping production at the time.

Walt received frequent visits from family members. Lilly and Diane made sure that these visits were cheery and brief. They didn't want Walt to get the idea that his family was on a "death watch."

Ron Miller recalled being impressed by Walt's relentless optimism during that time. "He said he thought he had the cancer licked," Miller said. "He was full of confidence. I think the thing that really helped him was a telegram that John Wayne had sent when he heard that Walt had his lung removed. It said, 'Welcome to the club. The only problem is height.'" (By "height," Wayne meant altitude—it was harder to breathe at high elevations with only one lung. John Wayne had lost a lung to cancer in 1963, and went on to live for sixteen more years.)

On Monday, November 21, just two weeks after the surgery, Walt was released from St. Joseph's Hospital. He went straight to the studio and resumed work.

Harry Tytle recalled, "I remember walking down the hall with him, seeing smile after smile greet him. Those employees he met were glad to see him back on his feet and told him so. Walt took the words graciously at first, but after awhile he became irritable. He glanced at me and said, 'You'd think I was going to die or something!'"

Whenever people saw Walt for the first time after the surgery, they couldn't help being shocked at his gaunt appearance. He had once filled out his well-tailored suits; now they hung on him like sacks. Walt pretended not to notice the stunned expressions. He plunged into his schedule as if nothing was wrong. Dick Nunis recalled, "Everybody was so amazed at how quick Walt came out of the hospital and got back to work at WED. He was calling meetings and talking about the future. I think he was trying to instill the vision as a road map."

Composer Robert Sherman recalled seeing Walt soon after his return from the hospital. "My brother and I ran into Walt in the hall," he said. "He looked ill and sort of shrunken. He was talking to director Norman Tokar and then he looked at us. He saw the concern on our faces—so he gave us a quick smile and said, 'Keep up the good work, fellas.' Then he winked and walked on. It was the first time he said anything like that to us. He never referred to anything we did as 'good.' He usually said, 'That'll work.'"

Walt spent the next ten days busying himself around the studio, checking on the progress of feature films, or overseeing the latest Imagineering projects at WED. He was particularly interested in his new Disneyland attraction, "Pirates of the Caribbean." Walt spent part of one morning with project supervisor Roger Broggie, who brought Walt up to speed on the attraction.

Later that day, Walt had lunch with John Hench and several other Imagineers in the Coral Room. "Walt said he was awfully tired of hospital food," Hench recalled. "His voice wasn't very good at first, but it got stronger and stronger. He talked about 'Pirates of the Caribbean.'"

At one point during lunch, someone asked Walt about the operation. "I think they got it all," Walt replied. "I'm convinced they got it all."

Walt tired easily, but whenever he talked about his latest projects, his spirit came alive. Winston Hibler, who produced numerous Disney films, recalled, "I saw him the Monday he came back from the hospital. He was quite weak and drawn. During the course of our conversation, however, his great vitality came back and his voice got firmer and firmer. He said, 'I had a scare, Hib. I'm okay, but I may be off my feet for a while. Now, I'm gonna be getting over this and I want to get on to Florida. You guys have to carry some of this load here. But if you get a real problem and you get stuck or something, why, I'm here.'"

Walt also visited the office of Imagineer Marc Davis, who had been with Disney since 1935. As Walt entered the office, Davis was creating sketches for an Audio-Animatronics country-western bear show for the Mineral King project. (The Mineral King project was later abandoned, so "Country Bear Jamboree" was built at Disneyland.)

Marc Davis was shocked at Walt's tired, thin appearance, but decided the best approach was to make light of it. "Boy," he said, "they sure knocked the weight off of you."

"That they did," Walt said, also keeping it light.

Walt flipped through Marc's drawings, chuckling at each one. Then he came upon a drawing that made him laugh out loud—a chubby baby bear playing a tuba. Walt turned to Davis and said, "You've got a real winner with this bear band."

Later, Walt and Marc Davis joined John Hench, Dick Irvine, and several other Imagineers to examine a moon-buggy attraction. The planned Tomorrowland ride would have taken guests on a trip across a simulated lunar surface, but was never built. As Walt looked over the mockup, he seemed to sag. "I'm feeling a little tired, boys," he said. "Dick, could you drive me back to the studio?"

"I was only four and a half when Walt Disney died, yet I vividly remember that day and the way it affected people around me. My mother and sister were crying. As I later learned, there was an outpouring of grief around the world. It affected everyone from children to adults alike."

TIM O'DAY
JOURNALIST AND DISNEY HISTORIAN

Marc Davis watched as Dick and Walt left the room and headed down the hall. Suddenly, Walt stopped and turned, as if he had forgotten something. "Good-bye, Marc," he said.

"Good-bye, Walt," Davis replied—with a sudden sinking feeling. In the thirty-plus years that Davis had worked for Disney, he had never heard Walt say, "Good-bye." It was always, "So long," or "See ya later." That night, Marc Davis told his wife Alice, "I think Walt's dying."

The next day, Walt made the rounds at various departments. He went to a sound stage where Robert Stevenson was directing the live-action feature *Blackbeard's Ghost*, starring Peter Ustinov, Dean Jones, and Suzanne Pleshette. Walt chatted with Ustinov and producer Bill Walsh. When the matter of his surgery came up, Walt dismissed the subject with a wave of his hand. "Oh, they took out one of my ribs so they could fool around in my chest, you know."

Later, while Stevenson directed Dean Jones in a brief scene, Walt stood behind the cameras, quietly observing. Jones finished a take and noticed Walt standing in the shadows. He knew Walt had been in the hospital, but had no idea how sick Walt was.

"Walt!" Jones called—then he saw how much Walt had changed since the last time they'd talked. The shock showed on Dean Jones' face. "Walt," he continued, trying to mask his dismay, "how are you doing? I heard they operated on your neck."

"Neck, hell!" Walt said bluntly. "They took out my left lung."

Jones was speechless. That could only mean one thing: *cancer.*

"Mr. Jones," someone called, "you're needed on the set!"

"Well, Dean," Walt said, turning to leave, "Enjoy your Thanksgiving holiday."

"Walt," Jones said, "wait just a minute, will you? We just need to get one take—"

"I have to go," Walt said, still walking.

"Please, Walt," Jones said. "There's something I need to tell you."

Walt paused.

Jones didn't know what he was going to say. He just knew he had to say something to Walt—something to express how much Walt's friendship had meant to him these past few years. Jones went back to the set, but he blew take after take. It was a simple little scene, but he couldn't concentrate. Finally, he got one good take, and started back to where Walt had been—

But Walt was gone. That was the last time Dean Jones ever saw Walt Disney.

A complete shock

On Wednesday, November 23, Walt went to his office at the studio, spent a few minutes dealing with correspondence, then sent for Hazel George. He went to the room next to his office, where Hazel had often massaged his neck, applied traction to his legs, and placed hot packs on his infected sinuses. In a nod to the Uncle Remus tales, Walt had dubbed that room his "Laughing Place." There, Walt had often checked in with Hazel on the latest gossip around the studio or confided to her his dreams and fears.

Hazel understood Walt and his moods very well. If he came into the Laughing Place feeling down, she could usually cheer him up. Her sense of humor had always been good medicine for Walt's soul. While he was in the hospital, Hazel had sent him a get-well card, and had written in it, "Walt, I'll see you in the Laughing Place."

When Hazel arrived, Walt was waiting for her. "Well," he said, "here we are in the Laughing Place." Then he watched her to see how she would react to his changed appearance.

Like everyone else, Hazel tried to mask her shock, but it was no use. Walt could see himself in everyone's eyes, as if in a mirror. He dropped his light-hearted facade and began, "Hazel, there's something I have to tell you—" But he couldn't speak. Neither could she.

They hugged and cried on each other's shoulders.

Sometime later, Walt stopped by Tommie Wilck's desk and told her, "I'm going to the screening room to watch some dailies. I'll be back after lunch."

Hours later, when Walt didn't return, Tommie called the front gate to find out if Walt had left the studio. The guard said that Walt had gone home early. Worried, Tommie called Walt's home. Lilly told her that her husband was exhausted and had gone to bed.

The next day, November 24, was Thanksgiving Day. Walt and Lilly spent the day at the Encino home of Ron and Diane Miller. After dinner, Walt sat with Ron and told him, "I had a big scare at the hospital. But I'm going to have to take things slower, you know—take better care of myself. So I've decided to turn the whole motion picture business over to you and Bill Anderson and Bill Walsh. I'm going to focus all my attention on building Disney World and EPCOT." Then he winked and added, "Of course, I'm still going to read every script!"

"The last time I saw Dad, he was very uncomfortable. We felt he didn't like people hanging around when he had moments of great pain. . . . He'd get very upset and would rather be alone then."

DIANE DISNEY MILLER,
WALT'S DAUGHTER

On Friday, November 25, Walt and Lillian flew in the company plane to Palm Springs. Walt realized he had overworked himself after coming home from the hospital. He decided that if he got some rest and breathed some dry desert air, he would soon be back on his feet.

It was just a twenty-minute hop from Burbank to Palm Springs. During the flight, Walt went to the cockpit and told his pilot, Kelvin Bailey, "Kel, I've been at old Saint Joe's Hospital for a while. I'm a pretty sick boy, but after a few weeks in Palm Springs, I'll feel a lot better. I'll call you when I want to come back. I don't know when that'll be, but wait for my call."

But Walt didn't spend a few weeks in Palm Springs—and he didn't get better. On Wednesday, November 30, Bailey received a call from Walt. The studio boss sounded so weak that Bailey didn't recognize his voice at first. "Kel," Walt said, "come and get me."

At the Palm Springs airport, Lilly and Kelvin had to help Walt into the plane. They flew to Burbank, and Walt was rushed to St. Joseph's Hospital.

The Disney studio announced that Walt had re-entered the hospital for a routine post-operative checkup. In reality, Walt was failing rapidly. Radiation treatment, intended to retard the cancer, served only to kill his appetite and sap his waning strength. Pain-control drugs left him disoriented and confused.

When he was lucid, Walt worried about his family's future. He had his attorney sell some Disney stock and set up accounts for his daughters. His family's visits cheered him, though it bothered him that Lilly and his daughters saw him in such a weakened state.

During one visit, Walt told his son-in-law, Ron Miller, "If I could live for fifteen more years, I would surpass everything I've done over the past forty years." By this time, both Ron and Walt knew it would never be.

Walt's brother Roy was a frequent visitor to Walt's bedside. Roy tried to keep his visits cheery and upbeat, bringing Walt daily reports on various studio projects. While Walt was in the hospital, Roy ordered that the lights be left on at the studio at all times. Walt's hospital room was on the Buena Vista Street side of the building, and when the nurses propped him up in bed, he could look out the window and see the studio he had built, busily carrying on in his absence. It was a comfort to him.

In his book *Ellenshaw Under Glass,* Peter Ellenshaw recalled, "I tried to see him in the hospital. But his secretary told me he would see no one. I decided to do a little picture of a desert smoke tree, knowing how much he loved the desert, hoping that I would be able to give it to him. I called his secretary, Tommie Wilck, who told me, no, he didn't want anyone to see him in the condition that he was in, but that she would take it to him. Later, she told me it was hung on the wall so he could look at it, and he would proudly tell the nurses how one of his boys painted it for him."

On December 5, Walt turned sixty-five. He spent most of the day sleeping. Over the next week or so, he slipped in and out of consciousness.

Around December 11 or 12, Walt's nephew, Roy E. Disney, visited and was dismayed by his uncle's appearance. "He was just so gaunt," Roy recalled. "He was unshaven, scraggly and gray. He looked up at me and said, 'Whatever I've got, don't get it.'"

On December 14, Lilly visited Walt during the day and was encouraged to see that he seemed to be rallying. The doctors, too, were encouraged. Walt was more comfortable, clear-minded and optimistic. He got out of bed by himself, and gave Lilly a surprisingly strong hug. Lilly and Walt talked about plans to take a vacation trip after he recovered. At one point, Walt kidded his doctors, saying, "Do you fellows know what you're doing?"

Lilly phoned Diane that night and said, "I know he's going to get well."

That evening, Walt's brother Roy came to visit. Walt seemed more energetic than he had been in days. He wanted to talk about the future, about building Disney World and EPCOT. Lying in his bed, Walt pointed up at the ceiling, using the ceiling tiles as a map grid. "Now Roy," he said, "you have this road here running north and south, and we can build on both sides of that. We need to put the new Disneyland park at the far end of that road. Then we need a road running east and west right here." For Roy, it was like the good old days, before Walt got sick. Walt's mind was clear, his imagination fully engaged, his voice strong and enthusiastic.

That night, Roy went home and told his wife Edna, "I think Walt's got a good chance of making it." Then he called Admiral Fowler. "Joe," he said, "I've just been over to see Walt at the hospital, and he's just wonderful. He's planning Disney World on the squares of the ceiling in his room. His spirits are great. I just had to tell you that I'm so encouraged."

It came as a complete shock to Roy, to Walt's family, and to the entire world when Walt died the next morning. Death came on Thursday, December 15, 1966, at 9:35 A.M. The official cause of death was "acute circulatory collapse."

His heart simply stopped beating.

"That's immortality for you"

It was unthinkable. Walt Disney was dead. Those he left behind gathered in the hallway outside his hospital room, hugging and consoling each other.

Least consolable was Roy O. Disney, who had spent his career looking after Walt—supporting him, sometimes battling him, but always helping him realize his dreams. Now, Walt was gone. It was as if Roy's entire reason for living had been ripped from him. When Roy's son and daughter-in-law arrived at the hospital, they found him standing alone in the hallway, weeping. Patty went to her father-in-law, wrapped her arms around him, and they wept together.

"A friend of Walt's told me about the day he died at St. Joseph's Hospital. Walt had passed away an hour or so earlier, and his foot was sticking out from under the blanket. His brother Roy was at the bedside, gently rubbing Walt's foot. Roy choked and said, 'Well kid, it looks like the end of the road.' Roy was still the older brother right to the end."

PAUL CARLSON
DISNEY ANIMATOR

Later that morning, Imagineer Harriet Burns was at her desk at WED Enterprises, chatting with Bill Cottrell about the new "Pirates of the Caribbean" attraction. Her phone rang. She answered it, then held it out to Cottrell. "It's for you, Bill," she said.

Cottrell took the call, listened for a moment, then paled. Hanging up the phone, he looked at Harriet and said, "Walt just died."

Harriet gasped. "That's not possible!"

"Don't say a word to anyone," Cottrell said, then he walked away, looking dazed.

Elsewhere in the WED building, Marty Sklar was at his desk when he received a phone call, summoning him to the office of Card Walker, then vice president of operations, in the main studio building. Sklar, who'd begun his Disney career as a twenty-one-year-old summer employee in 1955, was a writer at WED. The moment Sklar entered the room, Walker came to the point: "Walt's dead."

Sklar was shaken. Walt had been his friend and mentor. He had no idea Walt was so ill.

Walker told Sklar to write a news release about Walt's death and have it ready in an hour. Sklar was astonished. The company had no obituary of Walt on file. Nobody had prepared for this eventuality.

Sklar later recalled, "I was called that morning and asked to write a statement for Roy. I'm still resentful of it because somebody should have written that in advance—after all, we had to try to sum up his life. This was hard for me to write. Roy refused to talk."

Meanwhile, Dick Nunis, who was in charge of Disneyland, called Card Walker. The park was supposed to open in a matter of minutes. Nunis feared that opening the park on the very morning that Walt died would appear disrespectful to the founder's memory. "Should we open the park or not?" asked Nunis.

"I don't know," Walker said. "Let me get back to you."

Nunis didn't have to wait more than two or three minutes. Walker called back and said simply, "Open it."

"Card, are you sure?" said Nunis. "Our staff is going to be upset. And what will the media say? And then there's Lilly and the Disney family to consider."

"Don't worry about Lilly," Walker replied. "She's the one who made the decision. You know what she said? 'Walt would want the show to go on.' So on with the show."

Dick Nunis' eyes were moist as he hung up the phone. He gave the word to open the park—and lower the flag at Town Square to half-mast. Later that day, just as Nunis knew would happen, the newspapers blasted the decision to keep Disneyland open. But Dick Nunis knew it was the right decision, because it was the decision Walt himself would have made.

Throughout the park that day, Disneyland ride operators, shop clerks, maintenance workers, and street sweepers went about their business, keeping Walt's dream alive. As they worked, many wept openly and unashamedly, and so did many Disneyland guests.

At the WED machine shop, Bob Gurr and several other Imagineers were working on the "Pirates of the Caribbean" attraction. Roger Broggie walked into the room, looking pale and stricken. "Walt's gone," Broggie said. "Let's go home." Then he walked out.

Gurr looked around in stunned silence. Everyone else in the room had that same stunned look. No one spoke. People simply got up and filed out, looking more like robots than the Audio-Animatronics pirates they left behind. "That was the longest, most awful drive home," Gurr later recalled. "The world had stopped."

In the studio, directing animator Ollie Johnston was at his desk, working on drawings for *The Jungle Book*. A Disney staffer rushed into the office and blurted, "It just came over the news! Walt Disney's dead!"

Johnston sat still for a moment, trying to understand the enormity of what he'd just heard. For a moment, he felt as if he couldn't breathe. Finally, he quietly got up from his desk and went over to his longtime friend, Frank Thomas. "Let's go home, Frank," he said.

> *"Dick Nunis broke the news to the park staff that Walt had died. There were tears rolling down his cheeks as he told us. We were all in shock. We couldn't imagine living in a world without Walt Disney."*
>
> BILL SULLIVAN
> DISNEYLAND EXECUTIVE

Without a word, Frank Thomas got up and the two men went home.

In the studio shop, the announcement of Walt's death came over the PA system. Ub Iwerks was on the shop floor when he heard the news. At first, he couldn't believe it. Walt Disney—dead?

Ub and Walt had been together at the very beginning, back when they were first discovering together this amazing artform called animation. Ub and Walt had been teenagers when they became friends at the Kansas City Film Ad Company. They had worked together on the Alice Comedies and Oswald the Lucky Rabbit. They had even created Mickey Mouse together. Now, out of nowhere, a voice over the PA system said that Walt Disney had left this world. How could that be?

Ub went to the office of his son Don. He sat down heavily, his voice choking and eyes watering. "It's the end of an era," he said.

"My dad's view," Don Iwerks later recalled, "was that he didn't have anybody to please anymore. Not only had he lost a friend, but he had lost that person whom he was dedicated to please."

Annette Funicello was at her L.A.-area home on the day Walt died. During their last visit together, a year before, she had noticed how much his hair had grayed—yet, she recalled, "his eyes still twinkled and his spirit was still young." So the news of Walt's death came as a complete shock.

"I was cleaning the house and listening to the radio," Annette wrote in her autobiography. "I always had it tuned to a rock station. While polishing a table in the den, I felt myself jolted as if out of a dream when the announcer said, 'Walt Disney died today. . . .' My immediate reaction was to think that someone was pulling a horrible prank, that this was some kind of sick joke, maybe a mistake. But as the hours wore on and my phone began ringing with reporters asking my reaction, I knew it had to be true. I sank down onto a sofa and cried. . . . All I could think of was that I had lost a very dear friend, a guardian angel."

> *"It's funny, but sometimes when I feel discouraged or have a problem I can't work out, I find myself thinking, 'If only Mr. Disney were here, he would know what to do.'"*
> ANNETTE FUNICELLO
> ACTRESS AND MOUSEKETEER

In Los Angeles, *Life* magazine's film critic, Richard Schickel, was scheduled to meet Ray Bradbury for a luncheon interview about Walt Disney. When the news of Walt's death hit the airwaves, Schickel called Bradbury and said, "Did you hear the news about Walt?"

"Yes," Bradbury replied. "This is a terrible, terrible day. I'm devastated."

"Would you like to reschedule our lunch?"

"No," Bradbury said. "It's all the more reason to get together. I *want* to talk about him."

Disney matte artist Peter Ellenshaw was particularly heartbroken over Walt's death. Peter's son, Harrison Ellenshaw, told me, "Walt Disney died just ten days before Christmas. We didn't have a Christmas tree that year— we were all too upset. When my dad was only four, his father died, so Walt had filled a big void in his life. Walt was like the father my dad never knew. Suddenly, Walt was gone, and that left some big holes in my dad's life—in all our lives, really."

X Atencio started as a Disney animator in 1938, and Walt had personally made him an Imagineer, a writer and a songwriter. "I remember the day

Walt died," X told me. "John Hench came into my office and we talked about Walt and what he meant to us. We reminisced about projects we had worked on together, from *Pinocchio* to *Mary Poppins*. The office closed at noon, and they sent us all home. The tradition in my family was to bring home the Christmas tree on December 15. But Walt died on December 15. It was a terrible day, terrible. How could I buy a Christmas tree on a day like that?

"But I had the afternoon off, and I felt bad just sitting around the house. So I thought, 'Oh, I might as well go out and get the tree. So I bought the tree and came home. That evening, I started thinking again about Walt being gone. I was sitting in the living room and I started to cry. I cried and cried, just bawled my eyes out. It was as if I had lost my father."

Reflecting on Walt's death, Ward Kimball said, "I don't think Walt believed it would ever happen. I don't think he accepted it, knowing Walt. Not until he closed his eyes for the last time was he ever convinced."

The day Walt died was chilly and gray in southern California. All of Orange County was in the grip of an icy cold snap. The air over Disneyland was heavy with a damp, mournful fog. Late that afternoon, an announcer's voice came over the loudspeakers throughout the park, telling visitors what most of them already knew: Walt Disney had died that day. At Town Square, the Disneyland band played "When You Wish Upon a Star."

As dusk settled over the park, Disneyland cast member Don Payne was in a character costume, waiting with dozens of co-workers on the service road behind the Main Street firehouse gate. In moments, they would begin the premiere performance of the 1966 Disneyland Christmas Parade.

It was Don's eighteenth birthday, and for days he had been hoping that Walt would be there, perhaps in his apartment over the firehouse, watching the debut of the new parade. But as Don looked up at Walt's empty apartment, he felt only a disappointed sadness.

Grief wrapped the parade cast like a funeral pall. Ahead of Don, a female cast member pointed skyward. "Look!" she said. "It's snowing!" A soft sprinkling of snowflakes drifted from the sky, sparkling in the glare of a floodlight atop the Main Street Emporium. The delicate crystals melted instantly on contact with the ground.

> *"I remember my brother walking into my room on December 15, 1966, and blurting out, 'Walt died today.' I cried for weeks, not believing it could be true. Now I would never meet Walt."*
>
> PEGGY MATTHEWS ROSE
> LONGTIME DISNEY EMPLOYEE

Moments later, the parade music started and the voice of Disneyland announcer Jack Wagner rang out along Main Street: "Ladies and gentlemen, boys and girls, Disneyland proudly presents . . . !" The gate opened and the parade cast stepped out.

A large but subdued crowd lined the parade route. Many of them, no doubt, had chosen to be at Disneyland on that cold day just to feel a little closer to Walt. No one who was there thought it strange that there should be a parade in Disneyland on the day Walt Disney died. Walt was a showman, and the show must go on.

"One of the saddest things I have ever seen"

Bill Peet, who had left the Disney company two years earlier, didn't find out about Walt's death until the next morning when he picked up the morning edition of the *Los Angeles Times*. He was shaken to see Walt's picture on the front page beneath a headline that read "Wizard of Fantasy Walt Disney Dies."

Peet's first thought was one of relief that he hadn't been able to reach Walt by phone a few days earlier. "I would have felt really bad," Peet later recalled, "if I had told him to go to hell or something during what were the last few days of his life." Peet, who died in 2002, probably never realized that Walt's offer to buy the film rights to his books was actually Walt's way of saying good-bye.

Within twenty-four hours of Walt's death, his body was cremated and interred in a family vault at Glendale's Forest Lawn Memorial Park. The memorial service was held in Forest Lawn's Little Church of the Flowers at five in the evening on Friday, December 16. Only close family members were present: Lilly, Diane and Ron Miller, Sharon and Robert Brown, Roy O. Disney and his wife Edna, and Roy E. Disney and his wife Patty. The service was not announced until the next day.

The fact that Walt's final arrangements were conducted so quickly and privately contributed an aura of mystery to his death. A fantastic rumor later arose: Walt Disney, the Master of Tomorrowland, didn't really die; instead, his body was cryonically preserved by liquid nitrogen freezing. There is a certain irony in the idea that Walt Disney, the King of Animation, might be in a state of suspended animation. But there is no evidence to support that theory.

Walt hated funerals, especially the big-production celebrity funerals so common in the Hollywood community. His will specified a service that was simple, dignified and private, in keeping with his modest Midwestern values. But even such a simple service was too much for Walt's brother Roy. After the service, he told his son, "When I go, don't do that to me."

The day Walt was laid to rest, his friend, Ray Bradbury, went to Disneyland with his four daughters—a trip he had promised his girls long before Walt died. It was, as to be expected, a bittersweet day. When Ray arrived back home that night, his wife Marguerite told him, "CBS Radio called this afternoon. They wanted to interview you about Walt. I said you had taken the girls to Disneyland."

Ray broke into tears. "What greater tribute," he said, "than to celebrate his life at Disneyland!"

Bradbury later reflected, "There was a rumor that he had been frozen in a cryogenic mortuary to be revived in later years. 'Nonsense!' I said. 'He's alive now!' People at the studio speak of him as if he were present! That's immortality for you. Who needs cryonics?"

The death of Walt Disney caught the whole world by surprise. Even among those who knew Walt was sick with cancer, his death was simply unthinkable. "Walt had become a kind of mythical figure, especially to his own family," his nephew, Roy E. Disney, observed. "It was a sense of 'he'll be around forever'."

Roy Edward's father, Roy O. Disney, may have been the one hardest hit by Walt's death. Roy had spent nearly all of his adult lifetime looking after Walt. Now Walt was gone. It seemed impossible that Walt could actually die and leave Roy, eight years his senior, behind. Suddenly, Roy now faced the burden of being the sole custodian of Walt's accomplishments and dreams.

Disney writer Jack Speirs recalled seeing Roy in the studio parking lot one evening after Walt died. Roy was all alone, walking slowly toward his car—then he stopped and looked around at the studio he and Walt had built together after the success of *Snow White and the Seven Dwarfs*. Then he lowered his head, got into his car, and drove off.

"It was," Speirs concluded, "one of the saddest things I have ever seen."

How to Be Like Walt— Lesson 15: Accept Your Mortality

You are going to die. You don't need a fortuneteller to tell you that. You already know. Life hangs by the slenderest of threads. So you have to ask yourself: What am I doing with the time that remains? Am I using the time God has given me to complete my mission in life? Am I using that time to make my God-given dreams come true? To bring happiness to others? To build meaningful relationships? To build a relationship with the Creator?

These are the questions we should ask ourselves at the beginning of every new day, because we never know how long we have.

I'm not suggesting you should go through life feeling depressed about death. Fact is, a healthy awareness of death should make us more grateful for the time we have here on earth.

Walt certainly was a merry soul, full of laughter and a love of fun. The awareness of the inevitability of death didn't depress him. It energized and motivated him. It forced him to focus on what's important in life.

In his final days, when he knew his time was short, Walt wept and he hugged and he said good-bye. He made sure that he didn't leave anything unsaid that should have been said. A showman to the end, he made a good exit.

Walt showed us how to face our mortality—and he taught us to accept it. The awareness of death forces us to think about what is truly important in life. The reality of death forces us to deal with the realities of living—our search for meaning, our need to express love and seek forgiveness, our need for God.

As Jim Denney put it in *Answers to Satisfy the Soul*, "A cemetery is an excellent place to think about living. A funeral is a fine place to take a good, long look down our own road. We should live each day with a light heart but 'grave' minds, always conscious of our mortality. By staying connected

with our mortality, we stay connected with eternity."

When I look at the last days of
Walt Disney, I am impressed with
the courageous way he faced the end
of his life. There was no self-pity or
anger. There may well have been
fear—anyone would be afraid of
death. But when Walt faced his
death, he set an example for us all in
how to live and how to die.

I am absolutely certain that death
is not the end of our existence. We all

*"I was six and a half when my
grandfather died. I stayed with
my grandparents a lot when I was
young. After my grandfather died,
I slept with my grandmother,
Lilly, in her bed. She cried
a lot and I remember
staying real close to her."*

JENNY GOFF
WALT'S GRANDDAUGHTER

die—but we also live on. We were made by God, and he has prepared a
place where we can be with him and enjoy him forever. The Bible tells us
that God has "set eternity in the hearts of men; yet they cannot fathom
what God has done from beginning to end" (Ecclesiastes 3:11 NIV).

That longing for eternity is inside us all. We instinctively *know* that there
is something about us that is truly immortal. We all long for something
that we cannot have in this world. We catch glimpses of it every now and
then—in an achingly beautiful sunset, or a perfect evening with close
friends, or a day at Disneyland. But a glimpse is all it is. The sunset fades,
the friends say goodnight, the park closes. We had something beautiful and
perfect in our hands, but it slipped away. Heaven is a place where such
moments go on forever and ever—but we can only reach heaven by dying.

I know that Walt felt that longing for heaven. He had that longing when
he was a boy in Kansas City, peering through the fence at Electric Park,
wanting what he couldn't have because he didn't have a dime in his pocket.

I believe it was that same longing for heaven that drove Walt to build a
perfect place where children could ride merry-go-rounds and always catch
the brass ring, a place where yesterday and tomorrow are always within
walking distance, a place where anyone can be perfectly happy, if only for
a day. In Walt's mind, heaven is a beautiful park, all shining and clean, filled
with wonderful things to see and do, with a castle rising over it all, and a
train that goes around it.

Walt built his own heaven and called it Disneyland. It was the happiest place on earth, and he was always happiest when he could be there. The night before he died, Walt was looking at the ceiling of his hospital room, mapping out his dream of another, even bigger and brighter heaven called EPCOT. He didn't live to see that dream come true.

But God has set a dream in our hearts that is even bigger than anything Walt could imagine. God has set *eternity* in our hearts. He placed eternity in the heart of Walt Disney, and in your heart and mine.

Disneyland is a wonderful dream park—beautiful and shiny, full of joy and wonder. But compared with the dream of eternity that God has placed in our hearts, Disneyland is just a pale and imperfect reflection. The good news is that God has not only filled our hearts with this golden dream, but he has built this dream for us. It is a real place, a destination somewhere beyond death, somewhere beyond the walls of this world.

I believe it's the place Walt was searching for throughout his life.

I like to think that, in the end, he reached it.

Chapter Fourteen

❧

The *Real* Walt Disney

Was he a complex man—or uncomplicated and straight-forward? Was he a supreme egotist—or one of the most humble men who ever lived? Who was the real *Walt Disney?*

Walt once told one of his writers, "I am not Walt Disney anymore. Walt Disney is a thing, an image that people have. I spent my whole life building that image in the public mind. Walt Disney the person isn't that image. I drink and I smoke and there are a lot of other things I do that don't fit that image. But that image stands for something, and you don't have to explain to people what it means. They know what Disney is when they see our films or go to Disneyland. They know they are going to get a certain kind of entertainment. And that's what Disney is."

"Dad was careful about his image," Walt's daughter Sharon once said. "He wanted kids to look up to him. He never let himself be photographed with a drink in his hand and I don't think too many photos exist of him with a cigarette."

The real Walt Disney had his faults and frailties. He smoked way too much and he liked his Scotch (preferably with soda or over shaved ice with a twist). Among men, his speech was sometimes laced with profanity; in the presence of women, he was gentlemanly, even courtly.

Walt could be temperamental and moody. Story artist Bill Peet said "he was never the same two days in a row." Animator Jack Cutting described his personality as "like a drop of mercury rolling around on a slab of marble because he changed moods so quickly." When he was in a bad mood, people at the studio would warn each other, "He's wearing his bear suit today!"

Everyone who knew Walt saw him a bit differently. Disney scholar Jim Korkis told me, "Walt Disney's life reminds me of the old story of the blind men and the elephant. Each man touches a different part of the elephant. One touches the trunk and thinks the elephant is like a firehose. Another touches a leg and thinks the elephant is like a tree. If you talk to a hundred different people who knew Walt, you'll get a hundred distinct impressions. If you ask Diane Disney Miller, Ward Kimball, and Annette Funicello their views of Walt, you will get totally different answers. And each answer you get will be a life-changing lesson."

> *"Walt was easy to talk to, but not much for small talk. If the conversation pertained to his interests, his eyes would light up. He was always a kid at heart."*
>
> FULTON BURLEY
> PERFORMER, "GOLDEN HORSESHOE REVUE"

I collected a spectrum of varied impressions from the people I interviewed. But there was one consistent impression that came through every interview with those who knew Walt best: They all loved him. And the longer they knew him, the more they loved him.

Some critics have called Walt a supreme egotist. But those who knew him well, thought him the very soul of humility. Some critics called him cold and emotionless. But those who knew him best recalled how he laughed, hugged and even cried at sentimental moments. Some have said Walt never offered a word of praise, but those who knew him well knew how to read him. Two little words from Walt—"That'll work"—gave them a bigger lift than winning an Oscar.

Some say Walt was a complex man, an enigma, beyond comprehension. Those who knew him best said he was straightforward and unpretentious. There were no deep complexities to the man. Throughout his life, he maintained a Missouri farm boy's wide-eyed wonder about the world. The key to his personality was simply this: Walt knew what he wanted to accomplish in life, and he was intensely focused on those goals. Diane Disney

Miller put it this way: "Complex? Well, yes and no. Dad was consistently what he was, which was semi-innocent and very directed."

I asked people to describe Walt's distinctive habits and mannerisms. The first thing most people mentioned: Walt's eyebrow. Longtime Disney publicist C. Thomas Wilck (husband of Walt's secretary, Tommie Wilck) said, "When Walt lifted that eyebrow of his, you knew he was unhappy about something."

"Walt Disney was warm and friendly, but a tough taskmaster in the pursuit of perfection," said Disney artist Ralph Kent. "When his left eyebrow went up, he was thinking, 'This can be done better.' He had a very expressive face, and sometimes both eyebrows would rise—not a good sign. You always wanted to please Walt. You didn't want to let him down. The next time he came by, you didn't want to see that eyebrow go up!"

In an interview with Michael Barrier, animator David Hand recalled a meeting about a sequence for *Snow White and the Seven Dwarfs*. One of the dwarfs was supposed to perform several actions as he danced through a scene. The sequence needed to be exactly thirty seconds, not a second more, because it was timed to the music. Walt pantomimed the entire sequence, acting out all the movements of the dwarf.

When Walt finished, David Hand said, "Walt, it looked too long to me. The animator can't do all of those actions in thirty seconds."

"Yes, you can, Dave—look." And Walt went through the actions again. What Walt didn't know was that David Hand had a stopwatch in his pocket. Walt got to the end of the action and said, "There! You see? Thirty seconds."

David Hand pulled out the stopwatch and checked it. "Sorry, Walt," he said. "That was fifty-five seconds."

Walt gave Hand a hard stare. As Hand described it, Walt's eyebrow went up so high, it parted his hair. Without another word, Walt turned and stomped out of the room. That day, David Hand learned that Walt didn't like being proved wrong—not by stopwatches and not by uppity animators.

Michael Broggie, son of Imagineer Roger Broggie, told me a story about Walt's raised eyebrow. "Every Christmas," he said, "Walt gave a big party at his house for employees and their children. He would usually show some Disney feature films and cartoons, and they would put out a lot of food—

it was a great party. Then Walt would give all the kids a big box of Disney toys—all priceless collectibles today.

"One Christmas, when I was seven, Walt decided to do something different—no movies or cartoons. Instead, he had live entertainment—jugglers, comedy acts, live bands. He really outdid himself. It must have cost a fortune. When it was over, we were going out the door and Walt was seeing everybody out. I tugged on his sleeve and said, 'I really didn't like the party this year. I liked it more last year, when you had the movies and cartoons.'

"Walt looked down at me with that famous look of his—one eyebrow arched up. He said, 'Well, I guess you can't please everybody.'

"When we got home, my mother tore into me. 'How dare you be so rude? Mr. Disney gave us all that wonderful party and you criticized it! How could you do that?' She made me write a letter of apology. The next year, Walt gave another Christmas party—and it was movies and cartoons again. Walt always listened to his public, even though he didn't always like what he heard. And when he didn't like something, you could always see it on his face."

To Walt's daughters, the Disney eyebrow was more effective than any scolding. Sharon recalled an incident during her teenage years. Walt and Lillian were dining out with friends, and Sharon stayed home, tying up the phone for hours. When Walt tried to call home, he got a busy signal.

Later, Walt found Sharon lying on the floor with her feet stretched up on the wall, teenager-style, chattering away. He went over to the phone, cut the connection with one finger, and looked at Sharon with that single raised eyebrow. Sharon gulped.

"He didn't need to say a word," she said. "That raised eyebrow was a scolding in itself."

According to his brother Roy, Walt used his eyes to look into people's souls. "He had an eye that would grab yours when he was telling you something," Roy once said, "and if you would waver and look around, he'd say, 'What's the matter—aren't you interested?' Oh, he wouldn't let go of your eyes! He was so intent on everything he did, and that was his way of looking into you. You couldn't lie to him. You couldn't say you liked something if you didn't—it would show right in your eyes. People couldn't stand up to him if they weren't straight with him."

Walt's ability to assess character through eye contact was a skill he acquired and practiced. He was not a good judge of character in his twenties, when he trusted—and got cheated by—Charles Mintz and Pat

> *"When Walt made eye contact with you, he truly made eye contact."*
>
> RAY SIDEJAS
> LONGTIME DISNEYLAND EMPLOYEE

Powers. After his experiences with those men, the ability to size up people face-to-face became important to Walt. By the 1940s, he had become a good (some would say uncanny) judge of character.

Another distinctive Disney trait was his legendary smoker's cough. When making his rounds at the studio, Walt didn't like to barge in on his artists unannounced. At the same time, he didn't want to knock on doors—it was, after all, his studio. So while he was coming down the hall to someone's office, he would announce himself with a cough.

Some of Walt's artists—especially the lazy ones—dreaded that cough. But some looked forward to Walt's cough. Disney painter Peter Ellenshaw told me that he maneuvered to get his office on the same floor as Walt's because he enjoyed being close to the boss.

"Walt's office was at the other end of the floor," Ellenshaw said. "I can still hear him. His cough gave him away. I was always glad to see him. He'd ask, 'What are you working on, Peter?' I'd tell him and he'd encourage me and make me want to be a better painter. When he left, I'd think, 'That was great, that was encouraging,' and I'd be filled with enthusiasm once more."

"We could never lose Walt in a crowd," Lillian Disney once told an interviewer. "We could tell when he came home at night. If I was upstairs, I could hear him cough as he came through the gate outside. If we were in a crowd, I'd say 'Well, where's Walt?' Pretty soon, I'd hear that cough and say, 'Oh, yeah. There he is.'"

And then there were Walt's fingers. In *Walt Disney: An American Original,* Bob Thomas observed, "Walt's fingers were expressive and forever moving. He made eloquent use of his hands while he was describing a cartoon plot to an animator, or even a casual acquaintance. He had an artist's fingers, narrow and pliant, and hence he was good at making things.

"His animators learned that the fingers acted as a device to reveal his degree of approval or annoyance. If Walt was engrossed with the action on the screen in a sweatbox, his fingers would be motionless. If his interest started to drift, he began to drum on the arm of his chair. Animators listened for the sound, and if the drumming became a tattoo, they knew they would be sent back to their drawing boards."

Walt's drumming fingers could be unnerving. Animator Frank Thomas recalled, "There was this drumming of the fingers on the arm of the chair and that was when he'd just stare at you for as long as ten minutes or more. Usually, he wasn't thinking about you at all; you just happened to be in his line of vision, although you never knew for sure."

A good husband

A visitor to the Disney home would likely notice a stack of scripts in the living room, where Walt liked to read. Lilly would sometimes awaken in the middle of the night to find Walt with his brow furrowed, cigarette in hand, as he paced, sketched, or read a script. He had a work table in the bedroom to accommodate his bouts of creative insomnia.

Despite his workaholic personality, Walt maintained a healthy balance between his work and home life. He was in the office by eight, generally had lunch at his desk, took a break at five for a drink and a rubdown and traction from the studio nurse, after which he would attend a production meeting or an Imagineering session at six. After that, Walt would usually have his secretary call his house to inform Thelma Howard, the Disney cook-housekeeper, that he was on his way home. He would arrive at around seven or seven-thirty, give Lilly a hug and kiss, and sit down for dinner with the family.

One time, Walt's secretary forgot to phone home when he left. Arriving at his house, Walt was greeted by a look of horror on Thelma's face. "What are you doing here?" she said in a panicked voice. "Nobody called! I don't even have dinner on the stove yet!"

When Walt went into the living room, he received a similar greeting from Lillian. "What are you doing here?" his wife said. "Nobody called!"

"What kind of greeting is that?" Walt said. "Is this my house or isn't it?"

In June 1956, Walt and Lilly were driving near Colorado Springs when Walt spotted a sign near a farmhouse. It read PETRIFIED TREES FOR SALE. Walt stopped the car. "I won't be long," he said. Leaving Lilly in the car, he walked to the farmhouse and found the owner. Walt and the owner walked around the property, which was strewn with large pieces of petrified wood. He selected a large, symmetrical piece and arranged to have it shipped home.

When Walt returned to the car, he'd been gone about an hour. Lilly was fuming. Thinking fast, Walt said, "Lilly, I just bought you a wonderful anniversary present—a petrified tree!"

The five-ton tree arrived in time for their thirty-first wedding anniversary on July 13, 1956. It spent the better part of a year in Lilly's garden. Then, one year later, it was put on display next to the Rivers of America in Disneyland—where Walt had planned to put it all along.

There was one thing about Walt that drove Lilly crazy: his fondness for hats. He owned a large assortment—gray fedoras, feathered Tyroleans, white straw panamas, and tan Stetsons. Early in their marriage, Walt liked to tilt his hat at a jaunty angle; Lilly thought it made him look pretentious.

Later in life, Walt would put on his hat in such a way that the crown would get crushed. "Walt," Lilly would say, "fix your hat!" He would "fix" the hat by crushing it even more. Lilly would then grab the hat and toss it away. One year, he took one of the hats Lilly hated most, had it bronzed, filled it with flowers, and gave it to her as a Valentine's Day gift.

Walt's brother Roy once said, "Lilly worshiped him and anything he wanted to do was all right by her. She had a lot of patience with him and they used to fuss at each other in their own kidding way."

A typical American father

When Diane Disney was six, a school friend asked, "Is your dad really Walt Disney?" Diane didn't know, so she asked her mother. Lilly said, yes, her daddy was Walt Disney.

Diane stomped into the living room where her father was reading the newspaper. With her little jaw set in what Walt called "that dirty Disney look," she demanded, "Daddy, why didn't you tell me you're Walt Disney?"

For as long as they could, Walt and Lillian sheltered their daughters from Walt's fame. They wanted a normal family life for the girls. Sharon recalled,

> *"I always wished he was just ordinary people. From the first moment I became aware of his fame, I hated it. I didn't like the attention drawn to me."*
>
> DIANE DISNEY MILLER
> WALT'S DAUGHTER

"We weren't raised with the idea that this is a great man who is doing things that no one else had ever done. He was Daddy. He was a man who went to work every morning and came home every night."

"The world knew Dad from his movies and television shows," Diane Disney Miller told me, "but I knew him as my father. I still love him and miss him very much. I admired and valued his human qualities far more than the things he achieved in the entertainment world. He was simply a very good man. My sister, Sharon, and I loved him, delighted in his company, and trusted him completely. Even though he was a busy man and he accomplished so much in his career, he always gave us his time and attention. He was a very involved father."

Walt personally chauffeured the girls to school, dance lessons, and other events. Walt's role as Diane and Sharon's father always came first. He would take each girl to school before going on to the studio—a long morning commute that afforded him many father-daughter chats. Walt treasured those early years with his daughters, and the mere thought of watching them grow up and leave their childhood behind would cause him to mist up with emotion.

Though Walt was a demanding perfectionist at the studio, he was easygoing and affirming at home. Whenever his little daughters showed him a sheet of Crayola scribbles, he praised it as if it were an original Rembrandt. When Diane or Sharon appeared in a dance recital or school play, he would always be there with a hug and the words, "Great job, kid!"

"Daddy never missed a father-daughter event," Diane recalls, "no matter how I discounted it. I'd say, 'Oh, Daddy, you don't need to come. It's just a stupid old thing.' But he'd be there right on time."

One of Diane's favorite childhood memories is what she calls "the Sunday Routine." After taking Diane and Sharon to Sunday school, Walt would drive them to Griffith Park, where the Disney girls would ride the carousel. I've visited that carousel, and even though it's showing its age, it's a thing of beauty. The girls would ride around and around while Walt dreamed about building a park with a carousel beyond the castle.

"There was some apparatus that had rings sticking out from a slot," Diane remembers, "and you'd grab a ring as you went by. If you got the brass ring, you got a free ride. One day I kept getting that brass ring and I felt so clever. Years later, I asked Dad, 'How did I keep getting that brass ring?' He said, 'Oh, I gave the kid a few dollars and he kept putting the rings where you could get them.'"

"He took us for drives after Sunday School. We'd go to Griffith Park and play on the playground equipment and go on the merry-go-round for an hour or two or three. He never got tired. Sundays were so much fun and what made them so fun was that Daddy never got impatient with us. He was just there enjoying us. Yet at the same time, he was analyzing what we were enjoying and why."

DIANE DISNEY MILLER
WALT'S DAUGHTER

Though firm in discipline, Walt was also demonstrative and affectionate with his daughters. "My dad has been portrayed as an aloof person who didn't touch people," Diane told me. "That may have been true at the office, but at home with his family and friends, Dad was a hugger. I have many photos of Dad with his arm around me or Mom or Sharon. That's how I remember him."

Did Walt ever get grouchy or lose his temper around the house? Oh, yes. But with Walt, anger was a temporary condition. It blew over quickly, and was forgotten. "Nothing was ever under the surface in our family," Diane recalls. "He would blow up over little things. But when there was a crisis like a car accident, he'd say, 'Well, it's all right, kid. We'll get another car.' One time I skidded on a rainy street and bounced onto the curb into a palm tree. I was all shaken up, but Dad couldn't have been more calm and understanding."

Walt's grandchildren remember him as a wonderful man who enjoyed entertaining them and introducing them to new experiences and ideas. Walt's eldest grandson, Chris Miller, told me, "Granddad always made the most of his family time, even though he was very busy at the studio. We often spent weekends with our grandparents, and we sometimes went to visit Granddad at the studio after school. He would show us cartoons and films, and he'd let us do our homework in his office area.

"Granddad liked to involve us in his work and show us the latest projects his studio was working on. We toured the movie sets with him, and he took us out to Disneyland to see the new attractions. The most important thing I remember about him was that he made us feel loved

and important. I was ten when Granddad died, and I miss him to this day."

Jenny Goff has fond memories of Grandfather Walt and Grandmother Lilly. "My grandparents adored us," she told me, "and we were welcome in every nook and cranny of their house. Walt Disney was the best grandfather anyone could have. As a little girl I would take walks with him in the park. Even though I was only six and a half when he died, I'll always remember his warm smile and his wonderful laugh."

Longtime Disneyland employee Ray VanDeWarker told me, "One day, Walt came to the Indian Village with two of his grandaughters. Walt and the girls got in a canoe. Just then, another canoe came along, and the guy in the boat called out to Walt, 'Let's race!' So off they went! By the time Walt got back to the boat dock, he was soaking wet and grinning from ear to ear. He took his two granddaughters by the hand and walked off. He was like a kid who never grew up."

Mr. Avuncular

When Walt was "on-stage," greeting the public at Disneyland or hobnobbing with TV executives or corporate sponsors, he was witty, genial and charming. When he was "backstage" at his studio, he was reserved, quiet and reflective. Some found it unnerving to be around him when he withdrew into his private world of ideas.

Actress Ginny Tyler recalled, "You could tell when Walt was going to tune you out because his eyes went off to another field of vision. He was off in his own world and his own thoughts. You could feel his thoughts closing around the next idea he had."

Some Disney critics didn't understand this side of Walt's creative personality, so they pegged him as "cold" or "aloof." *Time* movie critic Richard Schickel, in a June 1998 retrospective called "Ruler of the Magic Kingdom," described Walt as "withdrawn" and a "complex and darkly driven man." According to Schickel, the man we know as Uncle Walt "didn't have an avuncular bone in his body"—a very different picture from the Walt Disney I've come to know through interviews with over two-hundred people who knew him well.

In case you had to look up the word *avuncular* as I did, it means "kind and benevolent in the manner of a loving uncle." It occurred to me that if I wanted to find out if Walt Disney was "avuncular" or not, I should talk to his nieces and nephews—those who have the best reason of all to call him Uncle Walt. So I did.

Walt's niece, Dorothy Puder (the daughter of Walt's brother Herbert) told me, "Walt was always very warm, friendly and outgoing to me

> "Walt was something very unusual: a family man in the world of Hollywood. He was very involved with his daughters' lives, their interests, and their schoolwork, despite the hectic pace of his life. That kind of commitment is sadly lacking today."
>
> LEE SUGGS
> HISTORY TEACHER AND ONLINE COLUMNIST,
> "DISNEY IN THE CLASSROOM"

and my family. I'll never forget the wonderful thing he did for my son, David. Walt loved to make things with his hands, and he built a beautiful train set—a very large set with little trees and houses, like a little town. He put hours and hours into that train set, and he gave it to David as a Christmas gift."

Walt's niece Marjorie Sewell told interviewers that Walt was a loving, doting uncle during the formative years of her life. Marjorie was the daughter of Lillian's sister, Hazel. "Aunt Lilly made me clothes for my dolls," she said, "and Uncle Walt gave me skates and scooters and all the exciting things."

Whenever Walt and Lillian came to visit, Marjorie always wanted Walt to tuck her into bed. "Uncle Walt fixed the blankets so that I never fell out of bed," she recalled. "He was the only one who had the knack. If he didn't tuck me in, I would always wake up the next morning on the floor."

Hazel and Marjorie lived in Walt's home for five years. As Marjorie became a teenager, Walt looked out for her, setting a strict curfew, then waiting at the top of the stairs to make sure she got home all right. As teenagers do, Marjorie occasionally challenged Walt's authority. During one of those challenges, Marjorie mouthed off to Walt, and he read her the riot act. After the blowup, Marjorie went to her bedroom while Walt sat in the living room and brooded. A deafening silence hung over the Disney household.

A few days later, Marjorie was in the study hall at her Catholic school when she was summoned to the office. Upon her arrival, she was met by Uncle Walt. "What are you doing here?" she asked.

"I had some film to deliver," he said, "so I thought I'd take you out for a treat."

At the ice cream shop, neither said a word about the argument. They just chatted about school and ate their ice cream. Afterward, Walt drove Marjorie back to school. "I knew he'd forgiven me," she later recalled, "and he knew I'd forgiven him. That was it. He didn't say 'I'm sorry' for anything. He just came by and took me out for ice cream."

Walt always had a hard time saying the words "I'm sorry," but he never had any trouble showing it. Those who were closest to Walt knew what was on his heart, even if he was reluctant to express it in words.

In his later years, Walt went out of his way to be "Uncle Walt" to the children of his employees. "Walt started an Explorer Scout post on the studio lot," recalls Bob Broughton. "He believed in the Boy Scouts and was very involved in it. He was always in the office when the troop met, and he sometimes came to the

> *"He'd get behind the counter of his soda fountain, which was his boyhood dream come true. He'd have all these different flavors of ice cream, and he'd make these big tall things with whipped cream and cherries. They'd be a mile high."*
>
> WARD KIMBALL
> DISNEY ANIMATOR

meetings. My son Danny was part of that troop. One night, Walt took the Scouts—about twenty of them—into his office for a three-hour session. He pulled out artwork, scripts and budgets to show them what his job as a movie studio executive was about. The kids were fascinated."

Former Disney employee John O'Connor, son of Disney artist Ken O'Connor, remembers the Boy Scout post at the studio. "When I was four-teen," he told me, "our Boy Scout pack met at the studio on Monday nights. We would see Walt in the halls—he put in long hours. He'd have a script in his hand and he'd stop and chat with us. Later, I became an Eagle Scout and Walt attended the ceremony."

Lynda Ellenshaw Thompson, daughter of artist Peter Ellenshaw, recalls, "I was four years old when the Disneys came for dinner one night. I was very shy as a child and hesitant to approach adults. That night, my mom was in the kitchen and my dad was in another room. When they came into the living room, they found me sitting in Walt's lap. He was telling me a story and I was captivated. That was so unlike me, but it says something about Walt's appeal to children."

I asked Mouseketeer Lonnie Burr to describe Walt in a word, and he responded, "Avuncular." That's right. He actually said, "Avuncular." Then he added, "He was always personable and relaxed when I talked to him. Jimmie Dodd was our surrogate dad on the show—but Walt was our easy-going, amiable Uncle Walt."

The stories of Uncle Walt's avuncularity go on and on. Marie Johnston, wife of Ollie Johnston, recalls the time Walt came to their home to see Ollie's backyard railroad. While Walt was in the living room, Marie was bottle-feeding her infant son. The phone rang, and Walt said, "Here, give him to me." Marie gave the baby and bottle to Walt and went to answer the phone. When she returned, her son was still feeding contentedly in Walt's arms. Marie offered to take the baby, but Walt said, "Oh, no, we're doing fine." Marie recalled, "Walt finished feeding him, put the towel over his shoulder, and burped him. He knew just what to do."

Clearly, Walt was as avuncular as they come. So where did Richard Schickel get the idea that Walt "didn't have an avuncular bone in his body"?

The gruff softie

I think Richard Sherman explained it well. "Walt had a Midwestern reserve about him," Richard told me. "He didn't gush, he was not a hugger—at least not around the office—but when you were in his presence, you definitely felt his warmth, as much as if his arm was wrapped around you. Walt was a very sweet and warm man. It wasn't always easy for him to show it, but he was. Working for Walt was a joyful experience for me."

Like most Midwesterners of his generation, Walt was uncomfortable expressing emotions. He was also uncomfortable around the emotions of others. He didn't even like to be thanked. Once, during the 1930s, Walt gave animator Milt Kahl a raise, and Milt thanked him for it—at which point Walt became embarrassed. His gruff response: "What are you wasting time thanking me for? Get back to your drawing board!"

Walt was also uncomfortable giving praise to his staff. Though he appreciated the contributions of his artists, he couldn't bring himself to say, "Good job!" (a trait probably learned from his undemonstrative father). Walt wanted his staff to know he appreciated their work, so he found an indirect way of telling them: He praised people behind their backs. He knew that if he told John Lounsbery or Woolie Reitherman what a great piece of animation Marc Davis had done, then Davis would get the word sooner or later. By passing his praise through third parties, Walt's commendations would ripple thoughout the entire organization.

"I was called to meet him about Mary Poppins, *and I found out why everybody called him Uncle Walt. He was the most old-shoe guy I ever met in my life. He was comfortable to be around. An avuncular personality is what he was."*

DICK VAN DYKE
ACTOR

On those rare occasions when Walt did give an artist a face-to-face compliment, the news spread like wildfire. Ollie Johnston recalls the time in the late 1930s when he was on a break, chatting with the secretaries. He spotted Walt coming down the hallway, looking right at him. *Uh-oh,* Ollie thought to himself, *he's going to say, "Why are you hanging around here when you should be working?"* But Walt didn't scold him. "Hey, Ollie," Walt said, "I sure like those Pinocchios you're doing!"

Ollie was stunned. The moment Walt was out of earshot, the secretaries were buzzing about it: Walt gave Ollie a compliment! By the end of the day, the whole studio was talking about it. "That was big news for an hour or two," Johnston said.

"Walt was not big on compliments," X Atencio told me. "He expected the best from you and that was it. One time our team did a presentation to a corporate sponsorship prospect in Ohio, and it went well. As we boarded the company plane to return to California, Walt said, 'X, you did a heckuva job—but don't let it go to your head.' That was good enough for me."

Disney Imagineer Sam McKim told me, "One day, after I completed a project, Walt said to me, 'Good job, Sam.' One of my bosses, Jim Alger, heard that and called me into his office. 'Sam,' he said, 'I've been here thirty-seven years and Walt has complimented me twice. Remember what he just said to you.' Later, after Walt had given me several more assignments, Jim Alger said to me, 'The greatest compliment from Walt is we're still working for him.' Walt would compliment you to other people and you'd hear back—that was the highest praise of all."

Ginny Tyler recalled, "One day I was at Disneyland with Walt. I was going on and on about how perfect and beautiful the park was. As I was raving away to Walt about how wonderful Disneyland was, he said, 'And that goes for my Disneyland storyteller, too.' That was me. I have never felt prouder in my entire life. I remember that moment like it was yesterday."

Director Ken Annakin told me, "It's been said that Walt never said 'Thank you' or 'Job well done.' It's true, I don't ever remember hearing that from Walt. But you knew if he approved of your work by the next project Walt assigned you to work on. That was his way of telling you 'Job done well.'"

Walt didn't readily give praise—and he didn't easily receive it. He distrusted people who lavished praise on him, taking it for empty flattery. On one occasion, Walt entertained a group of business executives at the Coral Room. Over lunch, they heaped praise on Walt with a very large shovel. Donn Tatum saw that Walt was uncomfortable listening to so many compliments, so he said, "Well, Walt, there's only one thing left for you to do—walk on water."

"I've already tried that," Walt replied with a wink, "and it doesn't work."

It always took people a little while to figure out how to read Walt. Songwriters Richard and Robert Sherman started with Disney in 1961. Their first project was "The Horsemasters," a two-part episode of *Wonderful World of Color* that starred Annette Funicello. The Sherman brothers wrote a song for that show, "The Strummin' Song," and showed it to Disney music director Jimmy Johnson. "Nice tune," said Johnson. "Let's show it to Walt."

Richard and Robert looked at each other in surprise. They had assumed that Walt Disney was remote and unapproachable by mere mortals. They never dreamed that they would actually get to meet Walt himself!

> "While in the 1930s Walt had been a lean young renegade with a subversive streak, by the 1950s he had turned himself into the genial host of the *Disneyland* television show—a soft, avuncular presence who promoted good values and wholesomeness."
>
> NEAL GABLER
> MEDIA CRITIC

Johnson led the Sherman brothers to Walt's office—and there was Walt, wearing a casual golf sweater, sitting at his desk. Johnson introduced them and Walt said, "So are you guys really brothers? I've seen vaudeville acts that call themselves brothers, but they're not related."

"Yes," Robert said. "We're really brothers."

"Well, fine, fine," Walt said. "Let me tell you about this picture we're making." And Walt told them all about a feature film with the working title *We Belong Together* (later released as *The Parent Trap*). While Walt talked, the brothers exchanged worried glances. Walt Disney was talking about the wrong movie. Finally, Robert cleared his throat and said, "Mr. Disney—"

"Call me Walt," he corrected.

"Okay, uh, Walt," Robert said. "The thing is, we weren't hired for that movie. We were hired to write songs for 'The Horsemasters.' You see, we wrote this song for Annette—"

"Well, why did you let me go on like that?" Walt said, rising from his desk. "Come with me. There's a piano in the next room. You can show me the song."

So the Sherman brothers and Jimmy Johnson followed Walt into the next room. Richard played and sang 'The Strumming Song' for Walt. Then Walt nodded and said, 'Yeah, it'll work.'"

Richard and Robert looked at each other, reading each other's thoughts: *'It'll work'? That's all he thinks of the song?* They were devastated.

Walt turned to Johnson and said, "Let's get these boys a couple of scripts for *We Belong Together.* Richard, Robert, read this script. I think there are a couple of places for a song. See what you think. Oh, and the title is *We Belong Together,* but I don't like it. See if you can think of a better one. Well, if you'll excuse me—"

And with that, the meeting was over. Out in the hall, Richard turned to Jimmy Johnson and said, "He hated the song."

"What are you talking about?" Johnson said, clapping the brothers on the back. "He loved the song! And he loved you guys! You were a hit! What a fantastic meeting!"

"What do you mean?" said Robert. "All he said about our song was, 'It'll work.'"

Johnson looked at them in astonishment. "You really don't understand, do you? Walt just accepted one of your songs—and he assigned you to the new Hayley Mills feature! You guys hit a home run! You just got the biggest break of your career—and you don't even know it!"

Walt could be difficult at times—but those who knew him best say he was just a gruff softie. Like a toasted marshmallow, Walt was crusty on the outside but a soft, sweet, warm human being underneath.

Fun, humor, sentiment—and "corn"

Walt loved fun.

After his daughter Sharon began dating a fellow named Robert Borgfeldt Brown, Walt and Lillian invited him over for dinner. Young Mr. Brown came from a prominent Kansas City family. He was in awe of Walt's reputation and a bit nervous on his first visit to the Disney home. It happened to be Walt's fifty-seventh birthday—and Walt did not enjoy birthdays. Lillian and Sharon treated the evening just like any other day—but they forgot to tell the cook, Thelma Howard, not to make a fuss.

Hoping to please Walt, Thelma baked a birthday cake—his favorite, a banana cake piled high with whipped cream. At the end of dinner, Thelma brought the cake into the dining room.

Walt frowned. "*That* is a birthday cake!" he snorted. "I don't *want* a birthday cake!"

The air crackled with suspense. Suddenly, Lillian scooped a handful of whipped cream from the cake and smooshed it in Walt's face.

Robert's eyes went wide. Sharon gasped. Walt scooped up a handful of whipped cream and tossed it back at Lillian. And the food fight was on! Moments later, Thelma's cake was in ruins, whipped cream was spattered everywhere—and everyone was laughing.

And Robert Brown? He got over his initial shock and later married Sharon Disney.

Walt was a barrel of fun. Disney writer Charles Shows recalls taking his parents to Disneyland soon after the park opened in 1955. Shows' father had worked on the railroad and was eager to check out the Disneyland train. So they boarded the train at the Main Street station and started down the tracks. Before long, Shows' father pointed and said, "Look!"

On the service road beside the tracks, a man was driving a Jeep, racing the train. It was, of course, Walt Disney. Walt waved and honked the horn, and the engineer answered with a blast from the steam whistle.

"Walt was a warm, genial host," Shows wrote, "and he insisted on personally escorting my mother and father around his new make-believe kingdom. This is the Walt Disney my parents will always remember and I will never forget."

Walt's granddaughter Joanna Runeare recalls Walt as a fun-loving man with a zest for life. "We have these old movies of my grandfather skiing or diving into the pool," she told me. "He liked all kinds of sports, even though he wasn't a great athlete. He just had a passion for life—all aspects of life."

Walt was witty, but he didn't tell jokes and he lacked the patience to listen to them. If anyone told a dirty joke in his presence, he responded with a chilly frown. Walt's approach to making people laugh was simple and unpretentious. When his daughter Diane was fourteen years old, she complained that Walt's movies were corny. "Of course they are," Walt replied, unfazed. "I like corn."

He once told his associates, "The critics think I'm kind of corny. Well, I am corny. As long as people respond to it, I'm okay." He believed his own tastes reflected the likes and dislikes of everyday Americans. "When I make a picture," he often said, "I play to my own tastes."

Critics attacked Walt's movies not only for their "corny" humor but for their "corny" sentimentality. Did his films cross the line from sentiment to sentimentality, from pathos to schmaltz? The cynics said so. The audiences didn't care. They flocked to the theaters and laughed, cried, and waxed nostalgic, then went home with a warm feeling in their hearts.

"I can't laugh at intellectual humor. I'm just corny enough to like to have a story hit me over the heart."

WALT DISNEY

"He gloried in sentimentality," Diane once told an interviewer. "Ron and I were married in a little church up in Santa Barbara. Naturally, Daddy led me down the aisle and stood with me. I heard this sob, turned around, and Daddy was standing there with tears streaming down his cheeks. I squeezed his hand and he gave me a soulful look."

Though Walt didn't like people to know it, he cried easily, especially at a sad scene in a movie—or even a movie script. Hycy Engel Hill, a flight attendant on the Disney corporate planes, once said, "On one of our plane trips, I walked to the back of the cabin to see if Walt needed anything. . . . He was reading a script, sniffing, and tears were rolling down his cheeks. He looked up at me and was embarrassed. He was fumbling for his handkerchief and said, 'How's that! A grown man like me can't even read a script without crying.'"

Walt's sentimentality was sincere, honest emotion—not manipulation. "That was the secret of Walt," Ward Kimball once observed. "He didn't do [sentimentality] with his tongue in his cheek. When he did *Flowers and Trees,* which had a tragic ending, he was sincere, he believed in it. And when he did *Snow White*—here are these gross cartoon figures, nothing like you'd see in real life, all the animals acting like people—he was completely serious. And to this day, the picture makes people cry when Snow White dies. The new generation sits there sobbing in their Kleenex."

Walt was no cynical manipulator of other people's emotions. He didn't resort to trite formulas to wring an audience's tear ducts. He demanded that his films affect his emotions first, genuinely and deeply. He knew that if a scene made him laugh or cry, then his audience would be affected as well. "In everything he did," Roy O. Disney once said, "my brother had an intuitive way of reaching out and touching the hearts and minds of young and old alike."

Disney historian Ron Stark told me, "Walt always wanted to see emotion on the screen, especially love. Even the Disney villains are portrayed with a sort of loveableness. Walt wanted his movies to touch the heart, and the deepest emotion of the heart is love."

How Walt's mind worked

Like his heroes, Abe Lincoln, Thomas Edison and Charlie Chaplin, Walt was a largely self-educated man. Though Walt's formal education only went as far as his freshman year in high school, he was a brilliant and well-educated man. At an early age, Walt mastered the art of self-education. While most people view education as something they passively receive from teachers, Walt viewed education as something to be aggressively pursued.

He exemplified an important life principle: Successful people are those who have learned how to learn. Whether college-educated or self-educated, successful people depend on themselves, not others, for their own knowledge, skills and wisdom. People who are committed to life-long learning have everything they need to shape their own destinies.

Like many self-educated geniuses, Walt had a few gaps in his knowledge—trivial flaws that became distinctive, even charming traits of the Disney persona. For Walt, these tiny flaws involved the pronunciation of certain words. His TV writers learned, for example, to avoid using the word "drama" in a script, because Walt would invariably pronounce it "drammer." Another word that gave him problems was "hover," which he would pronounce "hoover"—as in,

> *"You just can't please everybody. I don't want to please everybody. I'd get a little worried if I did something and everybody was pleased with it."*
>
> WALT DISNEY

"the flying saucers of Tomorrowland hoover on jets of forced air."

Because he was the host of a weekly television show, Walt was keenly aware that his verbal skills were on display before millions. So he hired a diction coach to help him with his pronunciation of words. He also initiated a ritual at the close of every workday. During his heat and traction treatment, Walt, Hazel George, and Tommie Wilck would play a skill-sharpening word game. Each day they would choose a new word, learn its meaning, origin, and usage, and try to work it into the next day's conversation.

Walt's memory for people, information and details was legendary. Disney artist Bob Moore recalled a conversation he had with Walt after a production meeting. "Walt," Moore said, "I'm a second-generation Disney employee. You probably don't remember my father, but he was one of the musicians who recorded the soundtrack for *Steamboat Willie*."

"I remember him," Walt said, "but it wasn't *Steamboat Willie*, it was *Plane Crazy*."

Walt's grandson, Walter Disney Miller, told me, "People who worked with my grandpa say that he seemed to be everywhere at once and he never forgot anything. He could remember things people did or said a decade or two earlier—and he would remember it in exact detail. My grandpa had an amazing memory and put it to good use."

Michael Broggie, was impressed by the way Walt would probe for information, then store, catalog and cross-reference that information in his mind. "When I was a kid of eight or nine," Michael told me, "I loved to visit Walt's office. I'd go to his office door and if he wasn't too busy, he'd say, 'Michael, come in, let's talk!' I'd sit in a chair and he'd start grilling me. 'What are you watching on TV? What are you reading?' He was probing for information on what my generation liked and enjoyed. His mind was like a giant computer and he was storing that information for future use. He was doing market research.

"Walt's recall was awesome. Many people would have a conversation with Walt, and then years later say, 'Walt, remember that time we were talking about such-and-such?' And Walt would not only remember every detail of that conversation, but he would challenge you and correct you if you mis-remembered any tiny point."

Imagineer Sam McKim told me about the first time he met Walt Disney.

"I started with Disney in December 1954," he said. "I was working during the lunch break, along with my friend, Fred Hartman. We heard footsteps coming down the hall and suddenly a face with a mustache appeared in the doorway. The man said, 'Hi, I'm Walt Disney. Who are you?' I said, 'I'm Sam McKim, and I just came over from 20th Century-Fox, and this is my friend, Fred Hartman, who came over from MGM. Walt said, 'Fine, fine. I appreciate you movie people coming to help build my park. I'll see you.' And he was gone.

> *"All you have to do is own up to your ignorance honestly, and you will find people who are eager to fill your head with information."*
>
> WALT DISNEY

"A few days later, I passed Walt in the hall—he was with a group of people—and he said, 'Hi, Sam.' That day, I really felt like part of the organization. I later learned that Walt had an incredible memory for names and faces."

John Matthews was a Disneyland cast member who often appeared as Mickey Mouse. "Walt had the memory of a politician," John told me. "I first met him when I was substituting for Paul Castle as Mickey. I was in the backstage area at Disneyland, and I had the Mickey suit on. It was early morning and we were going to do a photo shoot for a magazine ad. Walt saw me and said, 'You aren't Paul. Who are you?' Even with the head on, he could tell I wasn't the regular Mickey. I said, 'I'm John Matthews.' And he said, 'Well, John, you're doing a good job.'

"The next time I ran into him, I was in character as Mickey for the *Mary Poppins* premiere at Grauman's Chinese Theater in 1964. Again, I had the complete suit on, including the Mickey head. Walt came up to me and said, 'Hi, John!' That was just amazing. He recognized me and remembered my name, even though I was in the Mickey costume.

"The following year, I was in New York for the World's Fair, working as Mickey at 'It's a Small World.' There was no reason for him to even know I was there—I usually worked at Disneyland. But when he arrived, he came up to me and said, 'Hi, John!'

"That kind of memory doesn't come naturally to most people, but it really makes an impression. Here was a man who was king of the world—

yet he took the trouble to remember me and greet me by name. He brought me into his world and made me a part of it."

Walt's memory may have seemed super-human at times, but he also took advantage of memory aids. Mouseketeer Sherry Alberoni Van Meter told me, "I remember one day during a break from filming, my mom and I were standing in front of the administration building at the Burbank studio. I was wearing my *Mickey Mouse Club* costume, complete with mouse ears and my name written across my shirt in big letters. Uncle Walt came by with some other men and said, 'Hi, Mouseketeer Sherry!' I was so thrilled because he knew my name—not realizing that all he had to do was read."

Only rarely did Walt's memory fail him. Imagineer Rolly Crump remembers the first time he met Walt. They shook hands and Walt said, "Roland, it's nice to have you with us."

"Well," Rolly replied, "it's an honor to be working here, Mr. Disney."

"Oh, no, Roland—it's not 'Mr. Disney.' Call me Walt—and don't forget it."

"Okay, Walt."

For the next few days, Rolly would be working at WED and Walt would call him Roland. But after a week or so, Walt started calling him Owen—apparently confusing Rolly with Hollywood screenwriter Owen Crump. Later, Walt combined Roland and Owen and started calling him Orland. After a few weeks of being called Orland, Rolly was in a meeting with Walt, Yale Gracey, and some other Imagineers. Walt said, "Yale, you and uh, what's-his-name here—" And he pointed to Rolly. "I want you fellas to work on the 'Haunted Mansion' project."

Walt had a similar mental block when it came to Disneyland executive Jack Lindquist. "He always called me Bob," Lindquist said. "I'd wear my name tag and everyone else called me Jack, but Walt called me Bob. One day, Card Walker said, 'You know, Walt, that's Jack, not Bob.' Walt looked at me, raised that eyebrow and said, 'Looks like a Bob to me.'"

In the early days at the Disney studio, it was a lot easier for Walt to remember everyone's name, even without name tags. But as the list of Disney employees grew from scores to hundreds to thousands of people, Walt found it increasingly difficult to remember names. So he would go to the personnel department and study the employee files, matching people's names with their photos until he had memorized them.

Yes, Walt had an amazing memory—in part because he *worked* at having an amazing memory. If you want to be like Walt, then work on improving your mind and your memory.

A childlike curiosity

Walt was fascinated by the world of ideas. Disney historian Stacia Martin explains Walt's inquiring mind this way: "Walt wanted to know about everything. He had this relentless curiosity, and everything was interesting to him. He didn't sit back and wait for reports to cross his desk. He was constantly pursuing information by talking to people at the park, or at WED, or on the set at the studio. He had the ability to observe and retain everything around him—then he would take that information and put it to effective use.

"Walt would walk down to Mapo, the manufacturing arm of the company. The engineers would be building complicated robotic devices. Walt would ask one of them, 'What are you working on?' The man would give him a technical explanation. Weeks later, Walt would bring a visitor to the shop and explain in lay terms what was going on in that department—and everything he said was accurate, but translated into layman's terms."

> *"We keep moving forward, opening new doors, and doing new things, because we are curious—and curiosity keeps leading us down new paths."*
>
> WALT DISNEY

In the summer of 1949, the Disney studio was filming *Treasure Island* in England. Walt took Lilly, Diane and Sharon with him while he supervised the production. They spent five weeks in England and Ireland, then three weeks in France and Switzerland. One afternoon, Walt returned from a walking tour of Paris with dozens of mechanical wind-up toys.

"He wound them all up," Diane Disney Miller recalled, "and he put them on the floor of the room and just sat and watched them." There was a poodle that rolled over and a monkey that performed acrobatics. But the mechanism that fascinated Walt the most was a caged bird that flapped its wings, swished its tail, and warbled.

"Look at that!" Walt said. "Such a simple mechanism, but it looks like a real bird!"

Returning to the States, Walt handed the bird to studio technician Wathel Rogers and said, "Open this bird up and see what makes it tick." Rogers did so, and found an elegant arrangement of clockworks, a bellows and harmonica-like reeds. More than a decade later, these mechanical toys inspired a robotic technology called Audio-Animatronics.

At the time, Walt's family had no idea why he was so fascinated with wind-up toys. Only years later did it make sense. "He was studying," Diane said. "He could see Audio-Animatronics. We just thought he was crazy."

Walt's curiosity led him to experiment with new techniques and new technologies—just for the sake of learning new ways of doing things. Disney artist Ken Anderson recalled working on the optical effects for *Song of the South,* Walt's first color film combining animation with live action. This was before blue-screen matte photography made it relatively easy to combine different image elements onto a single piece of film. Walt footed the bill while Anderson experimented with one technique after another.

"We tried everything," Anderson recalled. "I was too stupid to realize that he was using everything as an experiment. I kept thinking he wanted problems solved. Then when I'd get something solved, he'd want to do something different. . . . He just wanted to find better and newer ways of doing everything."

"Walt had a deep curiosity about things," said actor Dean Jones. "He loved dealing with new technology. I remember my dad and mom visited the set once during something I was filming. I took them up to meet Walt, then I said, 'Okay, Dad, Mom, let's go. I've got to get back to the set.' Walt said, 'No, no, no, I'll show them around.' He spent all afternoon with my mom and dad, showing them the Audio-Animatronics figures they were designing for the park. He loved to talk about it and he was extremely curious about these things."

Walt believed that brilliant ideas were all around, just waiting for someone to ask the right questions. Disney executive Bill Sullivan told me, "I was a nineteen-year-old kid working on the 'Jungle Cruise.' It would be nine P.M. and no one was there. Walt would come and talk to us. He'd ask lots of questions. 'How is everything going at the attraction? What are the

> *"I happen to be an inquisitive guy,*
> *and when I see things I don't like,*
> *I start thinking, 'Why do they*
> *have to be like this and*
> *how can I improve them?'"*
>
> WALT DISNEY

guests saying when they get off the boats? How can we improve the attraction?' He wanted to find out what people thought. He listened carefully and was fascinated with everything we told him.

"We'd tell Walt what we were seeing and hearing, and he'd go back and give the V.P.s an earful at the Wednesday morning meetings. He knew more about everything that was going on than any of his paid experts. There was a guy whose job was to clean up the manure left by the horse-drawn vehicles on Main Street, and Walt talked to him, too."

Harold Bastrup was a detective with the Anaheim police force during Disneyland's early days (he became Anaheim's chief of police during the 1970s). He often walked around Disneyland at night, making sure the park was secure from intruders. During these visits, he became acquainted with Walt Disney.

"Walt always called me Sarge," Bastrup said. "Even after I was promoted to lieutenant, he called me Sarge. After a couple of years, he asked me what my name was. I said 'Harold Bastrup.' He said, 'I think I'll just call you Sarge.'

"I was always impressed with the way Walt asked questions and listened to what you had to say," Bastrup told me. "One night at about eleven-thirty, I was walking around the park with my partner. The place was closed, but there were park employees around. One man started toward us, and I realized it was Walt Disney. He asked us to sit and talk with him, and he sat down on a bench with one of us on either side of him, and he started asking us questions. 'What do you think of the park? How could we improve it?' He would ask a question, then listen intently, never interrupting. He was truly interested because he wanted to learn ways to improve the park. Walt was a good listener."

"Walt would get ideas from anyone," Michael Broggie told me, "from the places you'd least expect. One day, at an Imagineering meeting, Walt pointed to an open doorway and said, 'See that janitor out in the hall? He has as many ideas as any of us.'"

Bill Sullivan told me, "The janitor was Walt's best source of information because he would see all the work that was thrown away. The janitor knew what was in the waste baskets of every office in the building. Because Walt talked to the janitor, he knew everything that was going on throughout his organization."

Walt's curiosity about people and ideas goes back to his boyhood. His grandson, Walter Disney Miller, told me, "My grandpa always had this amazing curiosity. He stuck his nose into everything that interested him. He didn't have a shy bone in his body. As a kid growing up in Marceline, he would hang out with older people and ask questions about the old days. He spent a lot of time listening to a civil war veteran, Erastus Taylor, who told stories about the battle of Bull Run. He followed Doc Sherwood all around—the old doctor who paid him to paint a picture of his horse. From his boyhood to the end of his life, my grandpa was always asking questions."

Where does such insatiable curiosity come from? Disney writer Greg Ehrbar ascribes Walt's curiosity to his childlike spirit. "Walt had a childlike way about him," Ehrbar told me. "A four-year-old will stop and look at a blade of grass and think it's the greatest thing he's ever seen. Most adults lose that natural curiosity, but not Walt. He was always seeing possibilities and wonder in the simplest things. He never lost his childlike curiosity about life."

> *"Walt had the mind of a child. He was so curious."*
>
> ART LINKLETTER
> TELEVISION PERSONALITY

Paul Anderson, a Disney historian and a professor at Brigham Young University, told me that Walt's insatiable curiosity was one of the prime sources of his genius. He said, "I teach a senior course called 'Walt Disney and American Culture.' On the first day of class, I lecture on the genius of Walt Disney. I tell the students that genius must have its roots somewhere. But what were those roots? There was nothing special in Walt's childhood or his schooling. He was a daydreamer and a high school dropout. His parents led an itinerant life, chasing the American dream. He was not a great businessman; his first business venture ended in bankruptcy. So how did he become successful? After years of intense study, over two-hundred-fifty interviews with people who knew him, and reading over 25,000 books and magazine articles, I have boiled it down to six factors:

"First, *curiosity.* Walt was intensely curious about everything life had to offer. Diane Disney Miller told me that Walt was the most curious person on earth. If the family went to a ski resort, Walt would spend hours and hours asking questions of the ski instructors and the employees at the lodge. He wanted to know everything about how a ski resort worked. When Walt and Lilly went on a cruise, he talked to the kid who ran the shuffleboard court and the woman who ran the laundry operation. He was curious about every aspect of running a cruise ship. He had a childlike curiosity about anything and everything.

"Second, *knowledge.* Walt had a thirst for knowledge. He tried to impart this love of knowledge to everyone around him. In the 1930s, he gave out theater and concert tickets or museum passes so that his creative people could increase their knowledge about many fields. He knew that it would all pay dividends for the studio.

"Third, *experimentation.* Walt was always pushing the envelope and testing new ideas. He was on a continual quest for discovery, and he encouraged that same spirit in his staff.

"Fourth, *quality at all costs.* His philosophy was, 'Whatever you do, do it right.' He was always reaching for perfection, and his eye never missed a detail. One time, his staff had cut off the tail of Mickey Mouse in a single frame of a movie, just to see if Walt would catch it. After Walt watched the movie, he said, 'Put the tail back on Mickey before you release the film.'

"Fifth, *control.* Walt hired the best people and gave them a lot of creative freedom. But he always had control of the final results.

"Sixth, *vision.* That was Walt's special gift. He had a unique sense of what would sell, what the public wanted to see. He could envision Disneyland in every detail, and he pursued it relentlessly when everyone else predicted failure."

Those six qualities, Anderson told me, are the source of Walt's genius— but the greatest of these qualities was Walt's childlike curiosity.

Ego and humility

Over lunch at the studio, Ray Bradbury once told Walt, "I hear you're planning to redesign Tomorrowland. You know, I just helped design the United States Pavilion at the New York World's Fair. I have a lot of ideas. Would you hire me to consult on Tomorrowland?"

"Ray," Walt said, "it's no use. It'll never work."

Bradbury was crestfallen. "Why not?"

"Because," Walt replied, "you're a genius and I'm a genius. We'd kill each other before the end of the week." Bradbury later reflected that it was the kindest refusal he had ever received.

But Walt's words were more than just a polite turn-down. He had learned through disappointing experience that, in his business, there was only room for one genius. Two geniuses meant two competing visions.

Walt had tried working with geniuses before. He had brought Aldous Huxley to the studio to produce a script for *Alice in Wonderland.* Huxley wrote a brilliant script—but it was not a Disney script. Walt had brought Salvador Dali to the studio to work with John Hench on an animated project called *Destino.* Dali produced many marvelous paintings, but the project proved unfilmable at the time. Walt learned that there had to be one creative genius who had final and uncontested say over the finished product. At the Disney studio, that person was Walt Disney.

> *"Early in legendary Disney animator Ken Anderson's career, Walt Disney took him aside and described the reasons behind the selling of Walt Disney and that no picture would ever be a 'Ken Anderson' picture. It was always a Walt Disney Production. And while some in the organization took this branding as the effort of a vain man to promote himself, for those who got it and believed in it, the products that they put forth meant so much more to generations of fans than if they had gone it alone."*
>
> MATTHEW WALKER
> FOUNDER, STARTEDBYAMOUSE.COM

Does that make Walt an egotist? No. Walt was a man of great ego strength, but he was not an egotistical man.

Ego strength should not be confused with egotism or arrogance. To have a strong ego is not the same as having a big ego. Ego strength can be defined as confidence, initiative, decisiveness, persistence, and the toughness to endure difficult situations. Ego strength is a healthy sense of self that enables you to maintain your core beliefs and your core identity even amid pressure, opposition, criticism and temptation.

A person with healthy ego strength can also be quite humble. Such a person can say, in all humility, "I am good at what I do"—or even, "I'm a genius." Walt knew he was a genius, and he said so to Ray Bradbury. But when Walt said it, he was not bragging. He was simply (and even humbly) stating the obvious.

Critics have used words like "autocrat" or "despot" to describe Walt because he named his studio after himself, ran it on his own terms, and demanded final say on how everything was done. Even Walt's admirers sometimes described him in those terms. Former Disney executive Jim Cora told me, "Walt gathered opinions from everyone, then made his decisions, and his decisions were absolute. In that sense, he was a dictator—a benevolent dictator."

As Bob Thomas observed in *Walt Disney: An American Original,* "From all of his employees, Walt required a devotion to the collaborative effort, a sublimation of their own egos for the benefit of the studio product. . . . Those who were willing to contribute their work with selfless dedication remained and flourished. Some could not find gratification under such a system and left the studio to seek more individual achievement."

Even though Walt expected his employees to be team players, Walt had no patience with sycophants. He wanted the people around him to speak their minds and even challenge him during the creative, brain-storming phase. But once Walt arrived at a decision, the discussion was over.

Walt once chaired a story meeting for *Pinocchio*. After hearing several ideas, Walt announced his decision. Bill Cottrell spoke up and said, "I like my way better."

"Yes, I know," Walt said, "but let's do it my way."

"If we do it your way," Cottrell said, "we'll never know if my way would have worked."

"No, we won't," said Walt. Decision made, end of discussion.

This is not to say that Walt couldn't be reasoned with after he'd made up his mind—but it took guts. Actor Dean Jones recalls a lunch conversation with Walt in the Coral Room. The topic was the script for *Blackbeard's Ghost*. Jones wanted several changes made in the script on the grounds they were "corny and old-fashioned." The actor explained his problem with the first two items, and Walt grudgingly said, "Okay, we'll make those changes—but you're pushing your luck."

Jones ignored the warning in Walt's voice and plunged ahead. With each additional objection, Walt's annoyance mounted. On Jones' final criticism, Walt growled, "That joke was funny in 1923, and it's still funny today!"

"I'm not saying it's not funny," Jones said, "but I think it hurts the scene. We've already asked the audience to accept the premise that I've conjured up a ghost with a few magic words. Let's not pile on another implausibility so quickly."

> *"I am a patient listener, but opinionated to the point of stubbornness when my mind is made up."*
>
> WALT DISNEY

Walt leaned back, frowning. "You know, Dean," he said, "if there are so many things about this picture you don't like, maybe I should get another actor."

"Whoa!" Jones said. "Walt, please understand, I'm not asking for more money or more close-ups. All I want is to make the movie better. I know you want that, too."

There was a long pause. Dean Jones felt the tension subside.

Walt changed the subject. "Peter Ustinov is coming to the studio tomorrow," he said. "Would you like to have lunch with us?"

"If I'm still in the picture, Walt," Jones joked.

Walt didn't smile. He rose from the table, and the two men left the building together. They chatted on the way to the Animation Building, then they parted with a friendly good-bye, and Jones went on for a few steps.

"Oh, one more thing, Dean," Walt called after him. "About that last scene we talked about—"

Jones turned. "Yes, Walt?"

"We'll do it your way." Then he pointed his finger at Jones and added, "But you'd better be right!"

You see? Walt could be reasoned with.

Disney biographers often remark about the fact that Walt deliberately placed everyone at the studio—himself included—on a first-name basis. Why did he insist on that? First, because he wanted everyone in his studio to feel equally valued. Second, because he wanted everyone to feel that their ideas and contributions were equally valued. Walt knew that employees who feel like second-class citizens are afraid to speak up and offer ideas. First names helped to democratize the Disney studio and open the lines of communication.

One of Walt's favorite charities was the John Tracy Clinic for the Hearing Impaired, named for the son of actor Spencer Tracy, Walt's friend and polo buddy. Walt helped found the clinic in 1942, and he also employed John Tracy as an animator. In the late 1950s and early '60s, Walt volunteered his staff to cater and entertain at the clinic's annual fundraising event. And what did Walt himself do at those events? He wasn't the emcee. He wasn't the after-dinner speaker. No, Walt filled water glasses and cleared dirty dishes. Walt had the heart of a servant.

"Walt was just a plain, humble guy," said Ron Stark. "He never took the attitude, 'I'm Walt Disney and I can do anything I want.' Walt's genuine humility made him accessible to everyone. He didn't put on airs. He was just a regular guy who played in his backyard with greasy trains. He worked in Hollywood, but he never 'went Hollywood.'"

> *"Every year, Walt did a benefit lunch at the John Tracy Clinic in L.A. One year I finished eating and noticed a man was clearing my dirty dishes—and it was Walt! That's how committed he was to this benefit. He was an incredible person with a great perspective on humility and what's important in life."*
>
> KEVIN CORCORAN
> ACTOR

Animator Floyd Norman recalls an incident that occurred when he was at the Disney studio in the early 1960s. One morning, an unusual visitor showed up at the main gate: a little white-haired lady in a horse-drawn carriage. "I want to see Mr. Disney," she said.

"You can't see him without an appointment," the guard said. "He's a very busy man."

"I'm not leaving until I talk to Mr. Disney," the woman said.

The guard called the administration office, and word reached Walt that there was a nutty old lady at the gate who demanded to see him. So Walt walked out to the main gate. He talked to the woman, and learned that she had written a movie script. Walt accepted the script. "Thank you for bringing this to me," he said. "I will definitely read it." And he did.

"Walt treated everyone the same," said Jim Korkis. "It didn't matter if he was with a king or a ticket taker, he would give them both the same attention." And Imagineer Harriet Burns told me, "Walt was a humble man. He never talked about Walt Disney. He didn't put himself first." Actor Dean Jones agrees. "Walt had the common touch," Jones said. "He was very accessible. He seemed more like a tourist from Duluth than a studio head."

> *"I have no use for people who throw their weight around as celebrities, or for those who fawn over you just because you are famous."*
>
> WALT DISNEY

Though Walt was the boss of the Disney organization, he rarely pulled rank on people when they were doing their jobs. Disneyland employee Jim Haught tells about the time Walt came into a Disney warehouse smoking a cigarette. The warehouse worker didn't recognize him. "I'm sorry, sir," the man said, "but there's no smoking in this warehouse."

"Oh?" Walt asked. "Who says so?"

"Walt Disney himself," the worker replied.

"Well," Walt said, stubbing out his cigarette, "that's good enough for me."

Disneyland employee Ray VanDeWarker told me, "When we built New Orleans Square, it was fenced off with a security officer at the gate. Walt went up to the security officer and said, 'I'd like to go in.' The officer said, 'No one goes through that gate without a pass.' Walt said, 'I don't need a pass. I'm Walt Disney.' The officer said, 'Yeah, and I'm King Tut.'

"Walt saw me over at the 'Jungle Cruise,' so he walked over and asked me to explain to the security officer who he was. So I walked back and told the security officer, 'That man over there really is Walt Disney.' The security officer apologized and was terribly upset. Walt said, 'Don't worry about it. You were just doing your job.'"

Ron Stark shared a fascinating insight about Walt. He said, "Milt Kahl, one of Walt's 'Nine Old Men,' once told me, 'We made films for Walt as he envisioned them, but drawing for him was one of the most painful things we ever did. You know why we did it? Because we loved Walt Disney.'"

Ron went on to explain, "Walt would ask his artists to do the impossible, and they did it. Why? Because they loved Walt Disney. When the studio was racing to complete *Snow White,* Walt asked his artists to work nights and weekends without overtime pay. In fact, there were weeks they didn't get paid at all, because the studio had no money. And they sacrificed willingly, even eagerly. Why? Because they loved Walt Disney.

"When someone you love asks you for something, you find a way to deliver it—and that's when magic happens. But if you don't love this person, you're not going to work overtime, you're not going to sacrifice. If you don't love this person, you're just working for a paycheck. When five o'clock arrives, you say, 'I'm outta here.' Something as magical as *Snow White* only happens when people love the person they're working for. And people loved Walt Disney. With love, anything is possible. Even the impossible is possible when there is love."

> "Disneyland is like a time machine. You want to go back and have a glass of lemonade on a day that's been lost for a long time? Walt will do it for you."
>
> RAY BRADBURY

Ron is absolutely right. Walt achieved great things through people because they loved him and wanted to please him. Walt could be tough and abrasive—yet people chose to remain at his side for decades. What was it about Walt that inspired such loyalty and love?

I believe it was Walt's *humility.* Underneath his ego strength, his confidence, his drive to succeed, and his intense focus, there was a basic humility to Walt that people found irresistible. Those who knew him best understood that he was not a self-seeking egotist. They loved Walt Disney because they knew who he really was: a genuinely humble servant.

And a man like that is easy to love.

How to Be Like Walt—
Lesson 16: Make Family Your Top Priority

Walt once said, "A man should never neglect his family for business." And that was the way Walt lived. His top priority was his family—his wife, his children, his nieces and nephews, and grandchildren. "He was Daddy," said Sharon. "He was a very involved father," said Diane. Walt Disney was, first and foremost, a family man. And that is why the name "Walt Disney" still means "family entertainment" to us all.

Walt always made time for adventures with his girls. He didn't just love his family; he *enjoyed* his family. Sure, Walt made his share of mistakes, as we all do. But his children knew they were loved, and that their dad was proud of them. Love covers a multitude of mistakes. If children know they are loved and accepted by their parents, they have a good foundation for their lives. Authentic love builds stable, nurturing homes where children grow up emotionally healthy and strong. Here are some principles for making family *your* top priority:

1. *Love and forgive your spouse.* The best thing you can do to make your children feel secure is to make sure your marriage is strong and your home is stable. We are imperfect people, and we marry imperfect people. The only way for two imperfect people to live together is by loving each other, putting each other first, and forgiving each other.

2. *Make a priority of spending time with your children.* Don't just "find" time for them—*make* time! Walt set aside Sundays to spend with his children and made time for them throughout the week. He was home for family dinner every night. He attended every event, every recital—and that couldn't have been easy. But Walt made sure his children knew that they came first in his schedule.

> "Walt delighted in the role of Daddy to his two girls. He was a Hollywood rarity—a totally involved parent."
>
> ART LINKLETTER
> TELEVISION PERSONALITY

As you spend time with your children, be sure to enjoy them, get to know them, talk to them and listen to them. Give them your undivided attention. Look them in the eye, nod affirmingly, and repeat back to them what they say so they know they've been heard.

3. *Discipline your children.* To some people, "discipline" means punishment. But notice that the word "discipline" comes from the same root word as "disciple." Authentic discipline means training young people to become disciples—that is, to become people who embrace your values and beliefs. Authentic discipline involves love, affirmation, praise and positive reinforcement. At times, it may also involve punishment, but most of the training you do with your kids should involve reinforcing positive behavior, not punishing.

Walt was a firm disciplinarian—yet most of his discipline involved being affirming, demonstrative and affectionate with his daughters. Diane and Sharon remembered his hugs, his loving words, and the time he spent teaching them to swim and ride horses. Walt made "disciples" out of Diane and Sharon, and they loved him for it, cherished his memory, and embraced his values.

If you truly want to have the kind of influence Walt had, then begin where Walt began—in the home, with the people closest to you. Make family your first priority.

Chapter Fifteen

꧁꧂

Walt Lives!

Walt was a man of deep compassion, sincerity and simplicity; a man who loved his country and his God; a man with a utopian vision for the future. Had he lived a few years longer, how would he have changed our world?

In late June of 1955, a letter arrived at the Disney studio from a distraught mother on the East Coast. Her seven-year-old son was dying of leukemia. He had been following the construction of the park on the *Disneyland* TV show, and his only wish was to ride Walt Disney's train. Walt's eyes misted as he read the letter. He identified with the little boy's dream. Walt told his staff that the family would be calling soon.

When the family arrived, Walt was waiting for them. Walt took the boy in his arms and led the family up the stairs to the train station. There they watched the cranes transferring the railroad cars onto the tracks. The cars had only arrived from the Burbank studio that morning, and the engine had not even been tested yet.

Walt took the boy into the cab. As the train pulled out of the station on its maiden run, Walt pointed out the various attractions of the park that were still receiving their finishing touches. Along the way, the boy gave a few blasts on the steam whistle.

In parting, Walt gave the family a gold-framed piece of original art from *Lady and the Tramp*. After they left, he ordered his staff: "Don't mention this to anyone—and above all, *no publicity.*" Walt's instructions were obeyed, and his act of kindness was never mentioned in public until after his death.

One of the least-reported dimensions of Walt's many-faceted personality is the depth of his compassion. Despite his busy schedule, he continually made time for acts of personal kindness and caring. And unlike many corporate leaders who make a big show of their "charity," Walt wanted no publicity. His compassion for others was genuine.

Disney historian Chris Ihrig explains Walt's achievements as a function of his immense compassion.

> *"Walt cared about people. He was one of the kindest men I have ever known. One time, Walt was going to fly to San Diego with the media, and then go out to sea in a Coast Guard ship. He knew I had never flown before, and he thought I would enjoy it, so he said, 'Let's close the office.' I went in the plane with him, my first flight. He was just a very thoughtful man."*
>
> LUCILLE MARTIN
> WALT'S SECRETARY

"One of the greatest life lessons we can learn from Walt," Ihrig told me, "is that each of us has a responsibility to engage the world using our unique talents, gifts and passions. The core value that drove Walt was his compassion for people. His compassion started with his most important relationships, and it radiated out to people he had never met. This core principle of compassion created the complexity of his being.

"It was compassion that led him to change the date on his birth certificate, so that he could become a Red Cross ambulance driver, even though he was underage. Compassion for his fellow man was a moving force in every project he undertook, from animation to building his theme park. Everything he did was designed to bring happiness to people and enhance their lives.

"There are many words that describe the complexity of Walt Disney: A storyteller. A visionary and an optimist. A master communicator. An educator. A loving family man. A magical personality. But all of these spring from a core of compassion."

At Christmastime, Walt sent hundreds of Disney-themed gifts to the children of friends, associates and employees. Each December, one room at the Burbank studio looked like a set from *Babes in Toyland.* Tables were stacked high with toys. Like Santa's elves, Disney secretaries wrapped toys for mailing. Walt would sometimes drop by to watch the proceedings, like Santa watching over his shop at the North Pole.

Peter Ellenshaw's daughter Lynda told me, "The highlight of Christmas was when we got a package from Walt. He did that for all the children of the employees. The package had several items of the latest Disney merchandise, each item individually gift-wrapped. We loved Walt for his thoughtfulness."

Mark Kirkland, an Emmy-winning director and animator, told me, "My father was a photographer with *Look* magazine. On one assignment around Christmastime, he photographed Walt. When my dad came home, he gave me some gifts that Walt wanted me to have. Needless to say, from that point on I thought Walt Disney was Santa Claus."

To put it simply, Walt cared about people. Walt not only remembered his employees' names, he asked about their family members by name as well. When a baby was born to an employee's family, a bouquet of flowers from Walt invariably appeared at the hospital. Walt wrote lengthy letters to old friends and neighbors from Marceline and Kansas City. He sent personal, handwritten notes of condolence to Disney employees who had lost a parent or spouse.

> *"My wife Barbara and I had three daughters. After each birth, Walt sent us a porcelain Disney potty seat filled with flowers."*
>
> NORMAN "STORMY" PALMER
> LONGTIME DISNEY FILM EDITOR

Walt kept a sign-up sheet at the studio where employees could reserve time to vacation free of charge at his Smoke Tree Ranch home. On one occasion, when one of his young animators missed work for almost six months due to illness, Walt continued sending the man his full paycheck, week after week, no questions asked.

Actor Alan Young remembers Walt as one of the few Hollywood studio heads who was also a genuinely kind and thoughtful human being. He told me that he first met Walt in the late 1950s. "Walt took me to lunch," he said, "to discuss a part in the movie, *The Shaggy Dog*. I didn't get the part, and that was disappointing. Usually, when you are turned down for a part, you get a call from an assistant—very cold and impersonal. But Walt called me himself to break the news. I appreciated that. It may seem like a small thing, but it was an act of kindness that few studio bosses make time for."

Walt teaches us we can demonstrate compassion by simply being observant and noticing people's needs. Elizabeth Sherman, wife of composer Richard Sherman, told me, "I was about twenty-seven when I was pregnant with our first child. One day, I came to the set of *Mary Poppins*. There were people going in all directions, and Walt was in the middle of everything. Someone came up and wanted Walt's approval on a parrot umbrella for Julie Andrews, and Walt said, 'No, it won't do.' He glanced in my direction, then he said, 'Can't you see that Elizabeth is standing? Someone get her a chair right away!' Walt never missed a thing. He was very observant and very kind."

Walt was not only kind to people, but to animals as well. The sympathetic treatment of animals in films like *Snow White, Dumbo* and *Bambi* was an extension of Walt's genuine empathy for animals. "The critics say I personalize these little animals," he once reflected. "Well, I watch a little rabbit or I follow a cat or a dog, and I personalize them. It's just an intuitive thing with me."

One painful childhood event had a profound impact on his attitude toward animals. When he was seven years old, he was walking through the apple orchard on the family's Marceline farm when he came upon an owl perched on a low branch, sleeping. He remembered his father telling him that owls slept during the day and hunted at night.

Hoping to capture the bird, he crept toward it, then pounced, grabbing the bird with both hands. The terrified owl flapped its wings and struggled furiously in the boy's grasp. Walter panicked, threw the bird to the ground, and stomped it until it stopped moving.

When he realized what he had done, he wept bitterly. He went home and got a shovel, then he returned, dug a grave, and buried the owl. For months afterward, Walt dreamed about the owl. The incident so affected him that he was unable to speak of it until his later years.

That event influenced Walt's feelings toward all living things. Lillian recalled that Walt had a soft spot in his heart for animals for as long as she knew him. "Walt wouldn't allow the gardener to set traps for the ground squirrels or gophers," she once told an interviewer. "He would say, 'They're little creatures and have to live like anybody else. They're not hurting anything.'" When Lilly protested that the animals were poaching all of the berries, peaches, and melons in her garden, Walt replied, "You can go to the grocery store to buy food. They can't."

A simple, unpretentious soul

"I don't pretend to know anything about art," Walt once said. "I make pictures for entertainment, and then the professors tell me what they mean." As a filmmaker, Walt had no artistic pretensions. He was an everyman, and his common touch, as much as his storytelling ability, connected him with the broadest cross-section of the public.

Of course, to say he had no artistic pretensions does not mean he was not an artist. He certainly was. Walt Disney transformed his staff of mostly self-taught cartoonists into a vibrant community of the arts. He elevated "toons" to the level of animation art. His was the purest art of all, for it was free of the pretense, affectation and pomposity that characterizes most so-called "art" today. Walt created his art for the masses, not the critics.

Walt's art was dynamic, exciting, emotional and kinetic—not snobbish or elitist. "Art was always a means to an end with me," he once said. "You get an idea, and you just can't wait. Once you've started, then you're in there with the punches flying. There's plenty of trouble, but you can handle it. You can't back out. It gets you down once in a while, but it's exciting. Our whole business is exciting."

In the 1930s and '40s, Walt was lauded and acclaimed by the arts community. In 1937, surrealist painter Salvador Dalí told French poet André Breton, "I have come to Hollywood and am in contact with the three great American surreal-

> *"Walt Disney was a fascinating man. Down-to-earth, accessible, he had a genius for being himself."*
>
> DEAN JONES
> ACTOR

ists—the Marx Brothers, Cecil B. DeMille and Walt Disney." In the postwar years, Disney films lost some of their artistic boldness. The daring experimentation that gave us *Snow White, Fantasia* and *Bambi* gave way to safer movies constructed on proven formulas. Disappointed, even disillusioned, the critics and the arts community turned away from Walt. He had become (so they thought) merely a purveyor of family entertainment, or worse, "kiddie films."

But Walt had not sold out his art. He was still the same bold artistic soul he had always been. He had simply changed mediums. His primary focus moved from film to a totally new medium of expression. On July 17, 1955, Walt unveiled a radically innovative form of three-dimensional art. Some people called it a "theme park," but it was actually a full-immersion multimedia experience combining motion, light, color, texture, sound, music, taste, smell, story, adventure, thrills, nostalgia, futurism, fact, fantasy, and audience participation. It was, at that time, the world's largest art object, for it covered 160 acres of California real estate.

Walt's masterpiece, which he called Disneyland, was simple, unpretentious art—art for the masses, a feast for the senses and the imagination. The critics couldn't grasp the magnitude of what this everyman genius had created. They dismissed it as nothing but an "amusement park." But those who haven't lost their childlike wonder know that there is much more to Disneyland than mere "amusement."

When *Fantasia* was released in 1940, the critics accused Walt of being too highbrow. When Disneyland opened fifteen years later, they accused him of being too lowbrow. But the public—the only people whose opinion really mattered to Walt—didn't worry about the altitude of Walt's brow. They simply came and loved what he loved—trains and submarines, castles and merry-go-rounds, riverboats and rocketships.

Walt received plenty of honors in his lifetime, including forty-eight Oscars and seven Emmys. But his later films were largely shunned by the critics. Richard Sherman recalls one caustic review of *The Absent-Minded Professor.* "Walt just couldn't understand the response to this film," Sherman recalled. "*The Absent-Minded Professor* was such a funny idea."

He remembers watching Walt standing alone, looking out his office window. "Well," Walt said sadly, "I still think the majority of the people are going to like that picture." Sherman concluded, "The good reviews never went to his head, but the bad reviews went to his heart."

There were moments when Walt wistfully lamented the fact that he would never make a controversial, socially relevant film. In 1962, after viewing *To Kill a Mockingbird,* a powerful film about racial injustice, Walt confided to Ron Miller, "I wish I could make a movie like that—but the public would never accept it." As regrets go, however, it was a minor one. Walt didn't dwell on the few things he could never do. He was too busy working on his next big challenge.

Walt's lifestyle was a simple one, especially for a Hollywood mogul. Though he certainly lived comfortably (a house in Holmby Hills with his own backyard railroad), Walt was not wealthy by Hollywood standards. But then, he had no desire for luxuries, no ambition to amass great wealth. He only had two uses for money: creating new works of entertainment and meeting the needs of his family. Other than that, he was satisfied to live quite simply.

> *"We are not trying to entertain the critics. I'll take my chances with the public."*
>
> Walt Disney

At Christmastime, Walt enjoyed receiving simple, inexpensive gifts. "Hazel George had a good sense of what would please the boss," wrote Bob Thomas, "and she rarely spent over a dollar. One Christmas she gave him a dime-store kaleidoscope, and it fascinated him. He insisted that visitors to his office peer at the changing patterns of light and color."

On rare occasions when Walt bought himself an expensive luxury, he felt guilty for weeks. In 1964, after the tremendous success of *Mary Poppins,* Walt spotted a Mercedes two-seat sports car in the window of a car dealership. The price was $11,000—a lot of money for a car in those days. Walt's first thought was, "I don't need such an extravagance." He started to walk away—then he turned around and bought the car.

Though he could easily afford the car, he couldn't help feeling guilty. To assuage his working-class conscience, Walt rented the car to his studio for $100 a day as a movie prop. You can see Roddy McDowell driving Walt's Mercedes in the film *That Darn Cat.* The grand or two that Walt received in rent helped ease his conscience.

Walt preferred simplicity in everything, including his movies. Film editor Stormy Palmy told me, "One time I was getting too fancy on a project.

Walt passed me in the hall and said, 'Don't go arty on me, Stormy. Keep it simple. If you please me, you'll please eighty percent of the country.' Walt knew what the common man liked because he was a common man at heart."

Disney designer Wendell Warner told me, "Walt wanted everything simple and straightforward, not confusing. An engineer would refer to a 'kip,' and Walt would say, 'What's a kip?' The engineer would say, 'A kilopound, a thousand pounds of force.' And Walt would say, 'Why don't you just say a thousand pounds of force, then?' Walt liked simple, straight talk—say what you mean and mean what you say."

> "Walt didn't like the food over in London, so he'd bring chili and beans and other canned foods he liked to eat. At the Dorchester Hotel, where we always stayed, the waiters would serve him chili and beans and crackers."
>
> E. CARDON "CARD" WALKER
> FORMER DISNEY CEO

Walt had little use for ceremony and formality, and people were sometimes astonished by his blunt simplicity. Harrison Ellenshaw recalls a time his father, Peter, had Walt and Lillian over for dinner on a Sunday night. Walt wanted to see some of Peter's oil paintings. Mrs. Ellenshaw had prepared an elegant dinner, which she served in the formal dining room.

As the Ellenshaws and the Disneys sat down at the table, Walt looked around and said, "Don't you have a TV?"

"Well," Peter said, "yes, we do."

"There's a program from Disneyland on *Wonderful World of Color*," Walt said. "Weren't you planning to watch it?"

"Of course, Walt," Peter said. "We can watch it."

Though she said nothing, Mrs. Ellenshaw was horrified. The thought of her elegant formal dinner being intruded upon by *television*—!

Peter brought in the TV set and plugged it in. As the picture came on, Walt said, "It's black and white! Don't you have a color set?" On the screen, the NBC peacock was spreading its tail-feathers in glorious shades of gray.

"I'm sorry, Walt," Peter said. "We only have black and white." So the Ellenshaws and the Disneys sat and ate while watching *Walt Disney's Wonderful World of Color* on a black and white TV.

Walt's tastes in food were simple. He couldn't imagine a finer meal than chili and beans with crackers and a glass of V-8 Juice. If he didn't have a lunch appointment, he ate in his office. He'd mix a can of Dennison's Chili and a can of Hormel—he claimed that Dennison's had better beans but Hormel had more meat. Walt enjoyed simple, hearty foods: frankfurters, cheeseburgers, roast beef sandwiches, macaroni and cheese, or corned beef hash.

Perhaps the reason so many Disney critics and biographers have trouble understanding Walt is that they overcomplicate him. He was a simple, unpretentious soul, as his daughter Diane will attest. "Dad was very easy to read," she said. "He was always straightforward, never devious or complicated."

Renié Bardeau, who was Disneyland's official photographer for forty-three years, told me, "I took the photo that has become most people's favorite shot of Walt. It's called 'Footsteps,' and it shows Walt walking alone through the castle, early in the morning. The great thing about that picture is that it's candid, not a set-up. Walt is wearing a beat-up old sweater and a well-worn pair of pants. That picture says so much about Walt. He's the king surveying his Magic Kingdom—yet he's really just a regular old Joe."

Walt's patriotism

Walt and Ray Bradbury chatted over lunch about the future of American cities. At one point, Ray's face lit up and he said, "Walt, why don't you run for mayor of L.A.?"

"Ray," Walt said, laughing, "why should I run for mayor when I'm already king?"

A wise reply. Walt didn't have the patience for politics. At his studio, he'd say, "Do this," and it got done. Mayors don't have that kind of power, nor do presidents. I don't think Walt would have made a very good president, but he would have made an excellent king—a truly benevolent despot.

Some have called Walt a political conservative, but Walt didn't see himself in terms of left or right. Apart from voting, Walt was not politically active and never gave a political speech. He once said, "They say I'm a conservative, but I consider myself a true liberal."

Walt's legendary hatred of Communism was the flip-side of his love for America. On Friday, October 24, 1947, Walt appeared before the Committee of Un-American Activities. Asked if he believed that the strike of 1941 was instigated by members of the Communist Party, he replied, "I definitely feel it was a Communist group trying to take over my artists." He went on to tell the committee about Herb Sorrell, the union official who had organized the strike—and threatened to destroy Walt's reputation.

> *"Once a man has tasted freedom he will never be content to be a slave. That is why I believe that this frightfulness we see everywhere today is only temporary.*
>
> *Tomorrow will be better for as long as America keeps alive the ideals of freedom and a better life. All men will want to be free and share our way of life."*
>
> WALT DISNEY
> MARCH 1, 1941

Walt testified that Sorrell "laughed at me and told me I was naive and foolish. He said, 'You can't stand this strike. I will smear you, and I will make a dust bowl out of your [studio].' . . . When [Sorrell] pulled the strike, the first people to smear me and put me on the unfair list were all of the Commie front organizations. . . . They distorted everything, they lied; there was no way you could ever counteract anything that they did. They formed picket lines in front of the theaters, and, well, they called my plant a sweatshop, and that is not true."

The committee then asked if Walt had talked to Sorrell about Communism. Walt replied that Sorrell said, "You think I am a Communist, don't you?" Then Sorrell laughed and bragged, "Well, I used [Communist Party] money to finance my strike of 1937"—meaning the 1937 strike against the Max Fleischer studio.

Walt added, "I don't believe [the Communist Party] is a political party. I believe it is an un-American thing. . . . And I feel that they really ought to be smoked out and shown up for what they are, so that all of the good, free causes in this country, all the liberalisms that really are American, can [operate freely] without the taint of Communism."

Many people look back on the House hearings as a "witch hunt." However, Walt genuinely believed that the strike that nearly destroyed the

Disney studio was instigated by Communist agitators. That strike hurt Walt deeply and personally. It changed him forever.

Walt was raised on the left-leaning politics of his Socialist father, Elias Disney. In fact, he learned cartooning by studying the political cartoons in his dad's copies of the Socialist journal *Appeal to Reason*. Walt spent his early adulthood as a left-of-center Roosevelt Democrat.

After the strike of 1941, however, Walt voted Republican. His political views were not philosophical but visceral, shaped by painful personal experience. He never wavered from

> *"Before the strike, Walt thought socialism was about everybody pulling together. He was an extreme liberal at one time."*
>
> JOE GRANT
> DISNEY STORY ARTIST

his deep conviction that the common man deserved a fair shake in life. But after being smeared and nearly destroyed by the union, Walt could no longer support the Democratic Party, the traditional party of Big Labor.

Though the trauma of the strike changed Walt forever, making him more wary in his relationships with employees, there was one thing the strike could never change: Walt's simple belief in America and freedom. Michael Broggie told me, "Walt had a passion for preserving what is good and true in America. He was an unashamed American patriot. If you cut him, he'd bleed red, white, and blue."

In September 1959, Walt was delighted to learn that Soviet premier Nikita Khrushchev wished to visit Disneyland during his eleven-day U.S. tour. Walt's fervently anti-Communist soul relished the thought of standing beside the Russian dictator at the Tomorrowland lagoon and saying, "Mr. Khrushchev, take a look at the eighth largest submarine fleet in the world!" Unfortunately, the State Department decided that Khrushchev's safety could not be guaranteed in the crowded park, so he was not allowed to visit Disneyland.

At a 20th Century-Fox studio luncheon with Marilyn Monroe, Shirley Maclaine, Bob Hope, Frank Sinatra, and other stars, Khrushchev stood and shouted, "Just now I was told that I could not go to Disneyland! . . . For me, this situation is inconceivable! I cannot find words to explain this to my people!"

Walt was ecstatic! The leader of the most powerful totalitarian regime in the world had thrown a tantrum because he couldn't go to Disneyland! It was more than a public relations coup. It meant that the Russian dictator wanted something he could never have. Disneyland was the product of American ingenuity, imagination and freedom—and Communism would never produce anything as wonderful as Walt's Magic Kingdom.

Some critics have scorned Walt for his anti-Communism and his flag-waving patriotism. But the collapse of the Berlin Wall and the fall of the Soviet Union proved that Walt was on the right side of history.

Despite Walt's intense anti-Communism, he was never a McCarthyite or a "Red-baiter." He took a live-and-let-live approach to other political viewpoints. Herb Ryman recalled an incident that demonstrates the political tolerance of Walt Disney.

"Everyone knew that Walt was a committed anti-Communist," Ryman said. "Very patriotic and all that. So someone thought they would do damage to one of the writers on *20,000 Leagues under the Sea* by telling Walt that the writer was a Red. They thought that Walt would fire him or investigate him or kick him off the picture. Well, Walt's answer was, 'I'm glad to know that. It's a relief that he's a Communist. I thought he was an alcoholic.'"

Walt's utopian vision

In 1960, Walt produced the pageant-filled opening and closing ceremonies for the Winter Olympics in Squaw Valley, California. A few critics complained about the "Disney Olympics," but most of the athletes, officials and spectators thought it was the best-produced Olympic event in history. Walt brought some of the biggest stars in Hollywood to greet and entertain the Olympic competitors. The list included Bing Crosby, Roy Rogers, Red Skelton, Jack Benny, Danny Kaye, Jayne Mansfield, and Walt's longtime friend, Art Linkletter.

The opening ceremonies were scheduled to begin at ten o'clock on Thursday morning, February 18. The previous night, a blizzard had blanketed the Olympic site with snow. CBS was supposed to broadcast the event coast to coast, but the roads were snowbound, and network announcers and camera crews couldn't get to their locations.

Television broadcaster Chris Schenkel was part of the CBS broadcast team that day. He told me, "All of us, the announcers and camera crews, stayed in Tahoe and commuted back and forth. My broadcast partner was skier Art Devlin. Art and I got caught in a blizzard between Tahoe and Squaw Valley and we missed being on hand to broadcast the opening ceremonies. I was in a panic—I was sure I was going to be fired."

> *"My operations are based on experience, thoughtful observation, and warm fellowship with my neighbors at home and around the world."*
>
> WALT DISNEY

While Chris Schenkel was stuck in the blizzard, Walt and Art Linkletter were in Squaw Valley, ready to go on the air. "I was there as an entertainer, not a broadcaster," Linkletter recalls, "but CBS pressed me into service and I went on the air. The sky was overcast and threatening, and the snow was falling, and it looked like it was going to be a disaster. Walt was completely unfazed. He stood serenely and said, 'Well, we'll just go on with the show, and with any luck at all, the weather will clear and we'll get it on the air.'

"At about five minutes to ten, it stopped snowing, and the sun came out. At ten o'clock, exactly as planned, the ceremonies began and the broadcast went on the air. It was a beautiful event—the Olympic torch came down from the hills after making a nine-thousand-mile journey, and the marching bands played, and two thousand doves were released into the air.

"The ceremonies lasted half an hour. Five minutes after the broadcast ended, the sky closed up and it started snowing again. I looked at Walt in amazement, because it had gone exactly as he predicted. I pointed heavenward and said, 'Walt, you must have a connection!' He said, 'No. It's just that if you live right, things happen the way they're supposed to.'"

Minutes after the end of the ceremonies, Chris Schenkel and Art Devlin arrived in Squaw Valley. Schenkel recalled, "I went running over to Walter Cronkite, who headed up our broadcast team, and I apologized profusely. 'Walter,' I said, 'I'm so sorry I didn't make it in time!' And Walter Cronkite put his fatherly arm on my shoulder and said, 'Don't worry, Chris. Walt Disney took your place.' That was the biggest relief of my life!"

During the days that followed, Walt produced shows for the athletes in the Olympic Village. "These were real productions with big-name stars," Art Linkletter recalled. One night, for example, Roy Rogers did a singing cowboy act in an Old West saloon on the stage. The act concluded with a western-style saloon brawl, in which Roy duked it out with a dozen other cowboys—all Hollywood stunt men.

"I emceed the shows," Linkletter told me, "and it was an amazing experience. At every table, there was a different language spoken. One night, Walt looked around at all the tables, with athletes from around the world, representing every race and language. Walt's eyes were shining, and he said to me, 'Art, isn't this an amazing sight? Look at these people! They've come from all over the world, and they're all here, sharing the same hopes and dreams. This is how the whole world should be.' He was very moved by that. It was like a dream come true."

> "Disney himself had grown bored with movies; he had moved on to his true calling— the building of a better world."
>
> JAMES PINKERTON
> COLUMNIST

That Olympic experience *was* a dream come true for Walt Disney. His was a utopian dream of people from many nations, from diverse backgrounds, representing many faiths, all joined together in brotherhood and harmony.

Walt saw this same dream come true whenever he walked through Disneyland. Dick Nunis once told an interviewer, "In 1962, Walt was giving Billy Graham, the great evangelist, a guided tour of Disneyland. We got off the 'Jungle Cruise' boat, and Billy said, 'Walt, what a marvelous world of fantasy you've created!' And Walt said, 'Billy, take a look around you. Look at all the people, representing all nationalities, all colors, all languages. And they are all smiling, all having fun together. Billy, this is the real world. The fantasy is outside.'"

Walt's utopian vision of the future was more real to him than the "real world" of international tensions, racial tensions, and the Cold War. His vision of tomorrow was not just a futuristic city in the middle of Florida. He envisioned a better *world*—a world beyond hate, beyond divisions of race, ethnicity, religion and class.

Some revisionist critics have accused Walt of racism or anti-Semitism—and a lot of intellectually lazy people have repeated the accusation without bothering to check the facts. It's hard to know where these charges originated, but some Disney scholars believe they may have originated in the union smear campaign against Walt during the 1941 strike. In any case, there should be no doubt about this: Walt Disney was *not* a racist.

"Walt was sensitive to people's feelings," composer Robert Sherman told me. "He hated to see people mistreated or discriminated against. One time, Richard and I overheard a discussion between Walt and one of his lawyers. This attorney was a real bad guy, didn't like minorities. He said something about Richard and me, and he called us 'these Jew boys writing these songs.' Well, Walt defended us, and he fired the lawyer. Walt was unbelievably great to us."

Artist Joe Grant, who is also Jewish, agrees. "Walt was not anti-Semitic," Grant told an interviewer. "Some of the most influential people at the studio were Jewish. It's much ado about nothing. I never once had a problem with him in that way. That myth should be laid to rest."

Floyd Norman, an African-American story artist, also rejects the racism accusation. He recalls that, during the 1960s, several civil rights leaders tried to force the Disney studio to hire more minorities. "The funny part," he said, "was that minorities weren't knocking at the gates to get in. The jobs were there if they wanted them and if they were qualified. It's like the old ruse that Walt didn't hire Jews, which was also ridiculous. There were plenty of Jews at Disney. Personally, I never felt any prejudice from Walt."

> *"We have created characters and animated them in the dimension of depth, revealing through them to our perturbed world that the things we have in common far outnumber and outweigh those that divide us."*
>
> WALT DISNEY

Katherine and Richard Greene, authors of *Inside the Dream: The Personal Story of Walt Disney*, discussed this question in an article on The Disney Family Museum website. Like me, they interviewed hundreds of people who knew Walt well—and they, too, found that in all of those interviews, "not one recalled a single incident in which this alleged anti-Semitism reared its head." They observed:

> *Jewish employees like Joe Grant and the Sherman Brothers all violently defend Walt's memory. Meyer Minda, a Jewish neighbor of Walt's in Kansas City, didn't remember any evidence whatsoever of anti-Jewish feelings in Walt or the Disney family. Even when Sharon dated a young Jewish man, her parents didn't voice any objections. . . . In fact, the authors of this essay are Jewish, and from the outset of a decade of research into Walt Disney have looked carefully through the record—letters, memos, conversations with reliable sources—for any evidence that Walt may have harbored a dislike of Jews. None was found. Furthermore, in 1955 the B'Nai B'rith chapter in Beverly Hills cited him as their man of the year. Hardly an award likely to be presented to an anti-Semite.*

Those who truly knew the man will tell you—emphatically and unanimously—that Walt had a heart so big it embraced all of humanity, regardless of meaningless distinctions such as language or skin color. The only race he recognized was the human race, and nothing did his heart more good than to see people coming together from all over the world to share their hopes, goals and dreams.

Ralph Kent of the Disney Design Group told me, "Walt Disney was a humanitarian and a utopian. That's what his dream of EPCOT was all about. That's one reason he was so excited about producing attractions for the 1964 World's Fair. He was always thinking about tomorrow and how to make life better for the people of the world. He was promoting ecology in the 1950s, way before it was the thing to do. He was promoting peace, human understanding, and human progress. We'd tell him, 'No one will be interested in that stuff.' Walt said, 'I'll teach by entertaining people.' And he did."

I've often wondered just how much the whole world lost on that gray

December day in 1966, the day Walt Disney died.

Walt and his God

When Walt Disney passed out of this life, he passed into the presence of his God. What were Walt's beliefs about God? What sort of relationship did he have with God?

In matters of faith, as in so many other areas of his life, Walt was full of surprises—and paradoxes. He was a deeply religious man who never went to church. He drank and smoked and swore, but he was also a man of faith and prayer.

Raised in a strongly religious home, the son of a Congregational deacon, Walt got a heavy dose of Christianity in his early years. He was required to attend Sunday school and church every week until he was old enough to leave home. He was named Walter after the Congregational minister, Rev. Walter Parr.

Though Walt's belief in God never wavered from childhood until death, his strict religious upbringing left him with a distaste for institutional religion and sanctimonious church-men. The fact that Walt's own father could often be dogmatic, narrow-minded, and a severe disciplinarian was undoubtedly a factor in Walt's alienation from the church. Walt rebelled against his strict religious upbringing—but he didn't become a nonbeliever, as many rebels do. Instead, he became a nonpracticing believer. He had a faith in God, he lived by Christian principles, but he avoided church involvement.

> *"I believe firmly in the efficacy of religion, in its powerful influence on a person's whole life. It helps immeasurably to meet the storms and stress of life and keep you attuned to the Divine inspiration. Without inspiration, we would perish."*
>
> WALT DISNEY

Diane Disney Miller once told an interviewer that Walt was raised "in a strictly regimented church atmosphere. His father was a deacon at one time. I can understand why he had such a free attitude toward our religion. He wanted us [his daughters] to have religion. He definitely believed in

God—very definitely. But I think he'd had it [with organized religion] as a child. He never went to church."

Walt strongly believed in the role of religion in individual lives and in society. At the grand opening of Disneyland in 1955, Walt's nephew, Rev. Glenn Puder, led a silent prayer of dedication. Puder, a Presbyterian minister, represented the Protestant faith tradition in America; at his side were a Catholic priest and a Jewish rabbi.

In 1963, Walt contributed an essay to *Faith Is a Star*, a compilation of reflections on religion by famous people, edited by Roland Gammon. Walt's essay, "Deeds Rather Than Words," opened with a strong affirmation of the importance of prayer. "In these days of world tensions," he wrote, "when the faith of men is being tested as never before, I am personally thankful that my parents taught me at a very early age to have a strong personal belief and reliance in the power of prayer for Divine inspiration."

Those words were written in the shadow of the Cuban Missile Crisis of October 1962, so the world tensions he spoke of involved the very real threat of nuclear war. It was a time much like the post-9/11 era we live in today. People lived in fear that massive, civilization-wide destruction could take place at any moment, without warning.

Walt went on to express a wise and mature view of prayer—a view which says that authentic prayer is much more than merely asking God for favors. "My own concept of prayer," he wrote, "is not as a plea for special favors nor as a quick palliation for wrongs knowingly committed. A prayer, it seems to me, implies a promise as well as a request. At the highest level, prayer not only is a supplication for strength and guidance, but also becomes an affirmation of life and thus a reverent praise of God."

Walt was not nearly as impressed by what people said about their faith as by how they lived it out. "Deeds rather than words express my concept of the part religion should play in everyday life," he wrote. "I have watched constantly that in our movie work the highest moral and spiritual standards are upheld, whether it deals with fable or with stories of living action."

Disney historian Les Perkins told me, "There was a moral foundation to Walt's movies that people tap into. They're not heavy-handed messages, but moral threads that run through the story and weave their way into your heart. They have to do with simply showing kindness to others, serving others without expecting anything in return, and finding joy even in adversity. These themes reflect the Judeo-Christian values that Walt grew up with."

Most important of all, the Judeo-Christian values in Walt's movies were *not* simply injected in a cynical attempt to pander to a certain audience. Those values were Walt's own values, a reflection of who he was. Though not a church-goer, Walt was a moral, Christian man who lived out what he believed.

> *"He was a very religious man, but he didn't believe you had to go to church to be religious. . . . He respected every religion. There wasn't any that he ever criticized. He wouldn't even tell religious jokes."*
>
> SHARON DISNEY LUND
> WALT'S DAUGHTER

We've already looked at Walt's compassion, his humility and servant-hood, his commitment to being an involved and loving father, and his utopian vision for a better world for all people everywhere. These qualities all spring from Walt's Judeo-Christian worldview. And there is one more of Walt's Christian qualities that needs to be mentioned: his Christian view of morality. Walt was a moral and upright man.

"One thing I'm sure about Walt," said Ward Kimball, the Disney animator who knew Walt best, "he had no extramarital affairs. He had a wife, and that was it."

During the mid-1950s, Walt once commented to Ken Anderson that he was dismayed that some Disney staffers would spend their evenings womanizing. "Boy, I just can't understand that, Ken," Walt said. "It's like women are their hobby." Anderson noted that Walt simply couldn't imagine how a married man could be unfaithful to his wife—it was a completely alien concept to him. A Christian moral sense was woven into the fiber of Walt's being, and that's why Walt's movies are so rich in Christian moral virtues.

"We find Walt Disney's moral and spiritual vision expressed through the symbols in his films," says my writing partner, Jim Denney, author of *Answers to Satisfy the Soul* and the *Timebenders* science fantasy series. "Whether those symbols were placed there consciously or unconsciously doesn't really matter. What is important is that Walt's Judeo-Christian worldview drenches films like *Snow White and the Seven Dwarfs* and *Fantasia.*

"*Snow White* is based on the Grimm's fairy tale, 'Little Snow White,' and there's a lot of Judeo-Christian metaphor in the original tale. There is the prideful, satanic queen who is jealous of anyone who is more beautiful than she is. Like Satan tempting Eve in the Garden of Eden, the queen tempts Snow White by offering her a poisoned apple. Snow White succumbs to temptation, bites the apple, and tastes death.

"But there is a savior in this tale, just as in the biblical story. The king's son comes—a Christ-figure, like the Son of God—and he cancels the spell of death with a kiss. And what happens to the satanic queen? She is cast down by her own wickedness and pride, exactly as Satan fell in the biblical story.

> "*I ask of myself, 'Live a good Christian life.' Towards that objective I bend every effort in shaping my personal, domestic and professional activities and growth.*"
>
> WALT DISNEY

"Some of these symbols, like the poisoned apple, came from the original fairy tale, but others, such as the fall of the wicked queen, were Walt's own touches. The entire film, from the selection of the original story to Walt's additions and refinements, reflects Walt's spiritual and moral vision.

"You could say that almost every good story involves a conflict between good and evil. It doesn't require great moral vision to create a conflict between Mickey Mouse and Pegleg Pete. But Walt's vision of the struggle between good and evil goes much deeper than that, and we see it powerfully displayed in *Fantasia,* in the 'Night on Bald Mountain' sequence. That sequence comes straight from the imagination of Walt Disney, and it involves a chilling depiction of evil personified in the form of Chernabog, a Satan-like demon who rules over the lesser demons and damned souls of the dead.

"Set against this dark sequence is the tranquil conclusion, Schubert's 'Ave Maria,' which takes place in a cathedral-like setting. True to Walt's religious outlook, it is not the stone-and-glass cathedral of an organized religion. It is the cathedral of nature, the temple of the forest, where God can be felt and worshipped directly. When you watch *Fantasia,* you drink in Walt's own view of spiritual reality. The concluding sequence of *Fantasia* reveals

Walt's vision of good and evil, and how he related to God in the privacy of his own being. His was a very Christian worldview, though he distrusted church institutions and hierarchies.

"Much later in his career, Walt made a live-action movie that says a lot about his own view of God and religion. That movie was *Pollyanna,* which introduced Hayley Mills in the title role. Forget, for a moment, what that word 'pollyanna' has come to mean—someone who is naively optimistic. In Walt's film, Pollyanna is a spiritually strong young lady who has faced incredible adversity, including the loss of her parents. Yet her faith in the goodness of God remains undiminished.

"After being orphaned, she is sent to live with her Aunt Polly (Jane Wyman), a very unhappy rich woman. Aunt Polly uses her wealth to run the entire town, including the church. The pastor (Karl Malden) preaches what Aunt Polly tells him to preach—harsh, legalistic sermons designed to inflict fear and guilt on the congregation. Aunt Polly reflects Walt's view of the religion of his youth—the religion of his father, Elias Disney.

> *"When Walt screened* Pollyanna *for me, I wept out loud through the entire movie and he said, 'Great! Just go ahead and cry!' My reaction to his movie pleased him thoroughly."*
>
> PATTY DISNEY
> WALT'S NIECE, ROY E. DISNEY'S WIFE

"Into this situation comes Pollyanna, full of faith, grace and wide-eyed wonder. She is much like Walt himself. She has suffered terrible losses, yet she maintains her optimism—just as Walt has. Not only does Pollyanna refuse to knuckle under to the legalistic guilt of her Aunt Polly, but by the end of the movie, the town, the church, and Aunt Polly herself have been transformed by Pollyanna's infectious optimism. It's the triumph of authentic Christian freedom over soul-destroying legalism. That is pure Walt Disney theology. It's a parable of Walt's own spiritual journey."

As he raised his own children, Walt placed a high premium on religious tolerance and the celebration of diversity. In a January 1943 letter to his sister Ruth, Walt wrote, "Little Diane is going to a Catholic school now, which she seems to enjoy very much. She is quite taken with the rituals and is studying catechism. . . . I have explained to her that Catholics are people just like us and basically there is no difference. In giving her this broad view, I believe it will tend to create a spirit of tolerance within her."

Tolerance was one of Walt's most prized virtues. He believed in religious tolerance, racial tolerance, and political tolerance. He believed it is a good thing that people don't all look alike, think alike, and believe alike. Walt had a genuine love for the human race, and he made a deliberate effort to transmit his values of love and tolerance to his own daughters, and through his films, to the world at large. Yet, at the same time, he was reticent to discuss matters of religion outside of his own family.

One of the few people who tried to discuss religion with Walt was actor Dean Jones. Today, Jones is a committed Christian and president of the Christian Rescue Committee, which helps rescue Christians and Jews who are persecuted for their faith. In 1966, however, Dean Jones was a troubled atheist searching for meaning after a near-fatal motorcycle accident on Mexico's Baja Peninsula.

> *"He was also tolerant when an animator was arrested on a homosexual charge. 'Let's give him a chance; we all make mistakes,' Walt said. The animator continued at the studio for years afterward."*
>
> BOB THOMAS
> DISNEY BIOGRAPHER

A few months after the accident, Jones met Walt for lunch before filming the movie *Blackbeard's Ghost*. Walt asked the actor about his accident, and Jones told him what he could remember—which was almost nothing, due to a concussion.

"Lucky you weren't killed," Walt said.

"Yeah," Jones replied. "You know, Walt, an accident like that—well, it really makes you think. While I was in the hospital, I looked back a dozen times over every event in my life. It just seems to me that there's got to be more to this life than acting in movies, or—" He took a deep breath. "—running a movie studio."

Walt saw where Dean Jones was taking the conversation, and he didn't want to go there. Jabbing his finger at Jones, Walt changed the subject. "You just stay off that motorcycle," he said, "at least until we finish the picture."

Dean Jones had wanted to talk with Walt about his philosophy of life. Life is so short, so uncertain, and can end in an instant. What does it all mean? Is there something beyond this life? Or is this brief span of years all we get? Does God exist? Does He care? These were the questions Dean Jones wanted to discuss with Walt, but Walt wouldn't have it. So the conversation ended right there.

Six weeks later, Walt Disney died.

"Eight years after his death," Dean Jones reflected, "I came to realize that all of us need a Savior. And I prayed that Walt had found Him."

Walt lives!

I made a fascinating discovery while interviewing people who knew Walt: Many of them spoke of Walt in the present tense. It was as if he had never died, but continued to live on in their hearts and minds. Robert Sherman said, "To me, Walt is still alive. He will never die." His brother Richard told me how playing the song "Feed the Birds" always makes him feel that Walt is close by. "I feel his presence," Richard told me.

Buzz Price said, "After Walt's death, I dreamed about him for years. Once he was into your life, he never let you go, even after he died. His personality was so permeating. It was a baggy pants, old shoe kind of personality, but it was a penetrating force. Walt dominated my life without even trying."

Biographer Bob Thomas told me, "I was over at Disney Imagineering recently and you can still feel Walt's presence there. It's like he never left the building."

Disney master animator Glen Keane told me, "I don't do my animation for corporate reasons, or for money, or even for entertainment purposes. I do it for the same reason Walt did—for the pure enjoyment of bringing joy to others. I can't help feeling that Walt's heart is still beating deep down within me."

"Walt still walks the streets of the Magic Kingdom," said Tom Connellan, author of *Inside the Magic Kingdom:* "Not many people in any field of endeavor have the ability to leave a lasting legacy, but Walt's spirit is still there in every part of the company."

"Walt Disney will always live on," said Imagineer Alice Davis. "He created so much and now each generation falls in love with it all over again."

Walt lives! His impact on human lives was so great that it continues to resonate in the lives of those who knew him, and even in the lives of those who have only met him through movies, television and books. Walt lives—and the ongoing power of his personality continues to affect our world for the better.

Which brings us to our final lesson from Walt's life:

How to Be Like Walt—
Lesson 17: Be the Person God Made You to Be

"I believe that Walt Disney is God's gift to the world," said writer Greg Ehrbar. "God works through people like Walt to give the world what it needs at a given moment in time. Walt appeared at a specific time in history to bring stories to the world in a way that had never been done before. Walt told stories about our basic fears, our hopes and dreams, and our need for love. We all need these fairy tales. We need to believe that happy endings do happen, and that dreams really do come true. Walt's stories touch the child in all of us, and they awaken our faith in ourselves, in others, and in God."

> *"Walt is ageless and timeless. He just got stopped in time when he died in 1966. I'm over seventy now, and people still think I'm Walt's brother. My goodness, if I was Walt's brother, I'd have to be a hundred and twelve years old by now!"*
>
> ROY E. DISNEY
> WALT'S NEPHEW

Glen Keane agrees. "The only way I can explain Walt Disney is that he was meant to be. God gave Walt an incredible gift for visual storytelling, but without any guarantees that he would be successful. Walt had to gather up his talents and put them into action. He had to take risks and persevere so that God's gift in him could be revealed.

"At the point where Walt risked everything for his art, God kicked in and brought the right people to him at the right time to make those dreams come true. Walt needed those people in his life and they needed him, and it all came together at just the right moment in history. The story of Walt Disney has a lot to do with the grace of God."

Like Walt, you have been brought into this world by the grace of God. He has given you irreplaceable gifts and talents, and a personality that is uniquely *you*. As Ray Bradbury told me, "We are all born to be who we are. Walt Disney was a genetically unique individual who was born to be himself. His job—and ours as well—is to finish the job on earth that we were created to do."

God has given each of us a mission in life, and the gifts and talents with which to accomplish that mission. We have no guarantee of success. We must risk and work and persevere against obstacles and opposition. We may fail. But God has placed us here to dream big dreams, and by his grace, the dreams that we dream can come true.

The book you hold in your hands is a dream come true for me. I first suggested this book to my publisher, Peter Vegso, in August 2001. We had just published the first book in the "How To Be Like" series—*How to Be Like Mike,* about the life lessons to be learned from NBA star Michael Jordan. Peter liked the idea of a book on Walt Disney, but he said, "Before we can do a book on Walt, we need to get approval from the Disney family."

So I wrote a letter to Diane Disney Miller, explaining the nature of the project and asking for her approval. A few days later, I got a phone call and heard a warm, cheery voice say, "Pat? Diane Disney Miller! How are you? I just got your letter, and I read it with great interest. I have to tell you, my daddy was such a hero to so many people, and I've always thought that he was a great role model. So go right ahead with this project—you have my blessing."

We said good-bye, I put down the phone, and I let out a war-whoop! My assistant at the time, Melinda Ethington, poked her head into my office, wondering what I was yelling about. I said, "You'll never guess who just called! Diane Disney Miller! She just gave her blessing to a book about her daddy!"

I was so impressed that Diane still calls Walt "my daddy." That touched me. The loving way she says "my daddy" speaks volumes to me about how she views her father to this day. Walt Disney was a hero to Diane, and to his entire family. After that first phone conversation with Diane, I came away even more convinced that there is so much we can learn from the life of Walt Disney.

I have tried to write a book that is thoroughly researched and completely honest—a book that candidly speaks of Walt's human flaws as well as his greatness. I have wanted to write this book in such a way that I could show it to Walt himself without apology or embarrassment, and he would say, "It'll work."

This book has told the story of my hero—Diane's daddy—Walt Disney. We have looked at lesson after lesson of Walt's life. As Diane herself told me, "My dad's life teaches all of us to dream big dreams and believe in ourselves. When times get tough, don't be discouraged—keep working, keep trying. Be fair, generous, and compassionate in your dealings with others. Whatever you do, do it as excellently as you can. Be humble. Love your family. Trust God. And try to leave the world a better place than you found it."

> *"I believe that everyone makes his or her own destiny. On the other hand, one or two positive role models in your life can help influence your direction and goals, and help you to make better informed choices along the way. Walt has been that kind of influence in my life."*
>
> TOMMY COLE
> MOUSEKETEER

The final lesson we find in Walt's life is a simple one: *Be the person God made you to be.* This means you must be a *good* person—decent, moral, humble, tolerant, compassionate, loving, and full of faith. All of the other lessons of Walt's life are meaningless unless you have built those character traits into your life. Greatness begins with goodness. You must be a good person or you can never be great in any field of endeavor.

Be that wonderful, genetically unique individual you were born to be, the person God created you to be—then go out and change the world. Dream big dreams, then hammer those dreams into reality.

In closing, one final story:

For three decades, Thelma Howard was the cook and housekeeper for the Disney family. For Christmas and birthdays, Walt gave her bonuses consisting of shares of Disney stock. He told her, "Hang onto this stock, because it's going to grow in value."

So Thelma Howard clung to that stock. She lived a modest lifestyle for the rest of her life, and she kept those stock certificates tucked away in a safe place. She died in the early 1980s, seemingly very poor. In her will, she left half of her belongings to her only son Michael, who was in a home for the developmentally disabled. The other half she left to help poor and disabled children.

After her death, as her possessions were being itemized, the executor of Thelma Howard's estate found the stock certificates. The market value of those certificates was found to be $4.5 million. Thelma Howard died completely unaware that she was a millionaire.

Like Thelma Howard, you and I have received a great legacy from Walt Disney—a legacy much more valuable than cash or stock certificates. We have received the lessons of his amazing life. Do we truly understand what he has left to us? Do we grasp the rich lessons of his life? Have we taken those lessons to heart so we can become all that God created us to be?

Just as Thelma Howard had millions of dollars at her disposal and didn't even know it, you and I have

> *"Many young people today do not realize that Walt Disney was a real person. They think he was a made-up character like the Quaker Oats Man or Betty Crocker. A reporter once went to Walt Disney World and stood by 'Partners,' the famous statue of Walt and Mickey Mouse. He asked kids to identify the two figures in the statue. The kids all recognized Mickey, but had no idea who the man was. All too many people have no idea who the real flesh-and-blood Walt Disney was. If we could grasp the lessons of his life, the world would be a much better place."*
>
> TIM O'DAY
> JOURNALIST AND DISNEY HISTORIAN

so many riches at our fingertips—yet we don't even realize what we have! We have been willing to settle for so little. We dream our limited little dreams. We rein in our imaginations. We shrink back in fear from risks and tough challenges. We give up after the first or second try.

Walt's life challenges us to dream bigger, reach higher, work harder, risk more, and persevere as long as it takes. That is the rich legacy Walt left us. That is the supreme lesson of his endlessly instructive life. The riches of an incredible, adventure-filled life are within our grasp—if we will dare to be like Walt.

Acknowledgments

With deep appreciation I acknowledge the support and guidance of the following people who helped make this book possible:

Special thanks to Bob Vander Weide and John Weisbrod of the Orlando Magic.

I'm grateful to my assistant, Diana Basch, who managed so many of the details that made this book possible; and to my interns Doug Grassian, Katy Radkewich and Nicole Meunier, who were indispensible in managing the mountain of research that went into this book.

Hats off to three dependable associates—my adviser Ken Hussar, Vince Pileggi of the Orlando Magic mail/copy room, and my ace typist, Fran Thomas.

Hearty thanks are also due to Peter Vegso and his fine staff at Health Communications, Inc., and to my partner in writing this book, Jim Denney. Thank you all for believing that I had something important to share and for providing the support and the forum to say it.

I am also grateful to Howard Green, Lucille Martin, Peggy Matthews Rose, Peggy O'Connor, Tim O'Day and Paula Sigman who went far beyond the call of duty in helping me research and refine this book. It couldn't have happened without them.

Special thanks and appreciation go to my wife, Ruth, and to my wonderful and supportive family. They are truly the backbone of my life.

Finally, I wish to thank all of the people listed below who have generously shared with me their stories and personal reflections on the life of Walt Disney:

Chuck Abbott

Milt Albright

Bob Allen

Bob Allen Jr.

Wayne Allwine

Paul Anderson

Julie Andrews

Ken Annakin

Earl Archer

Frank Armitage

Alfonso Arribas

X Atencio

Bob Babcock

Buddy Baker

Steve Baker

Tony Bancroft

Renie Bardeau

Harold Bastrup

Tony Baxter

Katherine Beaumont

Rudy Behlmer

Greg Benford

Armand Bigle

Kevin Blair

Lucille Bliss

Hank Block

Wally Boag

Kevin Borg

Bo Boyd

Charles Boyer

Ray Bradbury

Michael Broggie

Bob Broughton

Dan Broughton

Bob Brunner

Bobby Burgess

Fulton Burley

Bill Burnes

Brian Burns

Harriet Burns

Lonnie Burr

Corey Burton

Bob Butler

John Canemaker

Tutti Camarata

Gary Carlson

Paul Carlson

John Catone

Ted Cauger

Mickey Clark

Peter Clark

Alan Coats

Evelyn Coats

Tommy Cole

Tom Connellan

Jim Cora

Kevin Corcoran

Mary Costa

Bill Cotter

Ralph Crite

Chris Crump

Rolly Crump

John Culhane

Pam Dahl

Alice Davis

Virginia Davis

Dean Day

John Debney

Mignonne Walker Decker

Tom DeWolff

Vincent DiFate

Roy Disney

Ron Dominguez

Dale Drummond

Buddy Ebsen

Greg Ehrbar

Harrison Ellenshaw

Peter Ellenshaw

Tom Elrod

Peter Emslie

Dorothy Eno

Don Escen

Bill Evans

Becky Fallberg

Orlando Ferrante

Christopher Finch

Richard Fleischer

Dr. Richard Foglesong

Joe Francis

Jamie Frederickson

Neil Gabler

Bob Garner

Tony Garrison

Blaine Gibson

Shav Glick

Jenny Goff

Bruce Gordon	Glen Keane	John Matthews
Joe Grant	Jack Kehoe	Peggy Matthews Rose
Howard Green	Ralph Kent	Ray Maxwell
Katherine Greene	Margaret Kerry-Wilcox	Virginia McGhee
Richard Greene	Betty Kimball	Ray McHugh
Bob Gurr	John Kimball	Dallas McKennon
Ryan Harmon	Virginia Kimball	Sam McKim
Jim Haught	Mark Kirkland	Dean McClure
Harry Hemhauser	David Koenig	Phil Meador
John Hench	Al Konetzni	Gene Merlino
Mark Henn	Jim Korkis	Chris Miller
Chris Hibler	Richard Kraft	Diane Disney Miller
Dottie Hibler	Bob Kredel	Rod Miller
Mike Hibler	John Lasseter	Ron Miller
Craig Hodgkins	Robbie Lester	Walter Disney Miller
Tim Hollis	Katheryn Levine	George Mills
Kay Hughes	Frank Liberti	Dianna Morgan
Chris Ihrig	Jack Lindquist	Becky Morris
Kim Irvine	Art Linkletter	Dick Morrow
Jean-Pierre Isbouts	Mary Lippold	Tom Moses
Don Iwerks	Bill Littlejohn	Keith Murdock
Leslie Iwerks	David Longest	Tom Nabbe
Fred Joerger	Howard Lowery	Ken Nadvornick
Inez Johnson	Arlene Ludwig	Floyd Norman
Kent Johnson	Irving Ludwig	Dick Nunis
Rich Johnson	Carol Luske	Tim O'Brien
Rush Johnson	Gary Lyons	Mary Alice O'Conner
Ollie Johnston	Kaye Malins	John O'Connor
Carol Jones	Leonard Maltin	JP O'Connor
Dean Jones	Linda Manack	Tim O'Day
Dick Jones	Steve Mannheim	Peter O'Malley
Volus Jones	Tony Marino	Stormy Palmer
Fred Judkins	Bill Martin	Bud Parker
Bill Justice	Lucille Martin	Fess Parker
Kim Justice	Stacia Martin	Don Payne
J.B. Kaufman	Bob Matheison	Bob Penfield

Pete Penoudet

Don Peri

Les Perkins

Larry Pontius

Buzz Price

Dorothy Puder

Greg Puder

Gary Quayle

Thurl Ravenscroft

Tom Ravenscroft

Janie Reitherman

Cicely Rigdon

Dodi Roberts

Jim Robinson

Mickey Rooney

Joanna Runeare

Ann Salisbury

Lorraine Santoli

Tammy Scheer

Chris Schenkel

Russell Schroeder

Elizabeth Sherman

Richard Sherman

Robert Sherman

Ray Sidejas

Paula Sigman

Dave Smith

Phil Smith

Jeff Southards

Robert Stack

Hal Stalmaster

Ron Stark

Dorothy Stratton

Lee Suggs

Bill Sullivan

Missy Hibler Sutton

Betty Taylor

Russi Taylor

Dennis Tenida

Bob Thomas

Frank Thomas

Jeanette Thomas

Ted Thomas

Lynda Ellenshaw Thompson

Ruthie Thompson

Randy Thornton

Ginny Tyler

Harry Tytle

Marion Tytle

Ray VanDeWarker

Sherry Van Meter

Mike Vaughn

Jim Verity

Dan Viets

John Waite

Ken Wales

Card Walker

Wendell Warner

Ray Watson

Stel Webb

Paul Wenzel

Tom Wilck

Don Williams

Tyrus Wong

Ilene Woods

Alan Young

Steve Zall

Bibliography

Aberdeen, J.A. *Hollywood Renegades*. Palos Verdes Estates, CA: Cobblestone Entertainment, 2000.

Anderson, Phillip Longfellow. *The Gospel According to Disney*. Minneapolis, MN: Augsburg Books, 2004.

Annakin, Ken. *So You Wanna Be a Director?* Sheffield, England: Tomahawk Press, 2001.

Bastrup, Harold. *One Police Officer's Experiences*. 1995.

Bright, Randy. *Disneyland: Inside Story*. New York: Harry N. Abrams, Inc., 1987.

Brode, Douglas. *From Walt to Woodstock: How Disney Created the Counterculture*. Austin, Texas: University of Texas Press, 2004.

Broggie, Michael. *Walt Disney's Happy Place*. Virginia Beach, VA: The Donning Company Publishers, 2001.

Broggie, Michael. *Walt Disney's Railroad Story*. Pasadena, CA: Pentrex Media Group, 1997.

Burnes, Brian, Robert W. Butler and Dan Viets. *Walt Disney's Missouri*. Kansas City, MO: Kansas City Star Books, 2002.

Canemaker, John. *Before the Animation Begins: The Art and Lives of Disney Inspirational Sketch Artists*. New York, NY: Hyperion Press, 1996.

Canemaker, John. *Walt Disney's Nine Old Men and the Art of Animation*. New York: Disney Editions, 2001.

Cotter, Bill. *The Wonderful World of Disney Television: A Complete History*. New York: Hyperion Press, 1997.

Culhane, John. *Aladdin: The Making of an Animated Film*. New York: Hyperion Press, 1992.

Culhane, John. *Walt Disney's Fantasia*. New York: Harry N. Abrams, Inc., 1983.

Disneyland, a souvenir book sold at Disneyland. *The First Quarter Century*. Burbank, CA: Walt Disney Productions, 1979.

Dunlop, Beth. *Building a Dream*. New York: Harry N. Abrams, Inc., 1996.

Ellenshaw, Peter, with Bruce Gordon and David Mumford. *Ellenshaw Under Glass* ©Disney Enterprises, Inc. All rights reserved. Santa Clarita, CA: Camphor Tree Publishers, 2003.

Finch, Christopher. *The Art of Walt Disney*. New York: Harry N. Abrams, Inc., 1983.

Finch, Christopher. *Walt Disney's America*. New York: Abbeville Press, Inc., 1978.

Foglesong, Richard E. *Married to the Mouse*. New Haven, CT: Yale University Press, 2001.

Ford, Barbara. *Walt Disney*. New York: Walker & Co., 1989.

France, Van Arsdale. *Window on Main Street: 35 Years of Creating Happiness at Disneyland Park*. Nashua, NH: Laughter Publications, Inc.

Funicello, Annette and Patricia Romanowski. *A Dream Is a Wish Your Heart Makes*. New York: Hyperion Press, 1994.

Grant, John. *Encyclopedia of Walt Disney's Animated Characters*. New York: Hyperion, 1993.

Green, Amy Boothe and Howard E. Green. *Remembering Walt: Favorite Memories of Walt Disney*. New York: Hyperion Press, 1999.

Greene, Katherine and Richard Greene. *Inside the Dream: The Personal Story of Walt Disney*. New York: Disney Editions, 2001.

Greene, Katherine and Richard Greene. *The Man Behind the Magic: The Story of Walt Disney*. New York: Penguin Books USA Inc., 1991.

Grover, Ron. *The Disney Touch*. New York: McGraw Hill, 1997.

Hall, Joyce. *When You Care Enough*. Kansas City, Missouri: Hallmark Cards, 1992.

Hench, John and Peggy Van Pelt. *Designing Disney: Imagineering and the Art of the Show*. New York: Disney Editions, 2003.

Hollis, Richard and Brian Sibley. *The Disney Studio Story*. New York: Crown Publishers, Inc., 1988.

The Imagineers. *The Imagineering Way*. New York: Disney Editions, 2003.

Iwerks, Leslie and John Kenworthy. *The Hand Behind the Mouse*. New York: Disney Editions, 2001.

Knowles, Rebecca. *Disney—The Ultimate Visual Guide*. New York: DK Publishing, 2002.

Koenig, David. *Mouse Tales*. Irvine, CA: Bonaventure Press, 1994.

Lefkon, Wendy. *Disneyland*. New York: Disney Editions, 2000.

Levin, Bob. *The Pirates and the Mouse*. Seattle, WA: Fantagraphics Books, 2003.

Maltin, Leonard. *Of Mice and Magic: A History of American Animated Cartoons*. New York: The Penguin Group, 1980.

Maltin, Leonard. *The Disney Films, 3rd Edition*. New York: Hyperion Press, 1973.

Merritt, Russell and J.B. Kaufman. *Walt in Wonderland: The Silent Films of Walt Disney*. Baltimore, MD: Johns Hopkins University Press, 1993.

Montgomery, Elizabeth Rider. *Walt Disney*. Champaign, IL: Garrard Publishing Co., 1971.

Mosley, Leonard. *Disney's World*. Chelsea, MI: Scarborough House Publishers, 1985.

Peet, Bill. *An Autobiography*. Boston: Houghton Mifflin Co., 1989.

Peterson, Monique, *The Little Big Book of Disney*. New York: Disney Editions, 2001.

Pontius, Larry. *Waking Walt*. New York: Writer's Showcase, 2002.

Price, Harrison. *Walt's Revolution by the Numbers*. Orlando, FL: Ripley Entertainment, 2003.

Rafferty, Kevin and Bruce Gordon. *Walt Disney Imagineering: A Behind the Dreams Look at Making the Magic Real*. New York: Hyperion Press, 1996.

Ryman, Herbert Dickens. *A Brush with Disney*. Santa Clara, CA: Camphor Tree Publishers, 2000.

Santoli, Lorraine. *The Official Mickey Mouse Club Book*. New York, NY: Hyperion Press, 1995.

Schickel, Richard. *The Disney Version*. Chicago: Irvin R. Dee, Inc., 1997.

Schroeder, Russell. *Walt Disney: His Life in Pictures*. New York: Disney Press, 1996.

Sinyard, Neil. *The Best of Disney*. Greenwich, CT: Twin Books Corp., 1988.

Sherman, Richard and Robert Sherman. *Walt's Time: From Before to Beyond*. Santa Clara, CA: Camphor Tree Publishers, 1998.

Shows, Charles. *Walt: Backstage Adventures with Walt Disney*. La Jolla, CA: Communication Creativity, 1979.

Smith, Dave. *Disney A to Z*. New York: Hyperion Press, 1996.

Smith, Dave. *The Quotable Walt Disney*. New York: Disney Editions, 2001.

Smith, Dave and Steven Clark. *The First 100 Years*. New York: Disney Enterprises, 1999.

Solomon, Charles. *The Disney that Never Was*. New York: Hyperion Press, 1995.

Thie, Carlene. *Disneyland . . . the Beginning*. Riverside, CA: Ape Pen Publishing Company, 2003.

Thomas, Bob. *Building a Company: Roy O. Disney and the Creation of an Entertainment Empire*. New York: Hyperion Press, 1998.

Thomas, Bob. *Walt Disney: An American Original*. New York: Hyperion Press, 1994.

Thomas, Frank and Ollie Johnston. *Bambi: The Story and the Film*. New York, NY: Stewart, Tabori & Chang, Inc., 1990.

Thomas, Frank and Ollie Johnston. *Disneyland Animation: The Illusion of Life*. New York: Abbeville Press Publishers, 1981.

Thomas, Frank and Ollie Johnston. *Disneyland Animation: The Illusion of Life*. New York: Hyperion, 1993.

Thomas, Frank and Ollie Johnston. *Too Funny for Words: Disney's Greatest Sight Gags*. New York: Abbeville Press Publishers, 1987.

Tytle, Harry. *One of Walt's Boys*. Royal Oak, MI: ASAP, 1997.

The Walt Disney Archives. Staff: Rebecca Cline, Dave Smith and Robert Thieman.

Wasko, Janet. *Understanding Disney*. Malden, MA: Blackwell Publishers, 2001.

Watts, Steven. *The Magic Kingdom*. New York: Houghton Mifflin Company, 1997.

Internet Resources

www.animationartist.com
www.awn.com
www.bcdb.com
www.disneypov.com
www.disneyshorts.toonzone.net
www.jimhillmedia.com
www.laughingplace.com
www.miceage.com
www.michaelbarrier.com
www.mouseinfo.com
www.mouseplanet.com
www.savedisney.com
www.startedbyamouse.com
www.waltdisney.org
www.waltopia.com
www.yesterland.com

DVD, Video, CD-ROM

Dumbo. Burbank, CA: Walt Disney Home Video, 2001.

Frank and Ollie. Burbank, CA: Walt Disney Home Video, 2003.

Snow White and the Seven Dwarfs, Platinum Edition. Burbank, CA: Walt Disney Home Video, 2001.

Walt Disney: An Intimate History of the Man and His Magic, written and co-produced by Katherine & Richard Greene. Santa Monica, CA: Pantheon Productions, Inc., 1998.

Walt: The Man Behind the Myth, written and co-produced by Katherine and Richard Greene. Santa Monica, CA: Pantheon Productions, Inc., 2001.

Walt Disney Presents 20,000 Leagues Under the Sea,. Burbank, CA: Buena Vista Home Entertainment, 2003.

Walt Disney Treasures: Behind the Scenes at the Walt Disney Studio. Burbank, CA: Buena Vista Home Entertainment, Inc., 2002.

Walt Disney Treasures: Disneyland USA. Burbank, CA: Buena Vista Home Entertainment, Inc., 2001.

Walt Disney Treasures: Silly Symphonies. Burbank, CA: Buena Vista Home Entertainment, Inc., 2001.

Periodicals

The E-Ticket Magazine, P.O. Box 800880, Santa Clarita, CA 91380

Disney News and *The Disney Magazine* (editorial offices currently in New York)

Storyboard, the Art of Laughter. (out of print, can't locate publisher information)

Backstage Magazine, published by and for Disneyland Cast Members. Burbank, CA: Walt Disney Productions, pre-1980.

The Disneyland Line, Disneyland Employee Newsletter. Burbank CA: Walt Disney Productions, archived issues 1977–1979.

The Disneylander, Disneyland Alumni Club Newsletter. Anaheim, CA: Disneyland Alumni Club, out of print.

Anderson, Paul, *Persistence of Vision: An Unofficial Historical Journal Celebrating Legacy of Walt Disney.* Salt Lake City, UT: Persistence of Vision #6/7, 1995.

Additional items from the personal collection of Peggy Matthews Rose.

You can contact Pat Williams at:

Pat Williams
c/o Orlando Magic
8701 Maitland Summit Boulevard
Orlando, FL 32810
phone: (407) 916-2404
pwilliams@orlandomagic.com

Visit Pat Williams' Web site at:
www.patwilliamsmotivate.com

If you would like to set up a speaking engagement for Pat Williams, please call or write to his assistant, Diana Basch, at the above address or call her at (407) 916-2454. Requests can also be faxed to (407) 916-2986 or e-mailed to *dbasch@orlandomagic.com*.

We would love to hear from you. Please send your comments about this book to Pat Williams at the above address or in care of our publisher at the address below. Thank you.

Peter Vegso
Health Communications, Inc.
3201 S.W. 15th Street
Deerfield Beach, FL 33442
(954) 360-0034 fax